Y0-CAV-329

Detroit Monographs in Musicology/Studies in Music, No. 56

Editor
Susan Parisi
University of Illinois

THE RUINED BRIDGE

Studies in Barberini Patronage of Music and Spectacle, 1631–1679

Frederick Hammond

Harmonie Park Press ◆ Sterling Heights, Michigan ◆ 2010

Cover:
Filippo Lauri–Filippo Gagliardi, *Giostra delle Caroselle* (1656), detail
(Museo di Roma)

Frontispiece:
G. L. Bernini (attributed), *Palazzo Barberini, The Ruined Bridge*
(Ponte rovinato) (Alinari Art Resource)

© 2010 by Harmonie Park Press

Printed and bound in the United States of America
Published by
Harmonie Park Press
Liberty Professional Center
35675 Mound Road
Sterling Heights, MI 48310-4727
www.harmonieparkpress.com

Publication Director, Elaine Gorzelski
Editor, Susan Parisi
Cover design, Mitchell Groters
Book design and Typographer, Colleen McRorie

Library of Congress Cataloging-in-Publication Data

Hammond, Frederick, 1937–
    The ruined bridge : studies in Barberini patronage / by Frederick Hammond.
        p. cm. — (Detroit monographs in musicology/Studies in music ; no. 56)
    Includes bibliographical references and index.
    ISBN 0-89990-151-4 (alk. paper)
  1. Music patronage—Italy—Rome. 2. Barberini family. 3. Urban VIII, Pope, 1568–1644. 4. Music—
Italy—Rome—17th century—History and criticism.   I. Title.
    ML1733.8.R6H355 2010
    782.10945 '63209032—dc22
                            2010031231

In memory of Théo Stavropoulos

"Heureux qui, comme Ulysse, a fait un beau voyage . . ."

Εῖν ὅλ᾽ αὐτὰ τὰ πράγματα πολὺ παληὰ
τὸ σκίτσο, καὶ τὸ πλοῖο, καὶ τὸ ἀπόγευμα

CONTENTS

ILLUSTRATIONS

FIGURES

Music Examples

ABBREVIATIONS

AB   Archivio Barberini
ASV   Archivio Segreto Vaticano
BAV   Biblioteca Apostolica Vaticana
CAB   Cardinal Antonio Barberini
CCB   Cardinal Carlo Barberini
CFB   Cardinal Francesco Barberini
Comp   Computisteria
CS   Cappella Sistina (=Pontificia)
DMB   Don Maffeo Barberini
DTB   Don Taddeo Barberini
gius.   giustificazione(-i)
LMG   Libro Mastro Generale

PREFACE

"The Rome that No One Cares to Write About"

"I see lots to say about the Rome that no one cares to write about—seventeenth-century Rome."

Edith Wharton to William Brownell
February 1904

At the end of his life, Cardinal Francesco Barberini undertook a number of major alterations to the family palace at the Quattro Fontane. Almost the last of these was the excavation of the area between the south wall of the palace and the garden, and the construction of a bridge across the ravine thus created. Perhaps designed by Bernini, it was known as "the ruined bridge" ("il ponte rovinato") owing to its trompe-l'oeil construction with caving voussoirs and a falling keystone in the arch (see frontispiece). The "ponte rovinato" struck me as an apt image of the last phase of Barberini patronage of music and spectacle in the years between the War of Castro and Urban VIII's subsequent death in 1644, and the death of Cardinal Francesco, his last surviving nephew, in 1679. The ruined bridge is a symbol of decay, but para-doxically a stable one, and its apparent collapse is a product not of nature but of art.

In a previous book, *Music and Spectacle in Baroque Rome*, I attempted to trace the musical patronage of the pope and his three nephews during the period of their hegemony. The problems involved were in large part historical, such as the examina-tion and coordination of large amounts of surviving archival and other material. The present collection might be considered at least in part a coda in a minor key to *Music and Spectacle*. Although it includes five chapters on events that occurred during Urban VIII's pontificate, the remainder of the text traces the increasingly fragmented support of music and spectacle on the part of the Barberini after the pope's death; its problems are as much literary as historical—despite Gibbon and Huizinga, decline has never been as easy or as gratifying to depict as ascent. By the end of his life, Cardinal Francesco, who a half-century earlier had emerged as the greatest patron of Roman opera, was instrumental in banning the entertainment and preparing the eventual destruction of the only public opera theater in Rome.

Edith Wharton's "the Rome that no one cares to write about" has become a thriving cottage industry, and this study would have been impossible without the work of scholars such as Giuseppe Adami, Maria Giulia Barberini, the late Franca Trinchieri Camiz, Joseph Connors, Dinko Fabris, Marc Fumaroli, James Gordon Harper, Irving Lavin, Marilyn Aronberg Lavin, the late Jean Lionnet, the late Georgina Masson, Margaret Murata, Laurie Nussdorfer, Roberto Pagano, Louise Rice, John Beldon Scott, Francesco Solinas, Patricia Waddy, Stefanie Walker, Karin Elizabeth Wolfe, and Agostino Ziino. I owe a particular debt of gratitude to Dinko Fabris for his revision of my transcription of the Floriani manuscript in Chapter 1—"grausam aber consequent," as Goethe said of Schiller's reworking of *Egmont*. Elaine Gorzelski, president of Harmonie Park Press, accepted the collection for publication, and Susan Parisi, the doyenne of students of music in seventeenth-century Mantua, edited the text; Colleen McRorie expertly set the text into type. John W. Lowell created the musical examples. To all of them I offer thanks and gratitude.

Other friends have contributed in less direct but no less important ways: James Bagwell, Cornelia Bessie and the late Michael Bessie, Victor Coelho, Gregory Harrold, Mariacarla and Roberto Pagano, Mary and James Ottaway, Carl Pritzkat and Anthony Travostino, the late Isabel and Laurance Roberts, the late Sandra Miller Sawyer, the late Théo Stavropoulos, and Emma Lewis Thomas. My Roman and Italian experiences over the last half-century inevitably recall friends now absent but still present to the memory: Elisabeth Mann Borgese, Ralph Kirkpatrick, James Moore, Pier Maria Pasinetti, Margherita Rospigliosi, Eugene Walter. My gratitude to Bard College and to its president, Leon Botstein, has only increased over the last two decades.

For archival materials I am particularly indebted, of course, to the Biblioteca Apostolica Vaticana and the Archivio Segreto Vaticano and their staffs. I am also grateful to the American Academy in Rome, in Ferrara to the Archivio di Stato, Archivio Storico of the Municipio di Ferrara, and Biblioteca Comunale Ariostea, the Harvard Center for Renaissance Studies at Villa I Tatti, the New York Public Library, and the libraries of Bard College (especially Jane Dougall), Vassar College, the University of California at Los Angeles, and the UCLA Music Library. Martayan Lan Rare Books provided a facsimile of *La maschera trionfante nel giudizio di Paride*. For permission to study and reproduce the Floriani documents I am indebted to Contessa Carla Compagnoni Floriani.

Visual materials appear by gracious permission of Her Majesty Queen Elizabeth II; Alinari Art Resource; Buffalo, New York, the Albright-Knox Gallery; Ferrara, the Biblioteca Comunale Ariostea; New York, the Metropolitan Museum of Art, the Pierpont Morgan Library, the New York Public Library; Rome, the Biblioteca Apostolica Vaticana, the Biblioteca Casanatense, the Direzione Generale I.N.P.S., I.N.G., and the Museo di Roma; Stockholm, the Nationalmuseum; Toronto, the Art Gallery of Ontario; Vienna, the Österreichische Nationalbibliothek. Every effort has been made to identify holders of copyright material. Additions and emendations should be communicated to the publisher and will be included in future editions. Unless otherwise specified, all translations are by the author.

The essay on *La contesa* was written for a congress on "Barocke Inszenierung" held at the Technische Hochschule in Berlin in 1996 and was published in *Barocke Inszenierung*, ed. Joseph Imorde, Fritz Neumeyer, Tristan Weddigen (Emsdetten/ Zurich: Edition Imorde, 1999), 146–57. "The Prince's Hat" first appeared in *"Et facciam dolçi canti": Studi in onore di Agostino Ziino in occasione del suo 65º compleanno*, ed. Bianca Maria Antolini, Teresa M. Gialdroni, Annunziato Pugliese, 2 vols. (Lucca: Libreria Musicale Italiana, 2003), I:629–54; the original version of "The Artistic Patronage of the Barberini and the Galileo Affair" was presented at a conference on Galileo at the University of Calgary and published in *Music and Science in the Age of Galileo*, ed. Victor Coelho (Netherlands: Kluwer Academic Publishers, 1992), 67–90; "Orpheus in a New Key" originally appeared in *Studi Musicali* 25 (1996): 103–25; "Barberini Entertainments for Queen Christina's Arrival in Rome" was read at an international conference at the Accademia dei Lincei in Rome in 1996 on Queen Christina and music and published in *Cristina di Svezia e la musica* (Rome: Accademia Nazionale dei Lincei, 1998), 133–60; the study of Barberini funerals was read at the Barberini Congress at the Palazzo Barberini alle Quattro Fontane on 7–11 December 2004 and has now been published in the congress report, *I Barberini e la cultura europea del Seicento*, ed. Lorenza Mochi Onori, Sebastian Schütze, Francesco Solinas (Rome: De Luca Editori d'Arte, 2007). I am grateful to all of the original publishers for permission to reprint this material. All these essays have been revised to take advantage of continuing scholarship and in several cases have been extensively reworked to fit their new context. The chapters *Le pretensioni del Tebro e del Po*, *La maschera trionfante*, and *Barberini Redux* are previously unpublished.

Bard College
Annandale-on-Hudson, New York

THE RUINED BRIDGE

Studies in Barberini Patronage of Music and Spectacle, 1631–1679

INTRODUCTION

The present essays on Barberini patronage are based on five hypotheses, now generally accepted in the remarkable development of Barberini studies during the last three decades. First, that all the important members of the family of Urban VIII personally influenced artistic projects. Second, that these artistic projects embodied identifiable goals for the papacy and for the family. Third, that these goals were specific and consistent enough to comprise what may be termed a program. Fourth, that this program was expressed in a coherent symbolic language. Fifth and last, that the Barberini program changed in emphasis and forum in response to political and intellectual events during the two decades of Urban VIII's pontificate.[1] In the early years of his reign the program was conceived largely in political terms and reflected primarily the pope's own ideals. In later years, it gradually shifted from the realm of practical politics to that of public relations, with symbolic events, such as the creation of Don Taddeo Barberini as Prince Prefect of the City, becoming correspondingly more important. This change accelerated at the period of the Galileo trial and its aftermath, and the Galileo affair played a part in this evolution.

The earlier stages of the Barberini program followed a traditional pattern. The crucial step in the upward mobility of the Barberini was taken by Urban VIII's uncle Francesco, an ecclesiastic who moved from Florence to Rome in the mid-sixteenth century. He obtained lucrative offices at the papal court, amassed and inherited a

---

[1] Aspects of the Barberini program are demonstrated in three fundamental studies: Patricia Waddy, *Seventeenth-Century Roman Palaces: Use and the Art of the Plan* (New York: The Architectural History Foundation/Cambridge, MA: MIT Press, 1990); John Beldon Scott, *Images of Nepotism: The Painted Ceilings of Palazzo Barberini* (Princeton, NJ: Princeton University Press, 1991); and James Gordon Harper, "The Barberini Tapestries of the Life of Pope Urban VIII: Program, Politics, and 'Perfect History' for the Post-Exile Era" (Ph.D. diss., The University of Pennsylvania, 1998; Ann Arbor, MI: UMI, 1999), 2 vols.

fortune, and purchased a small palace in the heart of old Rome. Since the Barberini were of undistinguished Tuscan origin, part of their program was recreating the family as a Florentine noble house. They changed the form of their name to encourage the impression that they had been territorial lords and altered their arms from three rather plebeian silver horse-flies (*tafani*, from the town of Tafano near Barberino Val d'Elsa) on a red field to three gold bees on a blue background, dropping in the process the wool-shears that indicated the original source of their prosperity. (A stone coat of arms of the family in the south cloister of Santa Croce in Florence still shows the horse-flies, but the wool-shears have been hacked off.)[2] A tenuous connection with the fourteenth-century poet Francesco da Barberino was revived to provide a patina of old culture.

The intellectual and literary ability of Francesco Barberini's nephew Maffeo (1568–1644)—the future Urban VIII—was ideal for building an ecclesiastical career on this solid foundation. After his graduation from Pisa with a doctorate of civil and canon law, Maffeo became successively governor of Fano, bishop of Spoleto, papal nuncio to Paris (where he received the red hat), and legate of Bologna. On returning to Rome he set himself up in princely, or rather prelatial, style, enlarging the family palace and commissioning a family chapel in Sant'Andrea della Valle. Maffeo was a poet of genuine gifts, working in Italian, Greek, and Latin, and published as early as 1606. His poetry was guided by the principle of *delectare et docere*, to inculcate moral instruction by the beauty of the poetry, and was often expressed in visual images. He was an early patron of Caravaggio, and by 1623 he had already received the dedications of several books of music and an important work on symbolic *imprese*. On 6 August 1623 Maffeo Barberini was elected to the papacy at the unusually early age of fifty-five.

The new pontiff's program was consciously expressed in symbols and images, beginning with his choice of the name Urbanus. Since the last prominent holder of the name had been Urban II, who preached the first Crusade, the new Urban linked himself both with the Roman civic heritage and with the Church militant and triumphant, while avoiding identification with any recent pontificate. This fusion of old and new Rome, a recurring theme of Urban's program, was embodied in his *possesso*, the ceremonial cavalcade in which a new pope took possession of Classical and Christian Rome. Starting from St. Peter's, the traditional site of the first pope's martyrdom and burial, the procession moved on to the Campidoglio, the seat of

---

[2] Irving Lavin, "Urbanitas Urbana. The Pope, the Artist, and the Genius of the Place," *I Barberini e la cultura europea del Seicento*, ed. Lorenza Mochi Onori, Sebastian Schütze, and Francesco Solinas (Rome: De Luca, 2007), 15–30, 16, fig. 2.

ancient Roman civil government, and culminated at the Lateran basilica with the pope's enthronement as bishop of Rome. The triumphal arch that the City hastily erected on the Campidoglio for the occasion—"Rome dedicating herself to Urban"— was approached up the hill by statues symbolizing the virtues of the new pope. It was decorated with his arms and with scenes of important events in his life, and was crowned by figures from Roman sacred and secular history illustrating the duties and powers of the papacy.

These symbols were still valid for Urban. The primary objective of his religious program was "the conservation of the Catholic religion where it is, and its restitution and propagation where it is not," as his cardinal-nephew Francesco instructed the papal nuncio to Paris.[3] Urban intended to restore the papacy to its historic influence and to guarantee the peace of Italy and of Europe by mediating between France and Spain, powers struggling for dominance in Italy while immersed in the wider ramifications of the Thirty Years' War. Urban even claimed the right, asserted in the decorations for his *possesso*, to depose secular rulers in defense of the Church. Armed force was an integral part of this program: the new universal pastor built fortresses in northern Italy, added breastworks to Castel Sant'Angelo, created a major harbor at Civitavecchia, installed an armory in the Vatican itself, and set up a foundry in the Vatican that served for casting both the bronzes for Bernini's baldacchino and the cannon for the papal army.[4]

Urban implemented his symbolic possession of Church and State in the promotion of his relatives. His immediate family in Rome consisted of two brothers, Carlo and Antonio, and three nephews: Carlo's sons Francesco, Taddeo, and Antonio the Younger, aged respectively twenty-six, twenty, and sixteen at their uncle's accession. Despite his unworldliness, the elder Antonio—an ascetic Capuchin monk—was named cardinal, librarian of the Vatican, Grand Penitentiary (the only great Church office not for sale), and eventually Cardinal Secretary of the Inquisition and thus a member of the committee that tried and sentenced Galileo. The pope's other brother, Carlo, became General of the Church, governor of Borgo, Castellan of Castel Sant'Angelo, and later duke of Monterotondo and prince of Palestrina. Carlo's brother-in-law, Lorenzo Magalotti, was also made a cardinal.

---

[3] Cardinal Francesco Barberini in Auguste Leman, *Recueil des instructions générales aux nonces ordinaires de France de 1624 à 1634* (Paris: Champion, 1920), 89: "E perchè la conservatione della religione cattolica dove ella è e la restitutione e propagatione dove non è, deve essere lo scopo principale del Sommo Pontefice. . . ."

[4] See W. Chandler Kerwin, *Powers Matchless: The Pontificate of Urban VIII, the Baldachin, and Gian Lorenzo Bernini* (New York, etc.: Peter Lang, 1997).

Of Carlo's three sons, the eldest, Francesco was made cardinal-nephew, Urban's first creation. Taddeo, like his father, remained a layman to perpetuate the family by marrying into the old Roman baronial nobility in the person of Anna Colonna, daughter of the Contestabile Colonna. Her brother, Girolamo, was made a cardinal and later became archpriest of San Giovanni in Laterano. On Carlo's death Taddeo inherited his father's military posts and their incomes as well as his titles and properties. In 1631 the Della Rovere family of Urbino became extinct in the male line, and Urban conferred their hereditary title of Prince Prefect of Rome on Don Taddeo. The third nephew, Antonio, became a cardinal in 1627, over Francesco's objections. Owing to the deaths of the nephews of two previous popes in the course of Urban's reign, the greatest benefices of the Church fell one by one to the younger Barberini cardinals: the abbacies of Pomposa, Farfa, and Grottaferrata; protectorates of countries, religious orders, and the Cappella Pontificia; the archypresbyteries of San Pietro and Santa Maria Maggiore; legations to France, Spain, and Urbino; the posts of Secretary of Breves, Vice-Chancellor of the Church (Francesco), including the basilica of San Lorenzo in Damaso and the palace of the Cancelleria, and finally Chamberlain of the Church (Antonio), who functioned as pope during the period of *sede vacante*.

These sacred and secular offices produced enormous revenues, much of which were spent on the magnificences appropriate to Renaissance princes: family churches, chapels, and palaces; the support of writers, artists, and artisans; the encouragement of knowledge in the form of learned academies, libraries, and publications; the collection and display of precious objects; the funding of public events such as processions, operas, dramatic performances, fireworks, banquets, religious ceremonies; and simple conspicuous consumption.[5] The Barberini vision could be described as a Renaissance papacy like that of Leo X Medici, ruled by a pope with the powers of the medieval Gregory VII, and establishing the papal family on the scale of Paul III and the Farnese.

---

[5] See Werner L. Gundersheimer, "Patronage in the Renaissance: An Exploratory Approach," *Patronage in the Renaissance*, ed. G.F. Lytle and Stephen Orgel (Princeton, NJ: Princeton University Press, 1981), 3–23; and Charles Hope, "Artists, Patrons, and Advisers in the Italian Renaissance," ibid., 293–343. On Barberini and papal revenues see Johannes Grisar, S.J., "Päpstliche Finanzen, Nepotismus und Kirchenrecht unter Urban VIII," *Miscellanea Historiae Pontificiae* (Rome: Libreria Herder, 1943), 207–366.

LA CONTESA (1631): A CHIVALRIC SPECTACLE FOR A BARBERINI CLIENT

For Emma Lewis Thomas

Armonica e per arte è la battaglia,
or s'intreccia, or fa testa ed or s'allarga
e, mentre contra quel questo si scaglia,
fan cozzar clava a clava e targa a targa
e, battendosi a tempo or tergo or petto,
fan di mezzo al'orror nascer diletto.

(Harmonious and artful is the battle,/now they intertwine, now they line up and now they widen/and, while this one hurls himself against that one,/they butt club against club and shield against shield/and, now striking the back, now the breast,/they arouse delight in the midst of horror.)

G. B. Marino, *L'Adone,* V/136 (1623)

THE CONTEXT OF *LA CONTESA*

In the course of research for an entry on the seventeenth-century soldier and military engineer Pietro Paolo Floriani (Macerata 1585-Ferrara 1638) for the *Dizionario biografico degli italiani*, Dottor Giuseppe Adami discovered in the hands of Floriani's descendants two manuscript codices in Floriani's hand. These illustrate and describe sets and machines by the great theatrical designer Francesco Guitti (1605–40), who served as Floriani's assistant for the military fortifications in Ferrara between 1629 and 1634, for four theatrical productions prepared for Ferrara and Parma between 1625 and 1631. The notebooks, previously described by Adami as unnumbered and designated by him as codex alpha and codex beta, have now been assigned the shelf-numbers a = 2.4.8. and ß = 2.4.528 bis in the Archivio Compagnoni Floriani in Macerata.[1]

Manuscript beta provides material for a *torneo a piedi,* a choreographed military exercise in the form of a mock battle executed on foot with swords or pikes. The text reveals that this was *La contesa,* which was performed as part of the wedding celebrations of Giovanni Francesco Sacchetti (1595–1637) and Beatrice Estense Tassoni (1613–33) in Ferrara on Monday, 3 March, the penultimate day of Carnival in 1631. (Their wedding had taken place on 23 February in the Castello.) An account or *relazione* of *La contesa,* including the text, descriptions of the action, and six engravings of the sets and costumes, was published by Guitti, the designer of the production, in 1632.[2] The engravings bear the inscription "Francesco Guiti Arch[itett]o" and "G[iovan] Battista Torre del[inxit]." The invention and libretto were by Giovanni Battista Estense Tassoni; the music was by an unknown composer and is mostly lost.[3] The author of the torneo choreography is unknown. The *mantenitore* or champion of the tourney was the architect and hydraulic engineer Count Girolamo Rossetti,[4] who also sustained a significant part of the expenses for the illumination, and the *padrino* (literally, godfather) of the event was Cornelio II Bentivoglio. The occasion was to have been celebrated also with a *quintana* or quintain-run, but this was rained out.[5]

---

[1] Giuseppe Adami, "L'ingegnere-scenografo e l'ingegnere-venturiero," *Barocke Inszenierung*, ed. Joseph Imorde, Fritz Neumeyer, Tristan Weddigen (Emsdetten/ Zürich: Edition Imorde, 1999), 158–89; Adami, *Pietro Paolo Floriani tra spalti e scene* (Loreto: Tecnostampa, 2006), 188–89. No complete inventory of the contents of ms. ß has yet been published. It contains thirty-seven folios of *La contesa* choreographies, two folios of designs for a 1625 entertainment, eleven folios of designs for *La contesa,* and four for the 1631 Bonacossi torneo.

[2] Ferrara, Biblioteca Comunale Ariostea, E. 12. 5. 20: "LA CONTESA/TORNEO/FATTO IN FERRARA PER LE NOZZE/Dell'Illustrissimo Signor/GIO: FRANCESCO SACCHETTI/Coll'Illustrissima Signora/ D. BEATRICE ESTENSE TASSONA./Dedicato/ALL' EMINENTISSIMO, ET REVERENDISSIMO/SIG. CARDINALE/GIVLIO SACCHETTI/LEGATO DI FERRARA, ETC./[stemma]/IN FERRARA./Appresso Francesco Suzzi Stampatore Camerale. 1632./*Con licenza de' Superiori.*" Guitti also wrote the *relazioni* for Ferrarese celebrations in 1625 and 1635.

[3] Giovanni Battista Estense Tassoni had been the author with Luigi Tasso of five intermedi for a play on the subject of "the flight of Aeneas from Queen Dido." This was prepared for a visit of Don Taddeo Barberini to Ferrara in early 1625; Guitti created the machines and the play was rehearsed up until the day before the performance but not presented. In 1627 Estense Tassoni, a cleric, became archpriest of the Ferrara cathedral (Giuseppe Adami, *Scenografia e scenotecnica barocca tra Ferrara e Parma (1625–1631)* [Rome: "L'Erma" di Bretschneider, 2003], 58–59).

[4] On Rossetti see Janet Southorn, *Power and Display in the Seventeenth Century: The Arts and Their Patrons in Modena and Ferrara* (Cambridge: Cambridge University Press, 1988), 131–34.

[5] Adami, *Scenografia,* 117, n. 6.

Pietro Paolo Floriani was connected with both the Barberini and the Sacchetti. In December of 1627 he was briefly appointed Vice-Castellan of Castel Sant'Angelo by Don Taddeo Barberini at the urging of Alessandro and Paolo Sacchetti.[6] In 1629 Floriani was named chief engineer of the States of the Church by Carlo Barberini, and in 1635 he would be sent by Urban VIII at the urging of Cardinal Francesco Barberini to reinforce the defenses of the island of Malta. Floriani's theatrical activities during his stay in Ferrara were intended to impress his patrons such as the Sacchetti and were ancillary to his main task, the perfecting of the great pentagonal fortress begun by Paul V Borghese, and the completion of the city walls, which he began in July of 1629.[7]

The Sacchetti were a Florentine mercantile family settled in Rome since the late sixteenth century. In the second Roman generation of the family Marcello Sacchetti was appointed Depositore Generale and Tesoriere Segreto of the Camera Apostolica by Urban VIII. The Sacchetti were assiduous clients of the Barberini; three of them, Marcello and his brothers Giovanni Francesco and Cardinal Giulio, were especially close to the pope and his nephews. The Sacchetti were patrons of art as well: Marcello and Giulio were both painted by their protégé Pietro da Cortona, whose works also decorated Beatrice Estense Tassoni's rooms in the Sacchetti palace in Rome, and they commissioned Giovanni Lanfranco to decorate the family chapel in San Giovanni dei Fiorentini. At the time of the Ferrarese wedding Cardinal Giulio was the popular Cardinal Legate there. The cardinal was present at the performance of *La contesa*, and Guitti dedicated his published account to him. The occasion was further adorned by the presence of the vice-legate Cardinal Spada, Enzo Bentivoglio's son-in-law Ascanio Pio of Savoy (an important librettist of chivalric combats: see below and Chapter 4), Sacchetti's protégé Fabio Chigi (the future pope Alexander VII), and the exiled Gonzaga de Nevers family of Mantua.[8]

---

[6] For a facsimile of the patent signed by Taddeo Barberini see Adami, *Pietro Paolo Floriani tra spalti e scene*, 64–65.

[7] See the article on Floriani by Giuseppe Adami in the *Dizionario biografio degli italiani*. Floriani's previous experience had included trips to Spain, Milan, Hungary, and participation in the battle of the White Mountain, a crucial Catholic victory in the Thirty Years' War.

[8] Agostino Faustini, G. Sardi, *Libro delle Historie Ferraresi* (Ferrara: Gironi, 1646; reprint, Bologna: Forni, 1967), 6:69–70: "Dimorava in questi giorni il Duca Carlo di Mantoa, con suo figlio e con la Principessa sua nuora, in Ariano . . . quando nel principio dell'anno che venne, per il matrimonio concluso tra la Signora Dona Beatrice Tassoni ed il fratello del Cardinal Sacchetti nostro Legato, dovendosi combatter alla sbarra e far nella Sala de' Giganti di questa nostra città, una bellissima festa con musiche, e recitar una pastorale con machine, fu invitato esso Duca Carlo, con la Principessa e suoi figli, a veder questa festa" ("In these days Duke Carlo of Mantua was staying in Ariano with his son and the Princess his

The bridal couple, Giovanni Francesco Sacchetti and Beatrice Estense Tassoni, were ill-matched. The Sacchetti clan had decided that one of their number had to marry in order to perpetuate the family, but they settled on an exogamic marriage only after Florentine possibilities fell through. The alliance was essentially arranged by Cardinal Sacchetti and the mother of the bride, Caterina Forna. Giovanni Francesco, who had enjoyed a distinguished career as papal soldier and diplomat, was thirty-six. His bride, who was plain and sickly, was eighteen. (She died two years after the wedding.)[9]

The Estense Tassoni were important Ferrarese and Modenese nobles with a long history of involvement in chivalric spectacle.[10] Despite their Roman connections (Count Ottavio Estense Tassoni had been a member of the Chapter of St. Peter's and took an active role in recruiting the Ferrarese Girolamo Frescobaldi as organist of the Cappella Giulia in 1608), they were not wholly reconciled to the papal annexation of Ferrara in 1598 after Alfonso II d'Este's death without legitimately descended male heirs. Beatrice's parents followed the unsuccessful claimant, Alfonso's cousin Cesare d'Este, to Modena.[11] Two years after *La contesa* a prominent participant, Nicolò Estense Tassoni, the bride's paternal uncle and Giudice de' Savi, the head of the communal council of Ferrara, was imprisoned in the Castello Estense under Cardinal Sacchetti's successor as the result of an attempted revolt.[12]

The celebrations for the Sacchetti-Estense Tassoni wedding fell at a low point in the history of seventeenth-century Ferrara, a moment marked by scarcity of

---

daughter-in-law . . . when at the beginning of the next year, for the marriage arranged between Donna Beatrice Tassoni and the brother of Cardinal Sacchetti our Legate, since they were to fight at the sbarra and perform in the Hall of the Giants [the *torneo Bonacossi* of Alfonso Chenda] of this city of ours a beautiful celebration with music, and recite a pastoral with machines, this Duke Carlo was invited with the Princess and her children to see this celebration"); Guitti, *La contesa*, 8.

[9] For a study of the Sacchetti and their relations of *clientela* with the Barberini see Irene Fosi, *All'ombra dei Barberini: Fedeltà e servizio nella Roma barocca* (Rome: Bulzoni, 1997); on the wedding see 214–21, 226, where she gives Giovanni Francesco's age as forty, while her genealogical table (242) gives his birthdate as 1595, making him thirty-six: the latter seems correct. On the Sacchetti as art patrons see Lilian H. Zirpolo, *Ave Papa Ave Papabile: The Sacchetti Family, Their Art Patronage, and Political Aspirations* (Toronto: Center for Reformation and Renaissance Studies, 2005). Curiously, there is a plaque commemorating Ottavio Estense Tassoni on Sangallo's Mint in Corso Vittorio Emanuele in Rome.

[10] Ercole Estense Tassoni published *relazioni* of tornei in 1561 and 1565 (Thomas Walker, "Echi estensi negli spettacoli musicali a Ferrara nel primo Seicento," *La corte di Ferrara e il suo mecenatismo 1441–1598/ The Court of Ferrara & its Patronage,* ed. Marianne Pade, Lene Waage Petersen, and Daniela Quarta [Ferrara: Panini, 1990], 337–51, esp. 340).

[11] Adami, *Scenografia*, 119, n. 9.

[12] Southorn, *Power and Display*, 116.

food, the sack of Mantua with the ensuing plague brought by the Imperial German mercenaries, the flooding of the Po, and the cutting of the canal of Modena. In his introduction to an account of a rival entertainment, the poet Francesco Berni (1610–73) lamented:

> This Year's Carnival, in the poverty of the past harvests lay famished, indeed extinct: In the ardors of enraged Mars it had found its funeral pyre: And, since even this was beaten down by the malignity of the Plague, it was buried there [. . .] They did not contemplate representing feigned, but real Tragedies of War.[13]

In June of 1631 the lutenist Filippo Piccinini wrote Enzo Bentivoglio that "a few months ago, I left Ferrara with the intention of never coming back, for the melancholy it gave me to see the wretchedness of that city, so different from when I set out for Spain."[14]

In his preface to his *relazione* of *La contesa* Guitti noted how these trials had fallen particularly hard on Cardinal Sacchetti as legate of Ferrara. The wedding celebrations were intended to raise the spirits of the entertainment-loving Ferrarese, since "that terrible Plague," Berni lamented, "which this year closed the eyes of mortals hereabouts, also kept the Theaters closed."

Chivalric spectacle is best seen in the wider context of what may be called the aristocratic crisis of the late Renaissance. Nobility was defined by birth and validated by military valor. Great princes, such as Odoardo Farnese, duke of Parma and Piacenza, were not too proud to serve as *condottieri*, paid commanders of the forces of kings and emperors. Aspiring nobles sought to distinguish themselves by achieving some striking military deed in the presence of their superiors. (Even the suave

---

[13] "Il Carnevale di quest'Anno, nella povertà delle passate messi famelico, anzi estinto giaceva: Negli ardori dell'adirato Marte aveva trovato il suo rogo: Ed, abbattuto pur'esso dalla malignità del Contagio, se ne stava sepolto [. . .] Non si vagheggianvano rappresentar finte, ma vere Tragedie di Guerra. Quell'orrido Contagio, che quest'Anno qui 'ntorno chiudeva gli occhi a' mortali, teneva chiusi pur anco i Teatri" (Francesco Berni, *Il torneo a piedi, e l'invenzione ed allegoria colla quale il signor Borso Bonacossi comparì a mantenerlo* [Ferrara: Gironi and Cherardi, 1631], quoted by Walker, "Echi estensi," 347 and 351 n. 14).

[14] Filippo Piccinini in Bologna to Enzo Bentivoglio in Ferrara, 9 June 1631: "Alcuni mesi sono ch'io mi partì de Ferrara, con animo di non ritornarvi più, per la malinconia che mi rendeva in vedere la miseria di quella città, tanto differente di quando io mi partì per Spagna" (Dinko Fabris, *Mecenati e musici: Documenti sul patronato artistico dei Bentivoglio di Ferrara nell'epoca di Monteverdi (1585-1645)* [Lucca: Libreria Musicale Italiana, 1999], 451).

and unwarlike Giulio Mazzarini entered the world stage as a soldier.) However, developments such as the reliance on artillery and the widespread use of mercenary soldiers lessened these opportunities.

An emblematic case of the growing disparity between the military man and the courtier is provided by the career of Giulio Cesare Brancaccio (ca. 1520-after 1585), a member of the *musica secreta* of Alfonso II d'Este of Ferrara, now remembered only as a virtuoso bass-singer with a range of three octaves. Brancaccio, a Neapolitan noble, considered himself rather a soldier and expert on fortifications than a performer, a man to whom the classification of "musico" with the *concerto delle dame principalissime* assigned him by Alfonso II was an affront.[15]

With the erosion of the military profession as a training-ground for noble youth, the chivalric spectacle became one way of employing young nobles in exercises that combined the military with dramatic entertainment.[16] The new role of academies and theatrical activity in the formation of young nobles is evident in the motto of the refounded Ferrarese Accademia degli Intrepidi, "Litteris armata, et armis erudita"—"armed with letters, and learnèd in arms."[17]

*　　*　　*　　*

The seventeenth-century chivalric spectacle fell into two broad categories. The *giostra* or joust was a combat of single mounted knights against an inanimate target, such as a ring, a quintain (*quintana*) or *saracino*, or a glove, or against another mounted knight. A *torneo* or tourney was a combat between squadrons of combatants on horse or on foot (*a piedi*)—often successive stages of the same event—in an enclosure

---

[15] See especially Richard Wistreich, *Warrior, Courtier, Singer: Giulio Cesare Brancaccio and the Performance of Identity in the Late Renaissance* (Burlington, VT: Ashgate, 2007).

[16] The gentrification of what was originally a serious military exercise was excoriated by G. B. Marino in the prologue to Canto XIV of *L'Adone*: "Deh, come fatta è vile a' giorni nostri/la milizia ch'un tempo era sì degna/. . ./Non vi manca guerrier ch'armato mostri/sovravesta superba e ricca insegna,/non già per acquistar nel mondo fama/ma sol per farsi noto a colei ch'ama" ("Ah, how vile the soldiery that once was so worthy has become in our days . . . There is no lack of warriors who display in arms proud surcoats and rich insignia, not to acquire fame in the world but only to show off before their beloved").

[17] Cf. the *Diario* of Cardinal Maurizio of Savoy's Roman Accademia dei Desiosi (1626): the "principal fine è l'impiegar chiunque in essa verrà ascritto, in vari esercizi si d'armi che di lettere, onde egli possa rendersi al cospetto de' suoi principi e per l'uno e per l'altro più amabile" ("the principal aim is to employ anyone who becomes a member of it in various exercises both of arms and of letters, whence he may render himself more pleasing in the sight of his patrons and for one another") (Mattias Oberli, *"Magnificentia Principis": Das Mäzenatentum des Prinzen und Kardinals Maurizio von Savoyen (1593–1657)*, Diss. Zurich 1998 [Weimar: VDG, 1999], 104).

or *recinto*, for possession of a field or *campo*. A typical *campo* had a portal with a triumphal arch at either end.[18] The *recinto* could be either an open outdoor space or an enclosed indoor space, as at Ferrara, where two theaters were employed for chivalric spectacles. A combat in a field divided by a wooden barrier or list was a *barriera* or *sbarra*. An undivided field was a *campo aperto*. The weapons employed could be lances, pikes, swords, and/or pistols.[19] The proliferation of such spectacles was extraordinary: at the court of Savoy alone some eighteen tourneys of various sorts are recorded between 1587 and 1645.[20]

A complete *giostra* or *torneo* consisted of a number of elements. These were all governed by a basic conceit or *invenzione*, the shaping theme of the combat. *Invenzioni* were created by gentlemen specialists, often through the mediation of a local academy, such as the Ferrarese Accademia degli Intrepidi. Among the best-known inventors were Ascanio Pio of Savoy, Pio Enea Obizzi, and Claudio Achillini, the *ideatore* and librettist of the 1628 Parma *torneo*, *Mercurio e Marte*, set to music by Claudio Monteverdi. Such specialists also devised a scenario for the *sfida* or ritual challenge to the event and the replies to it by the contenders. For the contest itself, further *invenzioni* were required for the costumes and appearances of the participants, including poetic compositions sung or recited by musicians and actors, who accompanied the entrance of the champions on *carri* (floats) or machines. These compositions were generally printed up and distributed to the onlookers. A *relazione* or account of the occasion, often lavishly illustrated, could be published as well.[21]

The *introduzione* to the event began several days before the actual performance (which usually took place during Carnival) with the proclamation to the city at large by heralds of a *cartello di sfida* or challenge embodying the *invenzione*, along with the *capitoli* or rules to be enforced by the *maestri di campo* or referees. In addition to the *maestri di campo*, the participants comprised the *mantenitore* or champion, the

---

[18] Such spectacles could also develop beyond combats into displays of dressage and even fully-choreographed horse ballets, as in Florence in 1637; on the Florentine events see Angelo Solerti, *Musica, ballo e drammatica alla corte medicea dal 1600 al 1637* (Florence, 1905; New York: Blom, 1968) and A. M. Nagler, *Theatre Festivals of the Medici 1539–1637* (New Haven and London: Yale University Press, 1964).

[19] The Floriani manuscript ß occasionally uses the word "stocco," which usually means a "spada da una mano e mezza con lama a forma di triangolo a sezione romboidale" ("a sword of a hand and a half with a triangular blade and a rhomboidal cross-section") (Benedetta Montevecchi and Sandra Vasco Rocca, *Suppellettile ecclesiastica* [Florence: Centro Di, 1988], 414), but it may also refer to the stock of a pike.

[20] *Le capitali della festa*, ed. Marcello Fagiolo (Rome: De Luca Editori d'Arte, 2007), 56. For early seventeenth-century paintings of a "Giostra di campo aperto a cavallo" and a "Giostra al rincontro" depicting Ferrarese armor and helmets see ibid., 47; and Adami, *Scenografia*, 15.

[21] See the entries "Giostra" and "Torneo," *Enciclopedia dello spettacolo* (Rome: Le maschere, 1954–1968).

avventurieri or challengers in their squadrons, their older *padrini* ("godfathers," like seconds in a prize fight), as well as actors, musicians, and servants. The participants might be presented to the public in a *corteo* or procession. In the actual combat the *mantenitore* entered the field through one triumphal arch, the *avventurieri* through the other, each challenger accompanied by his *padrino.*

Any chivalric spectacle presented in mid-seventeenth-century Ferrara—or anywhere else in Italy, for that matter—was overshadowed by one production and one personality: the 1628 celebrations in Parma for the Medici-Farnese wedding directed by Enzo Bentivoglio (c.1571–1639), who had presented chivalric spectacles in Ferrara in two theaters: from 1609 in the Teatro degli Intrepidi in a remodelled granary near San Lorenzo, and from 1610 in the Sala Grande di Cortile in the Palazzo Ducale.

Although the Bentivoglio were great nobles, former lords of Bologna and kin to other ruling families, they were plagued by numerous progeny and extravagant expenses. "Great pile[s] of debts and the chain of *fidecommesso* are notorious in the House of Bentivoglio," the legate of Ferrara, Cardinal Donghi, wrote in 1647.[22] Since the Bentivoglio could not afford the luxury of factional alliances, they practiced unusual diplomatic maneuverability, not to say slipperiness. At the devolution of Ferrara to the papacy in 1598, the elder Marchese Ippolito went to Modena with the cadet branch of the Este, while his half-brother Enzo remained in Ferrara as part of the papal bureaucracy. The Bentivoglio held fiefs from the Este, the Medici, and Ferrara, and also ranked as Venetian patricians. Enzo and his younger brother

---

[22] Southorn, *Power and Display*, 93. On Cornelio's debts for the 1634 joust see Ferrara, Archivio di Stato, Archivio Bentivoglio: b. 240 (1634), Marco, 4 March, c. 3: [a *setarolo* or silk-merchant dunning for an old bill]: "tanto maggiormente che l'Ill.o et ecc.o Sig. D. Cornelio suo fig[liol]o ha fatto prove stupendissime in questa Giostra e ne ha reportati tanti li honori con la sodisfatione de benevoglienza a tutta la Città di Roma" ("so much the more since the Most Illustrious and Most Excellent Sig. Don Cornelio your son has given stupendous proofs in this Joust and has carried off such honors with the satisfaction and good will of the entire City of Rome"); 8 April, c. 6: G. B. Bischi to Enzo Bentivoglio: "Se V. S. Ill.ma non soccore questi ss.ri suoi figliuoli con un poco di danari per pagare almeno i loro servitori, io gli veggo in necessità di non poter uscir di casa per mancamento di staffieri [. . .]" ("If Your Most Illustrious Lordship does not aid these sons of yours with a bit of money at least to pay their servants, I see that they will be forced not to leave their house for lack of servants"). On the 1634 *Giostra del Saracino* in Rome see Hammond, *Music and Spectacle in Baroque Rome* (New Haven and London: Yale University Press, 1994), 214–24, 270–71; and Pietro Della Valle's *Diario* (ASV, Archivio del Bufalo-Della Valle, n. 186, c.19r): "25 febraro [1634] fu fatta la festa in Piazza navona nella quale il Marchese Cornelio Bentivoglio mantenne al Saracino et io fui Padrino del Sig.r Angelo Incoronati, il quale vinse et con tutto quel che ci va" ("25 February was performed the festa in Piazza Navona in which Marchese Cornelio Bentivoglio was mantenitore at the quintain and I was padrino of Sig. Angelo Incoronati, who won with all that implies"). Cf. Agostino Ziino, "Pietro Della Valle e la 'musica erudita.' Nuovi documenti," *Analecta Musicologica* 5 (1967): 97–111.

Cardinal Guido eventually became artistic mentors of the younger Barberini, and Guido preceded Cardinal Antonio as Protector of France (1621–33). In 1641 Mazarin purchased Guido's Roman palace on the Quirinal, the present Palazzo Rospigliosi.

Enzo Bentivoglio developed the opera-torneo, a type of spectacle "in which scenes performed by professional singers (usually borrowed from other patrons) within scenic settings onstage alternated with pitched battles in the open space before the stage between a costumed champion or Mantenitore (Enzo himself) and his challengers."[23] Ferrarese spectacles almost always included a spoken pastoral or tragedy, with an introductory prologue and intermedi in music between the acts. The combats could take place before, after, or during the intermedi. Although the musicians were professionals, the challengers were noblemen who paid for their own costumes and could also contribute sets, machines, and verses to the entertainment.

In the years up to 1616, after which Enzo Bentivoglio was absorbed in planning the Parma celebrations (beginning with an abortive one scheduled for 1618), he did not produce any new entertainments for Ferrara. Instead, he created a "squadra ferrarese" for organizing tourneys, which could then be deployed outside of Ferrara: in Parma in 1628, in Rome in 1634, and in Modena in 1635. The poet responsible for the challenge, the texts of arias to be sung, and the intermedi, was for many years Alessandro Guarini (son of the more famous Battista Guarini, and a kinsman of Enzo). Claudio Achillini and Jacopo Cicognini also provided texts, as did the Modenese envoy to Rome, Fulvio Testi, in 1634 and 1635. Enzo's son-in-law Ascanio Pio di Savoia (1588–1648) produced libretti for the Parma celebrations and for later spectacles such as *La Discordia superata* (1635) with music by Antonio Goretti, *L'Andromeda* (1638), set by Michelangelo Rossi, and *L'Amore trionfante* (1641) and *Le pretensioni del Tebro e del Po*, both with music by Marco Marazzoli (see Chapter 4). The architect G. B. Aleotti alone designed the scenery until 1626, when the more up-to-date Alfonso Rivarola Chenda and Francesco Guitti were chosen for the 1628 Parma celebrations.[24] Antonio Goretti served as the general musical adviser for choosing composers (the star of the Parma celebrations was Claudio Monteverdi) and performers, and for coordinating the music, sometimes also himself functioning as both composer and performer. Crowds of specialized artisans formed part of

---

[23] Southorn, *Power and Display*, 81, where she calls this a *campo aperto*; for a synopsis of Ferrarese festivities see Chiara Cavaliere Toschi, "Tracce per un calendario delle manifestazioni dell'effimero," and "Appendice documentaria," *La chiesa di San Giovanni Battista e la cultura ferrarese del Seicento* (Milan: Electa, 1981), 144–53. My account relies heavily on Fabris, *Mecenati*.

[24] On Aleotti see Fagiolo, *Le capitali della festa*, 45–46.

the équipe: joiners (*marangoni*), carpenters, machinists, costumers, lighting and rope men, scene-painters and decorators (whose services Enzo could also commandeer for his own purposes at cut-rate prices), and engineers for flooding castle moats or even entire theaters to accommodate a concluding naumachia or naval battle. In Parma in 1628, in Rome in 1634, and in Modena in 1635 Enzo's son Cornelio rode as *mantenitore*. (In 1628 the Farnese duke himself rode as champion in the concluding torneo, *Mercurio e Marte*.)

Enzo's own contributions to such celebrations were twofold. First, he was an inexhaustible source of *invenzioni*. Enzo laid out his artistic credo in a letter of 1635 to the Duke of Modena: "The purpose of celebrations is to provide an increase of wonder and not a diminution."[25] Criticizing the lame conclusion of the duke's proposed *campo aperto*, he pulled out of his hat two possible brilliant finales. In the first, five of the challengers would join the two champions in a battle against the seven other challengers. The second proposal was to take five challengers and lower them to the piazza in a machine like a flame of fire that would open midway to show them surrounded by globes of flames, followed by the combat.[26]

In line with this love of effect, even in the *introduzione* to a spectacle Enzo tended to introduce scenic elements, personages with evocative names, machines, and short musical interludes. The spectacles themselves included magical appearances and disappearances, *son-et-lumière*, fireworks, and flooding for naval battles. Although a typical Ferrarese-style spectacle lasted about seven hours, the constant variety of such inventions could apparently hold the audience's attention throughout.

Enzo's other major contribution was to coordinate the entire vast enterprise of realising his *invenzioni* as artistic director or *corago*. (There is some suspicion that his chronic financial difficulties were in part owing to diverting income from the papal bond-issues, *monti*, intended for the ever-unfinished Bentivoglio land-reclamation projects, to such festivities.)

This tradition of the *torneo a tema* reached its fruition in the unparalleled opera-torneos of the Parma celebrations. Dinko Fabris has summarized their characteristics: transposition to a fixed space, a specially-constructed theater in a courtyard and Aleotti's colossal Teatro Farnese; closed and predetermined ambiences

---

[25] Fabris, *Mecenati*, 72–79 and #987: "Il fin delle feste vuol fornire con accrescimento di meraviglia e non diminutione."

[26] Ibid., #987: Torneo Bentivoglio, Modena, gennaio-settembre 1635: the letter continues: "these should be led by Malagigi" ("questi dovrìano esser condotti da Malagigi")—a minor character in the *Orlando Furioso*, but also the nickname of Cardinal Antonio Barberini's castrato Marc'Antonio Pasqualini.

instead of ephemeral settings in the open; development of the dramatic content within the spectacle, with ample space given to the poetic text, music, and recitation, as well as the clash of arms. The usual *relazione* had consisted of a plot-summary (*canovaccio*), the *sfida*, and descriptions of the scenes; this was now transformed into a full-fledged libretto.[27]

The 1628 Parma celebrations had been preceded a decade earlier by an abortive festival, *La difesa della bellezza*, prepared for a visit by Cosimo II de' Medici to Parma that never materialized. According to a manuscript text and directions, the festa was to consist of six intermedi and five battles on foot or horseback at the end of each intermedio. The entire entertainment was accompanied by music, performed by various instruments and two choirs above the two doors of the theater. Alfonso Pozzo was responsible for the iconographic program and the texts. Enzo Bentivoglio, assisted by Francesco Saracini, was the general coordinator or *corago*. The machines and architecture of the theater were the work of G. B. Aleotti, and the Ferrarese domination of the event was completed by the choice of Antonio Goretti as composer. Although the project fell through, Aleotti's immense theater was ready for performances by 1619.[28]

Several members of the original Ferrarese équipe took part in the final festivities of 1628. The first of the Parma spectacles took place on 13 December outdoors before a shivering audience in the *teatro provvisorio di cortile* erected in the court of the church of San Pietro Martire. It consisted of Torquato Tasso's pastoral *Aminta* with a prologue by Claudio Achillini and five intermedi by Ascanio Pio di Savoia, one after each act, ending with a combat featuring Enzo's son Cornelio as mantenitore.[29] The music, now lost, was composed by Monteverdi. The festivities concluded ten days later with the opera-torneo *Mercurio e Marte* of Achillini, again with music by Monteverdi. This was presented in a closed space, the gargantuan Teatro Farnese, on 23 December 1628 and consisted of five *azioni* with knights, "the most famous singers of Christianity," and musicians.

The torneo began with the appearance on "superbissime macchine" of Dawn, the Zodiac and the Months, and finally the Age of Gold, "singing the happiness of

---

[27] Ibid., 78–79.

[28] On the 1618 and 1628 celebrations see Paola Besutti, "Giostre e tornei a Parma e Piacenza durante il ducato dei Farnese," *Musica in torneo nell'Italia del Seicento*, ed. Paolo Fabbri (Lucca: Libreria Musicale Italiana, 1999), 65–79.

[29] On Ascanio Pio's contribution to the 1628 festivities see Roberta Ziosi, "I libretti di Ascanio Pio di Savoia: un esempio di teatro musicale a Ferrara nella prima metà del Seicento," *Musica in torneo*, ed. Fabbri, 135–65, esp. 138.

the present days."[30] Then Discord rose from the Inferno, accompanied by the Furies, boasting that she had sown strife between Mercury (representing the contemplative side of the duke's nature) and Mars (his warlike aspect) in order to impede the combat. Mercury appeared in the heavens on a chariot and announced that he had imprisoned the mantenitore in a castle at the bottom of the sea. The first squadron of challengers he had hidden within some rocks, the second in an infernal swamp, the third under Mount Etna, and the fourth in the bellies of sea-monsters. The rest of the action consisted of the progressive liberation of each squadron of combatants. The duke was rescued by Venus, who descended on a cloud accompanied by cupids. Apollo arose and called Orpheus from the Elysian fields, who by his singing freed the first squadron from their rocky prison. Juno, invoking Proserpina and Pluto, freed the second squadron. The third squadron was rescued from Etna by the God of Love, who descended on the coat of arms of the Medici, the bride's family. Each liberation was followed by a battle—"E qui si combatte." Through the joint efforts of Bellona, the goddess of war, Saturn, and Neptune, the last squadron was freed. "Suddenly water gushes out, which floods the theater. Galatea appears in the new sea, with two islets, and on one of them she receives the Mantenitore, and on the other the Challengers. And here they fight in the water." At the end of the sea-battle Jove and the council of the gods reconciled Mercury and Mars and expelled Discord from the heavens.[31]

The excitement of the creation of such wondrous machines (and probably some of their actual production methods) is evoked in the memories of the artist, actor, and writer Eugene Walter, who as a young man in the 1930s worked on the floats for the Mardi Gras in Mobile, Alabama:

> The warehouse was huge. . . . The walls were hung with life-size horses, dragons, giants' heads, urns, arches, wings, and cloud formations which could be used again.
>
> The wooden substructure for the float would take shape over this chicken wire, cunningly bent, stretched, and curved

---

[30] A design for this machine has been found among the Floriani papers: see Adami, *Pietro Paolo Floriani*, 140, 142–51. Adami, *Scenografia*, reproduces and discusses eighteen drawings by Floriani of Guitti's machines for the torneo, in many cases reworkings of Aleotti's 1618 contrivances.

[31] "Esce un'acqua improvvisa che allaga il teatro. Comparisce nel nuovo mare Galatea, con due isolette, e sovra l'una di queste riceve il Mantenitore, e sovra l'altra i Venturieri. E qui si combatte in acqua": Claudio Achillini, "Ristretto del Torneo" (Parma: Viotti, 1628) in Solerti, *Musica, ballo e drammatica*, 480–87. The sources for the torneo include Marcello Buttigli, *Descrittione dell'Apparato fatto per honorare la prima e solenne entrata in Parma della Serenissima Principessa Margherita di Toscana* (Parma: Viotti, 1629); for the opening festa, Ascanio Pio di Savoia, *Intermezzi recitati in musica* (Parma: Viotti, 1629).

to make the basic forms. Then a long two or three weeks of weaving strips of brown paper through all the chicken wire to give a base for the papier-mâché which came next. A great cauldron bubbled over a pile of pine knots: a vat of flour paste was cooked with cow-hoof glue and bluestone added. The sheets of brown paper were dipped in, wrung out, and smoothed over all the surfaces of the figures. What a stink! Several months of this, then the prime coats of paint were brushed on. This was made up as we used it, of dry powdered pigment, water, boiling cow-hoof glue, and was even stinkier than the paste . . . pounds of Dutch gold leaf were used on the floats. Sometimes crowns and thrones or certain details would be covered flatly, but usually the squares of gold leaf were applied onto a dab of glue so that the four corners were left fluttering. Mules drew all floats then. When the float moved down the street, the hundreds of moving scraps of gold leaf caught the light of the torches, and the float seemed literally to burn.[32]

LA CONTESA

La contesa belonged to the Ferrarese tradition of the opera-torneo, brought to fruition in the "unique and unrepeatable"[33] Parma spectacles. It was presented in a temporary theater set up in the hall of Camillo Bevilacqua's large palace "sulla Ghiara." The hall contained, "in figura ovale quattro ordini di palchi capacissimi, divisi in sette lati" ("in an oval shape four rows of most spacious boxes, divided into seven sides") like a miniature version of Aleotti's Teatro Farnese. It had a stage 5.4 meters deep raked in a proportion of 1 to 9 and was notable for the large back-stage area, 4.5 meters deep, to accommodate machines and machinists. Guitti's proscenium was flanked by statues and columns, and on either side stairs led from the stage down to the house. In the conceit familiar from the Palazzo del Te in Mantua, and later in Pietro da Cortona's frescoes in the salone of Palazzo Barberini and the ruined bridge in the palace garden, the faux marbre cornice of the theater appeared to collapse, revealing the arms of the bridal pair on the brick wall beneath, surmounted by Cardinal Sacchetti's arms (see fig. 1.1).

---

[32] Eugene Walter as told to Katherine Clark, *Milking the Moon: A Southerner's Story of Life on This Planet* (New York: Crown Publishers, 2001), 49–50.

[33] Fabris, *Mecenati*, 80.

FIG. 1.1   Francesco Guitti, engraved by G. B. Torre, *Prospetto della scena et ultima comparsa del Sig.r Mantenitore* from *LA CONTESA /TORNEO /FATTO IN FERRARA PER LE NOZZE /Dell'Illustrissimo Signor /GIO: FRANCESCO SACCHETTI / . . .* (Ferrara, Biblioteca Comunale Ariostea, E. 12.5.20)

*   *   *   *

Guitti's preface to *La contesa* states that the promotors of the torneo (presumably under the supervision of G. B. Estense Tassoni) began by parcelling out responsibilities for the performance. They invented a subject, composed the verses for the work, and put them in the hands of Guitti, who set to work on the sets in the hall of the Palazzone della Ghiaia on 3 February. The finished product was presented exactly a month later on Carnival Monday, 3 March 1631. A sheet of "Expenses for the machines and musicians and other things for the bariera" ("Spese p[er] le machine et musichi et altro p[er] la bariera") gives some of the costs of the production. Guitti received two payments of ten scudi each. Other payments were made for the drummers, the "balarino," the pikes, the *calzette* or hose, and the significant sum of 15.6 scudi "given to the Frenchman for the machines" ("dati al sig.r francese p[er] le machine").

The plot of the torneo was built on the familiar conceit or *invenzione* of personi-fying cities by their rivers. (The same idea was to serve for the joust *Le pretensioni del Tebro e del Po,* presented for Don Taddeo Barberini in Ferrara in 1642: see Chapter 4.) Florence, the ancestral city of the bridegroom, was symbolized by the Arno; Ferrara, the city of the bride, by the Po; and Rome, the seat of the papal government, by the Tiber. The allegory mirrored the political realities of Ferrara in 1631. The power of the Florentine Sacchetti had been achieved by their adherence to the Florentine Barberini. The knights and padrini of the event, on the other hand, comprised an anthology of the most prominent Ferrarese names: Estense Tassoni, Ariosti, Romei, Estense Mosti, Crispi, Rossetti, Bentivoglio. And, in power politics as in the torneo, Rome prevailed over both Florence and Ferrara.

La contesa consisted of a prologue followed by three acts—three *comparse* or appearances of challengers and champion. The sets comprised two basic scenes, a seashore with rocks and stones for the prologue and the first two scenes and a woodland scene for the appearances of the Dioscuri and the *mantenitore.*[34] In a unique survival, given the habitual secrecy of the professional machine-designer, the Floriani manuscript ß has preserved the details of Guitti's machines for *La contesa.*

For the prologue, after a triple trumpet-call the curtain disappeared to reveal the island of Cyprus and the temple of Heavenly Venus, with Venus, Heavenly Love (Cupid), and sixteen amoretti holding torches (fig. 1.2, LX-LXI [Roman numerals refer to Floriani's sketches of Guitti's machines]). The temple was constructed of wood and painted cardboard with colored glass, painted wax, and *talco* (colored phosphore-scent powders mixed with glass chips). After Venus and Cupid had sung in dialogue and duet "to the sound of most sweet instruments," celebrating their escape from the other, profane and lascivious aspect of Venus by virtue of the wedding, the temple rose, with the gods still singing. When the temple and its passengers had disappeared, the amoretti with their torches descended the stage steps to the floor of the hall or *campo* to illuminate the action there, the first appearance of the challengers.

After a "soavissima sinfonia, di vari strumenti" ("a most sweet sinfonia, of various instruments") the scene changed to the Lipari islands. The goddess Flora flew in, her cloud transformed into a silver seashell chariot as it touched the water (LXIX—"nuvola che si converte in conchiglia che portava flora"—"a cloud that

---

[34] Adami, *Scenografia*, 121.

Fig. 1.2   *Introduzione del S.r Mantenitore nel Torneo* from *La contesa*

changes into a seashell that carried Flora"). She complained that, because the wedding was being celebrated in Ferrara, Florence and the Arno were being ignored and asked for winds to defend her honor. A terrifying earthquake (a slightly gratuitous touch, since Ferrara was in fact seismic territory and had suffered a quake as recently as 1624) was heard, and a rock split open to reveal Aeolus, the god of winds, seated in state (LXII). (Guitti would employ the same mechanism two years later for Don Taddeo Barberini's Roman production of the Rospigliosi-Michelangelo Rossi *Erminia sul Giordano*.) Aeolus granted Flora's request, and the rock split again to reveal the first three challengers, costumed as the winds Aquilone, Euro, and Noto (fig. 1.3).

The three knights (all cousins) were Vincenzo and Alfonso Estense Tassoni and Giovanni Maria Crispi. Their *padrini* were, respectively, Francesco Ariosti, Girolamo Romei, and Ippolito Strozzi. The knights advanced to the edge of the stage and were lowered to the campo at floor level by a kind of proto-elevator that seemed to break from the stage front (LV-LVI). The knights, forming a squadron, "made their *passaggio* [procession] before the company, stopping at the top of the Hall opposite the Stage, and ending the first action, and Comparsa."[35]

---

[35] Guitti, *La contesa*, 15–26.

FIG. 1.3   *Prima Comparsa de' S.ri Venturier* from *La contesa*

The second appearance of the challengers presented the remaining three avventurieri, Ferrante and Francesco Estense Tassoni and Pietro Paolo Floriani. Their
padrini were another Francesco Estense Tassoni, son of the mastro di campo Nicolò,
Alfonso Rossetti, brother of the mantenitore, and Enzo Bentivoglio's son Cornelio.[36]

The scene changed to one of rocks and ocean waves. Tritons surfaced to escort
two sea-horses drawing the chariot of Neptune, adorned with pearls and coral. An
island surrounded by poplars (typical trees of the Po valley) appeared, and four
nymphs sang in praise of Beatrice Estense Tassoni, entreating the help of Neptune

---

[36] In 1624 Nicolò Estense Tassoni had put on a *torneo a piedi* (Fabris, *Mecenati*, 82, 132) in an attempt to
revive the glories of the Bentivoglio spectacles. The preface to the relazione gives some idea of the
scenic marvels of these events: "Più non vedeasi ne' sereni giorni di quelle famose notti l'aria piovar
Cavalieri, e la terra esalar torri, e con fecondità spontanea et inaudita produr palagi, e fruttar castella.
Più non erano scherniti i mari e navigate le scene. Non più squarciavasi l'Olimpo, né più dalle cerulee
bocche apriva glorie, e palesava paradisi, più non doleasi l'inferno di veder scoperti i suoi penosi secreti"
("No more in the calm days of those famous nights was the air seen to rain down Knights, and the earth
to exhale towers, and with spontaneous and unheard-of fecundity produce palaces, and bear forth castles.
The seas were no longer spurned and the stages sailed on. Olympus no longer split open, nor did glories
open from sky-blue mouths, and show paradises, the inferno no longer mourned to see its painful
secrets discovered").

to counter the winds of Flora. Neptune refused, and his chariot submerged. At this point a chariot rich with gold and jewels descended, carrying Pallas Athena. Continuing her age-old conflict with Neptune, she promised her aid to Ferrara as the new Athens and provided three warriors, Castor (Francesco Estense Tassoni), Pollux (Floriani), and Orione (Ferrante Estense Tassoni), "armed with beautiful crests." "When these [the nymphs of the Po] had disappeared, the clouds of Castor and Pollux were already seen to descend, and join from two into one, and bending, and the tempestuous and wonderful cloud of Orione descending, reached the sea . . ." (fig. 1.4), then moving on the elevator to the battle floor. The Floriani papers contain a design for the machine that lowered the challengers with directions in Guitti's hand.[37] For the second appearance of the challengers the temporary stage thus had to support the island with the nymphs of the Po, the chariot of Neptune, and three cloud machines: Pallas in the middle of the stage, the Dioscuri in front, and Orione at the back. The knights performed a "bellissimo passaggio," finally lining up opposite the first three knights for a combat. After the combat, the mastri di campo separated the knights.

To begin the concluding comparsa, that of the champion or mantenitore, the knights of the Arno and the Po made peace at the urging of the bride and bridegroom "in sign of this happy, and so dear union." At this point, the torneo was interrupted by a ballet, to which we shall return later.

After the ballet, the cavaliers saw the scene change again, this time to Latium, with the Tiber flowing through it. From the river arose the god of the Tiber, who implored the aid of heaven against the knights of the Arno and the Po. From the sky appeared a hydra with seven flaming heads, bearing on his back an armed deity, the Genius of Rome (fig. 1.5, LIX). In song, the Genius addressed the Tiber, who replied, and their dialogue developed into an encomium of the members of the Sacchetti family who had achieved glory in Rome. The scene changed to the Elysian Fields, where Aeneas, together with the Genius of Rome and the Tiber, persuaded Mars to retire in favor of Romulus. The forge of Vulcan appeared, where he and the cyclops were forging a new arrow for Venus, singing a bouncy canzonetta with a text in quinari—an innovation from the world of opera—to the clang of their hammers. At Aeneas' urging, they turned to forging a sword for Romulus, puffing their bellows and beating the iron on an anvil. Vulcan, seeing his ancient rival Mars, threatened him but disappeared in fright. Mars returned to the heavens, and the Elysian Fields vanished to the sound of a duet between the Genius and the Tiber. A "gagliardissimo, e bellicoso suono di Trombe" ("most lively, and warlike sound of Trumpets") resounded from

---

[37] Adami, *Pietro Paolo Floriani*, 164–66.

FIG. 1.4 *Seconda Comparsa de' S.ri Venturieri* from *La contesa*

FIG. 1.5 *Invenzione della Comparsa del S.r Mantenitore* from *La contesa*

the heavens, which grew brighter, with lightning flashing everywhere. A cloud descended with Romulus, the mantenitore, wearing a magnificent helmet and armed with sword and pike (fig. 1.6). The Tiber dove back into his river, and the Genius flew off on his hydra. Romulus descended to the campo, and the challengers united in battle order against him. The mantenitore began an elaborate passaggio in which he engaged battle facing the enemy knights. He returned to the stage, and the evening ended with a general combat.

FIG. 1.6   *Comparsa del Sig.r Mantenitore* from *La contesa*

THE FLORIANI MANUSCRIPT

The section of the Floriani manuscript ß related to the performance of *La contesa* consists of thirty-seven folios, which I have numbered autonomously 1–37, written in two hands. (The actual manuscript folios are numbered backwards and upside down beginning on my fol. 37v with "13" and ending on the verso preceding my fol. 1 with "56.") The opening hand continues until fol. 24. On fol. 25 the first hand has crossed out and rewritten the title of the combat or *partita* (commenting "oimè" in the margin) (fig. 1.7), and the second hand continues with the actual description. Hand 1 resumes on fol. 28, hand 2 takes over again at the middle of fol. 33v. Hand 1

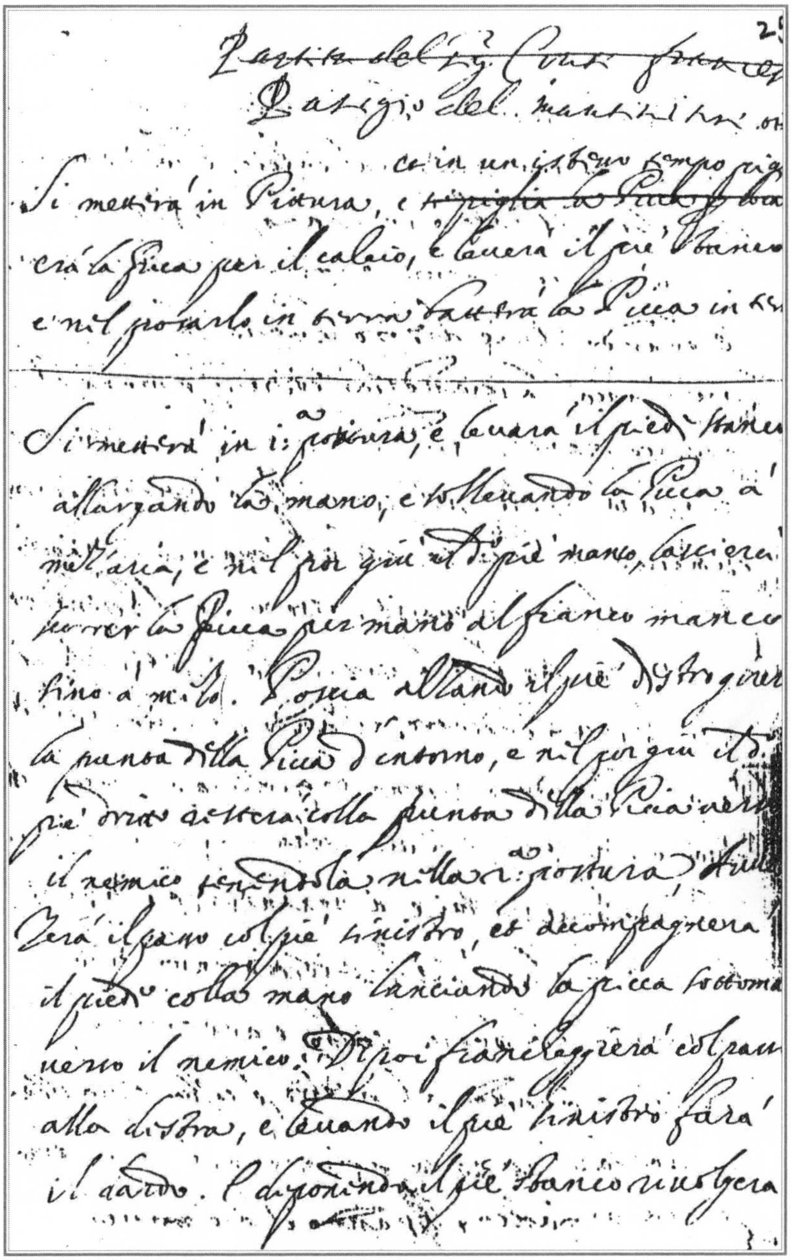

FIG. 1.7   Macerata, Archivio Compagnoni Floriani, manuscript ß, fol. 25

© Archivio Privato Compagnoni Floriani, Macerata.

All rights reserved. Used with permission

returns from fol. 34v to fol. 36, hand 2 copies fols. 36v–37, and hand 1 completes the section. The work is obviously a joint effort, and the corrections and alterations suggest that the manuscript is a private working notebook rather than a fair copy intended for circulation.

The first text-hand is cursive with certain orthographic peculiarities, such as "picha" for "picca," the omission of the second letter of a doubled consonant and the doubling of other consonants (e.g., "versso"), the replacement of "m" by "n" ("tenpo," "senpre"), and the reversal of the consonant pair "-gn." The word "stanco" (usually meaning "tired") is employed for "left" as well as "manco" or "sinistro." The first hand has been identified by Dott. Adami as that of Pietro Paolo Floriani himself, an identification supported by the fact that this is the hand that copied the partita "La Floriana." The difficulties in transcribing Floriani's text have been summed up admirably by Dottor Adami:

> Floriani's writing is a very irregular seventeenth-century cur-
> sive; in some points it is completely unintelligible. Punctuation
> is almost totally absent. Few abbreviations are present. The
> vocabulary is sometimes irregular with numerous variants and
> some imprecisions, surely owing to its personal nature and not
> being intended for the wider circulation of such documents.[38]

The second, more legible hand, with its characteristic back-slanting "d" and spiky "p," is that of Francesco Guitti. (The formation of the word "terra" here, for example, is virtually identical with that of the same word in a letter of Guitti written on 19 August 1627.)[39] The manuscript is illustrated with line-drawings of the various poses and movements described in the text. These are taken from an exhaustive treatise on the tourney by a Ferrarese nobleman, *Il Torneo di Bonaventura Pistofilo* (Bologna: Clemente Ferrone, 1627).

---

[38] Adami, *Scenografia*, 127: "La scrittura del Floriani, [è] una corsiva seicentesca molto irregolare; in alcuni punti risulta del tutto inintelligibile. La punteggiatura è quasi del tutto assente. Sono presenti poche abbreviazioni. Il lessico risulta talvolta irregolare con numerose varianti e alcune imprecisioni, sicuramente dovute alla natura affatto personale e non destinata alla divulgazione di tali documenti."

[39] Reproduced by Irving Lavin in "Lettres de Parmes (1618, 1627–28) et débuts du théâtre baroque," *Le lieu théatral à la renaissance* (Paris: Centre national de la recherche scientifique, 1968; reprint, 1986), 105–58, fig. 1. The identifications are supported by an unnumbered folio of "spese p[er] le machine et musichi et altro p[er] la bariera" ("expenses for the machines and the musicians and other things for the barriera") in hand 1 which refers to "il Guitti" in the third person. The items include sc. 2.2 "dati alli tanburi" and sc. 5.2 "data al balarino."

Like a seventeenth-century dance treatise, the Floriani manuscript first describes individual movements and then arranges them into choreographies. It opens with a section "Mutivi della picha per la bariera: Del passo" ("Movements of the pike for the barriera: Concerning the step"[40]) which assumes that each cavalier carries a pike, perhaps decorated as in the illustrations of halberds in the beautiful manuscript Ferrara, Biblioteca Comunale Ariostea, Ms. I, 708 (fig. 1.8). In his *Oplomachia* of 1621 Pistofilo described the pike as "an instrument of wood, which is generally nine *braccia* long [about six meters], straight, smooth, hard, flexible, and with a sharp iron at the point, suitable for offense, and defense."[41] In *Il Torneo* (1627) he distinguished between the war-pike and the half-pike.[42] The "mutivi" or "motives" are patterned movements, one for each step-unit, in which Floriani describes how the pike is held.

FIG. 1.8   Ferrara, Biblioteca Comunale Ariostea, Ms. I, 708

These instructions can be paralleled in military manuals of the period.[43] The often-reprinted *Wapenhandelinghe van Roers Musquetten ende Spiessen* (1607) of Jacob de Gheyn includes an entire section on the use of the pike. The pike is advanced, gripped vertically in both hands, the right foot forward; it is then lifted with the right hand under the butt; finally it rests against the right shoulder supported by the right hand, the feet spread. The rest position is "the pike ordered," with the weapon held in the right hand, the left hand on the hip, the feet apart with the weight resting

---

[40] The step (passo) was reckoned as 1/3 the height of the man (*OPLOMACHIA/DI/Bonauentura Pistofilo nobile Ferrarese/. . ./*In Siena 1621./Per Hercole Gori, 33).

[41] *OPLOMACHIA* i, 5: "La Picca è uno stromento di legno, ch'è lungo per ordinario nove braccia, diritto, liscio, duro, flessibile, e con acuto ferro in punta, atto all'offesa, e alla difesa. . . ."

[42] *IL TORNEO/DI BONAVENTURA PISTOFILO/NOBILE FERRARESE . . .* In Bologna per il Ferrone . . . M.DC.XXVI (dedication dated 1627) (New York Public Library, Spencer Collection), 145.

[43] See Jacob de Gheyn, *Wapenhandelinghe van Roers Musquetten ende Spiessen* (1607), edited rather cursorily by David J. Blackmore as *The Renaissance Drill Book* (London: Greenhill Books/Mechanicsburg, PA: Stackpole Books, 2003).

on the left leg. To order the pike it is lowered from the advanced position with the right hand under the butt, the weight resting on the right leg, then with both hands on the pike to reach the ordered position. The pike is shouldered and carried either level or sloping. To port the pike, it is held in both hands, then in the left alone. The pike is charged to a horizontal position at shoulder height in one motion from the advance. It may be checked and trailed, held at the head, whence it may be charged by palming it forward.

The next section of the Floriani manuscript enumerates eleven poses of body and pike in which the knight can enter the field of battle. Each of them is then described and illustrated by a line-drawing on the following recto. (The sources from Pistofilo's *Torneo* are indicated here by the Roman numerals of the plates in his text.) In the Floriani drawings, the performers wear plumed helmets (usually quite elaborately decorated, in one case surmounted by an Imperial eagle, an emblem of the Bentivoglio family) (fig. 1.9, XLII, "Positura, con la picca impugnata nel calcio"); such helmets also have their counterparts in the Ariostea manuscript. The knights wear in addition upper body armor covering the shoulders, torso, arms, and hands; short kilts; and slashed breeches and hose, with soft flat shoes, as in Pistofilo's *Torneo*. They carry pikes and wear swords. Several drawings show a favor floating from the knight's helmet. The mantenitore is depicted with a cloak over his costume ("mantinitore con il manto") (figs. 1.9, 1.10a, 1.10b = I, "Come debba il Cavaliero, mentre passeggia il Campo, portar la picca da Guerra in ispalla"). Rather sketchy insignia appear on some of the figures: a star for the mantenitore, fleurs-de-lis—another Bentivoglio emblem—on another knight. The drawings in the manuscript may be only schematic and fanciful representations of the actual costumes, however. The drawing of the mantenitore, for example, does not particularly resemble Guitti's engraving, "L'ultima comparsa del mantenitore" ("The final appearance of the mantenitore"), where the champion does wear a cloak but also a much more elaborate headdress. (Not only did the mantenitore not remove his helmet for combat, unlike the knights in the 1656 Roman giostra for Christina of Sweden [see Chapter 8], but Guitti informs us that "having laid aside his first headdress, [the champion] adorned himself with a greater one, more beautiful, and richer.")[44]

Here is a typically showy pose for the the entry of a challenger: "The sixth. The pike rests in the hand, that is, above the shoulder in height as much as the arm can reach with the butt [of the pike] in the hands, and the point on the ground behind

---

[44] Guitti, *La contesa*, 62–64: ". . . che deposto il primo Pennacchio, s'adornò di maggiore, e più bello, e più ricco."

FIG. 1.9   Macerata, Floriani manuscript ß, fol. 5r

© Archivio Privato Compagnoni
Floriani, Macerata. All rights reserved.
Used with permission

FIG. 1.10a   Macerata, Floriani manuscript ß,
fol. 8r

© Archivio Privato Compagnoni
Floriani, Macerata. All rights reserved.
Used with permission

FIG. 1.10b   Bonaventura Pistofilo, *Il torneo*,
plate I (New York Public Library,
Spencer Collection)

the shoulders, the which point must bend toward the left heel, nor must it ever be beyond the body [vita] on the right or left side."[45]

In the Floriani manuscript, the *pusture* or poses are followed by descriptions of *sbracciate*. Floriani introduces them without giving a definition: "Sbracciate: And because the importance of all the movements seems to consist in the varieties of the sbracciate, which are introduced for tacit challenges to the enemy, which are presented here below" [fol. 12v]. Pistofilo is more circumstantial: "the sbracciate are certain movements of the arm in a circular motion, which with the union of the hand and the pike planted in the fist, or held in some other manner, foot, and body show a mastery of the art, and sometimes an immediate action to offend the other."[46]

A typical description of a sbracciata in the Floriani manuscript runs as follows: "the first is the sbracciata which is made with the right foot and it is made in this manner. Raise the pike as high as the arm can go and at the same time raise the right foot which was behind and bring the hand and the foot forward together. At the same instant the hand and the foot draw backward, noting that as soon as the right foot touches the ground the left one must be raised forward and in the air with a slight semicircular motion."[47]

Folio 16v of the Floriani manuscript contains the single word "chiamata" ("call") illustrated on fol. 17. Pistofilo defines the chiamate as "according to me, certain movements of the hand, and of weapons accompanied by the placement of the body in an act of disdain" to invite the opponent to battle."[48]

The remainder of the manuscript consists of choreographies for single combats or *partite*. (The word can also mean both instrumental musical variations and sports matches.) I refer to the partite as choreographies deliberately, since the Floriani manuscript follows the pattern of contemporary dance manuals such as Fabritio

---

[45] "6 la sesta la picha si posa á mano cioe sopra alla spalla in altezza quanto pol andar il bracio con il ricalcio nelle mani, et la punta in terra dietro alle spalle la quel punta deve piegarsi versso il calcagno stanco ne mai deve esser fuor della vita dalla banda destra o sinistra" (fol. 7v).

[46] Pistofilo, *Il torneo*, 207: "Sono le sbracciate certi movimenti del braccio che tondeggiano, le quali con l'unione della mano e picca inarborata in pugno, od in altra maniera tenuta, piè, e persona mostrano una maestria nell'arte, ed alle volte un atto immediato di voler altrui offendere."

[47] "i é prima la sbracciata che si fa con il piede ~~dritto~~ destro et si fa in questa maniera si leva la picha ~~da terra~~ quanto po andar' alto il bracio et si leva in un istesso tenpo il piede destro quale era in dietro et la man et il piede portato in nanzzi nel medesimo istante ~~p[er] poco si sostenta et poi pur in un medesimo tempo~~ la mano et il piede si ritira in dietro avertendo che subito che il piede destro sara fermato in terra il sinistro con un poco di simi cerchio sia levato in anti et in aria" (fol. 12v).

[48] Pistofilo, *Il torneo*, 205: "Le chiamate . . . sono secondo me certi movimenti di mano, e d'armi accompagnati dalla positura della persona in atto di sprezzo. . . ."

Caroso's *Il ballarino* (1581) and his *Nobiltà di dame* (1600), and Cesare Negri's *Le gratie d'Amore* (1602), which give general steps and then employ them in specific choreographies, complete with music. Like a dance, the torneo takes place in the hall of a palace, here transformed for the occasion into a theater. (In one place the writer of the manuscript crosses out "sala" and substitutes "teatro.") The direction to the dancer to proportion his movements to the size of the room recurs in Italian dance-manuals from at least the mid-fifteenth century. The cavaliers perform before a prince and cardinals, called the "presence" in dance terminology, and they begin by making the same reverence that opened most social dances. The authors of the torneo employ "vita" not as "waist" but in Caroso's sense of "body." The description "in profilo" recalls Caroso's "in prospettiva"—"cioè all' incontro à'i circostanti" ("that is facing the bystanders") in which two dancers face each other on a diagonal. Conversely, in a dance-choreography Caroso orders "giostrando tutti insieme"—"all jousting together." The term "barriera" is employed generically in the manuscript for a torneo on foot, but it was also the title of two dances—one for a couple, the other a version for six dancers—notated by Caroso. Other terms in the manuscript descriptions have musical connotations: in addition to "partite," the "pasegio," the title of the last choreography, was both a musical term for chains of elaborate figuration, and a dance term meaning a "progress," or movement in a line.

The number of participants in each choreography is not always indicated, except for generic references to "il nemico," "the enemy." Given the prevalence of couple-formations in social dances, it may be that the "nemico" was another performer who repeated symmetrically the movements described. Even where the title of a partita specifies two performers—for example, Vincenzo Tassoni and the mantenitore in "La Vincenza"—only one performer's movements are notated. Other choreographies prescribe "3 cavalieri" or name three performers, and the manuscript ends with a *pasegio* for six cavaliers. Most of the choreographies end with a direction which, given the vagaries of Floriani's orthography, can be interpreted as "finire" ("to end") or "ferire" ("to strike"). The latter seems preferable for two reasons. First, a passage on fol. 37 in the more legible hand of Guitti clearly reads "ferisce," "strikes." Second, Pistofilo's *Torneo* contains an explicit reference to "striking," which he defines as "touching with the point of the pike that place, in which in the Capitoli [the rules of the engagement] one acquires the Merit of [being] the best striker . . . that is, in the head."[49]

---

[49] "[ferir] . . . toccar con la punta della picca quel luogo, nel quale ne' Capitoli s'acquista il Premio del meglio feritore . . . s'intende nel capo" (*Il torneo*, 231).

The Floriani manuscript transmits seventeen *partite*. Like instrumental canzonas and dance-choreographies, several of them have titles derived from personal names: "La Tassona," "La Vincenza," "La Floriana," La Crispa," "La Gesualda," and "La Ferdinanda." The first four *partite* refer to participants in the *torneo*. "La Gesualda" probably alludes to the marriage of Carlo Gesualdo, Prince of Venosa, with Leonora d'Este, the sister of Cesare d'Este, last duke of Ferrara, in 1594. The choreographies "La Ferdinanda" and the "Pasegio for six danced before the Grand Duchess" ("Pasagio fatto in sei avanti la gran duchessa") do not form part of *La contesa*. They were probably composed for a visit to Ferrara later in the same year by Maria Maddalena of Austria, Grand Duchess of Tuscany and mother of the Grand Duke Ferdinando II.

Floriani described the entertainment for the Grand Duchess in a letter of 4 October 1631 to his nephew Pompeo Compagnoni:

> A few days before the arrival of the Grand Duchess Cardinal Pallotta asked a group of knights here if they wished to do a barriera and a campo aperto, that is an encounter where the Cardinal also entrusted me to take part . . . in a villa of Marchese Tassoni called Casalecchio, six knights, that is Count Francesco, Count Ferrante, Count Vincenzo Tassoni, brothers, Count Alfredo Tassoni . . . and signor Borsio Bonacossi and I, armed, did a beautiful passaggio with beautiful crests and then we fought with three pike-strokes and five sword strokes, and then in a group of four we did a beautiful difficult ballet, where certainly I was greatly afraid of failing but God wished to favor our good will to serve the cardinal and that princess and princes, so everything went so well that her highness and everyone were most satisfied: Saturday morning sig. Cornelio Bentivoglio, sig. Francesco Ottavio Piccolomini, the nephews of Cardinal Bevilacqua, and Marchese Tassoni, and a Count Nosieti appeared in a theater made of beautiful trees and a facing box where were Madam and her sons and a group of ladies; these six knights appeared three by three all armed with beautiful crests and customary embroidered trappings and made a lance-stroke . . . and skirmished with the sword which was a splendid sight and her highness, most satisfied, got in her carriage and went on her way. . . .[50]

---

[50] "Il Sig. Cardinal Pallotta . . . giorni avanti della venuta della gran duchessa pregò qua una mano de cavalieri che si volesse far una barriera et un campo aperto cioè al in contro dove che il sig. Cardinale

The description of "La Gesualda" may stand as typical of the single choreo-graphies. "In the first position [of the illustrations] raise the left foot, and [raise] the Pike up to the left shoulder, and putting down the left foot, make the sbracciata forward. And putting down the right foot, and walking, make a sbracciata behind; and letting the Pike slide halfway through the hand while putting down the left foot, enfold it with the left [hand] and turning it, put it on the shoulder with the butt toward the enemy. And with the right foot raised and lowering [the pike], throw it from the shoulder, and quickly taking it with the left hand two palmi (about 5 cm.) above the butt without putting the right hand [on it] throw it toward the enemy, and place yourself in profile with the left foot forward, and take it with the right hand; and strike."[51] (Since the pike is retaken after being launched, this implies that it was not actually thrown, but that the throwing was mimed.)

Almost all published accounts of tornei (including Guitti's) display an anomaly. The action onstage is described in detail and texts are given, but the descriptions simply lead up to a combat and then resume afterward. The Floriani manuscript, on the contrary, describes only the combats and leaves us to fit them into Guitti's account. To the first comparsa, performed by Vincenzo and Alfonso Estense Tassoni and Giovanni Maria Crispi, we can assign the *passeggio della prima comparsa*, which mentions the three challengers by name, and the three solo partite, one for each avventuriero. The second *comparsa* was danced by Francesco and Ferrante Estense

---

mi affidò ancora a me entrarvi . . . in una villa del Sig. Marchese Tasone chiamata Casalecchio, sei cavalieri cioè il Sig. Conte Francesco, il sig. Conte Ferante il sig. Conte Vincenzo Tasoni fratelli, il sig. Conte Alfredo Tasoni . . . et il signor Borsio Bonacossi et io facemo armati un belissimo paseggio con belissimi cimieri et poi combatesimo a' di a' di 3 colpi di piche et 5 di stocco, et poi in 4 facesimo un belisimo baletto travaglioso, che certo io ne stavo con gran timore di falire ma dio volle favorire la nostra bona volontà di servire al signor Cardinale et a quella principessa et principi, che andò il tutto tanto bene che sua altezza et tutti ne restarono sadisfatisimi: la matina Sabato il sig. Cornelio Bentivoglio il sig. Francesco Otavio Picolomini li nepoti del sig. cardinal Bevilacqua et il marchese Tasoni et un Sig. conte Nosieti comparvero in un teatro fatto di belisimi arbori et in faccia con un palco dove era madama et di lei fig.lioli et una mano di dame; comparvero questi 6 cavalieri a tre a tre tutti armati con belisimi cimieri et bardature arecamate di uso et sortirono un colpo di lancia . . . et scaramucciarono di stocco che fece belisima vista et sua altezza sadisfatissima subito montò in carozza et se ne andò al suo viagio . . ." (Adami, *Pietro Paolo Floriani*, 141).

[51] Folio 36v: "In p[rim]a postura levará il pie' manco, e la Picca in alto alla spalla sinistra e deponendo il pie' manco in terra fará la sbracciata inanzi. e ponendo il pie' destro in terra, e camminando colla fará una sbracciata in dietro; e lasciando scorrere la Picca per la mano sino á mezo nel porre il pie' manco in terra l'infodrerá dalla sinistra e girandola la porrá in ispalla col calcio al nemico, e col pie destro alto e deponendola la gitterá dalla Spalla, e velocem[en]te colla sinistra pigliandola sopr'l calcio doi palmi senza por la mano dritta la lanciará [fol. 37] verso'l nemico, e si metterá in profilo col pie' manco avanti, e la prenderá colla mano dritta; E ferire."

Tassoni and Floriani, who are named in the *passeggio della seconda comparsa* and *passeggio secondo*, and Floriani has a solo. The *passeggio del mantenitore*, for Rossetti, is described at length and was clearly intended to be a virtuoso performance. The choreographies of Francesco and Vincenzo Estense Tassoni with the mantenitore presumably belong to the third part of the torneo, after the champion's appearance. The final general combat was most likely the choreography "La Tassona. Partite fatte da' Cavalieri con il mantenitore." Floriani summed up his judgment of the occasion in an undated letter to his nephew, Pompeo Compagnoni: "although I spent some scudi for this barriera, with all that I was particularly pleased to have been there since I showed that I am good at every thing to these Signori Sacchetti to whom I am so obligated. . . ."[52]

The Music

Traditionally, the music for Ferrarese chivalric spectacles comprised two types. The first was essentially martial noise, "musiche strepitose" produced by "high" or loud trumpets, fifes, cornetts, trombones, and drums. The second consisted of more delicate madrigalian concerted music performed "sometimes with flutes [recorders], sometimes with lutes, sometimes with viols, sometimes with voices alone, & sometimes with all those mixed together, either all, or a good part."[53]

Another element can be added to the jigsaw puzzle of reconstructing a complete chivalric combat. The "musiche strepitose" of trumpets, fifes, and drums were not merely generalized festive noise, but carefully defined signals to movement such as the Recall (Raccolta), the "far alta" for raising the pike, the halt (fermarsi), March, Change, invite the enemy to do battle, trot, to the death, the rejoicing, burying the dead.[54] Pistofilo notes that different countries employ different signals and notates the tamburo lines, even distinguishing left and right drum-strokes. To the notated signals he adds dotted lines that coordinate the movements of the knight with the signals, showing "when the Knight must begin to raise his foot from the ground, or

---

[52] "E di questa bariera ben che ci abbi speso qualche scudo con tutto ciò io ho gusto particolare esservi stato poiché ho fatto vedere che son bono da ogni cosa a questi Sig.ri Sachetti che li son tanto obligato . . ." (Adami, *Pietro Paolo Floriani*, 156).

[53] "Quando con flauti, quando con leuti, quando con viole, quando con voci sole, & quando con tutto ciò meschiato insieme, o in tutto, o in buona parte" (*Il monte di Feronia* [Ferrara: Panizza, 1562], quoted in Walker, "Echi estensi," 339).

[54] Pistofilo, *Il torneo*, 111.

lower it, to then raise it, or resting on the ground just on that note, in which that line ends, which has its stem up, or down."[55]

None of the vocal music for *La contesa* survives, and none of the known sources gives details about the vocal music or its performers. From an examination of the libretto in the light of contemporary materials, we can extrapolate some idea of the musical settings. Irregularly mixed seven- and eleven-syllable verses such as those that predominate in the libretto published by Guitti were set by contemporary composers in recitative style. Eight-syllable lines or alternations of eight and seven syllables, such as the final duet canzona of the Tiber and the Genius of Rome, prompted lively settings in hemiola rhythms alternating between triple and duple rhythmic groupings of six units (123 223/12 22 32). The five-syllable lines of the canzona of the four nymphs of the Po and the canzonetta of the cyclops also imply fast and rhythmic settings, as in the festive chorus "Lasciate i monti" in Act I of the Striggio–Monteverdi *L'Orfeo.*

The instruments are identified in Guitti's account only as "most sweet" or "varied." In seventeenth-century terminology "sweet" implied "low" or soft instruments, as we see them in Andrea Sacchi's drawing of the veglia or evening entertainment for the 1634 Barberini joust (fig. 1.11), or the painting by Filippo Gagliardi and Filippo Lauri of the 1656 Barberini carosello: violins, harpsichord, large lutes, and cornetti (see fig. 8.9). Harps, viols, chamber organs, and recorders were also included among the soft instruments. Like the operas of the period, *La contesa* was full of special sound-effects not included in the score. In the forge of Vulcan, for example, the new arrow for Cupid and the sword for Romulus were forged "to the sound of the striking of hammers on the anvil"—two centuries before *Il Trovatore* and *Das Rheingold.*

The real musical treasure of the Floriani manuscript consists of five rather insignificant loose sheets. Three are written by the same hand, which is firm, elegant, and literate (fig. 1.12a). The other two are also written by the same (second) hand, which is less literate both musically and verbally (fig. 1.12b): neither seems identical with either of the two text-hands. By contrast with the firm calligraphy of the first set, in the second sheets the note-stems are carelessly drawn, the beams waver, and the clefs are vestigial. The second scribe omits the dots at the opening of the first two dances, which makes nonsense of the rhythm, and confusingly transcribes the B-flats of the original as the number 6, improperly suggesting a continuo figuration.

---

[55] ". . . quando debba'l Cavalier principiar' a levare'l piè da terra, o a calarlo, per haverlo di poi alto, over posato in terra per appunto in quella nota, nella quale essa linea termina, che ha'l gambo all'insù, overo all'ngiù . . ." (118).

FIG. 1.11   Andrea Sacchi, *Veglia in Casa Falconieri* from *Festa, Fatta in Roma alli*
25. *di Febraio MDCXXXIV* (Rome, Biblioteca Apostolica Vaticana)

Both sets of parts contain the same three dances. The first (complete) set is written in trio-sonata texture (two treble instruments and bass). The dances are headed "Balletto Grave," "Galiarda," and "Corenta." Two parts in G clefs are designated "Primo soprano" and "Secondo soprano"; the third, unmarked, is a bass part in the customary F clef. The second set, now lacking the second soprano part, was clearly copied from the first, whose idiosyncracies of spelling it reproduces. Unlike its model, it is identified as part of *La contesa*: "baletto fatto nella bariera a Ferara p[er] le nozze del Sig.r Fran[ces]co Sachetti" ("balletto performed in the barriera at Ferrara for the wedding of Sig.r Francesco Sacchetti"). The bass part, whose player presumably directed the ensemble, indicates that the the sheets were employed in an actual performance, as anyone who has ever played for a dance troupe will recognize: the Balletto Grave is marked "va replicato 3 volte" ("gets repeated 3 times"), the Galiarda also "3 volte," and the Corenta "quanto e necessario" ("as many times as necessary"). In the other copied part the indefinite "Primo soprano" of the model parts is replaced by the specific indication "Violino," which instrument probably served also for the missing second treble of the performing parts.

FIG. 1.12a Macerata, Floriani manuscript ß,
separate leaves, first music hand

© Archivio Privato Compagnoni
Floriani, Macerata. All rights reserved.
Used with permission

FIG. 1.12b Macerata, Floriani manuscript ß, separate leaves, second music hand

© Archivio Privato Compagnoni Floriani, Macerata.
All rights reserved. Used with permission

These five sheets convey a surprising amount of information. They indicate that the instrumental forces for the barriera included two treble instruments, probably violins, and continuo instruments—harpsichord, organ, harp, or lutes of varying sizes. (Ferrara had produced a celebrated family of lute-players, the Piccinini, who worked for Enzo and Guido Bentivoglio.) Contrasted with these were the trumpets and drums of the military movements. Accounts of the 1656 Roman carosello for Christina of Sweden at the Palazzo Barberini alle Quattro Fontane similarly describe the alternation of sinfonie played by soft instruments—the lutes, violins, and cornetts visible in the painting—with the trumpets and drums that provided signals for the movements of the horses and the combat.

We know from financial records that instrumental parts were extracted from full scores, but they rarely survived. The present parts provide a precious example of actual performance materials, copied no more carefully than the occasion demanded by a hired instrumentalist, a category proverbially at the low end of the social and intellectual scale of musicians.

The music of the Floriani notebook reflects both social and theatrical dance. The Balletto Grave is a competently written little piece, if a little over-dependent on parallel tenths between soprano and bass. The Gagliarda is a triple-meter transformation of the Balletto, and the Corenta is written over the same bass, thus forming a miniature dance-variation set [ex. 1.1]. The proportional relationships of the torneo pieces are Balletto: 2 half-notes = Galiarda: 3 half-notes = Corenta: two dotted halves. This combination of dances is typical of Italian dance-manuals around 1600. Fabrizio Caroso's *Nobiltà di Dame* (Venice, 1600), for example, contains a choreography entitled *Laura suave* that was danced to the Aria di Fiorenza ("O che nuovo miracolo"). The melody is presented first in its original duple meter, then transformed into a galliard in triple meter, and finally becomes a "sciolta" or saltarello version in quicker triple meter, with a final short canario, also in triple, as a coda.[56] The same three-part scheme in increasingly faster tempi—a "Ballo piano adagio," "Trapasso un poco presto," and "Saltarello presto" all on the same bass—occurs in the first intermedio of the 1639 *Chi soffre speri* presented by Cardinal Francesco Barberini.

It is tempting to attribute the authorship of the music for the barriera to Antonio Goretti (c.1570–1649). Goretti was a distinguished Ferrarese amateur, the owner of an important collection of music and musical instruments in whose house the theorist Artusi heard the madrigals that prompted his notorious attack on Monteverdi and

---

[56] Fabritio Caroso, *Nobiltà di Dame (1600)*, trans. and ed. Julia Sutton (Oxford: Oxford University Press, 1986), 162–72.

Monteverdi's brother's celebrated reply. As a composer, Goretti was sufficiently accomplished to collaborate with Monteverdi for the 1628 celebrations in Parma (Francesco Guitti's apotheosis as a stage-designer) and to act as Monteverdi's assistant and agent for their preparation. Unfortunately, although there are some similarities between Goretti's script and that of the titles in the fair copy (the less literate script of the second copyist is clearly not his), Goretti's sensible handwriting lacks such features as the rather dashing backward-slashing "d" and the carefully closed double "t" of the music copyist.[57]

THE FUNCTION OF THE MUSIC

From the point of view of instrumental music and dance, the high point of *La contesa* was the ballet intermezzo. Perhaps this unusual feature, more character-istic of Florentine than of Ferrarese practice, was a concession to the origins of the Sacchetti. (A ballet intermezzo also formed part of the 1634 Barberini veglia in Rome, an occasion thick with Florentine associations.)

Guitti's description of the ballet allows us to put one more piece of our puzzle firmly in place:

> . . . in sign of so happy, and so dear a union they summoned the Drums, and the Violins; To the new and unaccustomed sound of which, the six Knights placed themselves in two ranks, and began a most beautiful ballet, which was divided into three parts. The first was a slow Ballo; The second a Gagliarda; The third a Corrente. Here various groupings were seen to form sequences: Nor did their arms keep them from now disordering themselves in ordered manner, now approach-ing, now moving away, & now turning in circles. Indeed, their sureness in arms was made known, since neither the weight, and inconvenience of their armor, nor the great elaboration of the feather Headdresses impeded them, not getting tangled up in approaching, or scattering in moving away. But above all it was an unexpected wonder to see that in the narrowness of the Field, owing to the number of the audience, the size of the Headdresses was not the cause of disorder in the interlaced

---

[57] For samples of Goretti's hand see the letters from Parma in 1627 in Ferrara, Archivio di Stato, Archivio Bentivoglio, and Lavin, "Lettres de Parme."

Ex. 1.1   *Baletto fatto nella bariera a Ferara p[er] le nozze del Sig.r Fran[ces]co Sacchetti* (Macerata, Floriani manuscript ß).

Ex. 1.1—*continued*

Ex. 1.1—*continued*

Ex. 1.1—*continued*

circles of the dance, since they were always loose, and free and not touching each other, nor getting tied up with the helmets. But most happily they ended with a beautiful Corrente, during whose vehemence one heard from the Stage a most lively call of Drums, which from the Clouds gave the signal of a proud invitation to battle. At the call, leaving the sound of the dances, the Drums of the dancing Knights responded brightly, & those of the Stage answered them, so that at the new trial of arms, and battle, the whole dance was upset, so that the Knights, almost challenging each other, not being able to guess the cause of the new noise, and laying hand to their swords, with beautiful advances and withdrawals, displayed a thousand unexpected surmises. But turning their eyes back to the Scene, they saw it all change, appearing there unexpectedly the beautiful, and pleasing Fields of Lazio. . . .[58]

Beyond its identification of the music in the Floriani manuscript, perhaps the most interesting point in this passage is that the barriers between the military combats in the hall and the elegant miniature opera on stage that had been established at the beginning of the representation are broken for artistic effect, a bit like the "collapsing" cornice of the proscenium. It is not surprising that the noble cavaliers are transformed into social dancers moving in what had been the space of their combat, since

---

[58] Guitti, *La contesa*, 40: ". . . in segno di lieta, e sì cara unione fecero venire i Tamburri, ed i Violini; Al nuovo, e non più usato suono de quali, li sei Cavalieri si posero in due schiere, e diedero principio ad un bellissimo balletto, il quale fù diviso in tre parti. L'una fù Ballo grave; La seconda Gagliarda; La terza Corrente. Quì si vedevano vari ravvolgimenti, e varie figure da loro concertati passi formarsi; Nè per l'arme si vietava loro ora ordinatamente disordinarsi, ora l'pressarsi, ora l'allontanarsi, & ora in giro volgersi. Anzi quivi la loro sicurezza nell'arme fù conosciuta, che nè il peso, & ingombro dell'armature, nè il grande invoglio de Pennachi fù loro d'impedimento, non intricandosi per l'appressarsi, non disperdendosi per l'allontanarsi. Mà sopra tutto fù in inaspettabile meraviglia il vedere, che nell'angustia del Campo per la quantità della gente, la grandezza de Pennachi non fù cagione di disordine frà gli intrecciati giri delle danze, restando sempre sciolti, e liberi, e non toccandosi l'un coll'al[41]tro, nè incatenandosi co' Cimieri. Mà felicissimamente si ridussero ad una bellissima Corrente, nella veheme[n]za della quale dalla parte della Scena si sentì una gagliardissima chiamata di Tamburri, che dalle Nubi davan segno di fiero invito à battaglia. A questa chiamata, lasciando il suon del ballo, risposero vivamente i Tamburri de Cavalieri danzanti, & à questi replicarono quelli della Scena, siche al nuovo trattar d'armi, e di battaglia tutto si pose in isgombiglio quel ballo. Onde i Cavalieri, quasi in atto di diffidenza l'un dell'altro, non congetturando la cagione del nuovo strepito, e ponendo mano sù brandi, con bellissime ritirate, & avvanzamenti, diedero segno di mille non preveduti sospetti. Mà rivoltando essi gli occhi alla Scena, la videro mutarsi tutta, apparendo quivi improvise le bellissime, & amene Campagne del Lazio. . . ."

a general dance was a traditional conclusion for masques, but here the genres are mixed. The loud drums of war introduce the violins of civil dance, and at its end the dance is broken up and the violins silenced by the intervention of the stage in the form of a dialogue with the drums in the hall. Almost at the same time as the production of *La contesa*, Claudio Monteverdi, in his festal mass for San Marco celebrating the end of the Plague of 1631 similarly broke convention by bringing trumpets and drums from their civic and quasi-military function in the Piazza into the sacred context of the ducal chapel.

THE MUSIC OF CHIVALRIC COMBATS

In addition to the Floriani manuscript, a few bits of music survive that might be connected with staged chivalric contests. Strangely, works entitled "battaglia" are not the most likely candidates for such attribution. Although battle pieces survive from as early as the fifteenth century, many later ones were based on Clément Jannequin's chanson "La Guerre," published in 1528. Subsequent battaglie were written for various instruments, including keyboard and lute, and instrumental ensembles. That the genre was by no means confined to situations depicting actual battles is confirmed by the fact that Adriano Banchieri recommended the performance of an organ battaglia during the Sequence of the Easter mass, "Victimæ paschali," to illustrate the verse "Mors et vita duello conflixere mirando" ("Death and life have contended in a wondrous combat"), and Maundy Thursday was celebrated at St. Mark's in Venice with a "messa della battaglia." The *Teatro armonico spirituale* (Rome: Robletti, 1619) of Giovanni Francesco Anerio ends with "Eccone al gran Damasco," a "Dialogo della Conversion di S. Paolo" that contains a "combattimento" for six instruments. Girolamo Frescobaldi, organist of the Cappella Giulia in St. Peter's and a member of the household of Cardinal Francesco Barberini from 1634, included a keyboard work titled "La Battaglia" in the 1637 Aggiunta to his first book of toccatas (to which the owner of one copy has added "navale").[59]

The score of the opera-torneo *Le pretensioni del Tebro e del Po* of Marco Marazzoli and Ascanio Pio di Savoia, presented at Ferrara for Don Taddeo Barberini in 1642 (Biblioteca Apostolica Vaticana, Chigi Q. VIII 191: see Chapter 4) provides no music for the combat itself, which the instrumentalists presumably improvised ("Quì si fà

---

[59] See Frederick Hammond, *Girolamo Frescobaldi* (Cambridge, MA: Harvard University Press, 1983), 23, 212, 334; James H. Moore, *Vespers at St. Mark's: Music of Alessandro Grandi, Giovanni Rovetta and Francesco Cavalli*, 2 vols. (Ann Arbor: UMI, 1981), 1:94–95.

il Combattimento"), as in the "Fiera di Farfa" intermezzo of Cardinal Francesco Barberini's 1639 *Chi soffre speri* ("Qui và il combattimento"). However, the *Pretensioni* score does open with a "Battaglia," of which only the bass part is given.

A rare example of what the musicians must have improvised for such a "Combattimento" occurs at the end of the second act of Monteverdi's *Il ritorno d'Ulisse in patria* of 1641 [ex. 1.2]. The score directs "Qui uà un tocco di guerra da tutti gl'istromenti" ("Here there goes a touch of war-[music] by all the instruments"). This is followed by a "Sinfonia da Guerra" in five parts that presents ever-faster figurations of a G major chord, followed by a furious aria for Ulisse, "Alle morti, alle stragi," in the same key and style.[60]

Other possible survivors of theatrical combat occur in seventeenth-century keyboard and lute manuscripts. A set of Florentine lute manuscripts in the German-isches National-Museum in Nuremberg containing music for the 1608 Florentine wedding celebrations (perhaps in the hand of the Medici court lutenist Lorenzo Allegri [1567–1648]) includes a "Barriera Balletto," a "Preludio della Battaglia" and "Battaglia," and an incomplete "Ballo de Cavalli."[61] Francesca Caccini's opera *La liberazione di Ruggiero dall'isola di Alcina* of 1625 ends with a complex consisting of a "Ballo Nobilissimo," a "Coro di Cavalieri Liberati" (knights freed from the enchantments of Alcina), a "Ballo a Cavallo" (for which no music is provided), and a "Madrigale per i Liberati."

The keyboard volume discovered by Adriano Cavicchi in the Biblioteca Comunale of Ancona contains a "Ballo del Cavallo per C." in triple meter and a "Ballo del cavallo" in duple meter.[62] The keyboard manuscript Ravenna, Biblioteca Comunale Classense 545, the "Libro di fra Gioseffo da Ravenna"—like Ferrara, a city belonging to the papal states—includes a work titled "La Barriera" (fols. 96v-98). The texture consists of a right-hand melody over block chords in the left hand. The harmonic

---

[60] See Ellen Rosand, *Monteverdi's Last Operas* (Berkeley: University of California Press, 2007), facsimiles 16–17.

[61] See Victor Coelho, *The Manuscript Sources of Seventeenth-Century Italian Lute Music* (New York: Garland Publishing, 1995), 110–15, 427–42.

[62] Adriano Cavicchi, "Appunti sulle relazioni fra Frescobaldi e l'ambiente musicale marchigiano: l'intavolatura di Ancona," *Girolamo Frescobaldi nel IV centenario della nascita*, ed. Sergio Durante and Dinko Fabris (Florence: Olschki, 1986), 87–106. This interesting manuscript deserves further study. Its concordances with works of Frescobaldi and G. B. Ferrini point it in the direction of Rome. Thus the two pieces headed "della Regina" may refer, not to the multiple royal wedding celebrations in Ferrara in 1598, as Cavicchi hypothesises, but to the passage of the Queen of Hungary, Maria Anna of Spain, through Ancona in 1631, escorted by Don Taddeo Barberini as the personal guest of the papacy on her way to wed the future emperor Ferdinand III; see Coelho, *Manuscript Sources*, 439, 610, 642.

structure is simple, employing both V-I and ii-I progressions. The meter alternates between duple and triple, with a three-measure section serving as a ritornello.[63] Guitar prints also contain pieces entitled "barriera."[64]

IMPORTANCE OF THE FLORIANI MANUSCRIPT

For the student of seventeenth-century spectacle, perhaps the central problem is the incomplete nature of the surviving source material. Few indeed are the celebrations for which we have complete visual, verbal, musical, choreographic, and financial records. Bernini's fireworks to celebrate the birth of Louis XIV in 1638 are known only through a payment record.[65] We have Claudio Achillini's gargantuan text for the 1628 torneo, *Mercurio e Marte*, in Parma, but not a note of Monteverdi's music. And, as we know from Venetian opera, even if a score survives it does not necessarily indicate the instrumentation that was so important in performance. (Monteverdi, daunted by the task of setting "more than a thousand verses" of Achillini's text, where he could not "find variation in the affetti" he sought to "vary the manner of concerting them.")[66]

Although we know that music played a central role in spectacles based on the metaphor of combat, key pieces of the puzzle are missing: the music for the seminal *Castello di Gorgoferusa* of 1561 in Ferrara, the score of Apollo's mimed combat with the dragon in the 1589 Florentine intermedi, the music for the Barberini jousts of 1634 and 1656, and for the *balletto a cavallo* in Florence in 1637.

In a sense, it is unrealistic to expect the survival of such materials. Accustomed to the availability of complete sets of scores and parts for standard works, we forget how such productions were created. They were often composed in a short time (supposedly three days for *La Maschera Trionfante*, Bologna, 1643: see Chapter 4), and such haste resulted in dashing off performing materials ad hoc. Singers memorized their parts, which were either worn out by then or thrown away soon after, and instrumentalists presumably worked from the seventeenth-century equivalent

---

[63] Alexander Silbiger, ed., *17th-Century Keyboard Music*, 12 (New York: Garland Publishing, 1987).

[64] Cf. Saverio Franchi, *Annali della stampa musicale romana dei secoli XVI-XVII: I/1: Edizioni di musica pratica dal 1601 al 1650* (Rome: IBIMUS, 2006).

[65] Hammond, *Music and Spectacle*, 333.

[66] Letter of 4 ii 1628 to Alessandro Striggio: "Le parole di esso *Torneo* le ha fatte il Sig.r Aquilini, et sono più di mille versi, belle sí per il *Torneo*, ma per musica assai lontane . . . et dove non ho potuto trovar variationi nelli affetti ho cercato di variare nel modo di concertarle. . . ."

Ex. 1.2   Claudio Monteverdi, *Il ritorno d'Ulisse in Patria*, II; "Qui uà un tocco di guerra
da tutti gl'istromenti"; Aria: "Alle morti, alle stragi" (Vienna, Österreichische
Nationalbibliothek, Picture Archives, Cod. Mus. Hs. 18.763, fols. 101v–103r).

Ex. 1.2—*continued*

of cheat sheets. When his brother asked for a score of the opera *L'Egisto*, Giulio Rospigliosi, the librettist, replied, "having it copied would be a very tedious undertaking, since it is full of replacements, and confusions, so that it would not be possible to succeed without the almost constant presence of the composer."[67]

Although we lack the vocal music for *La contesa* and all but one set of instrumental pieces, between the manuscript notebooks and Guitti's publication the surviving materials are unusually complete. The Floriani manuscript choreographies open up new vistas in the interrelationships of military exercise, mime, and both social and theatrical dance, and provide us with a unique repertory. The rediscovery in the Floriani manuscripts of Guitti's machines for the 1628 Parma festivities and *La contesa* is an almost unique survival of the most impressive aspect of these celebrations. Above all, for the music historian the instrumental dances so casually transmitted represent a rare survival of materials assignable to a specific Italian Baroque chivalric spectacle.

EPILOGUE: *IL COMBATTIMENTO DI TANCREDI E CLORINDA*

Claudio Monteverdi's *Combattimento di Tancredi e Clorinda* is unique in his surviving production. It is a dramatic setting of Canto XII (stanzas 52–62, 64–68) of Torquato Tasso's epic of the first Crusade, *Gerusalemme liberata* (with some contamination of the text from Tasso's revision, *Gerusalemme conquistata*). The same text had been set previously by Sigismondo d'India for solo voice and continuo in his *Le musiche . . . a una e due voci . . . libro quarto* (Venice: Vincenti, 1621). Instead of d'India's solo dramatic recitative, Monteverdi creates a miniature drama scored for three singers—the tenor Tancredi, the soprano Clorinda, and the *testo* or narrator, a tenor or high baritone. They are accompanied by soprano, alto, tenor, and bass viola da braccio, *contrabasso da gamba*, and continuo (harpsichord). *Il Combattimento* was first performed in the palace of the Venetian patrician Girolamo Mocenigo as part of an evening entertainment or *veglia* in Carnival of 1624–25.

As one writer has put it, "The chief problem of the *Combattimento* . . . lies in identifying its genre and function."[68] Various solutions to this problem have been proposed. For some writers it is an *opéra manqué*. The late Nino Pirrotta, on the other hand, wrote:

---

[67] Letter of Giulio Rospigliosi to his brother Camillo, 7 March 1637, quoted in Hammond, *Music and Spectacle*, 326, n. 13: ". . . il farla copiare sarebbe un'impresa di molto tedio, per esser piena di rimesse, e di confusioni, che non sarebbe possibile uscirne senza l'assistenza quasi continua di chi l'ha fatta. . . ."

[68] Tim Carter, *Monteverdi's Musical Theatre* (New Haven, London: Yale University Press, 2002), 188.

But the *Combattimento* is not a secular oratorio, nor an opera, nor a ballet, nor a torneo, although it shares a bit of the characteristics of all these genres. . . . It was therefore substantially an intermedio, probably performed without a set, of those that were interspersed between the courses of a banquet or between the dances and the refreshments of a veglia; and among the various forms of intermedi it is closest to those which were called *abbattimenti* because they included a combat between armed warriors, often stylized to the sound of music. . . . As an intermedio the *Combattimento* surpasses contemporary operas, which almost never succeeded in depicting the actions of the characters as effectively as their emotional reactions.[69]

To suggest an answer to such questions it is necessary to set the *Combattimento* in the context in which any upper-class seventeenth-century Italian audience would have placed it, the context of chivalric combat. Viewed in this light, the *Combattimento* can be understood as a sort of anti-*torneo*, beginning with the framing of the work. The *torneo* was preceded by a long buildup, consisting of challenges, cartelloni, handouts, and processions, in much the same rhythm that the procession preceding the Palio of Siena is still choreographed. In the case of the "*Combattimento*, in Music of Tancredi and Clorinda, described by Tasso; if you wish to perform it as a staged work, on the spur of the moment (after having sung some Madrigals without mime) there will enter from the side of the Room in which the Music will be performed Clorinda armed and on foot, followed by Tancredi armed on a Cavallo Mariano, and the Narrator will then begin to sing."[70]

As far as the music is concerned, what was naturalistic in the torneo, such as the movement of the horses, the sounds of trumpets and drums, and the clash of arms, is rendered allusively in the *Combattimento* by such devices as the rhythmic crescendo of Tancredi's galloping horse, the hammering sixteenth-notes of the *stile concitato* (often incorrectly described as a tremolo), and the brutal pizzicato produced by plucking the violin strings with two fingers to represent the clashing of swords. Even the use of the "Cavallo Mariano" — a hobby horse instead of a real horse — is a

---

[69] Nino Pirrotta, "Scelte poetiche di Monteverdi" in *Scelte poetiche di musicisti: Teatro, poesia e musica da Willaert a Malipiero* (Venice: Marsilio, 1987), 81–146, esp. 104–05.

[70] "Combattimento in Musica di Tancredi et Clorinda, descritto dal Tasso; il quale volendosi esser fatto in genere rapresentativo, si farà ala sprovista (dopo cantatosi alcuni Madrigali senza gesto) dalla parte de la Camera di cui si farà la Musica. Clorinda a piedi armata, seguita da Tancredi armato sopra un Cavallo Mariano, et il Testo all'hora comincierà il Canto."

Brechtian *Verfremdungseffekt* as well as a practical consideration.[71] If we compare Tasso's text with the elaborate conceits embodied in the thousand lines of Claudio Achillini's text for *Mercurio e Marte* we see that the *Combattimento* moves in a far different musical and emotional world.

The *Combattimento* must have had a rapid and broad circulation. Monteverdi's dedication of the *Madrigali Guerrieri, et Amorosi*, in which the *Combattimento* first appeared, to the Emperor Ferdinand II is dated 1 September 1638. By Carnival of 1639 the work was well enough known to be parodied in Rome in the intermedio *La Fiera di Farfa*, inserted in that year's revival of the 1637 *Chi soffre speri*, with a text by Giulio Rospigliosi and music by Marco Marazzoli. After a burlesque combat between two *commedia dell'arte* figures, the vanquished Zanni parodies Clorinda's final lines, "Amico hai vinto, io ti perdon, perdona . . ." ("Friend, you have won, I pardon you, do you pardon . . ."), concluding comically "in fatt nelle costui le par bella cosa esser poltròn" ("in such matters it appears it's a fine thing to be a coward").[72]

---

[71] A description of a banquet in Bologna in 1550 reports the entrance of "certi cavalli Mariani con huomini armati con lance in mano" ("certain cavalli Mariani with armed men with lance in hand"); the "cavalli" are glossed as "miniatures worn by the performers as part of their costume" (Sergio Monaldini, "'La montagna fulminata' Giostre e tornei a Bologna nel Seicento," *Musica in torneo*, ed. Fabbri, 103–33, esp. 116).

[72] See Frederick Hammond, "Bernini and the 'Fiera di Farfa,'" in *Gianlorenzo Bernini: New Aspects of His Art and Thought: A Commemorative Volume*, ed. Irving Lavin (University Park and London: Pennsylvania State University Press, 1985), 115–78.

THE PRINCE'S HAT
OSSIA *IL BERRETTINO DI PIETRO*

For Agostino Ziino

Our investigation begins with a hat. The object itself no longer exists, but its design and colors are known to us from prints, drawings, paintings, statues in terra cotta and marble, tapestries, and even architectural reliefs. We know the name of the artist who designed it—Pietro Berrettini da Cortona—but not that of the artisan who constructed it. The hat was the focus of a religious ceremony with political and dynastic subtexts: the creation of Don Taddeo Barberini, duke of Monterotondo and prince of Palestrina, as Prince Prefect of Rome by his uncle, Pope Urban VIII, in the Cappella Paolina of the Quirinal palace on 6 August 1631.

THE POLITICAL PROGRAM

The creation of Don Taddeo Barberini as Prince Prefect had three principal aims. First, the magnificence of the Barberini under Urban VIII was modelled on and rivalled the program of the Farnese under Paul III (reg. 1534–49): the construction of an immense Roman palace, the decoration of one of the largest enclosed spaces in the city, the attempt to create independent principalities for princes of the family. This rivalry was made explicit in Urban VIII's removal of Paul III's tomb to the apse of St. Peter's, opposite Bernini's tomb for Urban himself. (A canon of the basilica quipped that it was only necessary to add a crucifix in the middle to have Christ between the two thieves.) By bestowing on a Barberini prince an office previously held by the della Rovere and the Farnese, the Barberini—mere descendants of Tuscan wool-merchants—asserted a claim to equal status. Second, the semi-ordination of the Prefecture ceremonies conferred on Don Taddeo a secular rank roughly equivalent to the cardinalates of his two brothers, asserting precedence over all other Roman nobles and even foreign ambassadors. Like the ritual of creating a cardinal, the creation of the Prefect culminated in the imposition of a ceremonial hat by the pope. Third, the ceremony was carefully stage-managed to display Taddeo in two contexts: the ancient Roman baronial nobility, into which he had been grafted by his marriage to Anna Colonna, and the civil government of Rome, in which the Prince Prefect functioned as Prefect of the Annona, the official in charge of provisioning the city— an office symbolized by the seven loaves of bread on the Prefect's shield.

The Barberini had had their eye on the Prefecture for some time. The office had been granted by Sixtus IV to his nephew Leonardo della Rovere in 1471 and by Paul III to Ottavio Farnese in 1538. In 1631 it was held by the moribund Francesco Maria della Rovere, duke of Urbino. As early as 1625 Pietro Contarini, the Venetian ambassador, had reported: "The Pope has some plan to make him [Taddeo] Prefect of the City, after the death of the Duke of Urbino who presently enjoys this title."[1]

The news of the duke's death reached Rome on 26 April 1631, "and the following night the Pope's nephew Taddeo Barberino left Rome to take possession of [Urbino] in the pope's name."[2] Urban formally created Don Taddeo Prince Prefect by a *bollo concistoriale* announced at a Concistory on 12 May 1631.[3]

As Cardinal Francesco Barberini had done for the restoration of the Lateran triclinium for the 1625 Holy Year, through the Reverenda Camera Apostolica the Barberini published an opusculum on the Prefecturate: DE/PRÆFECTO VRBIS/LIBER/ auct./FELICE CONTELORIO.[4] The title-page shows Taddeo mounted and wearing

---

[1] Quoted by Scott, *Images*, 86, n. 89: "Qualche disegno vi è nel Pontefice di farlo Prefetto della città, dopo la morte del Duca di Urbino che hora gode questo titolo."

[2] Giacinto Gigli, *Diario di Roma*, ed. Manlio Barberito (Rome: Colombo, 1995), 2 vols. paged continuously, 206: ". . . e la notte seguente partì di Roma a pigliarne possesso per nome del Papa, suo Nepote Taddeo Barberino."

[3] G. Pisano, "L'ultimo prefetto dell'urbe, Don Taddeo Barberini," *Roma* 9 (1931): 103–20, 155–64 [p. 8 of offprint in BAV].

[4] *Nihil obstat* by G. M. Suarez, the day before the kalends of October [30 September], 1631. Dedication to "THADDÆO/BARBERINO, Duke of Ereti [Monterotondo], Prince of Palestrina, Captain General of the Holy Roman Church and Prefect of Rome." A letter from Giovanni Panziroli to an unnamed correspondent (presumably Contelori) requests: "Il principe Don Taddeo desidera di vedere il libro della Prefettura di Roma dove V.S. Ill.ma ha fatto dipignere l'habiti per restituirglielo subito" ("Prince Don

the insignia of the Prefect (fig. 2.1). Two flying putti draw back a curtain revealing Rome. A standing putto on the right supports the arms of the Prefecture, a shield charged with a crowned eagle holding a rose and and the seven loaves; on the left, another putto holds the Barberini arms. Coats of arms are read from the point of view of the wearer. What appears to the viewer to be the left, or lesser, side is in fact the side of greater dignity: here the Barberini outrank the Prefecturate. The Barberini bees are also employed as chapter ends.

FIG. 2.1   Felice Contelori, *De Præfecto Urbis* (1631), title-page

Taddeo wishes to see the book about the Prefecture of Rome where Your Lordship has depicted the habits depicted in order to return it to you immediately") (BAV, Barb. lat. 2609, fol. 23, quoted in Pisano, "L'ultimo prefetto").

The volume was intended to provide historical credibility for the Barberini claims. Its author, Felix Contelori (1588–1652), was a distinguished scholar, "one of the most able Archivists the Holy See has ever had," whom Urban VIII had appointed as director of the newly-founded Vatican Archive, which he separated from the Vatican Library in 1631.[5]

Contelori traced the dignity of Præfectus Urbis back to ancient Rome. It was later conferred by the Holy Roman Emperor, and from the twelfth century onwards the Prefect was designated by the pope, who often chose a member of his own family. In Chapter III of his book, "De Præfecti Officio," Contelori listed at length the ceremonial prerogatives of the Prefect. For the Barberini, the crux of these was precedence over all foreign ambassadors, including the ambassador of Venice, with which the papacy was constantly on bad terms. Chapter V consists of a long historical account justifying the Prefect's prerogatives, especially his precedence.

In seventeenth-century Italy questions of precedence had tangible political importance and were minutely regulated. The pretensions of the ambassadors of the great powers—the kings of France and Spain, the Emperor, Venice—created flashpoints of conflict. The so-called "royal treatment" afforded the Grand Duke of Tuscany by the Emperor ranked him above other reigning Italian dukes such as Savoy and Mantua. On formal visits, the distance the *padrone* went out to meet an honored guest and the point to which he accompanied the guest on his departure were precise indications of social position and influence and could also be employed to reward or reprimand (see below, n. 68).

The niceties of protocol were endless. For example, on her ceremonial entry into Rome, as a sovereign Christina of Sweden was flanked by two cardinals of ruling houses, Medici and Hesse; but because she was no longer a reigning sovereign the cardinals were drawn from the ranks of the cardinal-deacons rather than from the higher cardinal-bishops.

---

[5] Peter Burke, "Rome as Center of Information and Communication," in *From Rome to Eternity: Catholicism and the Arts in Italy, ca. 1550–1650*, ed. Pamela M. Jones and Thomas Worcester (Leiden, Boston, Cologne: Brill, 2002), 253–269, 256. In 1632 Contelori produced documentary proof controverting an inscription on a fresco in the Sala Regia of the Vatican stating that Alexander III "Pontifici sua dignitas Venetæ Reipublicæ beneficio restaurata est," the basis of the "myth of Venice." The Venetians had Contelori's book burned by the public hangman and promised a reward to anyone who would kill him.

THE VESTMENTS

Contelori devotes Chapter II, "De Urbis Præfecti Indumentis," to the various insignia of the Prefect, complete with engraved illustrations (fig. 2.2). The most important *indumenta* were three in number, all of whose names carry liturgical overtones. First was a dalmatic or tunicle (*tonicella*—the same names are applied to the vestments worn by a bishop, by the deacon and subdeacon at high mass, and by sovereigns at their coronation) with wide sleeves, of red silk bordered with gold and open on the side. Over this was placed a floor-length mantle, also called a Pallium (the white wool band ornamented with black crosses worn by an archbishop) or Pluviale, a liturgical cope. This again was of red silk decorated with gold, circular in shape and open down from the right shoulder, where it was held by a gold clasp, to give access to the prince's sword.[6] The ensemble was completed by a ceremonial hat, "which some call a Tiara, others a Crown, a certain cap in the shape of a Ducal bonnet."[7]

FIG. 2.2   *De Præfecto Urbis*, insignia of the Prince Prefect

---

[6] See Contelori, *De Præfecto Urbis Liber*, Appendix of Documents I.

[7] See Ibid., Appendix of Documents I. On the history of the mitre and the papal tiara see Benedetta Montevecchi and Sandra Vasco Rocca, *Suppellettile ecclesiastica* (Florence: Centro Di, 1988), 360–61, 369–70. For the Sacchi portrait see *Il principe romano: Ritratti dell'aristocrazia pontifica nell'età barocca* (Rome: Gangemi, 2007), 52–53.

The hat is depicted clearly in Carlo Maratta's portrait of Don Taddeo (fig. 2.3) and in Bernardino Cametti's terra cotta model for the bust on Taddeo's tomb in the Barberini church of Santa Rosalia in Palestrina (fig. 2.4) (1704). Andrea Sacchi's full-length portrait of Don Taddeo shows the hat, tunicle, mantle, and sword (fig. 2.5).[8]

FIG. 2.3   Carlo Maratta,
Portrait of Don Taddeo Barberini
(Museo di Roma, ex-coll. Barberini)

FIG. 2.4   Bernardino Cametti,
Terra Cotta Bust of
Don Taddeo Barberini
(Museo di Roma)

---

[8] For the Maratta portrait see Marilyn Aronberg Lavin, *Seventeenth-Century Barberini Documents and Inventories of Art* (New York: New York University Press, 1975), pl. 5; for Cametti's bust see Elena Bianca di Gioia, *Le collezioni di scultura del Museo di Roma* (Rome: Campisano, 2002), 12; on Santa Rosalia and the Barberini tombs see *I príncipi della Chiesa* (Milan: Charta, 1998), 174–76; for the Sacchi portrait see *Il principe romano*, 52–53. A smaller portrait of Don Taddeo as Prince Prefect in a private collection was published by Lorenza Mochi Onori, "Un ritratto di Taddeo Barberini di Carlo Maratta (1625–1713)," *Studi di storia dell'arte in onore di Denis Mahon* (Milan, 2000), 322–25. An inventory of Cardinal Carlo Barberini of 1692 lists "Un Ritratto del S.re D. Taddeo Barberini in habito di Prefetto in Tela da Testa Cornice nera, oro di Carlo Maratta" ("A Head Portrait of Don Taddeo Barberini in the costume of the Prefect on Canvas [in a] black and gold Frame by Carlo Maratta").

FIG. 2.5   Andrea Sacchi,
Portrait of Don Taddeo Barberini
(Rome, Direzione Generale I.N.P.S.)

The bulb-shaped hat was presumably constructed over a frame and was covered with shirred rose-purple silk held in place by a circlet and metal arches "in the manner of a cross." These were decorated with roundels containing the Barberini bees and solar disks, recalling Urban VIII's *imprese* of rising and setting suns. The paraliturgical nature of this hybrid object, resembling both a secular crown and the papal tiara or triregnum, is emphasized by the addition of prominent *infulæ*, the decorated and fringed cloth bands hanging from the back of the bishop's mitre and the papal tiara. The puntatore of the Cappella Pontificia, an annually elected official who fined singers for unexcused absences and other offenses which he recorded in a *diario*, was obviously struck by the "two Pendants similar to those of Bishops' Mitres, one on the side of the right ear, and the other on the left, and all this habit of a red color."[9] The

---

[9] BAV, CS 51, fol. 45r: see Appendix of Documents II.

papal master of ceremonies, Paolo Alaleona, also noted the ecclesiastical overtones of the hat, describing it as "resembling the papal Tiara with *infulæ*."[10] Urban VIII's biographer Andrea Nicoletti described the *beretta* as an ordinary hat without a brim, with two hanging strips like those of a bishop's miter and decorations forming a cross.[11] Giovanni Pesaro, the Venetian ambassador, called it bluntly "a tiara despoiled of its crowns."[12]

Contelori illustrated five forms of the hat (fig. 2.6). The shape closest to the one constructed for Taddeo is the bonnet that Francesco Maria della Rovere prized so much he ordered it to be placed on his head in his tomb. One source says that the Barberini had Francesco Maria exhumed to determine the exact form of his hat, which was reproduced by a local painter, Gerolamo Cialdieri.[13] The hat with which Don Taddeo was crowned was designed by Pietro da Cortona for Cardinal Francesco Barberini, who paid him three scudi.[14]

The creation of Don Taddeo as Prince Prefect was certainly the initiative of Urban VIII himself, but Cardinal Francesco's role in commissioning the hat and in paying more than one thousand scudi for Taddeo's ceremonial processions is emphasized by his prominent placement in the painter Agostino Tassi's rendering of the occasion (see fig. 2.10). While the hostility between Francesco and his youngest brother Antonio was notorious (Francesco had opposed Antonio's elevation to the cardinalate in 1627), Francesco felt a warm affection for Taddeo. Of Taddeo's premature death in 1647 Francesco wrote: "Because more than brotherly love drew me to him [. . .] having seen him born I lived with him, and it was God's wish that against my desires and the natural course of life I closed his eyes."[15]

---

[10] Alaleona, "ad similitudinem Regni cu[m] infulis": see Appendix of Documents III; "A somiglianza d'un regno Pontificio era il suo Diadema del medesimo colore" (Celio Talucci, *Relazione della Cavalcata*, Appendix of Documents IV). On Alaleona see *Päpstliches Zeremoniell in der frühen Neuzeit: Das Diarium des Zeremonienmeisters Paolo Alaleone de Branca während des Pontifikats Gregors XV. (1621–1623)*, ed. Günther Wassilowsky and Hubert Wolf (Münster: RHEMA, 2007).

[11] See Nicoletti, Appendix of Documents IV.

[12] Scott, *Images*, 87.

[13] Contelori, *De Præfecto Urbis*, 5: "ut eo caput suum ipso in tumulo contegi mandaverit"; Lorenza Mochi Onori, "Pietro da Cortona per i Barberini," in *Pietro da Cortona 1597–1669*, ed. Anna Lo Bianco (Milan: Electa, 1997), 73–85, esp. 76.

[14] See Appendix of Documents VI; see also John Beldon Scott, "Patronage and the Visual Encominum during the Pontificate of Urban VIII: The Ideal Palazzo Barberini in a Dedicatory Print," *Memoirs of the American Academy in Rome* 40 (1995): 197–234. Sketches of the hat are given in BAV, Barb. lat. 5009, fols. 108, 149.

[15] ". . . cosi perche l'amore più che fraterno mi strinse a lui . . . mà perche havendolo visto nascere seco son vissuto, e dio ha volsuto contro delli desiderij e corso naturale, che io gl'occhij chiudessi" (Francesco

FIG. 2.6   Contelori, *De Præfecto Urbis*, forms of the Prefect's hat

Without metamorphosing Don Taddeo's hat into King Charles' head, it is still notable how often its form recurs in seventeenth-century Roman art. The Prefect's hat, in a rudimentary rendering, forms part of Don Taddeo's heraldic claims as expressed in the frieze of Palazzo Barberini at the Quattro Fontane. The tiara, its *infulæ* prominently displayed, with which Divine Providence crowns the Barberini arms in Cortona's ceiling (1631–38) in Palazzo Barberini is simplified to its basic dome-shape in the splendid sketch now in the Morgan Library (fig. 2.7).[16] Countess Matilda of Tuscany, whose donation validated the papacy's temporal claims, clasps a tiara in Bernini's tomb statue in St. Peter's (1633–37). In Giuseppe Belloni's tapestry of the devolution of Urbino, from a series woven 1663–83, Matilda holds out to Urban VIII a pomegranate, the symbol of the dominions of which she indicates a map with her other hand while Don Taddeo genuflects, uncovered and clasping his ceremonial hat (fig. 2.8).[17] The dome-shaped *tempietto* common in Roman Baroque funerary monuments such as Bernini's displays for Paul V and for Taddeo Barberini's father Carlo was sometimes actually rendered as a papal tiara, as in projects for catafalques for Gregory XV and Innocent X.[18]

Barberini, *Life of Taddeo*, BAV, AB, Ind. IV, no. 1254, quoted in Waddy, *Seventeenth-Century Roman Palaces*, 331–41, esp. 333).

[16] Scott, *Images*, fig. 101.

[17] Ibid., fig. 112; see also Harper, "The Barberini Tapestries of the Life of Pope Urban VIII," 1:253–92.

[18] *La festa a Roma dal Rinascimento al 1870*, ed. Maurizio Fagiolo dall'Arco, 2 vols. (Turin: Allemandi, 1997), 2:28–31.

FIG. 2.7   Pietro da Cortona, sketch for *Divina Providenza*
(New York, Pierpont Morgan Library)

FIG. 2.8   Giuseppe Belloni, *The Devolution of the Duchy of Urbino*, tapestry
(Vatican Museum, Archivio Fotografico)

ASTROLOGICAL AND LITURGICAL CONTEXTS

The choice of August 6, the Feast of the Transfiguration of Our Lord, for the conferral of the Prefecture of Rome on Don Taddeo Barberini was dictated by a number of factors. In 1631 August 6 marked the eighth anniversary of Urban VIII's election to the papacy.[19] The election had been signalled in the heavens by a "mirabil congiuntura"—a wondrous conjunction of planets and stars. The concistory of 12 May 1631 may have been chosen for the initial announcement of Taddeo's appointment owing to another propitious conjunction, Leo and Jupiter, who with Venus played important roles in Taddeo's horoscope.

The astrological elements in the election of the Barberini were regarded as manifestations of Divine Wisdom and Divine Providence, both displayed in the great ceiling frescoes of Palazzo Barberini. The members of the family were "continually to be summoned to the administration of the Christian Commonwealth under the governance of Divine Wisdom" and to follow Urban VIII, "whose wisdom we know to be next to divine." In an answer to a letter of congratulation from Michelangelo Buonarotti the younger (30 August 1631), Don Taddeo stated that his appointment had to do with the success of Holy Church and therefore the praise was due to Divine Providence.[20] Both Taddeo and his father-in-law Filippo Colonna were in contact with the astrologer Tommaso Campanella, who may have been the author of the program of Andrea Sacchi's *Divine Wisdom*. The last sentence of the program, later crossed out, reads: "Such a painting is appropriate to the majestic edifice of the Barberini family to make it understood that since that happy family was born and elected to rule the Church in the place of God it governs with Divine Wisdom, equally loved and revered."[21]

The liturgical propers for the feast of the Transfiguration[22] harmonized with the particular significance of the 1631 ceremony in a striking manner. The central image of the texts for the mass and office of the feast is that of light, a light which proceeds from a father who is its source and which he makes evident in the Transfiguration

---

[19] This summary is based on Scott, *Images.* The Transfiguration occupied a prominent place in Barberini imagery. A tapestry depiction, now in the Cathedral of St. John the Divine, New York, was woven in 1642–56, and tapestries of the Transfiguration and St. Michael (the feasts of Urban's election and coronation) were woven in 1677 for the cycle of Urban's life (Scott, *Images,* 190; Harper, "The Barberini Tapestries," *passim*).

[20] Scott, *Images,* 144.

[21] Ibid., 201 and fig. 121: "Conveniva tal Pittura al Maestoso Edefitio della Casa Barberina, acciò che s'intendesse che, si come si felice fameglia è nata et eletta in luogo d'Iddio, per li primi governi della Chiesa, così, con divina Sapienza, parimenti amata e riverita, la governa."

[22] Cited according to the MISSALE/ROMANVM/EX DECRETO SANCROSANCTI/Concilij Tridentini restitutum/. . . VENETIS. APVD. IVNTAS, n.d. [1623], 427.

of his son, whose authority is thus both manifested and confirmed. The recurrent images of adoption, election, clothing with glory in a shining white garment, coronation, and illumination by a Sun-god are appropriate to Urban VIII as the chosen vessel of the Holy Spirit displayed in the supernatural character of his election.[23] By extension, these images are equally appropriate to Urban's "adoption" of his brother's son (Taddeo's father Carlo had died in 1630) as Prince Prefect of Rome, a secular dignity comparable to the cardinalates of Taddeo's brothers Francesco and Antonio.

Obviously, the propers for the Transfiguration existed long before the creation of Don Taddeo Barberini as Prince Prefect. However, the Barberini were masters of orchestrating what we can only call the multimedia photo-op. On one famous occasion Urban VIII visited the Quattro Fontane palace and dined under Sacchi's *Divina Sapienza* ceiling fresco while listening to a reading—supposedly chosen at random—from the Book of Wisdom: the dazzled onlookers saw Wisdom's "divine and lucid archetype in Holy Writ, her prototype in Urban, and her representation [ektype] in the paintings."[24]

The Transfiguration is recounted in Matthew XVII:1–13, the liturgical Gospel reading of the mass for the feast. Jesus took Peter, James, and his brother John to a high mountain, "and he was transfigured before them. And his face shone like the sun, his garments became white as snow." Moses and Elijah appeared, and Peter suggested making three tabernacles, one for each. A cloud covered the men, "and behold a voice from the cloud, saying: This is my beloved son, in whom I am well pleased: hear him." The liturgical Epistle, II Peter 1, repeats the words of the voice, adding "and we heard this voice from heaven when we were with him on the holy mount."

The verse for the Introit of the mass picks up the image of the tabernacles: "Quam dilecta tabernacula tua, Domine virtutum: co[n]cupiscit & deficit anima mea in atria Domini" ("How delightful are your dwellings, O Lord of hosts: my soul has a desire and longing to enter into the courts of the Lord"). (A few months later, in May of 1632, Don Taddeo did indeed enter into "the delightful dwellings [. . .] the courts of the Lord," when he moved into the new Barberini palace at the Quattro Fontane.) The Collect, "Deus, qui fidei sacramenta . . . ut ipsius regis gloriæ nos coheredes efficias, & eiusdem gloriæ tribuas esse consortes" describes the miracle of the Transfiguration as "adoptionem filiorum perfecta voce delapsa in nube lucida." ("O God, who in the glorious Transfiguration of your only-begotten Son did confirm the mysteries of the faith by the testimony of the fathers, and in the perfect voice

---

[23] For the tapestry of Urban's election see Scott, *Images*, fig. 111, and Harper, "Barberini Tapestries," 1:216–52.

[24] Quoted in Hammond, *Music and Spectacle*, 251.

which came down from the bright cloud did marvellously foreshadow the adoption of sons . . ."). The verse for the Gradual of the mass proclaims: "Candor est lucis eternæ, speculum sine macula, & imago bonitatis illius." ("Your bright-/whiteness is that of the eternal light, a mirror without spot, and the image of his goodness.") The only discordant note is struck by the Communio: "Visionem quam vidistis, nemini dixeritis"—"The vision that you have seen, tell it to no man"—hardly part of the Barberini program.

The same imagery is continued in the office propers for the feast. The Magnificat antiphon for first vespers refers to Christ as "splendor Patris, et figura substantiæ ejus [. . .] in monte excelso gloriosus apparere hodie dignatus est"—"the brightness of the Father and the express image of his person [who] on this day vouchsafed to show himself in glory on the high mountain." The responsory for terce proclaims, "Gloriosus apparuisti in conspectu Domini: Propterea decorem induit te Dominus" —"Glorious did you appear in the sight of the Lord, Therefore the Lord has clothed you with majesty." (The pope was regularly referred to as "Nostro Signore," "Our Lord.") The responsory for sext comments, "Gloria et honore coronasti eum," "You have crowned him with glory and honor." The chapter for none quotes the vision of the heavenly Jerusalem in the Book of Revelation, the source of the hymn "Urbs beata Jerusalem" which Urban VIII himself had reworked for this revision of the Breviary hymns.[25]

Anyone who thinks that these (mis)readings of scripture in a political context are far-fetched has only to recall the coronation ritual of the doge of Venice, who scattered handfuls of small change to the crowds in San Marco while the choir chanted with sublime inappropriateness the words of Peter to the cripple in Acts III, 6: "Silver and gold have I none, but such as I have give I thee." It may also be objected that these meanings had to be read in retrospect since the conferral of the Prefecture took place before the main liturgy. But throughout the mass Don Taddeo, dressed in royal and cardinalatial scarlet and gold over shining white, robed and crowned, was standing at the papal throne in a place usually reserved for cardinals.

THE CEREMONY

The Entry Procession. According to the diary of Paolo Alaleona, the papal master of ceremonies, Taddeo returned from Urbino on 2 July "incognito, and privately, and was not seen in public." Having been created *equis aureus* (knight of the

---

[25] See Hammond, *Music and Spectacle*, 177–80.

Golden Spur) by the pope the preceding evening,[26] Taddeo made his solemn entry into Rome on Sunday, August 3, at 22 o'clock (i.e., two hours before sunset). Owing to the plague, which had spread south from Florence, he entered from the Via Flaminia through the Porta del Popolo rather than from Villa Giulia. His procession followed the Corso as far as San Marco, turning right to pass the Gesù, following the Strada Papale (more or less the modern Corso Vittorio Emanuele) to Sant'Andrea della Valle, site of the family chapel, and past Palazzo Massimo alle Colonne. Turning left, the cavalcade entered Campo de' Fiori by way of Piazza della Pollarola and followed Via dei Giubbonari out of the Campo to Taddeo's residence, the old Barberini palace of the Casa Grande (fig. 2.9).

FIG. 2.9   Agostino Tassi, *Entry of Don Taddeo Barberini, 3 August 1631*
(Museo di Roma)

The weather was so hot that the street was watered by the *barilotti* or water-sellers. (Agostino Tassi's painting of the procession shows one of the participants wiping off his sweat.) There was a great concourse of people, and the windows along the way were adorned with hangings. The procession opened with *forieri* who cleared a path, followed by three mounted trumpeters and drums: "Never did more festive and sonorous notes come from the trumpets."[27] These in turn were

---

[26] Barb. lat. 2819, diary of Paolo Alaleona, 26 February 1630–3 December 1637, fols. 64–65v: "incognitus, et privatim, et publice non videtur"; see Alaleona, Appendix of Documents III; cf. BAV, Barb. lat. 5280, fols. 39r–42r: "Ordine dell'Entrata, che si farà dall'Ecc.mo Sig. Prefetto di Roma."

[27] Barb. lat. 2819, diary of Paolo Alaleona, fol. 65v: "Chelicines, et [fol. 66] timpaniste"; see Appendix of Documents III, IV.

followed by thirty-six carriages, variously covered in green velvet, red velvet, and gold brocade, and drawn by mules whose furnishings were all of silver. Then came the papal Light Horse (Cavaleggieri) with their own trumpets, followed by twelve pages with embroidered green liveries, more horses, and the mules of twenty-nine cardinals led by mounted grooms bearing their masters' ceremonial cardinals' hats. After more riders and four trumpets, there followed the papal court wearing red habits over scarlet cassocks, accompanied by many gentlemen. Sixteen drums led on more riders, followed by the Swiss Guards on foot with fifes and drums, surrounding bearers of two silver maces. Taddeo, in an "habito superbissimo," was mounted on a white charger whose bridle, shoes, and furnishings were all of gold, riding between two bishops and followed by a great number of bishops, prelates, the pope's Camerieri Segreti, and carriages drawn by six horses.[28]

The Creation. In our time the norm of great papal occasions is a pontifical mass celebrated by the pope at the high altar of St. Peter's. This was far from the case in the seventeenth century. The pope celebrated mass publicly only on rare occasions, such as Christmas, Easter, Pentecost, the feast of the Princes of the Apostles Peter and Paul, and canonizations. Most papal liturgical observances took place in the chapels and adjoining spaces of one or the other of the apostolic palaces, the Cappella Paolina in the Quirinal or the Cappella Sistina and Cappella Paolina in the Vatican.[29]

Even there, the pope did not necessarily celebrate himself. More often he presided from a throne raised several steps from the pavement, vested in cope and miter and attended by assisting cardinals, at a mass celebrated by another cardinal (who received a gift of money and a cake "for a mass well sung").[30] The ambassadors of France, Spain, the Empire, and Venice had the right of standing on the steps of the throne, and representatives of papal families and of the old Roman barony such as the Borghese, Orsini, and Colonna, attended as "Principi assistenti al soglio."

At the beginning of the mass the pope joined the celebrant at the foot of the altar for the Confession (Psalm 43, "Judica me, Deus," the Confiteor, and its verses) and then went in procession to the throne, where the cardinals ascended for their

---

[28] Gigli, *Diario*, 207–08. Cardinal Francesco's accounts record expenses of sc. 1013.63 for liveries and sc. 1000 for the "Cavalcata" (see Appendix of Documents VI).

[29] See T. A. Marder, *Bernini's Scala Regia at the Vatican Palace* (Cambridge: Cambridge University Press, 1997), 226–36. For ceremonial details I have employed the RITVALE/ROMANVM/PAVLI QVINTI/Pontificis Maximi . . . (Venice: Cieras, 1615) and the CÆRIMONIALE/EPISCOPORVM/. . . ./VENETIS APVD CIERAS M.D.C. XIII.

[30] Gigli, *Diario*, 39–40, n. 36; the papal *mazzieri* (mace-bearers) presented the cake.

ritual homage of kissing the pope's foot, hand, and mouth. The pope followed the mass privately: he said the Introit from a Missal held before him, then recited the Kyrie. He read the Epistle, Gradual, and Gospel to himself from the Missal and knelt at a movable faldstool before the altar for the consecration.[31]

Although the Feast of the Transfiguration is a feast of Our Lord, it ranked only as a Double of the Second Class without an octave, and the diarii of the Cappella Pontificia do not suggest that it was celebrated with any particular ceremonial elaboration. The Transfiguration is not mentioned in a detailed account of music performed by the Cappella Pontificia in 1616[32] nor in Andrea Adami's *Osservazioni per ben regolare il coro dei cantori della Cappella Pontificia* (Rome, 1711).[33]

The Cappella Sistina Diario 41 (1623) records the pope's election ("Creatione") on August 6 but succeeding diaries do not refer to the feast. The anniversary of Urban's coronation on September 29, the feast of St. Michael and All Angels, was celebrated as the principal commemoration of his election.[34]

The accounts of Contelori, the papal master of ceremonies Paolo Alaleona, the *diario* of the Cappella Pontificia, Andrea Nicoletti's manuscript biography of Urban VIII, and a manuscript *relazione* by one Celio Talucci all agree on the main outlines of Don Taddeo's investiture, in which, as in the creation of a cardinal, the culminating moment was the bestowal of a ceremonial hat (fig. 2.10). Each account, however, adds a particular touch.[35]

Contelori's Latin has a vaguely antique flavor: "In the Papal Chapel in the presence of the Sacred College of Cardinals, or in another Temple, the one to whom the

---

[31] For a faldstool see *Vatican Splendour: Masterpieces of Baroque Art*, ed. Catherine Johnson et al. (Ottawa: National Gallery of Canada, 1986), #38. A fine drawing by Pietro da Cortona of Urban VIII kneeling at a faldstool before the high altar of Cortona's SS. Luca e Martino is preserved in the Pinacoteca Comunale of Ascoli Piceno (Christie's, *Old Master Drawings*, auction catalogue, 1996, #48).

[32] Herman-Walther Frey, "Die Gesänge der sixtinischen Kapelle an den Sonntagen und hohen Kirchenfesten des Jahres 1616," *Melanges Eugène Tisserant* (Vatican City: Biblioteca Apostolica Vaticana, 1964, Studi e Testi, 236), 6:395–437.

[33] Andrea Adami, *Osservazioni per ben regolare il coro dei cantori della Cappella pontificia* (Rome: Rossi, 1711; fascimile ed. Giancarlo Rostirolla [Lucca: Libreria Musicale Italiana, 1988]).

[34] After mass on the anniversary of his coronation, the pope dined in public to the sound of motets sung by the Cappella from a "galleria" in an adjoining room (one of the few occasions on which the Cappella employed instruments); the choir drank to his health and sang the Polychronion, "Ad multos annos" (Frey, "Die Gesänge," 423–24). On Urban's devotion to St. Michael see Louise Rice, "Urban VIII, the Archangel Michael, and a forgotten project for the apse altar of St. Peter's," *Burlington Magazine* 134 (1992): 428–34.

[35] Other sources: Nicoletti, vol. 4 (BAV, Barb. lat. 4733), pp. 625–27; Celio Talucci, "Relazione della Cavalcata," Barb. lat. 5242, int. 7, 349–77; Barb. lat. 5280, int. 3.

Fig. 2.10   Agostino Tassi, *Investiture of Don Taddeo Barberini*
(Museo di Roma)

emblems of the Prefecture are to be given, is brought to the pope in the course of the sacred rites, accompanied by two of the most distinguished of the nobles: Then genuflecting on the lowest step of the throne he goes up to him [the pope], and having kissed his feet in the customary manner, kneeling he performs an Oath of fealty and subjection: Then returning to the foot of the throne he lays aside his mantle and cloak, and again ascending to the throne kneeling on his knees he is present at the blessing of his garments, while it is carried out by the Pope in an ancient prayer. Then he is garbed by [the Pope] with the Dalmatic and the Chalmys. Finally, when the hat has been placed on his head he is admitted to the kiss on the mouth: then he is placed by the Master of Ceremonies to the right hand of the Pope on the top step of the throne immediately after the Cardinal Deacon seated there, and he stands there until the end of the rite, leaning against the wall. Presently he supports the train of the pope's cope as he descends."[36] The admission to the final kiss placed the Prefect on a level with the cardinals, with their homage of a triple kiss.[37]

As a professional *ceremonarius*, Alaleona added a few liturgical details. The pope came to the Cappella Paolina in the sedia gestatoria, vested in the *falda* (a white linen vestment between a cape and a jabot, worn only by the pope), amice, alb, girdle, stole, white cope, and a precious miter. He prayed before the altar at a faldstool and recited the Confession with the celebrant, on this occasion Cardinal Caetani, representing the family of Boniface VIII. "The singers did not begin to sing the Introit, but they sang, when the Pope, having made the Confession went to his Pontifical seat at the throne, and sat, and received all the cardinals in the customary homage." When the homage was finished Taddeo "came to the Cappella from the nearby Rooms" between his supporters, "together with many nobles."

Talucci describes Taddeo's entering outfit in detail: "He was dressed this day all in cloth, artfully composed with strips of white silk taffeta [tabi] joined together but full of silver embroidery. In the same manner was the lining of his mantle of black taffeta which had at the shoulder a Hood crossed by large gold buttons full of shining diamonds. His Berretta of curled Velvet with a short hem and thick stripes, was enriched with gems of great price, and the finest plumes of heron."[38] Taddeo knelt with his supporters before the pope; after kissing the pope's feet he swore an oath "in the hands of the Pope," descended, and genuflected on the lowest step of

---

[36] Unlike the usual cope, the papal *manto* had a train (see the *manto* of Clement IX in *Bernini in Vaticano* [Rome: De Luca, 1981], 248).

[37] Gaetano Moroni, *Dizionario di erudizione storico-ecclesiastica*, 130 vols. (Venice: Emiliana, 1840–61), 9:82.

[38] See Appendix of Documents V.

the throne, where he knelt while the pope, uncovered, intoned a prayer over him from the Apostolic Sacristy book (in an edition reformed by Urban), held by the first assisting bishop. Taddeo left to remove his outer garments and returned between his supporters, dressed in white like a sovereign for his anointing, in preparation for receiving the scarlet insignia, which had been prepared on the credence table. These were described in more detail by Nicoletti.

The pope put the tunicle on Taddeo with the prayer "Induat te Dominus vestimento salutis" ("May the Lord clothe you with the garment of salvation"), then the mantle, and finally crowned him with the hat, concluding with the prayer "Deus pater eterne." Taddeo removed the hat, kissed the pope's foot and hand, "and was admitted to the kiss [on the mouth]." Holding in his hand the "infula[m], seù biretu[m]," he remained in the principal place at the throne, on the pope's right after the first Cardinal Deacon (Taddeo's brother Francesco). At the Kiss of Peace, he was given the pax by the celebrant's assisting priest immediately after the cardinals. "After the Lord prefect had been garbed with the garments of the Prefecture, the Singers began to sing the introit, and Kirie eleison." The pope blessed incense, "and the mass was sung in the customary manner." Don Taddeo remained at the throne "in the more worthy place," and at the end of the mass held the pope's train (an office frequently performed by an ambassador) when he descended from the throne.[39]

The account of Pietro Antonio Tamburini (d. 1635), the puntatore of the Cappella Pontificia, records what the singers in Agostino Tassi's painting of the event (fig. 2.10) actually saw from their vantage point in the cantoria opposite the papal throne. Tamburini records that the pope entered on the sedia gestatoria, recited the Confiteor with the celebrant, and received the homage of the cardinals at the throne. Don Taddeo appeared between his supporters, the governor of Rome, Mons. Grimaldi, on his right and his father-in-law, the Contestabile Colonna, on his left. He knelt before the pope, who administered the oath to him. After some prayers, the pope conferred the insignia of the Prefecture on his nephew. Taddo removed the hat and was admitted to kiss the pope's foot, hand, and mouth. He then stood at the pope's right throughout the sung mass that followed.

The propaganda aspect of the ceremony is reflected in the choice of Taddeo's supporters. Filippo Colonna (d. 1639) was not only the father of Taddeo's wife Anna, but was also Grand Contestabile and the head of one of the greatest Roman baronial families, the house of Pope Martin V. The genealogical importance of Anna Colonna,

---

[39] Alaleona, Appendix of Documents III; Nicoletti states that Taddeo stood before Cardinal [Ippolito] Aldobrandino [the younger], who was first Deacon; both Tassi's compositional sketch and the finished painting show Cardinal Francesco Barberini prominently placed at the pope's right hand (see below).

whose marriage grafted the parvenu Barberini onto the Roman patriciate, was enhanced by the gradual withdrawal of her mother-in-law, Carlo Barberini's widow Costanza Magalotti, from public life; Donna Anna thus became *de facto* hostess for Urban VIII. Monsignor Girolamo Grimaldi (d. 1685) was vice-chamberlain, governor of Rome, and a member of the Camera Apostolica: as such he was in weekly contact with the pope and had complex administrative relations with the representatives of the Roman civil government who took part in Taddeo's exit procession as Prince Prefect.[40]

The Exit Procession. The investiture was followed by a banquet at which Taddeo ate with the pope, seated "at a small table, lower and separated from the one where His Beatitude was eating."[41] He handed the pope his napkin for the ceremonial hand-washing and rose uncovered when the pope drank.[42] After the banquet Don Taddeo retired to his brother Francesco's apartments and left the Quirinal in procession about two hours before sunset. His cavalcade followed the Corso as far as the Gesù, to Palazzo Cesarini (at what is now Largo Argentina), turning toward Palazzo Vittori (attached to the Pantheon and later demolished) and the Dogana Vecchia; at the Palazzo of the Sapienza the procession moved toward Piazza Pasquino, Campo de' Fiori, Piazza Farnese, Piazza Capodiferro, Santissima Trinità dei Pellegrini, and Via dei Giubbonari to reach the Casa Grande in Via dei Giubbonari. Although the cavalcade could have gone directly to the Casa Grande from Campo de' Fiori, the detour to the Dogana and up through Piazza Farnese constituted a symbolic invasion of Farnese space (figs. 2.11, 2.12).

The procession was led by the papal Cavaleggieri with their trumpets, preceding the Giudici Capitolari, who with the Senator of Rome formed the Curia Capitolina. (The Senator himself, the nominal head of the civil government of Rome, was absent, either by reason of illness or in order to sidestep problems of precedence.) The Giudici were followed by a cavalcade of Roman nobility, "as many Barons and Princes, as were found in Rome," they and their entourages sumptuously dressed. The three trumpets of the Campidoglio, "which sonorous trumpets sounding from time to time advised the numerous populace from afar off, both in the streets and in

---

[40] Laurie Nussdorfer, *Civic Politics in the Rome of Urban VIII* (Princeton, NJ: Princeton University Press, 1992), 46–47, 51; on the Senator of Rome, 69–70. During the Barberini exile from Rome under Innocent X, Grimaldi (who had become a cardinal) was instrumental in protecting the Quattro Fontane palace for the Barberini.

[41] "[i]n un tavolino più basso et separato da quello dove magnava S[ua] B[eatitudi]ne." See Alaleona, Appendix of Documents III.

[42] Alaleona, fols. 68v–69.

FIG. 2.11   Giovanni Ferri, called Giovanni Senese (attributed),
Procession of Don Taddeo Barberini as Prince Prefect, 6 August 1631
(Rome, Banco di Santo Spirito)

FIG. 2.12   Giovanni Ferri, called Giovanni Senese (attributed),
Corteo del Prefetto di Roma Taddeo Barberini nel rione Ponte
(Museo di Roma)

their houses, to assemble together to watch" (as Gigli had described them in 1625),
heralded a group of Roman gentlemen, all dressed in long robes of black velvet with
black velvet caps.[43] A corps of fourteen drummers preceded a procession of the
Caporioni, the magistrates elected every three months to head the fourteen *rioni* or
districts of the City, riding in pairs and all dressed alike in white with a short robe

[43] Gigli, *Diario*, 147. On the Capitoline musicians see Alberto Cametti, "I musici di Campidoglio," *Archivio della Reale Società Romana di Storia Patria* 48 (1925): 95–135.

of red velvet, each accompanied by the banners of his rione and armed officers. (Gigli himself had been Caporione of Campitelli in January-March of 1631.) The three Conservatori, who worked with the Senator of Rome and the Priore de' Caporioni elected by the Caporioni, followed in senatorial habits of gold brocade, with the Fedeli (a guard of Vitorchiani) and the Swiss Guards.

Dulcis in fundo rode Don Taddeo wearing the insignia of the Prefecture—tunicle, mantle, and hat, enriched with gold and jewels. Of his two supporters, the Contestabile Colonna rode on his right and Grimaldi on his left (both paintings of the event reverse this placement—were they made from engravings?), followed by prelates. That evening and the next the Casa Grande and the Campidoglio—the seats of Taddeo's secular and civil dignities respectively—were illuminated.[44]

"IMAGES OF NEPOTISM"

The "visionem quam vidistis" has been preserved in a painting by Agostino Tassi (1578–1644) now in the Museo di Roma (fig. 2.10). This period was a low point in the career of the unappetizing Tassi, who was described by his half-sister Olimpia as "short, fattish, without much beard . . . a smartass and a mean good-for-nothing since he was a child."[45] Tassi fought with all his patrons—Paul V, Scipione Borghese, Gregory XV, Cardinal Ludovisi, Urban VIII, Cardinal Pamphilj, Maurizio of Savoy— but they were forced to put up with him because "no one could rival him in coordinating the work of several painters with such satisfying results."

Most of Tassi's oils are of modest dimensions, but two large canvases relating to the investiture of Don Taddeo were commissioned by Urban VIII and paid for by the pope through the Tesoreria Pontificia.[46] Their unusual size suggests that here also Tassi coordinated the work of several of his many assistants.

Tassi himself described the first canvas as "another picture of the same size and measurement [14 palmi long, 12 high: 1 palmo = 9 inches, i.e. 10'6" x 9'] where is painted the Papal Chapel at Montecavallo [=the Quirinal] in perspective, there is the entire vault with all the stucchi in perspective and painted therein when Our Lord gives the habit to the most excellent prince Taddeo with all their eminences

---

[44] Gigli, *Diario*, 208, 217. For Francesco's expenditures see Appendix of Documents VI.

[45] Patrizia Cavazzini, *Palazzo Lancellotti ai Coronari: Cantiere di Agostino Tassi* (Rome: Istituto Poligrafico e Zecca dello Stato, 1998), 177: "piccolotto, grassotto, di poca barba [. . .] un furbaccio e un tristo che non ha mai voluto fare bene sino da piccolo."

[46] Ibid., 163, 184–85, 226.

the cardinals and others who took part in the said function, scudi 300," twice the fee of the preceding pictures.[47]

The composition is the standard one for depicting the papal chapels, familiar from engravings.[48] The chapel, viewed head-on in a low vanishing-point perspective to give ample space for depicting the stucco vaulting by Martino Ferrabosco, is decorated with red hangings. The pope and his court are separated by the customary balustrade from the *profanum vulgus* — women, minor ecclesiastics, secular courtiers, exotic visitors — who are kept in order by guards. Inside the balustrade, the pope, in cope and miter, presides at a throne under a baldacchino on the Gospel side of the altar, surrounded by attendants. White, the liturgical color of the feast, is employed for the covering of the throne and the hanging behind it. Cardinals and other high ecclesiastics and secular figures (ambassadors were excluded on this occasion) are seated on three sides. The credence table, where the prince's vestments were placed, is visible on the upper right, loaded with ecclesiastical plate. In a balustraded cantoria high on the Epistle side of the chapel, at its center a lectern bearing a large volume of music, we see the choir, vested in cotta and cassock. Some sixteen singers are visible, all reacting in various ways to the ceremony that unrolls before them.

Tassi has chosen to depict the climactic moment of the ceremony: the pope crowns Don Taddeo, who is dressed in white and kneels before him flanked by his two noble supporters, with the ceremonial hat symbolizing the dignity of Prince Prefect of Rome. (Amid the bright colors of the other participants, the black and crimson of Grimaldi's short bishop's habit stand out.)

Two sheets of sketches show Tassi's alternate solutions for the final canvas (fig. 2.13, 2.14).[49] One, now in the Art Gallery of Ontario, Toronto (Inv. no. 69/34) depicts the central group of the final tableau. Urban VIII is enthroned, two clerics kneel on the steps of the throne, and the cardinal who appears prominently at the pope's right is identified properly as [Francesco] "barbarino." Taddeo's two kneeling supporters seem to be identified as "mons governatore" (Monsignor Grimaldi) and "Gran Contestabile" (Filippo Colonna). For the figure of "D Tadeo" Tassi sketched three possibilities. In the group sketch Taddeo kneels before the pope on both knees,

---

[47] Ibid., 226: "[U]n altro quadro dell'istessa grandezza e misura dove è dipinta la Cappella Papale di Montecavallo di prospettive, vi è tutta la volta con tutti li stucchi in prospettiva et dipintovi dentro quando Nostro Signore da l'habito all'eccellentissimo principe Taddeo con tutti li eminentissimi cardinali et altri che intervennero a dette funzioni, scudi 300." The reproduction in *Il Museo di Roma racconta la città*, ed. Rossella Leone et al. (Rome: Gangemi, 2002), 250, is unfortunately reversed.

[48] See, e.g., the engraving by Ambrosius Brambilla of a papal mass in the Cappella Sistina in 1582 (Hammond, *Music and Spectacle*, fig. 21).

[49] *Vatican Splendour*, ed. Johnson et al., 21.

FIG. 2.13   Agostino Tassi, sketch for *The Investiture of Taddeo Barberini*
(Toronto, Art Gallery of Ontario, Inv. no. 69/34)

FIG. 2.14   Agostino Tassi, sketch for *The Investiture of Taddeo Barberini*
(present whereabouts unknown)

bent forward; the pope's gesture seems to indicate that he is putting the tunicle or mantle on his nephew. The other versions on the sheet show Taddeo kneeling on one knee but almost standing, head up, wearing the ceremonial mantle; and kneeling on both knees, wearing the mantle and again with his head turned up. These may represent the swearing of his oath to the pope. A sketch whose present whereabouts are unknown depicts the pope enthroned, this time bending forward, with Taddeo kneeling before him and his two supporters kneeling behind. On the right stands a cardinal, the largest figure in the sketch.[50]

In the final version Taddeo is depicted in profile, kneeling on both knees and bending forward for the pope to crown him with the hat. The choice of the moment of the coronation for the final version was perhaps influenced by Raphael's *Coronation of Charlemagne* in the Vatican Stanze, where Leo III is represented as Leo X Medici.

Tassi described his other commission from Urban VIII as "another picture eighteen palmi long and eight palmi high [13'6" x 6'] of the cavalcade wherein is depicted the first cavalcade of the most excellent prince Taddeo, that is the first entry that he made in Rome returning from Urbino with perspectives of Rome in a great number of horses figures and perspectives and all at my own expense as above, 350 scudi" (fig. 2.9).[51]

Tassi's depiction of Taddeo's entrance procession on August 3 is now in the collection of the Banco di Roma. It shows the procession, curled around in the customary S-curve to fit onto the canvas, entering Piazza del Popolo through the porta Flaminia.[52] Tassi's bill for eight pictures, which totalled 1405 scudi, was discounted (as was customary) to 950 scudi and was paid on 10 October 1633.[53]

Taddeo's exit procession is depicted in two surviving canvases. The first, attributed to a collaborator of Tassi, Giovanni Ferri, and now in the collection of the Banco di S. Spirito, shows Taddeo in the garments of the Prefect and accompanied by his two supporters, preceded by the banners of the rioni of Rome (fig. 2.11). The procession is passing in front of Palazzo Aldobrandini on the Corso (now—greatly altered—Palazzo Doria-Pamphilj). A smaller version of the scene, attributed to Ferri and on display in the Museo di Roma, shows the procession from the opposite direction,

---

[50] On Tassi see *Agostino Tassi (1578–1644): Un paesaggista tra immaginario e realtà*, ed. Patrizia Cavazzini (Rome: Iride, 2008); for the sketch, fig. 7.

[51] Cavazzini, *Palazzo Lancellotti*, 226: "e più un altro quadro della cavalcata longo palmi deciotto e alto palmi otto dove è dipinta la prima cavalcata dell'eccellentissimo principe Taddeo cioè la prima entrata che fece in Roma tornando da Urbino, con prospettive di Roma in gran quantità di cavalli figure e prospettive a tutte mie spese come sopra, scudi 350."

[52] Fagiolo, *La festa*, 1:169; for an Avviso describing the procession see ibid., 1:231.

[53] Cavazzini, *Palazzo Lancellotti*, 226.

with Don Taddeo at the far left, preceded by three conservatori, and the rione banners at center stage (fig. 2.12). Between the conservatori and the rione banners there appears Duke Cesarini, Gonfaloniere of the Roman People, bearing their flag. The procession, coming from the Via dei Banchi Nuovi, passes in front of the Zecca, Sangallo's palace of the Mint, while the head of the procession is entering Via dei Banchi Vecchi.[54]

THE MUSIC OF THE CEREMONY

The musical practices of the Cappella Pontificia (now usually referred to as the Cappella Sistina) are described at length in Adami's *Osservazioni*, which can be supplemented by reference to the yearly *diari* kept by the puntatori of the Cappella.

The *Osservazioni* have no specific entry for the Transfiguration. For the anniversary of the pope's election Adami notes: "The Papal Cappella takes place in the Pope's residence, and the Mass is ordered like the other usual ones. At the Offertory there are two Motets, of which the Signor maestro will choose one to his taste, and they are *Tu es Petrus* [or] *Tu es Pastor ovium*, both by Palestrina. . . ."[55]

Agostino Tassi's depiction of the investiture shows some sixteen singers visible in the cantoria of the Cappella Paolina. However, Tamburini's *Diario* for 1631 states that, of the six pensioned and twenty-eight active singers of the Cappella, only two were absent. The large volume visible on the music stand may have been a chant-book or a manuscript of polyphonic music. In his account, the puntatore calls attention to a special point by a marginal "Annotatione": "Be it noted that in this service the Signori Cantori did not begin the Introit until after Our Lord had conferred the habit on the Prefect, and this Introit [was] in contrapunto while His Holiness was still reading it at the throne according to custom."[56] Alaleona's diary stresses the same point: "The Singers did not begin to sing the Introit, but they sang [it], when, having made his Confession, the Pope went to his Pontifical seat at the throne, and sat, and received all the cardinals to the customary obedience."[57]

The reason for this particularity was the fact that the pope's mass at the throne preceded largely independently of the one celebrated at the altar, so that the most

---

[54] Fagiolo, *La festa*, 1:230–31.

[55] Adami, *Osservazioni*, 127: "Si fa Cappella Papale nella residenza del Pontefice, e la Messa si regola come le altre ordinarie. All'Offertorio vi sono due Mottetti, de' quali ne scieglierà uno il Signor Maestro a suo gusto, e sono *Tu es Petrus, Tu es Pastor ovium*, ambi del Palestrina. . . ."

[56] See Appendix of Documents II.

[57] Barb. lat. 2819, Alaleona: see Appendix of Documents III.

important musico-liturgical coordination to be made was that of beginning the mass, signalled by the sign of the Cross made by the pope and the celebrant at the Introit. "The Signor Maestro must watch from the little window of the Choir" for the sign of the Cross, indicating the beginning of mass, "to be able then to direct the Contralti to intone the Introit immediately, which must last until the Pope has finished the Confession."[58] When the cardinals go up for their obedience, the Introit is repeated, "and the Kyries are begun, of which the Maestro will perform as many of them as he wishes, nor should he end them until the Pope has read the Introit."[59]

Adami describes similar ceremonies in the context of Holy Thursday. "All'Introito si fa il contrapunto," the Introit is sung with an improvised counterpoint to the Gregorian melody. Again, the Kyrie is ended when the pope or the celebrant has read the Introit. Kyries were sung to cover the censing of the altar and of the pope, his passage to the throne, and when "he will have finished reading the whole Introit there."[60]

At Don Taddeo's investiture the Introit of the mass was sung after the bestowal of the insignia, "and this Introit [was] in contrapunto while His Holiness was still reading [it] at the throne according to the usual custom."[61] The fact that the Introit was performed "in contrapunto," that is, in counterpoint improvised to the chant melody rather than composed polyphony, suggests that the feast did not enjoy a high ranking since such a performance implied that the occasion was not important enough to warrant polyphonic settings of the propers.[62] Taddeo "was present at the sung mass in the habit conferred on him by His Holiness [. . .] This mass is the one which is sung every year for the Election." In 1616, on the anniversary of the election of Paul V, the Cappella Pontificia had performed Palestrina's parody mass *Tu es pastor ovium* for the mass and its model, his motet on the same text, for the Offertory.[63]

---

[58] ". . . unito al Celebrante [il Papa] dà principio alla Messa col segno della Croce; per la qual cosa dovrà il Signor Maestro osservar dal Finestrino del Coro tutte queste Cerimonie per poter a suo tempo ordinar subito a i Contralti l'intonazione del Introito, che dee durar fin tanto, che il Papa abbia fatta la Confessione . . ." (Adami, *Osservazioni*, 6–7).

[59] ". . . e si principano i *Kyrie*, de' quali il Signor Maestro ne farà dire quanti vuole, nè gli deve terminare fin che il Papa non abbia letto l'Introito" (Adami, *Osservazioni*, 7).

[60] "All'Introito si fa il contrapunto . . ."; ". . . e dopo la replica dell'Introito si principieranno i *Kyrie*, i quali il Signor Maestro darà durare quanto richiederà il bisogno, fin che il Papa . . . avrà quivi finito di leggere tutto l'Introito . . ." (ibid., 38, 56).

[61] CS 41, fols. 44v–45v: see Appendix of Documents II.

[62] For an example of improvised contrapunto see Hammond, *Music and Spectacle*, 130.

[63] Frey, "Die Gesänge," 420. Arnaldo Morelli incorrectly states that Adami stipulates the Allegri *Missa Christus resurgens* for the coronation anniversary; the mass is scored SATB x 2, modelled on a motet of

The "messa cantata" that was performed as the mass ordinary for the investiture is unspecified. However, Tamburini, the puntatore for 1631, was also a prominent composer. Nine of his masses survive in manuscript in the Cappella Sistina archives. At least two of these, the *Missa quodcumque ligaveris* (the antiphon on the Benedictus for Lauds of the Feast of Peter and Paul, Christ's charge to Peter, "Whatsoever thou bindest on earth shall be bound in Heaven") and the *Missa tu es Petrus* would have been appropriate for an important papal occasion.[64]

Among the settings of the propers for the feast that might have been performed by the Cappella are two settings by Palestrina of the hymn for vespers of the Transfiguration, *Quicunque Christi*, or one of the two Palestrina motets specified by Adami, *Tu es Petrus* or *Tu es pastor ovium*. On one Coronation anniversary the mass ordinary was replaced by three motets, one at the pope's vesting, one at the Offertory, and one at the Elevation.[65] In 1628, on the anniversary of his coronation, Urban VIII had communicated to the Cappella through their protector Cardinal Lelio Biscia and Cardinal Francesco Barberini that "Our Lord [Urban] had great pleasure in the mass that was sung, which was, Ut, re, mi, fa, sol, la of Palestrina."[66]

That there was no fixed repertory for the Transfiguration is suggested by the fact that in 1627 one of the Cappella singers, Jacomo Razzi, proposed for performance on September 29 a mass and a motet of his own composition, both of which were rejected by the Cappella.[67]

* * * *

Felice Anerio; one of the three sources was copied in 1719 (Stephen R. Miller, "Music for the Mass in Seventeenth-Century Rome: Messe Piene, the Palestrina Tradition, and the Stile Antico," 2 vols., Ph.D. diss., University of Chicago, 1998, 1:310, n. 110).

[64] Miller, "Music for the Mass," 629–30.

[65] Alaleona, BAV, Barb. lat. 2818, fol. 73v, records an anniversary of Urban VIII's coronation, 29 September (St. Michael) "sine cantu," "without music"; fol. 74 states that Terce, Mass, and the remaining ceremonies were not sung: "qua[m]vis no[n] fuerit cantata Hora Terti, et Missa, et relicta Cerimonia"; fol. 78: "the singers of the Cappella sang three motets, the first when the pope vested, the second at the Offertory, and the third at the Elevation of the Most Holy Sacrament, when four lighted torches were brought" ("Cantores Cap:le cantaba[n]t tria motetta primu[m] q[uan]do Papa accepit paramenta 2.m ad offertoriu[m], et 3:m in Eleuatione S.mi Sacramenti in qua Eleuatione fuerunt portata quattuor funali accesa").

[66] CS 45, fol. 35v [29 September 1626]: "N.S. hà hauto grandissimo gusto della messa che si è cantata, quella è stata Vt, re, mi, fa, sol, la del Pren[estina]."

[67] CS 46, fol. 32 [29 September 1627]: "Il sig.r Jacomo Razzi Tenore voleua questa mattina cantare una messa à 8. quale lui haveva fatta per dedicarla à N[ostro] S[ignore] . . . fece il d[ett]o s.r Jacomo anco instanza di cantare un suo motetto auanti à S[ua] S[anti]tà" ("Sig.r Jacomo Razzi Tenor wished to sing this morning a mass à 8 that he had written to dedicate to Our Lord . . . the said sig.r Jacomo also requested to sing a motet of his before His Holiness").

Like the astrological conjunctions that had presided over Urban's election and Taddeo's investiture, with the passage of time the role of Prince Prefect tended to dissolve. Gigli noted that Taddeo's pretensions caused "much displeasure to Kings, and great princes [...] since it did not appear to them that he was a Prince comparable to the late Duke of Urbino."[68] The most severe conflict was with the Venetian ambassador, who was snubbed by both the pope and Cardinal Francesco Barberini for his reluctance to acknowledge Taddeo's preeminence. In September 1631 Taddeo bribed the ambassador's coachman to give him the right of way in the street and later sent the coachman to a country estate for protection from the enraged ambassador, but the man was murdered there two months later.[69] As a result of this and other provocations, Venice withdrew her ambassador to the Holy See from 1636 to 1639.[70] When the Farnese Duke of Parma came to Rome in 1639 he refused to enter the city until Taddeo had left.[71] The failure of an accommodation between the Farnese and the Barberini nephews in turn precipitated the War of Castro, in which Venice and other powers joined against the Barberini, who were besieged in Rome itself. The death of Urban VIII in 1644 and the election of Innocent X Pamphilj initiated a difficult period for the Barberini family (see Chapter 6).

Don Taddeo Barberini was not in fact "l'ultimo prefetto dell'urbe." Although Urban VIII had conferred the dignity on his family for three generations, it died out with Taddeo's unmarried eldest son, the unprepossessing Cardinal Carlo (the prefect's hat forms part of the decoration of his tomb in the family chapel in Sant'Andrea della Valle).[72] Carlo would be forced to renounce his father's titles of duke and prince to his younger brother Maffeo in exchange for a cardinalate so that Maffeo could marry Innocent X's great-niece.[73]

---

[68] Gigli, 209: "La dignità della Prefettura conferita nella persona del Nepote del Papa, diede cause di molto disgusto nelli Re, et Principi grandi: perciocché essendo questa la maggior dignità di Roma, ancorche D. Taddeo fusse Principe di Pellestrina, e Generale di S. Chiesa, e Nepote dell Papa, non pareva con tutto ciò a loro che fosse Principe da compararsi al Duca d'Urbino morto . . ." ("The dignity of the Prefecture conferred on the Pope's Nephew was the cause of much displeasure to kings, and great princes: since this was the greatest honor in Rome, even though D. Taddeo was Prince of Palestrina, and General of Holy Church, and the Pope's Nephew, with all that it did not seem that he was a Prince to be compared with the late Duke of Urbino . . .").

[69] Ibid., 209–20.

[70] Ibid., 282.

[71] Scott, *Images*, 194.

[72] Barb. lat. 5280, int. 3.

[73] The boy so prominently placed in Andrea Sacchi's depiction of Urban VIII visiting the Gesù for the 1639–40 centenary celebrations is commonly identified as Don Taddeo's second son Maffeo, the future

Appendix

Documents

Abbreviations: BAV = Biblioteca Apostolica Vaticana; AB = Archivio Barberini; CS = Cappella Sistina, Diario; CFB = Cardinal Francesco Barberini; gius. = giustificazione(-i)

I. DE/PRÆFECTO VRBIS LIBER/Auct./FELICE CONTELORIO . . . ROMÆ, EX Typographia Reu. Cam. Apost. MDCXXI./SVPERIORVM PERMISSV.

Nihil Obstat by Giuseppe Maria Suarez, dated the day before the kalends of October 1631. Dedication to THADDÆO/BARBERINO, Duke of Ereti [Monterotondo], Prince of Palestrina, Captain General of the Holy Roman Church, and Prefect of Rome.

p. 3: the Prefects "à Summis Pontificibus electi potestate, atq[ue] ornamentis ab eisdem donati sunt [. . .] Vtitur prætereà tunica Dalmatica laxioribus manicis, atq[ue] vtroque ex latere aperta, ex serico rubro, cuius oræ phrygio opere auro exornatæ sunt; Eam, qui de sacris Cæremonijs altero ab hinc sæculo scripsere, & alij antiquioris ætatis aliquando Tunicellam, nonnumquam aurifrigiatam, [4] aut Senatoriam dixerunt. Deindè Chlamydem, siue Paludamentum induit, quod aliqui Mantum, alij Pallium, nonnuli Pluuiale appellarunt. Id ex veste holoserica punicea confectum, auroq[ue] ad extremas oras distinctum circuli forma, vna tantùm ex parte apertum ad talos vsque dimittitur, ac suprà dexterum humerum aurea ligula nectitur. Iam verò capitis tegumentum, quod aliqui Tiaram, alij Coronam, quidam pileum ad modum Ducalis biretti, nonnulli Infulas vocant ex serico purpurei coloris non vnius sempre formæ fuisse compertum est."

p. 5: "Cæterum Ritus, quo Præfectus à Pontifice creatur huiusmodi perhibetur. In Pontificio Sacello præsente Sacro Cardinalium coetu, vel in aliquo Templo, qui Præfecturæ insignibus donandus est, inter sacrorum solemnia duobus ex procerum numero primoribus vtrinquè associatus ad Po[n]tificem ducitur: Tùm flexis in imo solij gradu genibus ad ipsum accedit, pedibusq[ue] de more exosculatis nixus [6] genibus, fidei, ac subiectionis Iuramentum præstat: Indè ad solij imum regrediens consuetum pallium, sagumq[ue] exuit, ac solio iterum conscenso genibus incumbens

---

Prince of Palestrina. In 1639, however, the heir was still his older brother Carlo (also misidentified in the entry in a Christie's sale catalogue for 1996 for Sacchi's drawing of the boy); as late as 1650 Maffeo was known simply as "l'abate Barberino"; see also Greuter's engraving of the *signorini*, Urban's three great-nephews (sometimes ludicrously misidentified as his three *nephews*, who at that point would have been forty-five, thirty-nine, and thirty-five years of age respectively) (Hammond, *Music and Spectacle*, fig. 26).

suarum vestium consecrationi interest, dùm à Pontifice veteri precatione peragitur: Tùm ab eodum Dalmatica, Chlamydeq[ue] induitur. Demum pileo capiti imposito ad osculum oris admittitur; exinde à sacrarum Cæmoniarum Magistro in supremo solij gradu proximè post Diaconum Cardinalem inibi adsidentem ad Pontificis dexteram collocatur, eisq[ue] ad sacri finem adstat parieti incumbens. Mox Pontificem discedentem assectatus pone pluuialis vestis oras sustinet. Postremò Pontifex eumdem nondum depositis Magistratus insignibus epulo publicè exceptum, collocutionèq[ue] coram omnibus in scamno sedentem dignatus dimittit; Et demùm solemni pompa reuertitur, vt inferiùs dicitur. Quæ modò diximus, ea tum à Sixto Quarto, cum Leonardus de Ruuere, tum à Paolo Tertio cum Octauius Farnesius Præfecturam iniere, ferè servata sunt. Hæc eadem superiores Pontifices imitatus seruauit Sanctissimus D. N. VRBANVS Octauus, cum die 6. Augusti Anno 1631. in Pontificio Sacello Quirinalis Palatij inter sacrorum solemnia insignibus Præfecturæ, quæ Francisco Maria Secundo postremo Vrbini Duce è vivis erepto cessauerat, D. THADEVM fratris Filium Principem Prænestinum, & Eretanorum Ducem donauit."

p. 28: 3 Kal. Aug., "qui dies festo illius ingressui dicatus erat, obuiam ad portam Flaminiam processere familiæ, tum Pontificis, tum Cardinalium, atque Oratorum, omnesq[ue] qui Romæ aderant Proceres, ac Dynastæ singuli ingenti famulorum peditum numero [29] stipati, equisq[ue] generosis, ac vestibus insignes.

"Pontifex inter Missarum solemnia eum, quem Vrbis Præfectum delegerit insignibus Magistratus vestibus, sacro, ac veteri ritu induere solet. Eumdem à Pontifice digressum, ijsdemq[ue] ornamentis insignem per Vrbem equestri pompa, magnoq[ue] apparatu illi ipsi, quos paulò ante commemoraui comitari solent, domumq[ue] deducere; huic tamen posteriori deductioni accedunt præterea omnes Populi Romani Magistratus suis singuli vestibus, ac peculiari dignitatis ornatu conspicui . . .

"Quo die Præfectus in Sacello Pontificio Præfecturæ Insignia suscipit ad osculum oris à Pontifice admittitur, atque eodem ipso ornatu in supremo solij gradu ad Papæ dexteram parieti innixus, consistit, Diacono Cardinali, qui adsidet proximus, idemq[ue] facit quotiescumque, vel in eodem [30] Sacello, vel in Templo coram Pontifice res sacra solemni ritu peragitur, consuetis vestibus indutis."

II. BAV, Cappella Sistina 51, 1631, diario of puntatore Pietro Antonio Tamburini, fols. 44v–45v: "VI/Mercordi/Trasfigurat[ion]e di N[ostro] S[igno]re/Creazione di S[ua] B[eatitudin]e/Habito co[n]ferito al Prefetto di Roma/Questa matt[in]a S[ua] S[anti]ta è uenuto portato in sedia nella capella della fe[lice] mem[ori]a di PP. Paolo V.o in Monte Cavallo, et fatta la solita or[ati]one in ginocchione sopra il faldistorio all'Altare hà fatto la confessione solita col celebrante, che è il Sig.re Card[ina]le

Guittano [Caetani] et di poi asceso sopra il solio, et in esso postosi a sedere li Sig.ri
Cardinali hanno fatto la solita adoratione à S[ua] B[eatitudin]e e doppo la quale è
comparso il Capella il Sig.re D. Taddeo Barberini prefetto di Roma [fol. 45r] in mezzo
a Mons.re Governatore cioè Mons. Grimaldi, et al Sig.re Contestabile Colonna, quali
fatta or[ati]one all Altare et Genuflessione à N. S. sono ascesi ai piedi S[antissi]mi
dove mentre tutti trè cioè il Prefetto di Roma in mezzo, Monsig.re Governatore à
mano diritta, et à mano sinistra il Sig.re Contestabile D. Filippo Colonna, stanno
flexibus genibus S[ua] S[anti]tà dato il giuram[en]to al Prefetto di Roma et dettoli
sopra alcune orationi gli hà conferito l'habito [in marg.: Habito dato al Prefetto]
che è una Tonicella, un Manto, et un Capello con due pendoni simili à quelli delle
Mitre Episcopali una dalla parte dell'orecchia dritta, e l'altro della sinistra et tutto
questo habito di colore rosso: et prima S[ua] S[anti]tà li ha messo la Tonicella, e poi
il Manto, et ult[im]o loco il Capello, quale poi levatosi di testa d[ett]o Prefetto ha
basciato il piede, la mano, et dato osculu[m] pacis à N.S. et poi ritiratosi à mano
dritta nel solio sotto il Baldacchino in piedi, è stato presente alla messa cantata
nell'istesso habito conferitoli da S[ua] S[anti]tà, et doppo il Prefetto il S. Contestabile
ancor lui è stato sù li scalini del solio presente à tutta la messa senza però nissuno
Ambasciatore. Questa messa è quella che ogni anno si ca[n]ta per la Creat[ion]e [in
marg.: Creatione di N. S.] poi ch[e] in tal giorno fù assu[n]to alla [fol. 45v] dignità
Pontificia, et hoggi comincia l'anno Nono del suo Pontificato, cioè di Papa Urb[an]o
VIII.o A queste funtioni sono stati presenti 29 Card[ina]li col sud[ett]o celebra[n]te.
De' Sig.ri Cantori tanto Jubilati, come [?illeg.] assistenti sono stati presenti eccetti li
S.ri Vincenzo de' Grandis Jubilato, che è in patria, et Loreto Vitorij, che si troua in
Zagarola [*sic*].   Notasi che in questa funtione li SS.ri Cantori no[n] hanno cominciato
[in marg.: Annotatione] l'Introito se non doppo ch[e] N.S. hà conferito l'habito al
Prefetto, et esso Introito in Contrapunto mentre ch[e] S. S.tà ancor lui leggeva sol
solio conforme al solito."

III. BAV, Barb. lat. 2818: Pauli Alaleonis Diarium à die 4 Maij 1622 ad diem 17.
Februarij 1630; fol. 73v: 29 Sept. the coronation of Urban VIII performed "sine cantu";
fol. 74v: "qua[m]vis no[n] fuerit cantata Hora Tertia, et Missa, et relicta Cerimonia";
fol. 78: "Cantores Cap[pel]le cantava[n]t tria motetta primu[m] q[uan]do Papa accepit
paramenta 2.m ad offertoriu[m], et 3:m in Eleuatione S.mi Sacramenti in qua
Eleuatione fuerunt portata quattuor funali accesa."
Barb. lat. 2819: Pauli Alaleonis Diarium à die 26 Feb. 1630 ad diem 3 Dec. 1637;
fol. 64r: Taddeo returns to Rome from Urbino 2 July "incognitus et privatim, et publice
non videtur"; fol. 67r, 6 August: "Cantores non inchoarunt cantare Introitu[m],

sed cantaverunt, facta Confess[ion]e Papa ivit ad sede[m] sua[m] Pontificale[m] in trono, et sedit, et recepit o[mne]s Card[ina]les ad solita[m] obedientia[m]. Absoluta obedientia venit ad Cap[pella]m discendens à Cameris contiguis Cappellæ [fol. 67v] [D. Taddeo] . . . associatus a multis nobilibus . . . et facta genuflex[ion]e ante Altare, et ante gradus solij, ascendit superius cu[m] suis ductoribus, et genuflexus ante Papa[m] in habitu suo ordinario . . . [68v] Post inductu[m] D. Prefectu[m] habitu Prefecture' cantores inchoarunt cantare intoitu[m], et Kirie eleison Papa imposuit Incensu[m] in thuribulo, et fuit cantata missa de more."

IV. BAV, Barb. lat. 4733, Andrea Nicoletti: Life of Urban VIII, p. 625, [6 August 1631], the pope goes to his chapel and is greeted with "ad multos annos" for the anniversary of his election. The Prefect enters with his supporters "et inginocchiati tutti trè nel primo grado del solio Pontificio, subito il Prin[ci]pe salì un grado più alto et inclinandosi baciò il piede al Papa; ritornato poi al luogo di prima pur sempre inginocchini, incominciò a spoliarsi leuandosi il mantello, e la casacca, e poi salì di nuouo in mano gli habiti della Prefettura, benediseli con alcune breui orationi, e uestillo. Era l'habito primo una Tonicella di rosso colore, in tutto simile à quella, che portar sogliono li Cardinali [p. 626] Diaconi, sopra la quale poseli il manto della Prefettura aperto dal destro lato. Era questo mantello una ueste lunga fino à terra, anche con un poco di strascino, aperta tutta d'auanti, e scollata; e affiiata d'una sola fibbia appresso al collo. Questo parimente era di drappo rosso, intorno agli homeri ornata di una ricca guarniggione di oro, che calaua poi à basso per le falde della ueste, tutta la circondaua; le aperture d'auanti dauano facil adito alle braccia di mostrarsi, e muouersi à loro uso e così allo scoprir dello stocco; su gli elsi del quale poteua senza alcuna sproportione ricalare et appoggiare quella parte di ueste, che alzauasi à tal effetto. In ultimo il Papa poseli in capo la berretta, la quale non può meglio descriuersi quanto alla forma, che assomigliaua ad uno degli ordinarij cappelli, à cui leuata sia la falda; in luogo della quale pendeuano dalle bande due fascie somiglianti à quelle delle mitre Vescouali, mà non così lunghi; era della med[esi]ma materia, e dello stesso color del manto guarnita anch'ella di alcuni fregi, che attrauersandosi nel mezzo, e for[627] mandoui una croce, ueniuano à diuiderla in quattro parti uguali. In questa forma uestito il Principe tornò al suo luogo primiero, oue leuatasi la berretta, salì più in sù, e baciò di nuouo il piede, e poi il ginocchio, e finalm[en]te la mano al Papa, e poi ritiratosi al luogo destinato in Cappella, che fù auanti al Card.le Aldobrandino, che in quel dì faceua l'ufficio di primo Diacono; al cui lato, mà un grado più basso fermosi il Constabile Colonna, et in questa forma terminò la funtione, alla quale gli altri Amb[asciato]ri de' Principi non intervennero."

V. BAV, Barb. lat. 5242, int. 7, fols. 349–377: Celio Talucci, "Relazione della Cavalcata"; fol. 361: sixty carriages with *suppellettili* of Don Taddeo; fol. 363r-v: Cardinal Francesco Barberini chooses four of his gentlemen to attend Don Taddeo (baroni romani). "Dalle trombe . . . non uscirono mai uoci più allegre, e più sonori"; fol. 367v: Taddeo goes to the Giubbonari palace; fol. 368r: 6 August: "Egli si uestì in questo giorno di calza intiera, artificiosam[ent]e composta con striscie di tabi bianco unite insieme ma ripiene di ricami d'argento. Nell'istessa maniera era la fodera del cappotto di tabi nero che all'homero haueua un Cappuccio attraversatto con grosse bottonere d'oro ripiene di lucidissimi diamanti. La Berretta di Velluto riccio con breue falda et spesse righe, era arrichita di gioie di gran prezzo, e con piume finissime d'[fol. 368v]arrione. . . ." After Don Taddeo's first obeisance, the master of ceremonies (Alaleona) took him back down the steps of the throne, where his cappotto was removed. Taddeo ascended the throne again and was vested by the pope with a "tonicella di drappo cremesino ricamato nelle parti estreme con oro. Il manto che lo copriua era di tabi parim[en]te cremesino, che gli scendeua fino à terra . . . A somiglianza d'un regno Pontificio era il suo Diadema del medesimo colore, hauendo le due be[n]de, che gli scendeuano all'homero, ma attrauersate in uece di corona da una Croce ricamato con oro, et con pietre pretiose"; fol. 370: after lunching with the pope, Taddeo went to the apartments of his brother, Cardinal Francesco, to await his return cavalcade.

VI. BAV, AB, CFB, gius. 1562–95, fol. 76: "Ristretto della spesa fatta dal s.r Carlo Gratiani m[aest]ro di casa nel Mese di sett[emb]re 1631 p[er] seru[iti]o del Em[inentissi]mo S. Card. P[ad]rone"; fol. 77r: "Spese di Arnesi [. . .] A Pietro di Cortona à conto del Cappello della prefett[u]ra che fa fare S. Em[inenz]a sc. 3.— fol. 77v: Spesa di liuree per la Cavalcata dell'Ecc.mo s.re D. Taddeo sc. 1013.63." [Small expenses for the anniversary of Urban VIII's coronation.] "Carlo deve dare per un man[dat]o per spese da farsi p[er] la caualcata del S.r Principe D. Taddeo, e prefetto di Roma sc. 1000" (Hammond, *Music and Spectacle*, 289, n. 60).

"A Pietro da Cortona a conto del cappello della prefett[u]ra che fa fare S. E. [. . .] scudi 3" (BAV, AB, gius. 1502–95, fol. 77r). M. A. Lavin, *Seventeenth-Century Barberini Documents and Inventories of Art*, 12, #97: 30 Sept. 1630, III LMB 30–34, fol. 65r: "sc. 3 à Pietro da Cortona, à conto della Cappella [!] della Preffetura che faciamo fare"; III. MC. 31–34, fol. 11r (31 Sept.): "A Pietro da Cortona a Conto del Cappello della prefett[u]ra che fà fare S.E. 26 d.o"; fol. 429: Inventory of Cardinal Carlo Barberini, 1692, "Un Ritratto del S.re D. Taddeo Barberini in habito di Prefetto in Tela da Testa Cornice nera, oro di Carlo Maratta."

THE ARTISTIC PATRONAGE OF THE
BARBERINI AND THE GALILEO AFFAIR

In memory of Isabel and Laurance Roberts

On 22 June 1633: Galileo Galilei, dressed in the white habit of a penitent, kneels in Santa Maria sopra Minerva in Rome to renounce his Copernican teaching. On 20 January 1634: in a Roman palace a brilliant audience watches enthralled as a female figure in armor descends on a trophy of antique weapons to greet a visiting prince. What connection can there be betwen the two events?

Both are embedded in a political context. Theoretically, in the chaotic events subsumed under the general heading of the Thirty Years' War, Catholic Europe opposed Protestant Europe. In fact, there were numerous cross- and sub-alliances on both sides (in addition to the Turkish threat on the borders of Christian Europe). Catholic France joined the Protestant Gustavus Adolphus in opposing Catholic Spain, with covert encouragement from the papacy. Anti-papal Venice tended to support the opponents of the pope. The Empire was allied with Spain, to the destruction of both their economies; their relationship was further complicated by the tension between the national and dynastic interests of Habsburg king and Habsburg emperor. In the opening decade of Urban VIII's reign conflicts erupted in Italy, first in the Valtellina, the main highway for the passage of troops from the north into Italy, and then in the War of the Mantuan Succession between French- and Spanish-supported claimants to the duchy; both conflicts were failures for papal diplomacy. The German mercenaries who sacked Mantua in 1630 brought with them the Plague, which spread north to Venice (through an embassy headed by Claudio Monteverdi's librettist

Alessandro Striggio) and southward to Bologna, Florence, and almost to Rome, literally decimating populations.[1]

In 1631, at the height of the Plague, all these knots began to come to the comb, as the Italians say. In January France had signed a treaty of alliance with Gustavus Adolphus against the Habsburgs. On Good Friday (April 18) the Jesuits opened their attack on Galileo and on the liberal francophile tendencies of Urban VIII in a sermon preached by the Jesuit Orazio Grassi before the pope in the Sistine Chapel. In case there was any doubt of his ultimate target, in flaying Galileo's *Dialogo sopra i due massimi sistemi*, Grassi—himself the architect of the immense new Jesuit church of Sant'Ignazio—took as his image "the edifice that Divine Wisdom had erected with her own hands." The Palazzo Barberini at the Quattro Fontane was still abuilding, and the paint was hardly dry on Andrea Sacchi's fresco of the *Divina Sapienza*. Grassi thundered, "We must weep, Most Blessed Father, for a terrible destruction and an immense ruin. The edifice that Divine Wisdom had erected with her own hands, that eternal temple of the peace between God and men, is demolished by impious pillagers, destroyed, razed to the ground."[2]

Urban's ability to resist Spanish and Jesuit pressure was eroded by the defeat of France in the War of the Mantuan Succession. In 1631–32 Gustavus Adolphus was more successful than his French allies had anticipated, charging into the Catholic German confederation with a success that surprised even himself, and taking Prague and half the Empire. In early March of 1632 the pope's negotiations with France were denounced before the College of Cardinals by Cardinal Gaspare Borgia, who also functioned as Spanish ambassador; the elder Cardinal Antonio Barberini, the pope's brother, had to be restrained from attacking Borgia physically.[3] By May, Gustavus Adolphus had invaded Bavaria and was ready to cross the Alps. Francophile intellectuals and artists in Rome such as Cassiano Dal Pozzo, Poussin, and Tommaso

---

[1] On the political history of the period see Geoffrey Parker, *Europe in Crisis 1598–1648* (Ithaca, NY, 1979). For descriptions of the Plague in Tuscany see Carlo Cipolla, *Cristofano e la peste* (Bologna: Il Mulino, 1976) and Eric Cochrane, *Florence in the Forgotten Centuries* (Chicago: University of Chicago Press, 1974). Colin Ronan, *Galileo* (New York, 1974) contains some interesting visual material, including a rare engraving of the treatment of the Plague in Rome (190) and a portrait of the hydrographer and Barberini familiar Benedetto Castelli (147).

[2] "Dobbiamo piangere, Beatissimo Padre, un'immane distruzione e un'immensa rovina. L'edificio che con le sue mani la Sapienza Divina aveva eretto, quel tempio eterno della pace fra Dio e gli uomini è demolito da empi predoni, distrutto, raso al suolo" (quoted by Pietro Redondi, *Galileo eretico* [Turin: Einaudi, 1983], 288). On Sacchi's fresco see Scott, *Images*, 34–35.

[3] See J. H. Elliott, *The Count-Duke of Olivares* (New Haven and London: Yale University Press, 1986), 431 and n. 109.

Campanella retired or fled. The Jesuits celebrated their return to power by banning the teaching of atomism, offering as a sop to Urban VIII a splended new edition of his poems on whose admonitory title-page Gian Lorenzo Bernini depicted David, the poet-king, strangling a lion—presumably representing Heresy—who dying generated swarms of bees.

Galileo's *Dialogo sopra i due massimi sistemi*, published in Florence in February of 1632, was precipitated into the midst of this political turmoil. Copies reached Rome by May, and by July the book was informally banned. Between mid-August and mid-September Urban's special commission on the *Dialogo* met five times in an attempt to keep the book out of the hands of the Holy Office, but the influence of the pope and the anti-Habsburg alliance plummeted anew in November with the defeat and death of Gustavus Adolphus at the battle of Lützen. The year closed with celebrations in Rome for the death of the king of Sweden and for the election of his Catholic cousin as king of Poland.

In April of 1633 Galileo arrived in Rome and his trial began. The ten Cardinal Inquisitors included Borgia, the pope's leading opponent in the Sacred College; the elder Antonio Barberini; the implacable Dominican Desiderio Scaglia, who had been suspected of attempting to invalidate the election of Urban VIII by concealing a ballot; Guido Bentivoglio as Supreme Inquisitor General; and Francesco Barberini himself as Secretary General of the Commission. On 22 June the trial ended with Galileo's abjuration.

What the Barberini got from the Galileo affair and the surrounding events was, to put it bluntly, a lot of bad publicity. Urban VIII had been accused of negotiating with the Protestants, he had been denounced as a virtual Antichrist by the Spanish-Imperial faction, and he had narrowly escaped being implicated with his former protégé Galileo in heresy. The Grand Duke of Tuscany through his ambassador Francesco Niccolini nagged the pope incessantly on Galileo's behalf, and the wires of the European intellectual network—the correspondences of luminaries such as Marin Mersenne, Nicolas Fabri de Peiresc, Giovanni Battista Doni, and René Descartes—were humming with criticism of the Barberini. Although Urban attempted to remain aloof from the situation, certainly Cardinal Francesco was aware of it. We might therefore expect a reaction on the part of the Barberini against the Medici and placating Spain, the Empire, the Dominicans, and the Jesuits; a retreat from scientific pursuits; a reaffirmation of sacramental doctrine; a public assertion of the family's power and clemency —and a few private revenges. All of these in fact occurred; but as a result of the shifting and declining power of the Barberini papacy, many of them had to be symbolic rather than political in expression.

The celebrations orchestrated by the three papal nephews during and immediately after the Galileo case were among the most brilliant of Urban VIII's reign. In Carnival of 1633 Cardinal Francesco sponsored, not an opera, but a *Quarantore* or Forty Hours' Devotion in his new basilica of San Lorenzo in Damaso, part of the palace of the Cancelleria that he had acquired along with the post of Vice-Chancellor of the Church, left vacant by the death of Cardinal Ludovisi, the nephew of Gregory XV, in 1632. In the new family palace at the Quattro Fontane, Don Taddeo Barberini produced the opera *Erminia sul Giordano*. In 1634 Cardinal Francesco presented a revised version of the Giulio Rospigliosi-Stefano Landi *Il Sant'Alessio* there, and Cardinal Antonio produced his *Giostra del Saracino* in Piazza Navona.

The 1633 Quarantore raises some interesting questions. The Forty Hours' Devotion celebrated the real presence of Christ in the Blessed Sacrament. Over a period of three days a consecrated Host was exposed in a monstrance placed in an elaborate stage-setting or *apparato* with incense and flowers while masses were celebrated, sermons were preached, and devotional music was performed.[4] In his study of the Galileo affair, Pietro Redondi attempted to reconcile the far-from-universal condemnation of heliocentrism—regarded in some circles (including the pope's own, judging from Andrea Sacchi's ceiling fresco of *Divine Wisdom* in Palazzo Barberini) as a venial offense—with Urban's repeated statements that Galileo had touched on the most perverse material possible, and with the pope's delaying action to keep the matter out of the hands of the Holy Office.[5] Redondi suggested that the whole question of Copernican heliocentrism was a smoke-screen thrown up to obscure a more serious charge; that the pope was in fact sentencing Galileo to a slap on the wrist for Copernicanism to avoid a possible death-sentence for advocating the forbidden atomism that undermined the whole doctrine of the Eucharistic Sacrament.[6]

The celebration of a Quarantore was nothing unusual in seventeenth-century Rome; each Advent the devotion began in the papal chapel and continued in succession around the churches of the city.[7] However, a surviving drawing by Pietro da Cortona

---

[4] The singer and composer Domenico Dal Pane, who performed in the Barberini *La vita humana* in 1656, published a volume of *Sagri concerti ad honore del Ss. Sagramento* for 2–5 voices and continuo in 1675, originally written for performance at the Corpus Domini celebrations in the Borghese chapel in Santa Maria Maggiore.

[5] On the heliocentrism of the fresco see Scott, *Images of Nepotism*, 38.

[6] Redondi, *Galileo eretico*, 289–344.

[7] On Quarantore in general see Mark S. Weil, "The Devotion of the Forty Hours and Roman Baroque Illusions," *Journal of the Warburg and Courtauld Institutes* 37 (1974): 218–48; on Cardinal Francesco's 1633 celebrations see Karl Noehles, "Architekturprojekte Cortonas," *Münchner Jahrbuch der bildenden Kunst*, dritte Folge, 20 (1969): 171–206; and Frederick Hammond, "Girolamo Frescobaldi and a Decade of

for Cardinal Francesco's *apparato*, coordinated with the expense records in the cardinal's accounts, shows that the 1633 occasion was unusually splendid, its solemnity further enhanced by the fact that the pope himself celebrated the closing mass (fig. 3.1).[8] Thus the 1633 Quarantore affirmed symbolically the sacramental orthodoxy of the Barberini in the wake of Galileo's condemnation.

FIG. 3.1   Pietro da Cortona, *Design for the 1633 Quarantore in S. Lorenzo in Damaso*

The Royal Collection. © Her Majestry Queen Elizabeth II. Used with permission

The secular event of 1633 balancing Cardinal Francesco's Quarantore, the fairy-tale opera *Erminia sul Giordano*, was appropriately staged during Carnival at the Quattro Fontane palace by the layman Don Taddeo Barberini (his only effort of the

Music in Casa Barberini," *Analecta Musicologica* 19 (1979): 94–124, esp. 123, and "More on Music in Casa Barberini," *Studi Musicali* 14 (1985): 235–61, esp. 254–55. There is a charming reminiscence of the devotion in a sonnet in Roman dialect by the nineteenth-century poet Gioacchino Belli, "L'affari da la finestra."

[8] On Cortona's 1633 Quarantore see Jörg Martin Merz, *Pietro da Cortona and Roman Baroque Architecture* (New Haven and London: Yale University Press, 2008), 43–46, 293.

sort), since its chivalric theme presented the Barberini in their alter ego as Renaissance princes. The story, a pastiche of episodes drawn from Torquato Tasso's *Gerusalemme liberata* by Giulio Rospigliosi, set to music by Michelangelo Rossi, was largely an excuse for Andrea Camassei's sets and Francesco Guitti's wondrous machines, which fascinated the Barberini (fig. 3.2). Guitti was introduced to the Barberini by Taddeo's artistic mentors, Cardinal Guido Bentivoglio—the Supreme Inquisitor of the Holy Office in the Galileo tribunal—and his brother Marchese Enzo, the *corago* or producer of the magnificent 1628 Parma wedding spectacles, which both younger Barberini cardinals had attended (see Chapter 1). A Venetian representative wrote the Senate on January 22 that Guitti had captured the humor of Cardinal Francesco and Don Taddeo with the setting-up of a theater with "various scene-changes," and that they were planning to spend five thousand scudi on the *Historia di Tancredi*.[9]

FIG. 3.2   Andrea Camassei (sets) and Francesco Guitti (machines),
            Erminia sul Giordano (Rome: Masotti, 1637)

---

[9] "Quel tal ingegnero Guiti venuto da Ferrara se ne stà tutto il giorno con il Card.e Barberino, e con il D. Taddeo, l'umore de' quali ha egli captivato nella constitutione d'un teatro, che con diverse mutationi di scene deve servire questo carnevale per rappresentare l'*Historia di Tancredi* del Tasso in musica. Nella quale opera questi signori spendono cinquemila scudi. Ed il Card.l Francesco n'è innamoratissimo, rubando ai negotii ed ai suoi proprii commodi tutto quel più di tempo che può assistere a detta costructione . . ." ("That certain engineer Guitti who came from Ferrara stays all day with Cardinal

The Bentivoglio lodged Guitti in their palace on the Quirinal, now Palazzo Rospigliosi, during the preparation of the opera. Guitti may have had other irons in the fire: the Modenese resident, Fulvio Testi, wrote to his master that the legate of Ferrara was pursuing a plan to extend a canal from Lagoscuro to within the walls of the city and had sent Guitti to treat with the pope and Cardinal Francesco "under the pretext of certain machines for a comedy that the Prince Prefect wishes to do."[10]

The 1634 celebrations, the revised *Il Sant'Alessio* and the Piazza Navona joust, were occasioned by the visit of Prince Alexander Charles Vasa, brother of the new king of Poland. As a strongly Catholic country ruled by cousins of Gustavus Adolphus of Sweden, Poland was much in the mind of the Romans at the time of the Galileo affair. The accession of King Vladislao Vasa had been celebrated in Rome at the end of 1632, and in November of 1633 the entrance of his ambassador had provided an exotic and brilliant spectacle recorded by the artist Stefano della Bella. By courting Poland the Barberini could reward a Catholic state outside the Habsburg alliance; by honoring a Catholic member of the Vasa dynasty the papacy could tacitly repudiate Urban VIII's embarassing flirtation with their Protestant cousin.

The 1634 joust presented by Cardinal Antonio Barberini in Piazza Navona was intended to relieve the understandable melancholy of the pope and to distract the Roman populace. The event tied together a number of strands in Barberini policy. The Piazza was hispanophile territory, adjacent to the Spanish national church, San Giacomo degli Spagnoli, and the Marquesa di Castel Rodrigo, the Spanish ambassadress, was honored with a box-seat and the homage of the concluding entry.

The joust was directed by Guido Bentivoglio's brother Enzo, the *corago* or animator of the 1628 Parma wedding celebrations. Enzo's son Cornelio II rode as champion or *mantenitore* in the combat, and the printed narrative of the occasion was included among the published works of his uncle Cardinal Guido (although his authorship has been questioned). The flower of Urban's intellectual establishment—what remained of it after the death of Virginio Cesarini and the exile of Giovanni Ciampoli and Pietro Sforza Pallavicino in the wake of the Galileo scandal—contributed conceits and verses. Cardinal Antonio's favorite castrato, Marc'Antonio Pasqualini, appeared triumphantly as Fame

---

Barberino, and Don Taddeo, whose humor he has captured in setting up a theater, which with various scene-changes must serve this Carnival to represent the *Historia di Tancredi* of Tasso in music. In the which opera these signori are spending five thousand scudi. And Cardinal Francesco is besotted with it, stealing from his business and his own convenience as much time as he can to be present at the said construction"): Hammond, "Bernini in Venetian Ambassadorial Dispatches," *Source*, 1986, 43, n. 42.

[10] "Il Legato ha mandato qua un tal Guitti, sotto pretesto d'alcune macchine per una commedia che vuol fare il signor Principe Prefetto . . .": Fabris, *Mecenati*, 453.

in the *veglia* or evening entertainment that preceded the joust. Francesco Guitti, fresh from his triumphs in *La contesa* and *Erminia sul Giordano*, designed the theater and the ship full of musicians that entered the Piazza at sunset to climax the joust, and wrote the words of the solo sung by Fame. Andrea Sacchi apparently designed the various entries of the joust, engraved by François Collignon, and painted a general view of the joust with the great ship ready to enter Piazza Navona (figs. 3.3–3.4).

For the opera *Il Sant'Alessio*, Cardinal Francesco's contribution to the "Prince's Carnival" of 1634, new sets were designed (perhaps the work of the ubiquitous Stefano della Bella), and a new Prologue—the easiest element to update—was commissioned from the librettist Rospigliosi and the composer Stefano Landi.[11] The Prologue was addressed to Alexander Charles Vasa, but it may have been intended as an indirect admonition to his brother, King Vladislao, whose liberal tendencies alarmed the Jesuits. More damning in the eyes of Urban VIII, Vladislao was an outspoken admirer of Galileo's champion the poet Giovanni Ciampoli, who had been driven from his office of Secretary of Breves into exile in a series of dreary provincial governorships. The Prologue's emphasis on the evangelization of the North was an indirect compliment to the Jesuits, whose Collegio Germanico held a monopoly on that effort.

The revised Prologue to *Il Sant'Alessio*, which was premiered on January 20, 1634 in Cardinal Francesco's antechamber in the Quattro Fontane palace, opens with a chorus of six slaves, who recount the virtues and travels of Alexander Charles.[12] They recall his brother Vladislao, who also came to Rome to reverence great Urban. The allegorical figure of Rome descends on a trophy of military spoils (fig. 3.5). To Alexander Charles and Vladislao, examples of secular heroism, she counterpoises the Christian hero Alexis. Turning to address Alexander Charles—"You, royal youth"— she compares him to Alexis as another devout pilgrim. Finally, she commands the chains to drop from the six slaves, "for I desire not a harsh rule but only a gentle rule of hearts," to which a slave replies prettily that chains may fall but the ties of

---

[11] For the original version see Margaret Murata, *Operas for the Papal Court 1631–1668* (Ann Arbor, MI: UMI Research Press, 1981), 21. The *avvisi* state that the opera was to be given in 1631, but owing to the Plague it may have been postponed until the performances documented in 1632. Cardinal Francesco's manuscript biography of Taddeo mentions only a performance of *Il Sant'Alessio* in 1632, followed by *Erminia* in 1633 and *Alessio* "con maggior apparato" in 1634 (Waddy, *Seventeenth-Century Roman Palaces*, 337).

[12] Despite being repeatedly demolished by a number of scholars such as Irving Lavin, Margaret Murata, Patricia Waddy, and myself, the legend persists that the production of *Il Sant'Alessio* inaugurated the immense Barberini theater and that the sets for the performance were designed by Bernini. Until the actual opening of the theater in 1639 the operas performed in Palazzo Barberini were given in a temporary theater set up in Cardinal Francesco's antechamber that accommodated at most a few hundred people, rather than the 3,600 of the great theater.

FIG. 3.3   Andrea Sacchi, engraved by François Collignon, *The Scythian Squadron*
from *Festa, Fatta in Roma alli 25. di Febraio MDCXXXIV*
(Rome, Biblioteca Apostolica Vaticana)

FIG. 3.4   Andrea Sacchi, *Joust in Piazza Navona with the Great Ship*
from *Festa, Fatta in Roma*

FIG. 3.5   Anonymous, engraved by François Collignon, *Il Sant'Alessio*, Prologue
(Rome: Masotti, 1634)

love cannot be undone. Addressing Rome, the chorus concludes, "Once, proud warrior maiden, you ruled our bodies. Now, dedicated to Christ, unfurling the great banner of the Cross, adored conqueror with tranquil rule, to our happy vows you are the queen of our devout hearts."[13]

This allegory of absolute power tempered by gratuitous clemency can be read as an attempt by the Barberini to change the general perception of their part in the Galileo affair. Was it intended as such? The Barberini had lost face above all with the intellectual community. Cardinal Francesco's friend, the venerable and distinguished humanist Nicolas Fabri de Peiresc, wrote the cardinal an eloquent letter at the end of 1634 begging for more lenient treatment of Galileo, "this good man in his seventies, in poor health, whose memory will scarcely be effaced by the future." Francesco answered dryly, "since I am one, although the least, of the Cardinals of the Holy Office, you will excuse me if I do not allow myself to reply to you in greater detail." Fabri wrote again more urgently, citing "the honor and reputation of this pontificate,"

---

[13] "Se libera è la mano, Restano i lacci al core; E indissolubil nodo ordisce Amore. Già fastosa Guerriera Domasti i nostri petti, Hor dedicata à Christo, spiega[n]do della Croce il gra[n] Vessillo, Con impero tra[n]quillo vincitrice adorata a lieti voti Reina sei de nostri cor devoti."

and adding that his own wishes "conformed to the desires of the most noble intellects of the century, who so greatly pity the severity and prolongation of the punishment," likening it to "the persecution of the person and wisdom of Socrates in his own fatherland."[14] For a private person to compare the treatment of Galileo by a reigning pope with the judicial murder of Socrates and to threaten the most brilliant papacy of the century with intellectual disgrace is breathtaking, especially when we recall the rage that the mere mention of the Galileo case provoked in Urban VIII. Not surprisingly, Cardinal Francesco did not answer Peiresc's second letter.

That the revised *Il Sant'Alessio* was a symbolic response to such criticism is suggested by the unusual diffusion of the printed score.[15] The opera was performed in January and February of 1634; the full score was in press by the following July, complete with eight handsome plates illustrating the sets and costumes.[16] (The score of *Erminia*, the only other Barberini opera to be printed in the reign of Urban VIII, took four years to appear and went largely unnoticed.) Copies of *Il Sant'Alessio* were distributed widely. Peiresc was sent one at the beginning of June 1635, and Cardinal Francesco's covering letter seems to have conveyed that praise from the intellectual community would be welcome.

The French musical scholar Marin Mersenne was in the process of writing his great treatise *Harmonie Universelle*, whose outline, presented to Cardinal Francesco by Jean-Jacques Bouchard, had received the cardinal's approval earlier in 1635. In July of the same year we find Peiresc writing to Mersenne: "I wished to take up my pen to write you and to accompany a book of new music for the comedies sung in the ancient style in Italy that the Most Eminent Cardinal Barberini has sent me, to see if you might not find it the subject for some small chapter in your great work, knowing that this mode was not practiced in France, as it is in Italy. . . . And if you could take some small occasion of speaking of it and of giving a bit of praise to this good cardinal, that would not at all hurt your work." The slightly patronizing phrase, "un peu d'éloge

---

[14] *Le opere di Galileo Galilei*, ed. Antonio Favaro (Florence, 1890–1909), 16:169–71, 187, 202; cf. Stillman Drake, "Galileo Gleanings XII: An Unpublished Letter of Galileo to Peiresc," *Isis* 53 (1962): 201–11, esp. 202. I am indebted to Professor Drake for this reference.

[15] Franchi, *Annali della stampa musicale romana dei secoli XVI-XVII*: I/1, lists twenty-one surviving copies of the score, while only ten of *Erminia* exist.

[16] In July 1634 Cardinal Francesco paid 100 scudi "nella stampa della rappresentazione di 'S. Alessio' in musica, con l'intaglio delle prospettive in rame dedicateci da Stefano Landi" ("for printing the rappresentazione of 'S. Alessio' in music, with the engraving of the sets on copper dedicated to us by Stefano Landi"); the engravings were by François Collignon and the printer was Paolo Masotti (Bav, AB, Comp. 80, c. 218r, quoted in Franca Petrucci Nardelli, "Il Card. Francesco Barberini senior e la stampa a Roma," *Archivio Romano di Storia Patria* 108 [1985]: 133–98, esp. 143–44).

à ce brave cardinal" suggests that Francesco was indeed anxious for reassurance.[17] Mersenne obliged by praising "the great Cardinal Barberini, most worthy nephew of his Holiness, to whom every science and particularly harmony will be obliged, as long as will last the excellent account that he has had made and printed at Rome of the heroic deeds of S. Alexis, whose life is recounted by excellent voices."[18]

An otherwise inexplicable fact can be fitted into this puzzle. The composer and keyboard virtuoso Girolamo Frescobaldi spent the years from December of 1628 to April of 1634 in Florence, in the service of Galileo's patron the Grand Duke of Tuscany; indeed, his collection of *Arie musicali*, the first volume of which was dedicated to Ferdinando II, was printed by Landini, the publisher of Galileo's *Dialogo*. When Frescobaldi returned to Rome to enter the service of Cardinal Francesco Barberini, the cardinal paid Frescobaldi one hundred scudi for his family's trip from Florence, subsidized the rent of their new house in Rome, raised Girolamo's salary as organist of the Cappella Giulia in St. Peter's from seventy-two to ninety-six scudi per annum, gave him occasional gifts of money, and even supplied him with music paper. In 1635 Frescobaldi dedicated the reworked version of his instrumental canzoni to the Dominican Cardinal Desiderio Scaglia. (The first edition of 1628 in parts had been dedicated to Ferdinando II of Tuscany.) There is no evidence that Frescobaldi ever encountered Scaglia, or that the grim prelate had any interest in music.[19] The only

---

[17] "Je voulois prendre la plume pour vous escripre et accompagner un livre de nouvelle musique des comedies chantées à l'antique en Italie que l'Em.me Cardinal Barberini m'a envoyé, pour voir si vous n'y trouveriez pas de sujet d'en fair quelque petit chapitre dans vostre grand oeuvre, n'ayant pas appris que ceste mode ayt esté pratiquée en France, comme elle est en Italie . . . Vous verrez dans ce libvre de la musique infernale aussy bien que de la celeste, dont la beauté des intermeses ordinaires tiroit, je m'asseure, les assistanz à plus d'admiration que la difference de l'armonie. Tant est qu'on demeure d'accord que ça esté des plus belles pieces qui ayent esté representées en ce siecle. Et si vous pouviez prendre quelque petite occasion d'en parler et de rendre un peu d'eloge à ce brave cardinal, cela ne nuiroit pas à vostre ouvraige et vous seroit un passeport d'importance, si vous persistez à passer les monts pour aller voir M.r Dony . . ." (Nicolas-Claude Fabri de Peiresc at Aix to Marin Mersenne in Paris, 23 July 1635, *Correspondance du P. Marin Mersenne, religieux Minime*, ed. Cornélis de Waard [Paris, 1933–77], 5:328–29).

[18] *Correspondance*, 6:84, quoting the *Harmonie universelle*, vol. 2 (1637), VII, Des Instruments de percussion, Prop. 30, pp. 58–59: "[le] grand Cardinal Barberini, tres digne nepveu de sa Saincteté, et auquel chaque science et particulierement l'harmonie sera aussi longtemps obligee, comme durera l'excellent recit qu'il a fait fair et imprimer à Rome des actions heroiques de S. Alexis, dont la vie est exprimee par d'excellentes voix."

[19] However, the cardinal's train bearer, Girolamo Navarra, had entered the Cappella Pontifica in 1624 as a bass singer and performed in *Il palazzo incantato* of Luigi Rossi and Rospigliosi, presented by Cardinal Antonio Barberini in 1642 in the Barberini theater (Jean Lionnet, "Una svolta nella storia del Collegio dei Cantori Pontifici: Il decreto del 22 giugno 1665 contro Orazio Benevolo; Origine e Conseguenze," *Nuova Rivista Musicale Italiana* 17 [1983]: 72–103, esp. 101). He did own a Boni harpsichord.

known connection between the two men is Francesco Barberini, with whom Scaglia had served on the Galileo tribunal. It is perhaps not too fanciful to conjecture that the Barberini, who paid for every other publication by Frescobaldi from his return to Rome until his death in 1643, in return for underwriting the revised canzoni requested that its dedication be offered to Scaglia.

The diminishing echoes of the Galileo affair can be heard in other events of Barberini patronage: in Cardinal Francesco's refusal to save the Accademia dei Lincei after the death of Federico Cesi, and his promotion of his own intellectual and artistic academies in the second half of 1630s;[20] in Francesco's publishing activities, filling the gap left by the Lincei;[21] in the widespread festivities for Ferdinand III as king of Rome, the Imperial heir, in 1637, in 1637 and in Cardinal Antonio Barberini's rival celebration for the birth of the Dauphin in 1638; and in Antonio's brilliant commemoration of the centenary of the Jesuit Order in 1639–40. But let us rather end where we began, at the high point of Barberini patronage of the arts and, whatever its causes, the saddest moment of Urban VIII's papacy as a human institution.

---

[20] See Enrica Schettini Piazza, "I Barberini e i Lincei: dalla *mirabil congiuntura* alla fine della prima Accademia (1623–1630)," *I Barberini e la cutura europea del Seicento*, 117–26; Ingo Herklotz, "The Accademia Basiliana. Greek Philology, Ecclesiastical History and the Union of the Churches in Barberini Rome," ibid., 147–54.

[21] Petrucci Nardelli, "Il Card. Francesco Barberino senior e la stampa."

LE PRETENSIONI DEL TEBRO E DEL PO: FERRARA ENTERTAINS DON TADDEO BARBERINI

For Dinko Fabris

Tension between the Barberini papacy and the Duke of Parma, Odoardo Farnese, a descendant of Pope Paul III, had begun in 1638 as a dispute over the revenues of the city of Castro, which Farnese had leased to tax-farmers to pay the interest to the holders of his papal *monti* or loan-shares; his debts amounted to 1,500,000 scudi. Farnese's visit to Rome in 1639–40 in the face of Don Taddeo Barberini's pretensions as Prince Prefect accomplished nothing except to increase the anger of the Barberini. Farnese was so rash as to burst into the pope's chamber with an armed escort, declaring that the pope was a good old man but was misled by his nephews. (In fact, the power behind the prosecution of the war was not Cardinal Francesco Barberini, who typically was of two minds about the venture, but the aging pope himself, who was described as "seeming to increase in spirit and vigor in these wars."[1]) In March of 1641 Urban revoked the right of Castro to export grain, and in August he began to assemble an army to defend the northern possessions of the papacy against Farnese, who was arming Castro and Ronciglione. In September the pope excommunicated the duke's followers. In early October the news arrived in Rome that the papal forces had taken Castro, and at the end of the month Urban sent Don Taddeo, General of the Church, to Bologna to review the state of the papal fortifications. The papal army

---

[1] Alberto Morone to Cardinal Panciroli, 3 April 1643: "il Papa pare che in queste guerre cresca in animo e vigore . . ." quoted in Claudio Costantini, "Fazione Urbana: Sbandamento e ricomposizione di una grande clientela a metà Seicento" (January 2006 version online at *Quaderni* [www.quaderni.net], i2c).

was split up into three units, one sent to Bologna, one to Ferrara, and one to winter quarters in Rome.[2]

In January of 1642 the pope excommunicated the duke himself, and the following July the Barberini took the military initiative. In August Urban announced the war in a concistory, prompting an alliance in September of the Empire, France, Spain, Venice, Tuscany, and Modena against the papacy. Farnese burned two abbeys of Cardinal Francesco in Bolognese territory, sending the pope into a rage with the cardinal, who had falsely assured him that there were thousands of soldiers in the area. (Don Taddeo, who had been given money to hire thirty thousand soldiers, had enrolled ten thousand at most.) Farnese countered the Barberini initiative by invading the papal states, entering the city of Forlì in the Romagna. By October the duke's army had almost reached Rome, which was in a state of panic. Civic militias were raised in the rioni of Rome, barricades were erected, a curfew was imposed, and there was a run on the banks. The pope moved from the Quirinal palace to the Vatican, close to the treasury and bolthole of Castel Sant'Angelo, which was newly fortified. Unexpectedly, Farnese turned back in the face of a second papal army commanded by Cardinal Antonio, and papal troops were sent to Bologna.

As a result of the potential danger to the states of the Church in the north, in December of 1642 Urban had appointed Antonio to superintend action on the Lombardy front as Legate of Bologna, Ferrara, and Romagna, territories which usually had separate legates.[3]

Despite the increasingly tense political situation, the Ferrarese continued their tradition of festive entertainment. Cardinal Antonio Barberini's musician Marco Marazzoli, the virtuoso harpist and composer known as "Marco dell'Arpa," sojourned in Ferrara as a "servitore" of Cornelio Bentivoglio from 7 July 1640 to February 1641. An unsigned minute of a letter (possibly from Giovanni Bentivoglio to his brother

---

[2] For a lucid account of the War of Castro see Nussdorfer, *Civic Politics*, 203–28; see also Faustini, *Delle historie di Ferrara*, 84; Gigli, *Diario*; and Costantini, "Fazione Urbana."

[3] In 1630 Antonio had replaced Cardinal Sacchetti as Legate in Ferrara. He was fêted despite the unfortunate impression he made: "un ragazzo imberbe, piccolo, pallido, non bello, se ben compito di creanza . . . il nostro Comune, non restò, secondo lo stile dell'adulazione, di applaudire alla sua venuta con apparenza di fuochi e macchine ingegnose, eccitati dalla vivacità dello spirito del Marchese Nicolò Tassoni, Giudice de Savi; le quali ad altro non servirono, che ad accrescere le spese al publico erario, ormai destituto e fallito" ("a beardless boy, small, pale, not handsome, although good-mannered . . . our City, in the manner of adulation, did not delay applauding his arrival with fireworks and ingenious machines, prompted by the lively spirit of Marchese Nicolò Tassoni, Giudice de Savi; which served for nothing else than to increase the expenses of the public exchequer, now empty and bankrupt" (C. Ubaldini, *Storie*, quoted in *La chiesa di San Giovanni Battista e la cultura ferrarese del Seicento*, 59).

Cornelio in Ferrara) dated from Scandiano, 25 September 1640, explains Marazzoli's prolonged stay:

> Sig.r D. Ascanio Pio [di Savoia], Sig.r Marchese Martinengo, and many other cavalieri to the number of twelve, among whom am I also, have resolved to give a bit of cheer to the present Carnival by making a festa in music and with machines; and because Sig.r Marco Marazzoli Your Excellency's servant, with his compositions has given such proof of his valor, that no greater could be desired, these cavaliers would desire to be honored by Your Excellency that Sig.r Marco might stay on to give life and spirit to the festa by setting it to music.[4]

The festa has been identified as *L'Armida/L'Amore trionfante dello sdegno*, an opera in a prologue and five acts on a libretto of Ascanio Pio of Savoy, Cornelio Bentivoglio's brother-in-law,[5] based on material drawn from Tasso's *Gerusalemme liberata*. *L'Armida* was commissioned by the Bentivoglio for a wedding between the Bonelli and Martinengo families (cousins of the Bentivoglio) and was premiered in the Teatro Grande di Corte during Carnival in February of 1641.[6]

Marazzoli's extended stay in Ferrara was necessary for the production of *L'Armida*, which required his personal supervision. On 9 November 1640 he wrote to Cornelio that Ascanio Pio had advised him to ask Cornelio to come to Ferrara because the festa risked being a failure, "since there are more difficulties to overcome than had been supposed."[7] The "architect in the same theater" wanted to know what carpenters

---

[4] "Il Sig.r D. Ascanio Pio, Sig.r Marchese Martinengo, e molti altri cavalieri al numero di dodici, fra quali sono ancor io risoluto di dare un poco di allegria al carnevale presente con fare una festa in musica e con machine; e perché il Sig.r Marco Marazzoli, servitore di V. E., con le sue compositioni ha dato saggio tale del suo valore, che non può desiderarsi maggiore, desidererebbero questi cavalieri d'esser honorati da V. E. che il Sig.r Marco potesse trattenersi per dar vita e spirito alla festa con metterla in musica" (Fabris, *Mecenati*, 474).

[5] On Ascanio Pio see Southorn, *Power and Display*, 131–33; and Roberta Ziosi, "I libretti di Ascanio Pio di Savoia: un esempio di teatro musicale a Ferrara nella prima metà del Seicento," *Musica in torneo*, ed. Fabbri, 135–65.

[6] See Roberta Ziosi, "L'Amore trionfante dello sdegno": *un'opera ferrarese del 1642* (Ph.D. thesis, University of Ferrara, 1987). For payments for *L'Armida* see Municipio di Ferrara, Archivio Storico, Sec. XVII, 29, "Allegrezze e commemorazioni 1: Spettacoli" (recently transferred to the municipal archive from the Archivio di Stato) such as the payment of sc. 3,200 by the Giudice de' Savi "p[er] serv[iti]o della festa d'Armida e q[uest]e saranno p[er] compir la sud[dett]a festa e regalar musici" (item #32, "for the service of the festa of Armida and these will be to fulfill the said festa and to give to the musicians").

[7] ". . . essendoci più difficoltà da superare di quello si era presuposto" (Fabris, *Mecenati*, 475).

and painters Cornelio had engaged, and the choreographer ("il ballerino") reported that prospective dancers were already engaged elsewhere and did not wish to come.[8] ("L'architetto nel medesimo teatro" is not further identified but letters in the Bentivoglio archive make it clear that the "architetto" —also "Pittore o Ingeniero" —was Giovanni Burnacini [ca. 1605—55], set- and machine-designer for the Teatro di SS. Giovanni e Paolo, who arrived in Ferrara from Venice in December 1640, and who also supervised the 1642 repeat of *L'Armida*.[9]) The production was a success, according to a letter of Giovanni Bentivoglio to Cornelio from Rome, 13 March 1641:

> I already wrote you in previous letters that I had found, concerning Signor Marco, quite the opposite of what had been represented to you in Ferrara: afterward I always found that he does nothing but proclaim your generosity, and the good treatment that he received. Indeed he shows that if the occasion arises, he would come most willingly to serve for another Carnival.[10]

Marazzoli continued in correspondence with Cornelio about singers for the next Carnival, especially a young Roman woman named Veronica Santi. (The ambiguous role of female singers in noble households is underlined by Marazzoli's observation to Cornelio that "I believe that the Signora Marchesa [Cornelio's wife] will be pleased with her, both for her modesty, which to me seems too much for a singer, as also because she is ugly, which is a quality which cannot but be of satisfaction to the Signora").[11] By 21 August 1641 Marazzoli was listing singers who had performed in the previous production of *Armida* and was beginning to worry about obtaining a leave of absence (licenza) from his employer and from the Cappella Pontificia. (Dinko Fabris suggests Cardinal Francesco Barberini as the patron, but a letter of 18 October 1641 from Annibale Bentivoglio in Rome to his brother Giovanni states: "I have dealt

---

[8] Fabris, *Mecenati*, 475.

[9] See the letters by Burnacini and others quoted by Ziosi, "I libretti."

[10] March 13, 1641: "Io di già le scrissi con le lettere pasate che havevo trovato, circa al Sig.r Marco, tutto l'opposto di quello che le era stato rapresentato a Ferrara; doppo sempre ho trovato ch'egli non fa altro che predicar la sua generosità, e buoni trattamenti ricevuti. Anzi egli mostra che venendo l'occasione, verrebbe volontierissimamente a servire un altro carnevale" (Fabris, *Mecenati*, 479).

[11] Marazzoli to Cornelio Bentivoglio, 3 August 1641: "Credo che la Signora Marchesa ne havrà gusto, sì per la sua modestia, la quale per haver a cantare la mi par troppa, come anche perché è brutta, che è qualità che alla Signora non potrà esser se non di buona satisfatione" (Fabris, *Mecenati*, 481).

with the S.r Cardinal Antonio for the permission for S.r Marco, whom I have already told that His Eminence is content that he come to serve my brother the Marchese."[12] Marazzoli was not only a member of Antonio's household, but from 1639 Antonio was also Cardinal Protector of the Cappella Pontificia, which Marazzoli had entered as a tenor in 1637.)

On 16 October 1641 Marazzoli wrote Cornelio about the new work for Carnival, which would be the torneo *Le pretensioni del Tebro e del Po*:

> . . . Carnival is shorter than last year and time is brief: if my licenza cannot be had before the [Christmas] celebrations, I don't see how the thing can succeed unless they send the work to me here, so that I could compose it in the meantime. And when this should happen, it is necessary to send me the distinction of the parts, how high and how low each one goes in its *genere* and its voice, and the poet himself should inform me of how the whole thing is linked together and his thoughts about the work.[13]

(The poet in question was again Ascanio Pio of Savoy.)

Three days later Marazzoli reported that he had unexpectedly been granted a leave through the efforts of Monsignor Annibale Bentivoglio at the papal court.[14] By 23 October Marazzoli was planning the carriage accommodations of the trip to Ferrara for himself, one Antonio Sonzino with his wife and daughter, Veronica Santi, and Marazzoli's servant. "If Your Excellency wants me to bring my harp, tell me, because we will need at least one mule; if Your Excellency does not wish it, I won't bother to bring it, since I don't play any more: because it's too much trouble."[15]

---

[12] "Ho trattato col S.r Card.le Antonio p[er] la licenza del S.r Marco, al quale ho fatto già sapere che S[ua] E[minenza] si contenta ch'egli venga a servire il S.r Mar[ches]e mio fr[ate]llo" (Ziosi, "I libretti, 162).

[13] ". . . il carnovale è più corto dell'anno passato ed il tempo è breve: se la mia licenza non si potrà havere avanti le feste, non veggo cosa riuscibile se non mi mandassero l'opera qui, che intanto la potrà comporre. E quando questo fosse, bisogna mandarmi la distintione delle parti quanto va basso ed alto ciascheduna nel suo genere e nella sua voce, e che il medesimo poeta m'informasse di tutta l'incatenatura ed i suoi pensieri della stessa opera . . ." (Fabris, *Mecenati*, 485).

[14] In 1626 Annibale had been involved in a disreputable adventure with Taddeo Barberini; by 1655 he was an archbishop, welcoming Christina of Sweden to Ferrara and accompanying her to Rome (see Chapter 8).

[15] "Se V. E. vorrà ch'io porti l'arpa, me l'avvisi, perché bisognarà almeno una soma; se V. E. non la desidera, non mi curo di portarla, perché non sono più: ch'è troppa fatica" (Fabris, *Mecenati*, 487).

Marazzoli left Rome on 20 November 1641. He became ill and arrived in Ravenna on December 3, where he was operated on. On December 10 he left for Venice by way of Ferrara on a Bucintoro from Primaro and was in Venice by the end of December.

On January 6 of 1642 Don Taddeo Barberini visited Ferrara from Bologna. His reception was described by a local chronicler, Agostino Faustini:

> . . . in that time Prince Don Taddeo Barberini having come to Ferrara, he was received by the City with signs of esteem, of honor, and great rejoicing, there being made fireworks out of the ordinary, & a Castle of painted wood, representing Castel Sant'Angelo in Rome, which being full of fireworks, when they were lighted they performed in the Piazza of the Magistrato a military combat; & on the following day, when they had made a Theater in the Courtyard [of the ducal palace], there they made a combat of twelve armed Knights, a *Campo aperto*, which succeeded with the great satisfaction of the Spectators.[16]

The spectators included the newly-created Cardinal Francesco Machiavelli, bishop of Ferrara.

Faustini may have conflated Taddeo's visit to Ferrara in January of 1642 with a second visit in March of the same year. Another chronicler, Nicola Leccioli, describes three evenings of illuminations and fireworks, 7–9 January, with the Castel Sant'Angelo display ("so-so") on the fourth and the performance of *L'Armida* on 11 January. The *campo aperto*, the "combat of twelve armed knights," took place on 4 March.[17]

Faustini does not give a precise date for Taddeo's visits, but Leccioli gives 6–14 January and 3–9 March 1642.[18] *L'Armida*, not mentioned by Faustini, was performed on 11 January in the Teatro Obizzi, G. B. Aleotti's old Teatro degli Intrepidi. Since

---

[16] ". . . nel qual tempo essendo venuto à Ferrara il Principe Don Taddeo Barberino, fù ricevuto dalla Città con segni di stima, d'honore, & d'allegrezza grandissima, essendosi fatti fuochi non ordinari, & un Castello di legnami dipinto, rappresentante il Castello Sant'Angelo di Roma, il quale essendo pieno di fuochi artificiati, accesi che furono, rappresentarono nella Piazza del magistrato un combattimento militare; & nel giorno che seguì, essendo stato fatto un Theatro nel Cortile, quivi si fece un combattimento di dodici Cavalieri armati, à Campo aperto, che riuscì con molta soddisfattione de' Spettatori" (Faustini, *Historie*, 84). For payments for the Castello and a bill of sc. 4152:12:10 for "diverse dimostrationi d'Alegrezze p[er] occas[io]ne della Venuta dell'Ecc.mo Sig.re Prencipe Prefetto" see Municipio di Ferrara, Archivio Storico, Sec.XVII, 29, "Arrivo di Personaggi illustri," item #14.

[17] *Libro d'alcune memorie scritte io per curiosità* (Ferrara, Biblioteca Comunale Ariostea, Ms. I, 359, quoted in Ziosi, "I libretti," 150–51).

[18] A. Frizzi, *Memorie per la storia di Ferrara*, cited by Wolfgang Witzenmann, "Autographe Marco Marazzolis in der Biblioteca Vaticana (I)," *Analecta Musicologica* 7 (1968): 36–86, esp. 50.

Don Taddeo was present, the libretto printed for the performance contains added passages in praise of Taddeo in the prologue and the final scene (both lacking in the one surviving musical score of the opera).[19] These textual alterations for the second performance may have been set in a separate score by a pupil of Marazzoli.[20]

After the performance of *L'Armida*, Marazzoli returned to Venice, where he had been engaged to revise Filippo Vitali's opera *Eco e Narciso* for the Teatro di SS. Giovanni e Paolo. Marazzoli may have returned to Ferrara for *Le pretensioni*, which was presented on 4 March 1642 to frame the combat fought in the Cortile Ducale.[21] Giovanni Burnacini may have been chosen by Cornelio Bentivoglio to design the production—perhaps with Marazzoli, who was working in the Venetian Teatro di SS. Giovanni e Paolo, as an intermediary—to fill the gap left by the recent deaths of Francesco Guitti and Alfonso Rivarola il Chenda. The *relazione* of *Le pretensioni* refers to Burnacini's recent staging of *L'Armida*, on the basis of which he was entrusted with the "care of the new Theater, and of the Set." The theater, in the court of the ducal palace, "which is the heart of the City," was most handsome and capacious, covered with a cloth awning and decorated with tapestries, and illuminated by many torches.[22] The *relazione* notes in passing the brevity of the *Pretensioni* and the small number of machines employed in it.

Burnacini's print of the torneo shows the pastoral stage erected in the courtyard of the Castello Estense and identifies the participants, all of them Ferrarese noblemen: the *maestro di campo*, two mounted squadrons of five each, two *padrini* for each

---

[19] BAV, Chigi Q. VIII. 189; the surviving score seems to have been used for an actual performance, as witness the indication "Ritornello se bisognerà per aspettare la machina" ("Ritornello if necessary to await the machine") (fol. 79v). The libretto of *L'amore trionfante dello sdegno* is preserved in Ferrara, Biblioteca Comunale, MF 54. 3–4. Folios 82–84 of the score contain an untexted soprano recitative and an untexted chorus (Witzenmann, "Autographe," 49).

[20] See Witzenmann, "Autographe," 50, who cites BAV, Chigi Q. IV. 4. as showing the same hand as the final scene of Q. VIII. 189, with emendations by Marazzoli.

[21] BAV, Chigi Q. VIII. 191; see Eleanor Caluori, "Marco Marazzoli," *New Grove Dictionary* (1980). See also Toschi, "Tracce per un calendario," *La chiesa di San Giovanni Battista*, 144–65. On *L'Amore trionfante* and *Le pretensioni* see Witzenmann, "Autographe," 48–51. In a letter from Rome of 12 IV 1642 to Annibale Bentivoglio Marazzoli reminded him of ". . . that which was assigned to me for the celebrations made there before Christmas, which was 80 scudi . . ." ("quello che mi fu assegnato p[er le feste fatte costì avanti Natale, che furono 80 scudi") (Ziosi, "I libretti," 153).

[22] Page 20: "Gioanni Bornacini, che, pochi giorni sono, . . . volle [p. 21] rappresentarle come effetti d'una Maga; Di quale Armida . . . Al Bornacini dunque fu dato la cura del nuouo Teatro, e della Scena . . . quell'azione, per causa della breuità, e del poco numero delle macchine . . . [p. 22] . . . in quel Cortile, ch'è il cuore della Città. [p. 24] Trouerai nel Cortile un Teatro di vaghissima, e capacissima forma ordinatamente disposto. Sarà egli con una gran tela coperto."

FIG. 4.1   Giovanni Burnacini, set for *Le pretensioni del Tebro e del Po*
(Biblioteca Apostolica Vaticana)

squadron, and twelve palafrenieri (fig. 4.1).[23] The librettist Ascanio Pio doubled as
mastro di campo, and Cornelio Bentivoglio rode as the first "Knight of the Tiber."[24]

    The text of the entertainment was published as *The pretensions of the Tiber, and of
the Po, sung and fought in Ferrara, for the arrival of the most Eccellent Prince Don TADDEO
BARBERINI Prefect of Rome, Generalissimo of the Armies of Holy Church, etc. [Poetic]
Composition of DONN'ASCANIO PIO OF SAVOY, and description by FRANCESCO BERNI"*
[1610–73]) (fig. 4.2).[25]

---

[23] For Burnacini's print see Jarrard, *Architecture*, 37, where it is attributed to Ludovico rather than Giovanni
Battista; Jarrard gives the location of the print only as BAV: it is not in the relazione in Ferrara, Biblioteca
Comunale Ariostea. In his *Memorie* Leccioli gives the names of eight knights, which do not always
agree with the ten listed in Burnacini's print.

[24] [IX]: Maestro di Campo: Ascanio Pio di Savoia; Padrini of the Caualieri del Tebro: Carlo Vanani, Lodivico
Beuilacqua; Caualieri del Tebro: Cornelio Bentivoglio [1], Francesco Gilioli, Francesco Tassoni, Ippolito
Strozzi, Onofrio Beuilacqua; Padrini of the Caualieri del Po: Gherardo Martinenghi, Girolamo Rossetti
[2]: Caualieri del Po: Camillo Rondinelli, Francesco Fiaschi, Gioanni Villa, Giulio Sacrati, Mario Calcagnini.

[25] *Le pretensioni del Tebro, e del Po, cantate, e combattute in Ferrara, nella venuta dell'Eccell. sig. Principe Don
TADDEO BARBERINI Prefetto di Roma, Generalissimo dell'Armi di S. Chiesa, etc. Componimento del sig.
DONN'ASCANIO PIO DI SAVOIA, e discrizione di FRANCESCO BERNI.* In Ferrara, per Francesco Suzzi
Stamp[atore] Camerale, 1642 (Ferrara, Biblioteca Comunale Ariostea MF 54.4).

LE PRETENSIONI
DEL TEBRO, E DEL PO
CANTATE, E COMBATTVTE
IN FERRARA.
NELLA VENVTA
DELL'ECCELL. SIG. PRINCIPE DON
TADDEO BARBERINI
PREFETTO DI ROMA,
GENERALISS. DELL'ARMI DI S. CHIESA, ETC.
COMPONIMENTO DEL SIG.
DONN'ASCANIO PIO DI SAVOIA.
E DESCRIZIONE
DI FRANCESCO BERNI.

In Ferrara per Francesco Suzzi Stamp. Camerale.
CON LICENZA DE' SVPER. 1642.

FIG. 4.2   *Le pretensioni del Tebro e del Po*, title-page
(Ferrara, Biblioteca Comunale Ariostea MF 54.4)

The author of the account, Francesco Berni (1610–73), had previously published a relazione of the 1631 Torneo Bonacossi (see Chapter 1). His account of *Le pretensioni* was comissioned by Enzo Bentivoglio, "a Knight well worthy of that name, who was pleased to confer the Festa on me, that I might describe it."[26] From Berni's dedication to Taddeo Barberini:

> . . . There appeared in that bustling about, that Your Excellency deigned to honor, the extreme devotion of the Ferrarese nobility so full of pomp, that others might perhaps have believed it to be haughty pride, if now, being presented again to You, in the lowliness of these leaves of mine it did not show the extremes of their humility. Therefore Marchese Cornelio Bentivoglio, from whose great House it appeared that in every period the theaters learned magnificence, has desired me to describe the celebration, and dedicate it to you . . .

Speaking in the person of Pallas Athena, Berni continued:

> So that poetry should be accompanied by her sister [music], the composition was assigned to the hands of the famous Marco Marazzoli, who can make [even] those who are not Pythagoreans hear the harmonies of the Heavens on earth. With his musical pen he immediately made the happy accompaniment under the generous and shining shade of the great House of Bentivoglio, in which, if I had to have my dwelling down there among you mortals, I would wish to immortalise my abode. Of that House, in order not to offend its past glories, which are vaunted as unsurpassable, I do not wish to reverence the present [glories] with other than only the soul. The parts were then handed out to the singers. . . .[27]

---

[26] ". . . un Caualiere ben degno di quel nome, che si compiaque di conferimi la Festa, a fine, ch'io la descriuesi."

[27] "(. . .) Comparve in quell'armeggiamento, che l'E. V. si degnò d'onorare, l'estrema divozione della nobiltà ferrarese così pomposa, che altri forse l'avrebbe creduta superba, se ora, di nuovo a Lei presentandosi, nella bassezza di questi miei fogli non ostentasse gli estremi della sua umiltà. Perciò il Marchese Cornelio Bentivoglio, dalla cui gran Casa parve che apprendessero in ogni tempo la magnificenza i teatri, ha voluto che io descriva la festa, e la dedichi (. . .)

"Perché poi la poesia fosse accompagnata con la sorella, fu la compositione consegnata nelle mani del famoso Marco Marazzoli, che sa far qui in terra sentire a chi non è pitagorico le armonie de' Cieli. Fe' subito egli, con la sua musica penna, il felice accompagnamento sotto l'ombra generosa e

Marazzoli's composing score of *Le pretensioni*—the unique surviving opera-torneo —is preserved in BAV, Chigi Q. VIII. 191. In its crossings-out, ad hoc indications, and occasional missing instrumental parts, the manuscript gives a strong sense of a work in progress. After the descent of a cloud bearing the Barberini bees and the roses of the family of the cardinal-legate Ginetti [Berni, pp. 25–26], an improvised trumpet fanfare announced the beginning of the performance. The score omits these elements and begins with a slow "dolcissima sinfonia" [p. 27], followed by an increasingly rhythmically active "Bataglia," for both of which only the bass part is given. To this music there appeared the Inferno, a "Scene with four great loggias of the Doric order, burning and collapsed, joining in the middle and terminating in a most distant, and most deep smoky portico" ([p. 27] "Scena con quattro gran logge ardenti, e dirupate d'ordine Dorico, con[p. 28]giundendosi nel mezzo con un terminare in un lontanissimo, e profondissimo portico affumicato"). In Marazzoli's score this is indicated as a "Scena Infernale": Pluto, a bass, is throned "in a Royal seat, with courtiers of Demons" ("in seggio Reale/Corteggiato da Demoni"). He turns and strikes the throne with his foot, "and with tuneful but lamenting voice, complaining of the happiness of mortals" ([p. 28] "e con voce canore sì, ma lamentevoli, querelandosi dell'allegrezza de' mortali)" he sings an aria. This consists of four strophes with trio-sonata (SSB) ritornelli that have been crossed out but which are nonetheless repeated, again crossed out, between the verses. (Are the crossings-out perhaps the work of a copyist to mark the passages that he had already copied for the instrumentalists?)

In the manner of Milton's Satan, Pluto summons the gods of the underworld to avenge their defeat by the powers of heaven on the unwelcome celebrations for Taddeo. A bass line with two empty staves above it is repeated at the bottom of the page, crossed out, and followed by a ballo danced by six demons: "Play until the 6 demons come out to the cross + first Ballo play the dance seven times up to the sign" ("Si sona fin che escan gli 6 demoni alla croce + Ballo p[rim]o si suona la danza sette volte al segno") (fig. 4.3). The demons and various monsters perform "That ingenious dance, in which those Demons, reviving the ancient and famous custom of imitating in number alone" (p. 32: "Quella danza ingegnosa, onde quei Demoni, col rinovare l'uso antico, e famoso d'imitare col solo numero"). Does this indicate a choreography based on harmonic numerical relationships, in the tradition of Balthazar de Beaujoyeulx' *Balet Comique de la Royne* of 1581?

---

chiara della gran Casa Bentivoglia, nella quale, si io dovessi avere quaggiù fra voi mortali l'albergo, vorrei eternar la mia stanza. Di quella Casa, per non offender le cui passate glorie, che si vantarono d'insuperabili, non voglio riverir le presenti con altro che solo con l'animo. Furono poi divisate a musici le parti (. . .)" (Fabris, *Mecenati*, 489).

FIG. 4.3   Marco Marazzoli, *Le pretensioni del Tebro e del Po*
(Rome, Biblioteca Apostolica Vaticana, Chigi Q. VIII. 191, fols. 2v–3)

In a long recitative Pluto announces that after his expulsion from heaven he and his followers can expect no hope there; instead they will disturb the peace of others: "The souls [that are] handmaids of my enemy applaud such bright and clamorous honors, every joy of Heaven pains Hell and the glory of Urban is our derision" ("A' così chiari e strepitosi honori applaudon l'alme al mio nemico ancelle ogni gioia del Ciel penasi d'Inferno e la gloria d'Urbano è nostro scherno"). Pluto plans to disrupt the festivities by inciting armed conflicts between the rivers of Italy: the rival claims of the Roman Tiber and the Lombard Po thus symbolise the two sides in the War of Castro.

Pluto summons up two Furies, tenors; one enters with a torch of sulphur, the other with a whip of snakes ("sferza di serpi"). Their virtuoso duet, preceded by a crossed-out ritornello marked "A," describes their task as tormenting the world. A bravura passage in 6/2 illustrates the words, "Quei lumi ardenti fochi d'amor dispenderemo ai venti e di Bellona accenderemo ardor" ("We will scatter those lights, burning fires of love, to the winds, and inflame the ardor of Bellona [the goddess of war]") [ex. 4.1]. This is followed by a chorus of four Demons (TTTB) with touches of rather old-fashioned counterpoint and a virtuoso conclusion. They exit "with varied movements of a new ballo" (p. 37: "col vario moto d'un nuovo ballo"), a "Balletto 2" of which again only the bass line is given in the score. The Inferno disappears, there appear the Po, bosky paths ("boscarecci viali"), and a spotless sun with three bees. Three spacious perspective sets (lontananze), right, left, and center, show the banks and waters of the Po, with Ferrara in the middle.

The Tiber enters from the right, mounted on a fish. (On the representation of river gods such as the Tiber see Chapter 5.) Like Pluto a bass, the Tiber presents his credentials, details his travels in a long recitative, extolls Don Taddeo fulsomely ("a single TADDEO is worth a hundred Augustuses" — "vale per cento Augusti un TADDEO solo"), and challenges the Po. He then sings a vaguely strophic aria with a ritornello over a walking bass, punctuated with an admonition to the Po and its tributary the Reno ("give me back my Hero, unworthy rivers" — "rendetemi il mio Eroe, fiumi non degni"), echoing the refrain "rendetemi il mio ben, Tartarei numi" from Monteverdi's *L'Orfeo*. The aria ends with a triple-meter coda [ex. 4.2]. On fol. 12 of the manuscript there appears another ritornello bass, marked "B" and different from the one appearing on fol. 13.

Yet another cancelled ritornello precedes a "Coro di Ninfe" (presumably the "ancelle" of Pluto's recitative), an elegant duet sung by soprano Nymphs of the Po costumed in "scanty silver skirts" (p. 44: "succinte gonne d'argento"). One sings, "Such a proud voice threatening and praying is not prayer if accompanied by threats"

Ex. 4.1   *Le pretensioni del Tebro e del Po*, Duet of Furies, fol. 6.

Ex. 4.2   "Rendetemi il mio Eroe," fols. 12v–13.

("Qual voce altera qui minacciando e così pregando và non è preghiera se di minaccie in compagnia si stà"). The second answers, "Mars and Bellona have their seat on the banks of the Po, let not the voice that thunders fear to arouse ridicule" ("Marte e Bellona tengono i seggi loro in Ripa al Pò, voce che tuona derision non tema eccitar può"). After a repeat of the ritornello bass, again cancelled, the two join in "Each of us laughed at your foolishness when we heard of it, but you will bewail your fate if you stay here longer; our arrows precede the arms of our King, and perhaps you will flee too late" ("Di noi ciascuna rise di tua follia quando t'udì ma' tua fortuna piangerai tu' se più ti fermi quì i nostri dardi l'armi precorredan del nostro Ré, e forse tardi ricorso havrai al fuggitivo pié") [ex. 4.3]. This is again followed by a cancelled repeat of the ritornello bass.

In a recitative the Tiber admonishes the nymphs of the Po that needles and spindles are more appropriate to their hands than the arrows of war. After another statement of their ritornello, again cancelled in the manuscript, the nymphs defy the Tiber, and the slanging match continues as he replies in recitative, "I came girded for dignified battles, not to squabble with Women, who would not run out of words until the sun set, and I would be humiliated whether conqueror or conquered" ("À battaglie civili io venni accinto, non à garrir con Donne che parole non mancarian pria che mancasse il sole e scorno havrei ò vincitore ò vinto"). In a triple-time aria of three strophes with Passacagli ritornelli, Tiber challenges the Reno and the Po, ending with a final echo of "rendetemi il mio Eroe fiumi non degni" [ex. 4.4].

Aroused by the Tiber, the Po answers in a disdainful recitative whose text is dense with geographical and astrological references, to which the Tiber replies that power is unique and indivisible: "One Tiber on earth, one Jove in paradise" ("Un Tebro in terra un Giove in paradiso"). In a duet the Tiber and the Po prepare for battle: "now that the mouth is silent, let the sword speak; let him who is not strong in harsh Battle fall on the bosom of his mother earth" ("muta la bocca si parli la spada; da chi non sarà forte in dura Guerra della sua madre terra in seno cada"). They conclude, "Let the sound of songs give way to the sound of trumpets, and let the trumpets sound "to arms, to arms" ("Ceda al suon delle trombe il suon de carmi, E tocchin gli oricalchi à l'armi, à l'armi").

The two nymphs summon up the warriors, and all four join the cry "to arms, to arms!" At this point the score directs simply, "Quì si fà il Combattimento"— "Here they do the Battle." This is presumably the "combat of twelve armed Knights" between the knights of the Tiber and of the Po. No music is provided in the score. On the evidence of *Le pretensioni* and the *Fiera di Farfa*, the music for staged combats was generally not written out but improvised. In the *Fiera di Farfa* four breves in the bass bear the indication, "Qui và il combattimento" (see Chapter 1).

Ex. 4.3   Duet of Ninfe, fol. 14v.

EX. 4.4   Tebro: "Rendetemi il mio Eroe," fol. 17.

Ex. 4.4—*continued*

The *relazione* fills in the missing combat. "Now here . . . when the harmonious voices have given way, they will make the air resound with a warlike challenge, and trumpets. You will see directly those two lontananze, which will be on the sides, advancing with two large bridges toward the Stage of the Theater" (p. 70: "Hor qui . . . cedendo le voci armoniche, faranno risonar l'aria, con bellicosa disfida, e trombe. Vedrai diritto a quelle due lontananze, che saranno dalle parti avvanzarsi con due gran ponti verso il Teatro la Scena.") From the Tiber side comes a squadron of five knights, arranged in the four corners of a square with the fifth knight in the middle, preceded by two padrini. "To the reciprocal sound of the trumpets" (p. 71: "al vicendevole suono delle trombe") the knights first fire off pistols and then brandish swords (stocchi), moving two by two in changing formations, which unfortunately are not described.

"Then unexpectedly by main force the breath will fail the Trumpets, and their motion [will fail] the Knights. You will turn your eyes and ears to the Stage, and you will realize, that the harmony of his sphere will have carried Mercury to the place. Flying through the air this winged Messenger with the wand of his caduceus will have enchanted the throng of those Champions, who united in orderly fashion will join to bow with a half turn to the presence of the Princes, as if Ferrara bows in the form of a moon of iron" (p. 78: "Quando all'improviso mancheranno per forza sovrana il fiato alle Trombe, il moto à Caualieri. Volgerai l'occhio, e l'orecchio uerso la Scena, e t'accorgerai, che in quel luogo avrà portato l'armonia dalla sua sfera Mercurio. Per l'aria questo alato Messagiere volando avrà, con la verga del caduceo, incantato la schiera di quei

Campioni, che ordinatamente unite giungeranno a piegarsi con un mezzo giro alla presenza de' Principi, facendo quasi, che Ferrara in forma di una luna di ferro s'inchina.")

In a long recitative Mercury stops the battle and urges peace on the opponents, since they are of equal valor. He admonishes the Tiber and the Po, "And you, Gods of the waves who bathe the noble and happy fields of Italy, you are not less famous than she is. Forever friends, you will soon see before your eyes that prohibition of arms that the great peaceful Thunderer imposes" ("E voi ò Numi ondosi che dell'Ausonia i campi almi e felici irrigate non men di lei famosi siate p[er] sempre amici tosto vederete a gl'occhi vostri avante qual ch'impone dell'armi il gran divieto pacifico Tonante"). Mercury breaks into lyrical triple meter for his concluding admonition, "Listen, obey the great decree" ("Ascoltate, obedite al gran decreto"). Tiber and Po give their consent in a duet, again ending in a flourish of joyful triple meter.

Apparently the Furies still resist the general peace, since Jove appears, condemns them and Pluto, and hurls the Furies down to the "blind prison" of Hades. He praises the rivers and directs Taddeo to return "there where your great uncle holds the throne of the world" ("là dove il suo gran zio del mondo hà il trono"). In a tutti all the personages recognize that what seem evils to mortals are good to the immortals in the heavens. A final speech is addressed to the departing Prince Prefect Don Taddeo, "Eroe prefetto grato." He is to return "to reverence the foot of [the holder of] the Keys of Heaven . . . Let us sing in harmony and let the universe sing, One Jove in Heaven and one Urban on earth" ("à venerare il piede delle Chiavi del Cielo . . . Cantiam concordi e l'universo canti, Un Giove in Cielo et un' Urbano in terra") [ex. 4.5].

An examination of *Le pretensioni* leads one to consider the role of Marco Marazzoli, which runs like a red thread (to employ Manfred Bukofzer's simile) through the musical life of the Barberini family. In 1631 he accompanied Cardinal Antonio on his mission to repossess Urbino after the death of Francesco Maria della Rovere. From 1637, the year of his entrance into the Cappella Pontificia, he was employed as an aiutante di camera for the Barberini. Marazzoli contributed to the 1639 reworking of *Chi soffre speri* that opened the Barberini theater. For the Barberini celebrations for Christina of Sweden in 1656 he provided the principal opera, *La vita humana*, as well as the two other operas presented, *Dal male il bene* and *Le armi e gl'amori* (see Chapter 8). His output of 379 extant cantatas, a genre particularly favored by Cardinal Antonio Barberini, is greater than that of any of his contemporaries, and his oratorio production, although smaller, ranks him with Carissimi.[28] In *Le pretensioni del Tebro e del Po* we see him as the fluent composer of the unique surviving opera-torneo.

---

[28] Twenty-one cantatas for 1–3 voices and continuo are reproduced in facsimile in *The Italian Cantata in the Seventeenth Century*, vol. 4, ed. Wolfgang Witzenmann (New York: Garland Publishing, 1986); two

Ex. 4.5   Final chorus, fol. 32v.

oratorios appear in *The Italian Oratorio 1650–1800*, vol. 1, ed. Joyce Johnson and Howard E. Smither (New York: Garland Publishing, 1986).

Ex. 4.5—*continued*

Ex. 4.5—*continued*

Ex. 4.5—*continued*

Ferrara, Biblioteca Comunale Ariostea MF 54.4; BAV, Chigi Q. VIII. 191

The text that follows is a currently-unfashionable conflation that combines Marazzoli's manuscript text and the text of the printed *relazione*. It follows the punctuation, capitalization, and form of the printed libretto in order to clarify the poetic structures of the text. Material found only in the musical manuscript is indicated by < >, material found only in the *relazione* by [ ]. Pagination in brackets refers to the printed *relazione*, foliation in brackets refers to the manuscript, which is written across an entire opening rather than in separate recto and versos of a folio. While Marazzoli's manuscript text follows the *relazione* text closely, he often writes "dell'" where the printed text employs "de l," "degli" instead of "de gli," etc., and he often adds an initial "h" to words such as "[h]orribile."

<[fols. 1v–2] Scena Infernale / Plutone in seggio Reale / Corteggiato da Demoni>
    Dalle sponde d'Acheronte,
È di stige e Flegetonte
Tutti, tutti quà venite,
Numi d'Inferno, alla Città di Dite. <Ritornello con . . . e Tromboni a 7>

<Plutone 2.a strofa>
    Nelle piagge luminose
Spargon gigli e gittan rose;
Tutto è riso, tutto è festa;
È la gioia del Mondo à noi molesta. <Ritornello a 7 Voltate>

<[fols. 2v–3] Pluton 3.a strofa>
    Aspra ben fù la percossa,
Che gittoci in questa fossa.
Ma trapassa ogni martire
Il veder chi ci offende <h>ora gioire. <(Ritornello)>

<Plutone 4.a strofa>
    Il sentir l'altrui diletto
Troppo annoia un mesto petto;
Onde quì con aspro ciglio
Chiamo ad udirmi l'infernal Consiglio. <Ritornello>

< Si sona fin che escan gli 6 demoni alla croce + Ballo p[rim]o> [p. 31: Various monsters come out and dance; p. 32: "Quella danza ingegnosa, onde quei Demoni,

col rinovare l'uso antico, e famoso d'imitare col solo numero"; Pluto incites flames in the breasts of the most noble rivers]

[fol. 3v–4] [Plutone] Ò da la mano ripida, e severa,
Che prevalse al valor gent'abbattuta;
Ò Deità de l'ombra orrida, e nera,
Compagni fidi alla crudel caduta,
Poiche alcuno di noi pace non spera
Dal Cielo, che p[er] noi tempore non muta,
Turbiam' la pace altrui, diamoci il vanto
D'affogare ogni riso in sangue, e pianto.

Sù la sponda del Pò
Gioiosi ardori s'alzano alteri ad emolar le Stelle,
Tuonan concavi bronzi, e quei rumori
Voci di calma son, non di procelle.
À così chiari, e strepitosi onori
Applaudon l'alme al mio nemico ancelle
Ogni gioia del Ciel, pena è d'Inferno,
E la gloria d'URBANO è nostro scherno.

Più non si tardi, ò Numi, e quanto vale
Nostro valore, e nostra industria, et arte
Tutto s'adopri. Sorga incendio tale,
Che sian festive fiamme à terra sparte.
Esca dal tuono fulmine mortale,
[fols. 4v–5] Fulmine non di Giove, mà di Marte.
Del ferro la Città sia ferrea Scena
Di morti orribilissime ripiena.

Voi, voi del Regno mio,
Ò potenze maggiori,
Furie, ministri eleggo à miei furori.
Voi p[er] mio gusto à turbar gusti invio.
Frà i capi ogn'or fumosi
Degl'Italici fiumi amor destate;
Nè prima ritornate
Che'l sangue de guerrieri
Estingua de la gioia i fuochi alteri.

Destino armate liti
Nostri pestiferi angui
Tanto, che i corpi esangui
Formino nuovi Monti, e nuovi liti. <Ritornello A>

[p. 35: two Furies enter, one with a torch of sulphur, the other with a "sferza di serpa"]

<Due Furie / Furia P.a / Furia 2.a>
  È nostra gran ventura,
Qualor ci sciogli tù
[fols. 5v–6] Da la prigion crudel, ch'habbiam quà giù.
Nostra fattura
E quando usciam' da questo duro carcere
Il torme[n]tare il Mondo, e non mai parcere.
Quei lumi ardenti,
Fuochi d'Amor
Disperderemo ai venti,
[fols. 6v–7] E di Bellona accenderemo ardor.
Per seminar i mali
Ecco pronte le mani, aperte l'ali [they fly off].

<Coro a 4. di Demoni. [fols. 7v–8] Coro Infernale a 4.>
  Ite à turbar il cor
Di chi languir ci fà.
L'altrui pena, e dolor
Qualch'ombra di piacer pure ci dà.
[fols. 8v–9] Infelici piacer, mà naturali
Dell'anime infernali.

[p. 37: they leave "col vario moto d'un nuouo ballo"; the Inferno disappears, the Po appears; boscarecci viali, sun with three bees = no sun spots appear; three spacious lontananze with banks and waters of the Po; middle lontananza shows Ferrara; p. 39: the Tebro enters from the right, mounted on a fish]

Tebro:
[fols. 9v–10] <Balletto 2 Sinfonia Presto/Tebro>
  Io, che dono al Tirreno gli argenti miei

Del gran Padre Appe[n]nin figlio più degno.
Io, che già stesi al Gangi, al Tago il Regno,
E tributario l'Ocean mi fei.

De la Città d'ogni Città Reina
Liquido Nume, irrigator famoso,
Il Tebro son, del cui cristallo ondoso
Specchio si fà la Maestà Latina.

Dè la Città immortale, e del mio letto
Le pompe, e le delitie abbandonando,
Umido Peregrin quà vengo errando
Tanto può giusto sdegno in nobil petto.

[fols. 10v–11] Col Regio albergo il trionfal mio fiume,
Co[n] lo ciel purpureo, e l'aureo suol lasciai,
Nel Tosco mare passaggiero entrai,
E solcò l'acque amare un dolce Nume.

Di Mongibel mirai l'alta favilla:
Vidi il lito gentil de la Sirena;
À dietro mi lasciai l'onda Tirrena
Et i latrati disprezzai di Scilla.

D'Adria nel mar' entrai, scorrendo il lido,
Ch'à l'Epirotta, e Dalmatin s'oppone,
Al fin l'acque incontrai del Pò, che pone
La Giustitia in non cale, ond'io lo sfido.

E sfido insieme un'altro Rio rapace,
Che de la gioia mia s'adorna il seno.
Tù dunque, Pò superbo, e tù, vil Reno,
Più non godrete il mio tesoro in pace.

Per adornar mie sponde à l'Vniverso
I più bei fregi i figli miei furaro
Or che tolto mi vien fregio il più raro,
S'io'l soffrissi, sarei dá mé diverso.

Portar le glorie mie da Polo à Polo,
Emilio, Scipio, Cesare, e Pom[fols. 11v–12]peo.

Questi mi tolse il Ciel, dièmmi TADDEO:
Vale p[er] ce[n]to Augusti un TADDEO solo.

Schiera al pugnare, al trionfare accinta
Di Romani guerrier seguì il suo Tebro.
Se'l Pò no[n] basta, e'l Ren, dia[n] l'Istro, e'l Ebro
Schiera contraria, e fia battuta, e vinta.

Sostrerran questi miei, che degna stanza
Del Prefetto di Roma è sola Roma
Su'l Pò, sù'l Ren se buon guerrier si noma
Venga al cimento, e perderà baldanza.

Ma pria, che'l foro, e'l ferro apran la strada;
De' miei seguaci al bellicoso ardire,
Sian precursori i preghi miei de l'ire;
Pria s'adopri la lingua, e poi la spada. <Ritornello>

Ò Reno ò Pò rendete
Rendetemi sù, sù
Il fiore degli Eroi, che mi tenete;
E non si tardi più.

A l'armi, à l'armi gridano
Di [fols. 12v–13] Roma i forti figli,
Bramosi di far gl'argini vermigli
Del Reno, e dell'Eridano. <Ritor[nell]o:>

À guerrier vostri vita
Salvate, ò Reno, ò Pò.
Rendetemi il mio bene, et io partita
Pacifico farò.
Preghi accettate, e non vogliate sdegni,
Rendetemi il mio Eroe, fiumi men degni.
[p. 44: nymphs of the Po appear, glad in "succinte gonne d'argento"]

[fols. 13v–14] <Coro di Ninfe / Ninfa P.a / Ritornello>

Qual voce altera
Qui minacciando, e non pregando và
Non è preghiera
Se di minaccie in compagnia si stà.

<Ninfa 2.a> Marte, e Bellona
Tengono i seggi loro in Ripa al Pò.
Voce, che tuona
Derision non tema eccitar può.

<Ninfa P.a Ninfa 2 a2>

    Di noi ciascuna
Rise di tua follia, quando t'udì.
Mà tua fortuna
Piangerai tù, sè più ti fermi qui.

[fols. 14v–15] I nostri dardi
L'armi precorreran del nostre Rè;
E forse tardi
Ricorso havrai al fuggitivo piè.

Tebro:
    Amazzoni novelle,
Col Pò male cangiaste il Termodonte.
Cessate omai da'l onte,
E gentili non men siate, che belle.
Voglino pugne d'Amor visi sì vaghi,
E non dardi le man, mà fusi, et Aghi. <Ritornello>

[*Ripigliano animose le Ninfe*]

<Ninfa P.a Ninfa 2.a>
    Al dardo, al fuso
Al[fols. 15v–16]ternamente diam la destra, e'l cor;
E non è escluso
Da le Ninfe del Pò maschio valor. <Ritornello>

[*Soggiugnerà disprezzante il Tebro*]

    Serbate il valor vostro,
P[er] quand'io condurrò Clelia, o Camilla.
Io di cianice non giostro, <?posso>
Nè bastaria con voi lingua di squilla.
À battaglie virili io venni accinto;
Non à garrir con donne, che parole

Non mancarian pria che mancasse il Sole.
E scorno havrei ò vincitore, ò vinto.

<Ninfa P:a>
    Chi miste à prieghi le minaccie semina,
Sdegnar no[n] deve di garrir con femmina.

Tebro:
    Voi tenete in sù la sponda,
Ninfe, homai la lingua [fols. 16v–17] à freno.
Et il capo fuor de l'onda
Il Pò cavi, et esca il Reno.

<2.a strofa / Passacagli>
    Le mie doglie, e le querele
Voi sprezzate, ò Numi vili,
Che non ponno in cor crudele
Trovar porta voci humili.

<3.a strofa / Passacagli>
    Cangiarò dunque costume;
Trovarò mezzo migliore.
Io vi sfido, umidi Numi.
Reno, ò Pò, non più dimore.

    Forza è, ch'à forza cortesia v'insegni.
Rendetemi il mio Eroe fiumi non degni.

Pò [Enters from left]:
    Eccomi ò Nume altero,
Ingiusto turbator del mio riposo.
Tù, non uso ad uscir dal proprio impero,
Sei anche nel pregar ingiurioso.
Duri incontri riceve ogni orgoglioso
In pa[fols. 17v–18]ese straniero.
Mà, prima di punir, risponder chero.
P[er] me, p[er] l'honor mio
À parlar son venuto.
Non già p[er] quel già tributario Rio,
Che sino m'offenda col suo tributo.

Mentre ogn'un l'odiava,

Mentre scacciato, e vagabondo andava,

Io gli diedi pietoso almo ricetto,

Et egli ingrato m'occupò il mio letto.

Non fia mai più, ch'io mi raccolga in seno

Quel mostro tortuoso,

Quel serpe insidioso

Il cui fiato è veleno.

E se voler del Ciel, se forza humana

Uniranno à mie Linfe i fanghi suoi,

Lasciarò questi liti, andrò'a'gli Eoi,

Occorrerò à cercar l'Istro, e la Tana.

Per mè, per l'[h]onor mio solo rispondo.

Io, che da l'Alpi innondo

Sino al mar d'Adria la più bella Terra;

Io, che porto la Guerra

À lo stesso Nettuno;

Io, ch'à miei cenni adduno

Tanti Vassali miei di te maggiori

Dovrò lasciare[ti] à [fols. 18v–19] me dovuti honori?

Qual ragion, qual possanza,

Otterrà, vincerà, che'l nostro Sole

Faccia in un segn<i>o sol perpetua stanza?

Pur Febo in Cielo suole

No[n] premer sempre del Leone il tergo,

Nè sdegna haver co' i pesci umile albergo.

D'ogni modestia ornato,

Non d'alterigia armato

Io mi voglio appagar di gratia alterna.

Mà s'in un loco sol sua stanza eterna

Scritta è del Ciel ne' solidi volumi,

Non fia, che mia virtù ceda à l'orgoglio.

Et à provarti, che si deve, io toglio

Il Prence degli Eroi al Rè de' fiumi.

Tebro:

    Frà gl'altri io son di pregio unico al Mondo.

Stanche le penne son ne le mie lodi.

Conosco le tue frodi.
Sdegno d'haverti eguale, anzi secondo.
Quel, ch'è mio di ragion, non vuò diviso.
Un Tebro in Terra, un Giove in Paradiso.

[*Ecco le conclusioni del Pò*]
    Ormai sembra viltà l'esser cor[fols. 19v–20]tese.
Così và, se s'onora ogni superbo.
Mà pure intatto i'serbo
L'honor, che più risplende à le contese.
Or', ora i miei guerrier di ferro cinti
Te cingeran de' tuoi campioni estinti. <Ritornello. A>

<a 2 / Tebro Pò>
    Muta la bocca sia, parli la spada;
E da chì non sarà forte in dura guerra,
Della sua Madre Terra in seno cada.

[fols. 20v–21] <Tebro>
    Voi decidete, ò miei Guerrier, la lite,
E col ferro, che fulmina, ove tocca,
Chiudete al Pò la temeraria bocca,
E'l pazzo cor de' suoi Campioni aprite.

[Eridano=]Pò
    Il cor de' miei campioni è sempre aperto,
E può gl'affetti suoi veder chi vuole;
Così fosse d'ogn'altro. Or le tue sole
Canginsi in fatti, e sia['l] valore esperto.

<Tebro Pò a 2.>
    Ceda al suon delle trombe il suon de carmi,
E tocchin gli oricalchi à l'armi[, à l'armi] [fols. 21v–22].

<Ninfa P.a Ninfa 2.a>
    Suonin cavi metalli
De l'equestre battaglia il fiero invito.
Apran guerriero udito
Cavalieri, e cavalli.
Esca da chiusi valli

Ogni Campion di forte acciar coperto

À scoprir sua virtute in Campo aperto.

Vengano à farsi i [fols. 22v–23] Cavalier più forti

Immortal frà le morti.

Gli spettatori,

Da gli stupori

De' fieri colpi, sia[n] ca[n]giati in marmi.

A'l armi, a'l armi.

<Qui entrano a 4. li Tebro e Pò>

All'armi all'armi

Gli spettatori,

Da gli stupori

De' fieri colpi, sian cangiati in marmi.

[fols. 23v–24] <Qui si fà il Combattimento.>

[p.70: "Hor qui . . . cedendo le voci armoniche, faranno risonar l'aria, con bellicosa disfida, e trombe. Vedrai diritto a quelle due lontananze, che saranno dalle parti avvanzarsi con due gran ponti verso il Teatro la Scena." From the Tiber side comes a squadron of five knights, arranged in the four corners of a square with the the fifth knight in the middle, preceded by two padrini; p. 71: "al vicendevole suono delle trombe" the knights first shoot pistols then brandish stocchi, moving two by two in changing formations (which are not described).

p. 78: "Quando all'improviso mancheranno per forza sovrana il fiato alle Trombe, il moto à Caualieri. Volgerai l'occhio, e l'orecchio uerso la Scena, e t'accorgerai, che in quel luogo avrà portato l'armonia dalla sua sfera Mercurio. Per l'aria questo alato Messagiere volando avrà, con la verga del caduceo, incantato la schiera di quei Campioni, che ordinatamente unite giungeranno a piegarsi con un mezzo giro alla presenza de' Principi, facendo quasi, che Ferrara in forma di una luna di ferro s'inchina."]

Mercurio:

Fermate, omai fermate

Le destre fulminanti.

Frenate, omai frenate

I destrieri anelanti.

Ultimate i conflitti,

O del Tebro, ò del Pò

Guerrieri invitti.
Io Messagero alato
Del Sovrano Monarca
Noto vi fò, che non concede il Fato,
Ch'oggi alcun filo in voi tronchi la Parca.
Pari è il valore, é pari
Seguirebbe trà voi lunga tenzone.
[fols. 24v–25] Oggi ogni legge impari,
Che la battaglia è un' empia prova ingiusta,
In cui la man robusta
Sovente abbatte la miglior ragione.
Il Rè del Ciel m'impone,
Che questa verga riverita io stenda,
E la pace vi renda.

    Non desio di Vittoria,
E non sete di Gloria
Rappresenti odioso al petto audace
Il bel nome di Pace.
In van, Guerrieri, in vano,
Mentre frà voi pugnate,
La Vittoria cercate.
Stendete pur la mano,
Per empirla di Palme, in altra parte,
Che frà voi sempre indiferente è Marte.
Senno, forza, destrezza, ardir prevale
In voi sopra ogni gente;
Mà senno, forza, ardir, destrezza e quale
Fra voi non ponno far vinto, ò vincente.
Abbracciate la pace, e'n segno vero
Di pacifica mente, e cor sincero
Lasci l'acuto ferro il destro braccio,
E s'incurvi à' l'abbraccio.

[fols. 25v–26] Mercurio
    E voi, ò Numi ondosi,
Che dell'Ausonia i campi almi, e felici
Irrigate non men di lei famosi,

Siate p[er] sempre amici.

Tosto vedrete a gl'occhi vostri avante

Quel, ch'impone dell'armi il gran divieto,

Pacifico Tona[n]te.

Ascoltate, obedite il <al> [suo] gran decreto.

[fols. 26v–27] Tebro Pò a 2.

    Volante Messagero

Ch'à noi la pace imponi,

Vànne, chè obbediremo al sommo impero.

Cedan n[ost]re ragioni

E cedan tutte le guerriere prove

Solo al cenno di Giove.

Al suo divin precetto, ed al consiglio

Apra l'orrecchia [fols. 27v–28] il Mondo e chiuda il ciglio [ms. is inconsistent

    here]

Giove:

    Ancora, ancora, ò temerarie, ò sciocche,

D'innestar risse à riste ardir havete?

E sol con la presenza ire accendete,

Ond'altri in nuovo ardor cada, e trabbocche?

    Indarno, ò gran Rubelle, <ribelle> indarno tenti,

Tù ch'l reggi l'Abisso e denso, et atro

Di far il chiaro Cielo à Teatro,

Che machine n'havrai d'alti spaventi.

    In [fols. 28v–29] queste, che dal Ciel caderro teco,

Novo esempio darò, Dite s[e]guaci.

Impari ogn'uno à noi turbar le paci.

Precipitate, ò cieche, al carcer cieco. [The Furies are banished to the Inferno]

E tù d'Etruria, e Lazio,

E tù maggiore

De l'insubria, et Emilia adornamento,

Tranquilli state à versar vostro argento,

Et ogni ingiuria omai cancelli Amore.

    Habbia il Tebro il suo Eroe illustre, voglio che torni

Là, dove il suo gran Zio del Mo[n]do hà il freno.

Mà renda in tanto il Rè de' fiumi e'l Reno
D'olivi armati, o ver di palme adorni.

Tutti:
    Giustissima sentenza
Di chì, potendo il tutto, errar non puote.
Giran l'eterne Rote,
Che [fols. 29v–30] sempre effetti son di providenza
Del vero Dio, non di falaci Dei,
E gl' influssi delle stelle or buoni, or rei.
Buoni, ò rei sol gli crede
Ochio che poco vede.
Mà la pupilla, che trapassa i veli,
Che cingono i mortali,
In sembianza di mali [fols. 30v–31]
Riconosce ogni ben sempre ne' Cieli.

[tutti] Questi hanno dall'Immoto ogni lor moto.
L'adamantino fuso ei torce à Cloto.
<. . . in Cielo et in terra a 5. Tutti>

Giove:
    De la Donna del mondo
Con sovrana virtute Eroe Prefetto,
Grato ricevi i voti
De' popoli de[fols. 31v–32]voti, ò mio Diletto.
Rendi con lieto aspetto
Questo Suol, Questo Ciel lieto, e giocondo.
Indi ritorna à venerare il Piede
De le chiavi del Cielo al sommo Erede,
Vero ritratto mio,
Giove, che giova à tutti, il tuo gran ZIO.

<Tutti:>
    In eterna amistà volta la guerra,
L'inguine in lodi, e le querele in canti.
Cantiam concordi, [fols. 32v–34] e l'universo canti
Un Giove in Cielo et un URBANO in Terra.

5 *LA MASCHERA TRIONFANTE*: DON TADDEO BARBERINI ENTERTAINS HIS BROTHER CARDINAL ANTONIO

For Cornelia Bessie and in memory of Michael Bessie

The tourney *La maschera trionfante nel giudicio di Paride* was performed in Bologna on 16 February, the penultimate day of Carnival in 1643.[1] It was presented by Don Taddeo Barberini, Prince Prefect of Rome and commander of the papal forces in the War of Castro, for the entertainment of his younger brother, Cardinal Antonio, who had been appointed legate of Ferrara, Bologna, and the Romagna.

As *La contesa* of 1631, Cardinal Antonio Barberini's joust in Piazza Navona in 1634, and *Le pretensioni* of 1642 had demonstrated, the many components of a full-fledged chivalric spectacle generally demanded elaborate preparation. According to the printed account of the event, however, *La maschera trionfante* was run up in three days. It seems even more surprising that so complex a celebration could be created at the height of a disastrous war. However, February was on the early side for military action (it even snowed at the end of the performance). A spectacular

---

[1] [Costanzo Ricci] LA/MASCHERA TRIONFANTE/NEL GIVDICIO DI PARIDE/RAPPRESENTATO/DALLA MAGNANIMITA' DELL'ECCELL.O/PRINCIPE PREFETTO/BARBARINO./ALL'EMINENTISS. PRINCIPE IL CARD./ANTONIO BARBERINO/LEGATO &c. (Bologna, N. Tebaldini, 1643). Copies are preserved in London, British Library; Paris, Bibliothèque Nationale; Rome, Biblioteca Nazionale; Glasgow, Stirling Maxwell Collection; New York, Metropolitan Museum of Art (Dept. of Drawings and Prints); New York, Public Library, Tilden and Lenox Collections; Washington, DC, Folger Shakespeare Library. A copy was sold by Martayan Lan Rare Books, to whom I am indebted for a facsimile of the volume, to the Marquand Art Library at Princeton University.

event climaxing the celebration of Carnival would have provided a diversion for the beleaguered populace of Bologna, a city famous for its production of Carnival masks. The symbolic content of the hastily-assembled *La maschera* was hardly coherent, but it did touch on familiar themes of magnanimity, integrity, loyalty, right choice, and the greatness of the Barberini.[2]

La maschera trionfante nel giudicio di Paride is preserved in a long printed account by one Costanzo Ricci, lavishly illustrated with engravings.[3] The frontispiece of the *relazione* (fig. 5.1) depicts two armed females resembling the figure of Fortezza or Strength in Cesare Ripa's *Iconologia*. The one on the left rests her hand on the head of a lion who bears in his paw the arms of Bologna. The right-hand figure tramples an illegible coat of arms—presumably that of one of the members of the princes' coalition against the papacy. She stretches out her arms to three putti who descend with heraldic symbols of the Barberini nephews, each putto accompanied by a bee: the cardinal's *galero* and legatine cross of Francesco, Antonio's cross as Prior of Malta, and the prince's crown of Don Taddeo. In the middle distance a river god, based on a statue now in the Capitoline Museum in Rome, pours water from a jar. (The same figure appears on the title-page in Vincenzo Galilei's *Discorso* [Florence, 1589] and symbolizes Rome in the form of the Tiber in the 1600 print of Giulio Caccini's opera *L'Euridice*; to the Romans the statue was known as Marforio, one of the talking statues of which the most famous was Pasquino).

After the title-page there appears as a dedication an engraved portrait of Cardinal Antonio rich in Barberini symbols familiar from Giovanni Ferro's *Teatro d'Imprese* (Venice, 1623, dedicated to Cardinal Maffeo Barberini, the future Urban VIII) and such creations as Bernini's baldacchino (fig. 5.2). Cardinal Antonio's head is surrounded by laurel branches issuing from the mouths of two lions holding banners. The laurel branches spring from a crown like the one used by the Medici, indicating both Antonio's princely rank and his family's Tuscan origins. Two arms of the cardinal's cross as Prior of the Order of Malta are visible, and the ensemble is surmounted by a rayed sun and three bees.

The dedication to Antonio is dated Bologna, 10 March 1643, by Ricci. In the following letter to the reader he states that "[the Performance] was planned, & carried out in only three days, and Machines were also involved, which did not facilitate,

---

[2] The propagandistic use of such spectacles is evident in the 1644 production by the Farnese and Francesco II of Modena of *Le risse pacificate di Cupido* as a gesture of triumph over the Barberini after the War of Castro (Jarrard, *Architecture*, 35).

[3] The portrait of Cardinal Antonio seems to be by a hand different from that of the other engravings. The name of one of the Siraini, probably Giovanni Andrea, has been suggested.

but impeded the execution."[4] (A *torneo, I furori di Venere,* had been performed in the Sala del Podestà in Bologna on 26 May 1639 for the Cardinal-Legate Sacchetti; perhaps materials from this were re-used for the hurried creation of *La maschera.*)[5]

Ricci asserts that pleasure is valid "for lifting up human weakness" ("per solleva-mento dell'humana fralezza," 3–4). Carnival celebrations are the "confused and indistinct" descendants of the classic festivals of Dionysus and Saturn. The masks of Lombardy and especially Bologna do not resemble the shameful ones of antiquity, above all in this year when Don Taddeo wanted to renew in Bologna the greatness of Roman spectacle. Don Taddeo's choice of the judgment of Paris about which of three goddesses to award the golden apple as the subject of *La maschera* allegorizes three roads to happiness: that of Pallas Athena, the Contemplative way, turning to wisdom and seeking truth; that of Juno, the Active way: ease, riches, studying to possess and not to know; and the way of Venus, the path of Voluptuousness, which only approves as good that which persuades by means of pleasure. The performance took two hours and was done out of doors, the processions traversing various streets and piazzas and ending in the main piazza of Bologna.

La maschera was divided into eight squadrons: Paris, Helen, and Amor on a fiery chariot (fig. 5.3); the triumph of Venus on a swan (fig. 5.4); Juno and Don Taddeo on a peacock (fig. 5.5); Pallas and Ulysses on a dragon (fig. 5.6); Agamemnon and Chriseis on a harpy (fig. 5.7); Achilles and Briseis on a sphinx, signifying Ignorance (fig. 5.8); Hector and Andromache on an eagle (fig. 5.9); and Aeneas and Creusa on a griffon (fig. 5.10). Each squadron was preceded by two mounted heralds with trumpets whose forms were different for each entry (for example, the trumpets for the triumph of Venus were in the form of the ancient tibia, a less martial instrument). The heralds of each squadron were followed by four mounted knights preceding a decorated *carro* drawn by a horse and accompanied by twenty men on foot, all costumed in accordance with the theme of the entry. Each *carro* had a different form and featured different personages mounted on it. The *relazione* gives strophic verses for the various entries, in a variety of forms and usually in the standard mixture of seven- and eleven-syllable lines.

---

[4] "Fù quella [l'Azione] ordinata, & eseguitta in tre soli giorni, e pure v'intervennero Machine, non da facilitare, ma da impedire lo scioglimento," *La maschera* [1].

[5] *Del torneo ultimamente fatto in Bologna all'Emin. Sacchetti descrittione panegirica del Comm. Gio. Battista Manzini all'Em. padrone il Sig. Card. Capponi* (Bologna, 1639); the *invenzione* was by Ascanio Pio di Savoia, the scenes and machines by Alfonso Chenda-Rivarola: see *Le capitali della festa,* 19–20.

Personages	Carro	Accompaniment, colors
1. Paris, Helen, Amor	fire and gold	4 satyrs, purple, red, gold fiery sorrel horses, moving to the sound of the trumpets 9 verses ABCABCCDD
2. Triumph of Venus	swan = Orfeo Venus w/ golden apple, Amor	silver and carnation tibia in place of trumpets; white horses, 4 blindfolded cupids 10 verses ABBACC
3. Juno, Don Taddeo	peacock chaste love, prudence	marine horses, 4 nymphs sky blue, silver 12 verses ABBA
4. Pallas, Ulysses	dragon machine	yellow, gold 4 Greek soldiers on blond Spanish horses 13 verses ABBA
5. Agamemnon, Chriseis	harpy	black silk, gold, burnished steel 4 Greek heroes of the Helen story no poem

A space after Agamemnon's carro to "keep the awareness of the spectators clear" ("tener ben distinta la notizia de' circostanti")

| 6. Achilles, Briseis | sphinx (=Ignorance) Fabio della Cornia | silver, tawny 4 Frisian horses of ripe date color 4 Trojan heroes |

While the two Greek squadrons were parading around the field, printed challenges (the poem or *cartello*: 4 verses ABABABCC) were handed out

| 7. Hector, Andromache | eagle | green, gold, M. A. Pasqualini as Pentasilea no poems |
| 8. Aeneas, Creusa | griffon | burnished armor w/gold *cartello* distributed while Aeneas parades 4 verses ABABABCC |

The role of music in the *Maschera* seems to have been minimal. Owing to the shortness of time it would not have been able to write a text, compose music for it, and have it memorised by performers, even assuming that there were competent poets, composers, and singers available. Ricci cites the musical instruction of the centaur Cheiron, tutor of Achilles and Aesculapius, "to evade boredom, and compose the passions of the agitated mind" ("per ingannare il tedio, e ricomporre le passioni della mente agitata," 54). Here, however, the kithara of Homer and the lyre of Timotheus have been replaced by the trumpet: the only music mentioned in the *relazione* is that of the two mounted trumpeters who preceded each of the eight squadrons, whose function was as much martial as musical. The great castrato Marc'Antonio Pasqualini, who was travelling with Cardinal Antonio, appeared as the Amazon queen Penthesilea on the *carro* of Hector [fig. 5.7], as he had appeared as the allegorical figure of Fame delivering the *sfida* at a *veglia* or evening entertainment preceding Antonio's 1634 Roman joust in Piazza Navona. Ricci devotes an elaborate passage to Pasqualini:

> As a conclusion to the group, in the warlike semblance of the Amazon Penthesilea, [was] Sig. Marc'Antonio Pasqualini, who makes the harmony of the spheres audible on Earth, even to non-Pythagorean ears. Nor was the Fable exaggerated, that said that Harmony was the daughter of Mars, and of Venus, and proudly boasted the title of truthful, showing Charm, Harmony, and Valor closely joined together in that fierce Amazon; as it also proved, that the very anvil of Vulcan, who administered the Arms to Achilles, & Æneas, suggested to Love the tones for the invention of Music: tones, that have the power of lethal thunders, when they loose themselves from two flaming red lips.[6]

Despite this flowery gloss on the legend of Pythagoras' discovery of musical consonances from the sound of hammers on anvils of various sizes, there is no suggestion that Pasqualini sang a note.

---

[6] "Da compimento alla schiera, in guerriero sembiante di Pentasilea Amazone, il Sig. Marc'Antonio Pasqualini, che fà sensibile in Terra, anco all'orecchie non Pittagoriche, il concento delle sfere. Ne superbì la Favola, che disse l'Armonia figlia di Marte, e di Venere, e va[n]tò superbamente il titolo di verace, mostrando in quella feroce Amazone strettamente congiunti Vaghezza, Armonia, e Valore; come anco verificò, che l'istessa incude di Vulcano, che somministrò l'Armi ad Achille, & ad Enea, suggerì ad Amore i tuoni per l'invenzione della Musica: tuoni, che han forza di fulmini mortali, ove da due labra infocate di porpora si disprigionano" (59–60). Pasqualini was still (or again) in Bologna on 16 May 1643, when he wrote to the Cappella Pontificia "Havendo io creduto che i presenti motivi di guerra fussero p[er] terminar di mese in mese . . ." ("Since I believed that the present grounds for war were about to end from one month to the next . . .") (BAV, CS, Diario 62, fol. 21). This adds a second surviving letter of Pasqualini to the one published in Fabris, *Mecenati*, #1009.

"With such order the long, and majestic pomp, after having slowly circled some of the principal streets, came to the Corso, where it was awaited at the windows, and in the Coaches by the rarest Nobility."[7] Ricci judged that the spectacle surpassed all others in the City, in the same way that the position of those who command surpasses that of their subjects. The celebration showed that the Barberini magnificence could employ gold even for the servants' costumes. Avarice, Envy, Greatness, Luxury, Power, and Magnanimity were all conquered. Even the heavens showed their approval by chasing away the clouds that had covered the city for days, and a crescent moon was supplemented by a thousand torches of white wax, produced by bees who recalled the omnipresent Barberini symbol.

The procession had reached the central piazza, where the actual combat was to take place, when a sudden snowfall forced the spectators to quit their bleachers, leaving the theater of the tourney empty, and to take refuge on the balconies of the palaces lining the exit route. The verdict of the failed combat between Greeks and Romans was left in doubt, through the action of the "Reigning Bees," who had as their only intention Innocence and Peace. "And from the entire Action, beginning with Paris, concluding with Æneas, we learn an allegorical, and sound teaching, That the Great must direct their Pleasures to the end of Piety."[8]

---

[7] "Con tal'ordine la lunga, e maestosa pompa, doppo di havere à lento passo girato alcune delle principali strade, pervenne à quella del Corso; dove era attesa alle fenestre, e ne i Cocchi dalla più rara Nobiltà" (69).

[8] "E dall'Azione tutta, principiata in Paride, terminata in Enea, s'apprese allegorico, e sano documento, Che devono i Grandi indrizzare i Diletti loro al fine della Pietà" (72).

FIG. 5.1 *La maschera trionfante,*
Frontispiece

FIG. 5.2 *Portrait of Cardinal Antonio Barberini*
from *La maschera*

Fig. 5.3 *Paris and Helen* from *La maschera*

Fig. 5.4 *Triumph of Venus* from *La maschera*

FIG. 5.5 *Juno and Don Taddeo* from *La maschera*

FIG. 5.6 *Pallas and Ulysses* from *La maschera*

FIG. 5.7   *Agamemnon and Chriseis* from *La maschera*

FIG. 5.8   *Achilles and Briseis* from *La maschera*

FIG. 5.9   *Hector and Andromache* from *La maschera*

FIG. 5.10   *Aeneas and Creusa* from *La maschera*

ORPHEUS IN A NEW KEY:
THE BARBERINI FLIGHT TO FRANCE
AND THE ROSSI–BUTI *L'ORFEO*

For Mariacarla and Roberto Pagano

THE VICISSITUDES OF POWER

Pope Urban VIII died on 28 July 1644. His reign of nearly twenty-one years had brought to his family, especially his nephews Cardinal Francesco, Don Taddeo, and Cardinal Antonio, extraordinary honors and incomes. In reaction against the Barberini, the ensuing conclave chose Giovanni Battista Pamphilj, who took the name Innocent X: according to the diarist Gigli "he was held to be a severe man, and not very liberal."[1]

Cardinal Francesco's ostensible candidate was Cardinal Sacchetti, an able and attractive prelate with close ties to the Barberini (see Chapter 1). It appears, however, that Francesco was playing a double game. He secretly supported Pamphilj, who as a creation of Urban VIII and was thought to be friendly to his family, with the aim of protecting the Barberini by a matrimonial alliance with the Pamphilj. Francesco quit the conclave with the excuse of indisposition, leaving his brother as leader of the Barberini faction. As Cardinal Protector of France, Antonio had originally advised the French crown to exercise its right of exclusion to eliminate the hispanophile Pamphilj. When Antonio became convinced of the choice of Pamphilj bolstered by a marriage with the prospective pope's family, his volte-face secured the election for Pamphilj but enraged Mazarin, who deprived Antonio of his post of Protector and

---

[1] "[E]ra tenuto per huomo severo, et non molto liberale": Gigli, *Diario*, 431.

its income.[2] (It has been conjectured that another of Francesco's motivations was to make his brother the instrument of his own ruin by electing Pamphilj in opposition to Mazarin.) The election was further tainted by the suspicion of simony owing to an "exchange of notes, true and proper *pagherò* ["I shall pay"] between the French ambassador and Antonio Barberini on behalf of the future Innocent X and through the intermediary of the Teodoli Brothers."[3]

By reason of their power and their temperamental differences with the Pamphilj, the cultivated Barberini were an obvious target for the new pope—"enemy of Poets and Orators"—and his rapacious sister-in-law, Donna Olimpia Maidalchini. As Don Taddeo had warned his brothers in the conclave, "the Kinship of the Popes must end and we have seen others remain without being relatives."[4] Innocent conspicuously favored the enemies of the Barberini such as Spain, the Venetian Republic, and the Farnese dukes of Parma—the princely league of Urban VIII's opponents in the War of Castro, which had darkened and impoverished the last years of his reign.

The first sign of a fracture between the two papal families occurred in November of 1644, when Innocent raised his nephew Camillo, the only son of Olimpia Maidalchini, who had taken the name Pamphilj, to the cardinalate, thus blocking Camillo's proposed marriage with Lucrezia Barberini. An auditor from the Medici-Spanish-Pamphilj faction was assigned to look into the financial records of the papal Monti, to move from thence to those of the Camera Apostolica for the War of Castro. By January of 1645 the Venetian ambassador could write that the central projects of the papacy included "precipitating the fortunes of the Barberini."[5] Innocent's new cardinal creations were anti-Barberini and pro-Spanish and were intended to pack the Sacred College in order to block any future candidacy of Sacchetti.

The first overt act of Innocent's campaign against the Barberini was the blocking of their port of Santa Marinella with the excuse that the Turks might take it. A sentence of the Sacred Rota in favor of Olimpia Aldobrandini Borghese, princess of Rossano and future wife of Camillo Pamphilj, rejected Barberini claims on the state

---

[2] A. Merola, "Barberini, Antonio," *Dizionario biografico degli Italiani* (Rome: Istituto della Enciclopedia Italiana, 1964), 6:166–70. A limited revaluation of Pamphilj as a patron of architecture has been undertaken by Stephanie C. Leone, *The Palazzo Pamphilj in Piazza Navona: Constructing Identity in Early Modern Rome* (London and Turnhout: Harvey Miller Publishers, 2008).

[3] ". . . l'episodio centrale del Conclave del 1644 è stato lo scambio di biglietti, veri e propri *pagherò*, tra l'ambasciatore di Francia e Antonio Barberini per conto del futuro Innocenzo X e per tramite dei fratelli Teodoli" (Costantini, "Fazione Urbana," Fazd3).

[4] "Il Parentado de Papi ha da finir et havemo visto altri restar senza esser parenti": BAV, Barb. lat 10042, fol. 52.

[5] ". . . di precipitar le fortune de' Barberini" (Costantini, "Fazione," Faz2c).

of Meldola. In June of 1645 Innocent ordered the review of the accounts of the Camera Apostolica for the last part of Urban VIII's reign. He refused to acknowledge the chirographs by which Urban had exempted his nephews and any other payer from the obligation of documenting expenses. Adherents and household members of the Barberini were harassed and jailed, and a plan was afoot to seize Cardinal Antonio "mentre capitava in casa di certa donna" ("while he happened to be in the house of a certain lady") and imprison him in Castel Sant'Angelo. In December of 1644 Cardinal Antonio consigned a copy of the documents of the recent conclave, which supported accusations of simony in Pamphilj's election, to the French government.

The knots began to come to the comb in September 1645, when Antonio, disguised as a barrel-maker, fled by boat from Ostia with the authorization of Mazarin, and Innocent "began with great rigor to have reviewed the accounts of the expenses made in the time of the war, which add up to many millions."[6] (There is some suspicion that Innocent's anger was partly due to the arranged death of a kinsman, a member of Antonio's household, who on being summoned to the cardinal's presence remarked, "I have him up the ass all night, he could leave me alone in the daytime.") Antonio arrived in Genoa, which had given the Barberini notable financial support in the War of Castro, on 1 October:

> Yesterday, Sunday 1 October at 3:30 at night [three and a half hours after sunset], there appeared by sea at the villa of Albaro in the house of Signor Gio. Battista Raggi Cardinal Antonio, who had left Rome on the 27th of September without the permission of the Pope, nor having said goodbye to anyone, he even claims and says that he had not even confided it to Cardinal Barberino, his brother. When he arrived he was dressed as a layman in a short robe, he had embarked with only two people on an armed lighter of 22 men . . . He left Rome on Wednesday on the pretext of going hunting and embarked at Ostia. On the trip owing to bad weather he had to stay for 28 hours in the port of Leghorn, where he always lay low, without ever raising his head in an anxious fear not to be discovered . . . I do not doubt that he left Rome for fear that the Pope could even be reduced to desiring to proceed against his person.[7]

---

[6] ". . . cominciò con molto rigore a farli rivedere i conti delle spese fatte al tempo della guerra, che importano molti milioni": Gigli, 456.

[7] Giannettino Giustiniani in Genoa to Mazarin, 2 October 1645: "Hieri sera domenica primo d'ottobre alle tre hore e mezza di notte, comparve per via di mare alla villa d'Albaro in casa del signor Gio Batta

Traveling by way of Varazze, Savona, San Remo, and Nice, Antonio left Turin on 21 December and arrived in Paris on 6 January 1646.

On 15 October with great fanfare (literally) Francesco and Taddeo Barberini had ordered the arms of France to be set up again on the façades of their palaces. Invoking a papal bull against any cardinal who put himself under the protection of a secular prince, Innocent suspended Antonio from his most important offices in absentia and ordered his return under a fine of a thousand scudi a day.[8] The pope imprisoned members of Taddeo's and Francesco's households, and the Barberini palaces were surrounded by police and spies; it was even rumored that Cardinal Francesco was to be arrested when he went to St. Peter's as archpriest of the basilica for the feast of the Cathedra Petri on 18 January.

On the night on 16 January 1646, Francesco and Taddeo, disguised as hunters, together with Taddeo's three sons, Carlo, Maffeo, and Nicolò, and daughter Lucrezia, all dressed as pages, embarked for France from Ripa, the Roman port of the Tiber, leaving Taddeo's wife, Donna Anna Colonna, as a rear-guard in Rome. At the news of their arrival in France at the end of the month after a dangerous journey, Innocent sequestered the revenues of all three brothers and suspended Francesco from the Chancellorship, "to deprive him of all the abbeys and benefices that he enjoys threatening to proceed also against the whole House to indeed ruin it."[9] A summons of all cardinals to Rome within four months under pain of losing the income of their offices provided another turn of the screw. On 23 April Anna Colonna set off for France, where she arrived in early October. She had secured the movable valuables of her family, and Antonio's palace at the Quattro Fontane was saved by placing it under the protection of the French crown, but the Camera Apostolica had taken possession of the other Barberini palaces and lands.[10] In August of 1646 the French in Rome

---

Raggi il signor cardinale Antonio, partito alli 27 di settembre da Roma, senza né licenza del Papa, né d'havere detto adio ad alcuno, anzi che prettende e dice di non haverlo tampoco conferito al signor cardinal Barberino, suo fratello. Quando giunse era vestito alla curta da secolare, con due sole persone imbarcato sopra d'un liuto armato di 22 huomini che di qua di suo ordine fu inviato molto secretamente da Tobia Pallivicino, nostro gentilhuomo, il quale in queste ultime guerre di Papa Urbano ha contratto e servitù e gran confidenza con tutta casa Barberini. Si partì di Roma in mercoredì sotto prettesto di andare alla caccia et s'imbarcò ad Ostia. Nel viaggio per il mal tempo li è convenuto trattenersi nel porto di Livorno 28 hore, dove sempre stette basso, colcato, senza mai alzare il capo in una ansiosissima passione di non essere scoperto . . . Di Roma non ho dubbi ch'egli si è partito per timore che il Papa si pottesse anche ridurre a voler procedere contra la sua persona" (Costantini, Faz2e, n. 21).

[8] Gigli, 456–58; other sources put the penalty at sc. 500 per day for each Barberini.

[9] "E non lo facendo di privarlo di tutte le abbatie e beneficii che gode minacciandosi di proseguire anco contra tutta la Casa per affatto rovinarla" (Costantini, Faz2f).

[10] A. Merola, "Barberini, Taddeo," *Dizionario biografico degli Italiani*, vol. 6, 180–82.

celebrated the feast of their patron saint in his church of San Luigi de' Francesi, with decorations costing 12,000 scudi, "Musica maravigliosa," and a defiant show of the arms of the francophile cardinals headed by those of Urban's brother, the cardinal of Sant'Onofrio, the only adult male member of the Barberini family left in Rome.[11]

A number of factors combined to alter the political situation, including the deployment of French troops in Italy to besiege Piombino and Orbetello and the deaths of Cardinal Sant'Onofrio and the duke of Parma. The Parlement of Paris invalidated the papal bulls against the Barberini, and Mazarin threatened an ecumenical council to depose Innocent X. On 12 September 1646, Innocent issued a *motu proprio* absolving the Barberini and reinstating them in their possessions and dignities. However, the Venetian ambassador quoted the pope as saying that "when the Barberini had performed all the foregoing humiliations and other satisfactions owed to our dignity . . . that is, that the Barberini come for the said purpose to Rome to be jailed in Castel S. Angelo and that His Holiness was free to make them render the accounts of the money spent during the war and to submit to justice as it appeared to him, without the French Crown intervening."[12] A month later the two cardinals' had left Paris, retired to papal territory in Avignon, and had sent their submission to the pope. On 29 March 1647 Innocent gave Cardinal Francesco permission to return to Rome and allowed Cardinal Antonio to remain in France.

The chronology of the Barberini flight is thus as follows: Antonio arrived in Genoa on 1 October of 1645, was received in Paris on 6 January 1646 and went to Provence in March. (His return to Paris was awaited in May of 1647.) Francesco, Taddeo, and his children arrived in France at the end of January 1646. Anna Colonna left Rome for Paris in late April of 1646, arrived in Paris in early October accompanied by her husband and children, and returned to Italy at the end of June of 1647. Francesco left Paris for Avignon with Antonio in October of 1646. Don Taddeo died in Paris on November 14, 1647.[13] Francesco returned to Rome in February of 1648 with his nephew Maffeo; his elder nephew, the new Prince Carlo, returned only in June of 1653, and Cardinal Antonio (who had become bishop of Poitiers in 1652) returned in July of the same year.

---

[11] Gigli, 479.

[12] "Facendo i Barberini tutte le sodette humiliationi et altri sodisfationi dovute alla nostra dignità . . . cioè che li Barberini varriano per detto effetto a Roma a constituirsi carcerati in Castel S. Angelo et che restava libero a Sua Santità di farli rendere li conti dei denari spesi nella guerra e di stare a giustitia come li paresse, senza che la Corona di Francia vi si interponesse . . ." (Costantini, "Fazione Urbana," Faz3e).

[13] Carlo Claudi from Paris to Cornelio Bentivoglio, 6 October 1646: ". . . quì arrivò l'altra sera il s.r P[ri]n[ci]pe Prefetto con la s.ra D Anna e loro figliuoli che furono ricevuti da S M[aes]tà con dimostrat[io]ni

THE CARDINAL-IMPRESARIO

Two figures with musical connections seem to have played a role in Giulio Mazzarino's entrance into the household of Cardinal Antonio Barberini, where he became *maggiordomo* in 1632: Cardinal Guido Bentivoglio and the celebrated singer Leonora Baroni. (The appointment was in fact rather a comedown for Mazzarino, who had already achieved the rank of papal nuncio.) Guido was the former patron of Girolamo Frescobaldi and the Piccinini family of lutenists, and the brother of Enzo Bentivoglio, the great Italian *corago* of the period. After service in France, Mazzarino returned to Rome from 1637 to 1639 for the golden age of the Barberini opera productions.[14] The Barberini employed opera as a spectacle for diversion, a display of wealth and power, and as a form of political and ideological statement. The transplant of Italian opera into France for the same purposes became an important element in the policy of Mazarin (as we should now call him) as prime minister for Anne of Austria, queen regent for her son Louis XIV after the death of Louis XIII.

As early as 1640 Mazarin was attempting to bring Italian opera to France.[15] One of his first moves was to recruit the sculptor and designer Nicolò Menghini, to whom Bernini had promised to teach his famous sunrise-sunset machine. Francesco Guitti was also approached. Although a production équipe was assembled and sent to Paris, the project fell through, in part owing to Guitti's death.

The French musicologist Henry Prunières' reading of Mazarin's abortive attempt in 1642–43 to engage the harpist and composer Marco Marazzoli for an Italian opera troupe in Paris is not quite accurate, since here as elsewhere he confuses the two younger Barberini cardinals.[16] "Il Cardinal Barberino" *tout court* was Francesco, the senior; his brother was "il Cardinale Antonio." (Their uncle, the elder Antonio, was "il Cardinal Sant'Onofrio" from his titular church.) Ordinarily, Mazarin's Roman

---

grand[issi]me d'affetto e di stima . . . la sera avanti gli fece vedere un bellissimo balletto, che si fece fare aposta per il loro arrivo . . ." (". . . there arrived here the other evening the Prince Prefect, with Signora Donna Anna and their children who were received by Her Majesty with great demonstrations of affection and esteem . . . the next evening she showed them a beautiful ballet, which she had made especially for their arrival . . ."): Sergio Monaldini, *L'Orto delle Esperidi: Musici, attori e artisti nel patroncinio della famiglia Bentivoglio (1646–1685)* (Lucca: Libreria Musicale Italiana, 2000), 7.

[14] Henry Prunières, *L'Opéra italien en France avant Lulli* (Paris: Champion, 1913; reprint, 1975), 43, is misleading: he lists as works that Mazarin could have seen in 1637–39 *Il falcone* and *Chi soffre speri*, which are two versions of the same opera; *Erminia sul Giordano*, which was produced in 1633 and *La Galatea*, which—as far as we know—was never performed.

[15] See Margaret Murata, "Why the First Opera Given in Paris Wasn't Roman," *Cambridge Opera Journal* 7 (1995): 87–106.

[16] Prunières, *L'Opéra italien*, 45–55. Neal Zaslaw falls into the same trap (see n. 24).

agent, Elpidio Benedetti, would have treated with Cardinal Antonio. Not only was Cardinal Antonio Marazzoli's employer, as a singer in the Cappella Pontificia, Marazzoli was also under the cardinal's authority as Protector of the Cappella. (Monsignor Fausto Poli, Urban VIII's *maggiordomo*, served as liason between the Barberini and the cappella and acted as Antonio's surrogate.) In March of 1642 Marazzoli's opera-torneo *Le pretensioni del Tebro e del Po* was presented in Ferrara for Don Taddeo Barberini (see Chapter 4).

In the summer of 1643, mired down in the War of Castro, the Barberini had other things on their minds than opera singers. Cardinal Antonio was absent with the papal forces in Bologna, and therefore Benedetti and Mazarin applied to "il S. Card. Barb."—Francesco—through Poli, who gave his permission for a leave of absence from the Cappella, and Marazzoli went to take a formal *congé* of Urban VIII and Cardinal Francesco. Poli's permission was countermanded by the pope, the ultimate head of the Cappella, who remained unmoved by the examples of other singers of the Cappella who were permitted to absent themselves from Rome, such as Marc'Antonio Pasqualini, who was traveling with Cardinal Antonio in the war zone up north.

The real reason for Urban's refusal was that the French continued to aid the duke of Parma in the War of Castro and "they think of being of good cheer and celebrating while leaving the Holy See in a thousand afflictions."[17] Mazarin blamed Cardinal Francesco, who "did not want to let Marco de la Harpa [Marazzoli] come to France for the simple reason that I had wanted him."[18] When Antonio returned to Rome, he reproached Benedetti for not having consulted him instead of Francesco, with whom Antonio was on notoriously bad terms. This omission was repaired, and Benedetti wrote Mazarin that "it was indeed made clear to me that Cardinal Barberino had no blame whatsoever for it."[19] With the granting of Antonio's permission, Marazzoli was free to leave and arrived in Paris in mid-December of 1643. He left to return to Rome on 10 April 1645.

Late in 1644 Mazarin began to receive applications from Italian musicians to enter the service of the French court, probably prompted by the death of Urban VIII

---

[17] ". . . ben pensano a stare allegramente e far feste con lassare in mille afflitioni la sede apostolica": Prunières, 49.

[18] ". . . n'a pas voulu laisser venir en France Marco de la Harpa pour la seule raison que je l'avois désiré": Prunières, 50.

[19] ". . . mi sono veramente chiarito che il sig. card. Barberino [Francesco] non vi haveva colpa alcuna": Prunières, 50, n. 2. Benedetti also attempted to recruit Giuseppe Bianchi, a soprano castrato formerly in the service of Don Taddeo Barberini (Prunières, 47, 63, 377).

and the election of a pope notoriously unsympathetic to the arts. (There seems to have been an exodus of Roman musicians into the Imperial service about the same time.) One of the applicants, presented in a letter to Mazarin, was "a certain Giulio Cesare Burzio, gentleman of Parma [. . .] organ builder, who was sent by the father of this Duke to put together an organ for the father of the present Emperor, who is an expert engineer for making movable machines for theaters." This adds a few significant touches to the biography of G. C. Burzio, the builder of one of the two new organs commissioned by Cardinal Francesco Barberini for his titular basilica of San Lorenzo in Damaso.[20]

Mazarin was angling for bigger fish, however. He wished to attract to the French court the great Leonora Baroni (fig. 6.1), not only one of the most famous singers of the period but also a woman of remarkable cultivation. His plan involved Enzo's son the *abbate* Bentivoglio and both Barberini cardinals (as well as Leonora's lover, Camillo Pamphilj, about to become the cardinal-nephew of Innocent X). Francesco was the employer of Leonora's husband, Giulio Castellani, and Antonio frequented Leonora and her family and supported them so generously as to arouse the jealousy of his pet castrato, Marc'Antonio Pasqualini (fig. 6.2).[21] On her arrival in Paris in the spring of 1644 Leonora became the favorite of Anne of Austria, who was just emerging from formal mourning for Louis XIII. In November of 1644 there arrived in Paris the young Pistoiese castrato Atto Melani, together with his brother Jacopo and a singer from the Florentine court, Anna Francesca ("Checca") Costa.[22] In April of 1645 Baroni returned to Rome, accompanied by her husband and Marazzoli, bearing jewels, money, and a pension of a thousand écus; Atto Melani followed a month later.

On Shrove Tuesday (28 February) of 1645 Mazarin's preparations bore their first fruit. An Italian opera and a ballet danced by noblemen were performed in the Palais Royal before an audience including the young king, members of the royal family, and Louis XIII's sister Henrietta Maria, wife of Charles I of England, as part of the first Carnival celebration since the death of Louis XIII. The gathering was a select one, since the theater of the Palais Royal was a small room without elaborate stage-machines. (Anne had moved her family into the palace, which Richelieu had

---

[20] Postscript to a letter of Pietro Mazzarini to his son Giulio, 7 August 1644: "un tal Giulio Cesare Burtio gentilhuomo di Parma [. . .] compositor d'organi, che fu mandato dal Padre di questo Duca [di Parma] a comporre un'organo al padre del presente Imperatore, che è ingegniero esperto per comporre macchine movibili per teatri" (Prunières, 58, n. 3). On Burzio see Patrizio Barbieri, "I 'doi bellissimi organi' di S. Lorenzo in Damaso," *Amici dell'organo* (September 1984): 46–53.

[21] Hammond, *Music and Spectacle*, 86.

[22] Roger Freitas, "*Un Atto d'ingegno:* A Castrato in the Seventeenth Century," Ph. D. diss., Yale University, 1998 (Ann Arbor: UMI Research Press, 2000), 56.

FIG. 6.1   Fabio della Corgna, *Leonora Baroni* from
*Applausi poetici alle glorie della
Signora Leonora Baroni* (Bracciano, 1639)

FIG. 6.2   Andrea Sacchi, *Portrait of Marc'Antonio Pasqualini*
(New York, Metropolitan Museum of Art)

left to the Crown, in 1643; her own rooms were behind Richelieu's theater. A few months later, Mazarin also moved in.)[23] The opera, untitled in the two sources that mention it, has been tentatively identified as *Il giudizio della Ragione tra la Beltà e l'Affetto*, a *dramma in musica* on a libretto by Francesco Buti (Cardinal Antonio Barberini's secretary), set by Antonio's musician Marco Marazzoli and first performed in Rome at Palazzo Roberti near Sant'Eustachio in 1643.[24]

Ironically, despite Leonora Baroni's presence in Paris, contemporary sources are silent on the identity of the performers, except for Atto Melani, who reported only that "each of us acquitted himself well in his role."[25]

The opera consists of a prologue and three acts, with dance-interludes between the acts and a *canzonetta del ballo* at the end. The characters are all allegorical: the plot chronicles the vicissitudes and final union of True Love, who is counselled by Reason, with Beauty, who is misled by Caprice. On the grounds that Palazzo Roberti may have been the French embassy, Neal Zaslaw attempted to link the first production of the opera with the French circle in Rome, reading True Love as France, Beauty as the papacy, and Austria as Caprice. While there is no evidence that Palazzo Roberti had any relationship with the French embassy, the Roberti family did have Barberini connections, since a Roberti accompanied Cardinal Antonio to Castro in autumn of 1643.[26]

As I have suggested elsewhere, Antonio's production of the Giulio Rospigliosi-Luigi Rossi *Il palazzo incantato/Lealtà con valore* in Carnival of 1642 can be interpreted as a rallying-cry for adherents of the Barberini in the War of Castro. If *Il giudizio*, created by two members of Antonio's household, is to be considered a political allegory, it is probably to be read in the same context. True Love would then represent the papacy (ROMA=AMOR), as in the prologue to the 1634 version of Landi's *Il Sant'Alessio*, which presents Rome as wishing to rule by love and not by coercion (see Chapter 3). Beauty might then be France, Reason the Barberini (Reason was a standard allegorical element in the Barberini productions, including *Il palazzo incantato*, where it was

---

[23] Ruth Kleinman, *Anne of Austria* (Columbus, OH: Ohio State Press, 1985), 175–76.

[24] Saverio Franchi, *Drammaturgia romana: Repetorio bibliografico cronologico* (Rome: Edizioni di Storia e di Le Heratura, 1988), 252; the scenario is given in Alessandro Ademollo, *I teatri di Roma nel secolo decimosettimo* (Rome: Pasqualucci, 1888; reprint, Borzi, 1969), 52–55; Neal Zaslaw, "The First Opera in Paris: A Study in the Politics of Art," in *Jean-Baptiste Lully and the Music of the French Baroque: Essays in Honor of James R. Anthony*, ed. John H. Heyer (Cambridge: Cambridge University Press, 1989), 7–24. On Palazzo Roberti Conti Datti see Claudio Rendina, *I palazzi storici di Roma* (Rome: Newton and Compton, 2005), 268–69.

[25] Quoted in Zaslow, "The First Opera," 16.

[26] Gigli, *Diario*, 361.

personified by the heroine Bradamante), and Caprice, the Farnese of Parma—a scheme that represents the political situation somewhat more accurately. (Zaslaw's interpretation is unlikely in another respect: it is unthinkable that an opera produced in seventeenth-century Rome could represent the papacy, incarnated by Andrea Sacchi on the ceiling of Palazzo Barberini as *Divine Wisdom*, as deluded, even momentarily.)

In Mazarin's 1645 revival the allegory may have been meant to refer to the consolidation of his power by becoming head of the Queen's household in 1644, and to Anne's loyalty to France despite the blandishments of her brother, Philip IV of Spain.

With the fall of the Barberini, Mazarin could expect little help from the new hispanophile pope and turned to other patrons. In response to a request from Anne of Austria (i.e. Mazarin) in March of 1645 the new duke of Parma sent to France three Italian comedians and the choreographer Giovanni Battista Balbi, adding for good measure Giacomo Torelli, the greatest living designer of sets and stage-machinery. Balbi had choreographed the first Venetian opera, *L'Andromeda* of Benedetto Ferrari set by Francesco Manelli, in 1637, and their *Maga fulminata*, presented the following year.[27] Torelli had worked with Enzo Bentivoglio for the Farnese and dedicated the engravings of ten of his sets for *Il Bellerofonte* (Venice, 1642) to Ferdinando of Tuscany and the engravings of the sets for *La Venere gelosa* (Venice, 1643) to Cardinal Antonio Barberini.[28]

In December of 1645 Balbi and Torelli demonstrated their art in the first public French operatic spectacle, a production of the opera *La finta pazza* (Venice, 1641). It was performed in the great hall of the Palais du Petit Bourbon, which offered more scope for sets, machines, and dancing than the small theater of the Palais Royal. *La finta pazza* was presented not as an opera sung throughout but as a comedy with music, combining spoken dialogue with recitative and airs. The interest of the work for the audience lay almost exclusively in Torelli's astonishing (and astonishingly expensive) machines and Balbi's ballets, which were striking enough to be published as *Balletti d'Invenzione nella Finta Pazza* (Paris, Bibliothèque Nationale, Rés. V. 2566).

As the scholar of Venetian opera Ellen Rosand has shown, *La finta pazza*—"the first, and possibly the greatest operatic 'hit' of the century"—was a significant choice. Created by the Accademia degl'Incogniti to open their Teatro Novissimo, it constituted a manifesto for Venetian opera. The original text was part of a trilogy of libretti by Giulio Strozzi and was set by Francesco Sacrati. The machines were by

[27] Irene Alm, "First steps on the Venetian stage (1637–1640)," unpublished paper.

[28] See Cesare Molinari, *Le nozze degli dèi: un saggio sul grande spettacolo italiano del Seicento* (Rome: Bulzoni, 1968), 69–77.

Torelli, and the leading role was sung by the celebrated Anna Renzi. In part owing to the publicity machine of the Incogniti, the work received twelve performances in seventeen days during Carnival and was repeated after Easter. Not only was the libretto published, but the visual aspects of the production were the subject of another volume, Maiolino Bisaccioni's *Il Cannocchiale per la finta pazza* (1641). *La finta pazza* created a vogue for disguise, mad scenes, and other operatic conventions. In its projection of the Venetian self-image, it not only "laid the groundwork for the political interpretation of the development of Venetian opera" but prompted other nationalistic uses of opera. Its later performances — Piacenza in 1644, Florence and Paris in 1645 — served as "a model of the new Venetian genre to the world at large."[29]

The pot began to boil more fiercely — to borrow Don Taddeo Barberini's metaphor — with the arrival of Urban VIII's nephews in France. In February of 1646 Mazarin revived, on a much more modest scale, another Venetian success, the Cavalli-Faustini *L'Egisto* (Vienna, 1642; Venice, 1643), which also included a spectacular mad scene. The production coincided with Cardinal Antonio Barberini's reconciliation with Mazarin through the mediation of Francesco Buti and Antonio's triumphal entry into Paris of 11 January. Mazarin lodged Antonio in his own palace, and the cardinal's presence at *L'Egisto* with the royal family and the queen of England sealed his rehabilitation with Mazarin.

ASSEMBLING ORPHEUS

At the beginning of 1646 Torelli set to work on machines for a great ballet for the Duc d'Enghien, in which the choreographer Balbi was to have "the means to work with a free talent in an enterprise of greater importance."[30] Somehow, this project was transformed into the opera *L'Orfeo*. The choice of the subject may reflect a number of considerations: the re-use of the story of the earliest surviving Florentine opera, written for the wedding of Louis XIV's grandparents; an appeal to the powers of the new Italian music, which Mazarin wished to impress on the French; even a compliment to the Barberini, since Orpheus was the son of Apollo and both figures were connected with the poet-pope Urban VIII, the "Christian Apollo," and other members of the Barberini circle. (The choice of a different version of the Orpheus

[29] Ellen Rosand, *Opera in Seventeenth-Century Venice: The Creation of a Genre* (Berkeley: University of California Press, 1991), 90, 112, 121.

[30] ". . . les moyens d'agir avec un libre génie en entreprise de plus haute conséquence": Balbi, preface to *Balletti d'invenzione*, in Prunières, 79, n. 2.

myth may have carried yet another message—see below.) The Barberini musician Stefano Landi had set *La morte d'Orfeo* in 1619, and Marc'Antonio Pasqualini was depicted by Andrea Sacchi as a new Orpheus, crowned with laurel by Apollo himself.

Previously, Mazarin had simply borrowed members of the Barberini musical establishments. For *L'Orfeo* he cast his nets wider, even among enemies of the Barberini. The composer and the librettist, Luigi Rossi and Francesco Buti, were members of Cardinal Antonio's household, as was Pasqualini. (The intense anti-Spanish feeling in France and the anomalous position of a Queen-Regent of Spanish birth perhaps explain why another Barberini adherent, Monsignor Giulio Rospigliosi, nuncio to Madrid and author of the other Barberini opera libretti, did not write *L'Orfeo*.) Mazarin charged two agents with assembling the rest of the troupe, Elpidio Benedetti in Rome (aided by Marazzoli) and Cornelio Bentivoglio in Florence, with his brother Giovanni as a liason in France.[31] When Luigi Rossi arrived in Paris in mid-June he took over the direction of the recruitment.[32] In the late fall of 1646 Benedetti was writing Cornelio Bentivoglio every few days about the transport of the singers; by the end of December they had arrived.[33]

As the son of Marchese Enzo Bentivoglio (d. 1639), Monteverdi's *corago* for the 1628 wedding celebrations in Parma, Cornelio II Bentivoglio was no stranger to the theater,[34] demonstrated in his participation as champion in Cardinal Antonio Barberini's joust in Piazza Navona in 1634 and *Le pretensioni del Tebro e del Po* in Ferrara in 1642 (see Chapter 4). Cornelio's own wedding to Costanza Sforza in 1638 was celebrated with the *Andromeda*, a magnificent collaboration of the librettist Ascanio Pio di Savoia with the composer Michelangelo Rossi and the designer Francesco Guitti. For Cornelio II, his father's avocation was part of his livelihood. In 1640 he had leased the Sala delle Commedie in Ferrara, where he presented professional theatrical troups and organized jousts.[35]

---

[31] A letter of 29 September 1646 from Giovanni Bentivoglio at Fontainebleau to Cornelio shows Mazarin's detailed planning for the transport of the Costa sisters (Monaldini, *L'Orto*, 5–6).

[32] See Atto Melani's letter of 15 November 1646 to Bentivoglio (ibid., 10).

[33] Monaldini, *L'Orto*, 8–13. On 29 September 1646 Giovanni Bentivoglio had written Cornelio from Fontainebleau, "Havendo la M[aes]tà della Regina risoluto di volere havere in Parigi quest'inverno una buona mano di musici tanto per la camera quanto per il teatro . . ." ("The Queen's Majesty having resolved to have in Paris this winter a good handful of musicians for the chamber as well as for the theater . . .") (ibid., 5).

[34] Dinko Fabris has stated categorically that Enzo Bentivoglio's operatic ventures were inspired not by a love for the genre but by political calculations (*Mecenati*, 83).

[35] On the Bentivoglio see Southorn, *Power and Display*, 75–96; Fabris, *Mecenati, passim*; and Monaldini, *L'Orto*, which contains much material on Cornelio's theatrical ventures.

In the War of Castro against the Farnese of Parma, the Barberini had been opposed by the Medici of Florence, Francesco I d'Este, duke of Modena (whose first
two wives were Farnese), and the Venetian Republic. All of these made significant
contributions to Mazarin's production. The duke of Parma had already provided
the Venetian dancing-master Balbi and Torelli, "le grand sorcier." From Prince Mathias
de' Medici came the castrato Atto Melani, accompanied by his brother Jacopo,[36] in
the service of the Grand Duke, and the soprano Rosina Martini. From Prince Leopold
de' Medici came another leading soprano, Anna Francesca Costa, with her sister
Margherita; an "Alessandro fiorentino" (still at the French court in 1650) was probably
also a Medici retainer. Francesco d'Este sent two Roman boy sopranos, Marc'Antonio
and Domenico, under the supervision of Venanzio Leopardi.[37] Although Leopardi
was in the service of the Este, he had previously served Anna Colonna Barberini's
brother, Cardinal Girolamo, who was legate in Bologna. The castrato Pamfilo
Miccinello, who traveled with Pasqualini, was a contralto at the Seminario Romano
and was also in the service of Cardinal Colonna; he was recommended by Marazzoli.
The most striking contribution was that of Innocent X, who not only permitted
Pasqualini to absent himself from the Cappella Pontificia at the end of 1645 but
charged him to assure Cardinal Antonio that "in the future he must remain assured
of the great affection that he bears him."[38]

Although Pasqualini had been summoned by Cardinal Antonio on the latter's
arrival in France, with the usual generous financial provision, Rossi left Rome without him; Pasqualini did not move until entreated directly by Mazarin. In March of
1646 Cardinal Antonio wrote from Aix to G. B. Bonghi, sending a *polizza* or bank
draft of five hundred scudi. From a rather breathless item in Cardinal Antonio's
papers it appears that of this Pasqualini was to receive sc. 300 for his pension and he
and Luigi Rossi sc. 100 as well:

> . . . to come to France and the other half to Marc-Antonio in
> Rome to come with Luigi and soon[,] do me the favor of not
> letting it be known that of the two hundred scudi, that is one
> hundred apiece for the journey[,] and charge Marc-Antonio

---

[36] Freitas, "Un Atto," 46–67.

[37] On Alessandro see Prunières, 150; on Venanzio Leopardi, ibid., 377. Marc'Antonio [Sportonio] later
became an important figure in Sicilian musical life. There seems to be some confusion as to whether
the singer Margherita Costa was also the author of the *Tromba di Parnasso*, see Prunières, 133–34.

[38] ". . . in avvenire deve restar sicuro del molto affetto che gli porta" (Prunières, 90–91, n. 4).

that for now he not know of the three hundred having wished
to put right in such manner those things that happened with
him against my order so that by another way you put it right
still with the others that then one can know about all together
with every other[.] I beg Your Lordship to do me the favor of
keeping everything most highly secret having wished to remedy
that if M. Antonio wishes to come up there for some time that
he make his own provisions.[39]

In September of 1646 the Queen had asked for the Costa sisters in order "to
have in Paris this winter a good handful of musicians for the chamber as well as for
the theater."[40] Benedetti arranged this, sending also Stefano Costa and Atto Melani.

The musicians arrived in Provence on 1 December and reached Paris on the
26th. Their lodgings were casual and money was initially short. As often happened
in seventeenth-century operas (and not only then), things were delayed. "As far as
the performance is concerned," wrote Stefano Costa, "we are very much behind
schedule and nothing is composed except the first act of the words and also of the
music, and it is believed that we will surely do *Il Nerone* before but in the little theater
without machines, only with the beautiful costumes, and afterwards we will do the
big opera whose words are by Sig. Buti."[41] (The composition of "the big opera" may
have been held up by the death of Rossi's wife Costanza in Rome on 27 November
of 1646.[42]) The *Nerone* that the company was contemplating performing, presumably
in the small theater of the Palais Royal, was the Monteverdi opera better known as
L'incoronazione di Poppea.[43]

---

[39] BAV, Barb. lat. 8806, unnumbered, item #25: "per venir in francia et l'altra meta a Marc-Antonio à
Roma venire con Luigi et a presto mi faccia favore non far saper' che delli ducento scudi cioé cento per
uno per il viaggio et incarichi a Marc-Antonio che per hora non si sappia cosi delli trecento havendo
voluto rimediare in tal modo a quelle eseguito contro mio ordine con lui fin ch'per altra strada lo rimedij
ancora con gl'altri che allora poi si potrà saper' di tutti insieme con ogn'altro prego V.S. favorirmi di
tener il tutto con sommo segreto havendo voluto rimediare che si M. Ant.o vol venirsem' lasù per qualche
tempo provisa i suoi."

[40] See n. 33.

[41] "In torno alla recita, siamo addietro assai et non è con posto altro che il primo atto delle parole et
anco della musica, et si crede che faremo il Nerone sicuro in anzi pero nel piciolo teatro senza machine,
solo con li abbiti belli, et doppo poi faremo l'opera grossa quale le parole sono del sig.r Buti": Monaldini,
L'Orto, 13.

[42] Letter of Elpidio Benedetti in Rome to Mazarin, 1 December 1646 (Prunières, 98 and n.).

[43] See now Rosand, *Monteverdi's Last Operas*, 126.

Despite the vicissitudes of war and the attempts at a peace, which was not concluded until 1648 with the Treaty of Westphalia, the French court gave itself to lighter matters. As Zongo Ondedei wrote to Cornelio Bentivoglio from Paris on 8 February 1647, "in the meantime we attend only to plays, and music." The imported Italian singers performed often at court, soon developing their own partisans, right up to the throne. "Signora Checca does herself honor, and is praised to the stars by the Chevalier de Jars," wrote Ondedei, "Marc Antonio makes great proof of his knowledge, and of his art. But Atto [Melani] bears off the palm, and his party of knights, and ladies is the strongest, and the queen herself belongs to it."[44]

L'ORFEO

Two sources exist for L'Orfeo. The libretto copied on French paper that is now in the Biblioteca Apostolica Vaticana (Barb. lat 3803, L'ORFEO/Tragicomedia/Per/Musica) is possibly the version from which Rossi worked, but it was altered for the musical setting. The only existing score of the opera is Biblioteca Apostolica Vaticana, Ms. Chigi Q. V. 58, L'ORFEO/Poesia del sig. Fran.co Buti/Musica del sig. Luigi Rossi, which according to Jean Lionnet could not have been copied before 1659.[45] (The series of operas collected for Cardinal Flavio Chigi now in the Vatican Library begins with Rossi's earlier opera, Il palazzo incantato of 1642.) This version differs from the synopsis of the original production given in the relazione of Biblioteca Apostolica Vaticana, Barb. lat. 4059. There also exists a French synopsis, Orphée tragi-comédie en musique (Paris: Cramoisy, 1647; Paris, Bibliothèque Nationale, Yf. 946), which I have been unable to consult. The Ms. Kassel, Landesbibliothek, Mus. fol. 61 (ca. 1650–70) contains an instrumental fantaisie, Les Pleurs d'Orphée ayant perdu sa femme, perhaps for the use of the Vingt-quatre violons du Roy. (Only the bass is given in the Chigi score, at the end of Act II.) The opera was also described by Claude-François Ménestrier

---

[44] ". . . frà tanto noi non atendiamo che à comedie, e musiche . . . La sig.ra Checca si fà honore, et è portata alle stelle dal cavalier de Jars. M. Antonio fà gran prove del suo sapere, e della sua arte. Mà Atto porta la palma, et il suo partito di cavalieri, e di dame è il più forte, e la regina medesima vi adherisce": Monandini, L'Orto, 14–15).

[45] Jean Lionnet, liner notes for Luigi Rossi, Orfeo, Harmonia Mundi France 901358,60. In his article "Les événements musicaux de la légation du Cardinal Flavio Chigi en France (1664)" (Studi Musicali 25 [1996]: 127–53), Lionnet states that the cardinal had a copy made of L'Orfeo, presumably in 1664, but does not identify it with the Vatican volume. For information on these materials and a copy of the Vatican score I am indebted to Professor James Tyler of the University of Southern California, Los Angeles, who has made a performing edition of the opera.

(1631–1705) in his *Des Représentations en musique anciennes et modernes* (Paris: Guignard, 1681; reprint, Geneva: Minkoff, 1972). The *relazione* of Barb. lat. 4059 is given here in translation and in the original in the Appendix, with the comments of Ménestrier interspersed.

L'Orfeo was presented, after much delay, on 2, 3, and 5 March 1647 and repeated after Easter on 29 April and 6 and 8 May. The performances were given in the theater of the Palais Royal, rebuilt by Torelli to accommodate his machines. On 10 May Carlo Claudi wrote to Annibale Bentivoglio that "the *comedia* has been done several times, and it has always gone from good to better, and the queen said the last evening that the only thing that displeased her about leaving Paris was not being able to hear the *comedia* any more, of which she wanted a copy in music of the ariettas that are in it, to have sung by the four singers who will remain."[46] The day after the last performance (Lionnet, "Les événements," says after the first performance) a ball was given by the Duc d'Orléans in the same room in honor of Anna Colonna Barberini on the eve of her departure for Rome.

> The following day in the same theater the stage was converted into a great hall, being all well painted and gilded with twelve chandeliers of rock crystal, it made the most beautiful sight ever seen. And there descended a machine where there were 24 violins to play, adorned with 30 or 40 ladies, or rather goddesses, for such they seemed, both for their beauty and for their ornaments of inestimable jewels. Mademoiselle d'Orléans alone wore three million in jewels, between diamonds and pearls, however, they were the queen's, and the other women were equally covered with diamonds. I believe that in all the rest of Europe there are not so many. They entered the beautiful hall by a bridge, and there went also as many gentlemen, who were not less adorned than the ladies since one cavalier had in his hat a great braid of large pearls, and his outfit all embroidered with pearls was said to be worth 200 thousand scudi. To sum it up, the riches cannot be described. They danced all night, the king danced and the Prince of Wales, and Prince Rupert of the Palatine.
>
> Make allowances for this report written in haste.

---

[46] ". . . si è fatta diverse volte la comedia, e sempre è andata di bene in meglio, e la regina disse l'ultima sera, che non per altro gli dispiaceva di partire da Parigi, che per non poter intendere più la comedia, della quale ne hà voluta una copia in musica, per far cantare a' quattro musici che qui resteranno delle ariette che sono in essa": Carlo Claudi in Paris to Annibale Bentivoglio, 10 May 1647 (Monaldini, *L'Orto*, 18).

(The Duc d'Orléans was Louis XIII's brother, the troublesome Gaston d'Orléans; Mademoiselle d'Orléans was his unfortunate daughter, the Grande Mademoiselle. The Prince of Wales was the future Charles II, and Prince Rupert was his first cousin, son of James I's daughter Elizabeth and Frederick V of the Palatine, the Winter King and Queen of Bohemia.)

In Anna Colonna's presence the queen praised a Roman singer, sometimes identified as Margherita Costa (who was in fact Tuscan) but more probably Leonora Baroni. Donna Anna, "that proud woman, daughter of the Contestabile Colonna," replied, "'If she had come, I would have had her thrown out the window.'"[47]

The manuscript Barb. lat. 4059 provides a virtually complete list of performers for *L'Orfeo*, not all of whom can now be identified. The soprano castrato Atto Melani sang the leading roles of Victory in the Prologue and Orpheus in the opera, while his brother the tenor Jacopo ("Giacomo") sang Jove. Rosina (incorrectly listed as "Caterina") Martini was Venus. Anna Francesca Costa sing the female lead, Eurydice, and her sister Margherita the important role of Juno. Aristaeus, the most succulent role in the opera since it included a spectacular mad scene of the type made famous by *La finta pazza* and Cavalli's *L'Egisto*, was allotted to the most celebrated of the singers, Cardinal Antonio Barberini's castrato Marc'Antonio Pasqualini. "Alessandro fiorentino" doubled the bass roles of Pluto and the Augur. "Stefano di Bentivoglio" sang the roles of Bacchus and Endymion, the lover of Diana here transformed into Eurydice's father: since the former is a soprano while the latter is a bass, Alessandro probably performed Bacchus in falsetto. Atto Melani says that "il castrato dei Bentivoglio" sang "una vecchia," presumably the Nurse, otherwise unnamed in the *relazione* cast-list. Venus as an old woman was a tenor ("Francesco Venetiano"). Jealousy was sung by the Roman castrato Pamfilo Miccinello. Leopardi wrote the duke of Modena that "Your Highness' boy servants each sing six parts [. . .] I too am employed in something to perform"—presumably Charon, sung by "Venantio d'Este."[48] In fact, of the *putti*, Domenico d'Este doubled not less than one of the Graces, one of the Parcae, Suspicion, and Hymen.

The *relazione* lists the instruments and performing forces. The orchestra comprised four violins and twenty *viole*, presumably the Vingt-quatre violons du Roy; these consisted of first violins, violas scored in three different clefs, and *basses de*

---

[47] ". . . cette femme superbe, qui était fille du connétable Colonna . . . 'Si elle y fut venue, je l'aurois fait jeter par les fenetres'": Prunières, 139.

[48] "Li putti servitori di V. A. fanno sei parti ciascuno . . . io ancora sono impiegato in qualche cosa da recitare": Prunières, 99, 381.

violon, violoncelli with a low B-flat string which gave a 16-foot sonority at 8-foot pitch; four harpsichords, four theorboes, two lutes, two guitars, four trumpets, and drums. The strings, where notated in the score, are written in four parts: treble clef, second- and third-line alto clefs, and bass (in one case there are two bass lines, suggesting an independent theorbo part.) Fifes, cornetts, and bagpipes provided music for an Infernal ballet. All of these could have been furnished from the various divisions of the royal musical establishment (winds and percussion from the Écurie or stables, other instruments from the Musique de Chambre, and keyboards and voices from the Musique de Chapelle). The twenty-four violins also performed at the ball for Anna Colonna, descending on a machine.

In addition to the solo singers, the vocal forces consisted of sixty performers on stage for the French army in the Prologue, a chorus of sixteen for the attackers and eight for the defenders. The chorus of nymphs and shepherds, Imenei, and Baccanti comprised six singers and twenty-four dancers, the Infernal chorus, ten singers; the final Celestial chorus was a *tutti*.

The extent to which Francesco Buti fleshed out the original story of Orpheus into a three-act "Tragicomedia" by adding characters, incidents, and subplots, as well as a Prologue and a miniature epilogue, is apparent from the synopsis in the Vatican manuscript Barb. lat. 4059.

The Prologue to the opera depicted the assault of a stronghold by the French army. Victory descended on a chariot-machine covered with trophies, reminiscent of the descent of Roma in the 1634 prologue of the Barberini *Il Sant'Alessio*. The ritornelli of her aria were played by the twenty *viole* with the rest of the instruments. Ménestrier commented that, according to Italian practice, the Prologue was a separate piece, not part of the action. It described Orpheus' victory, which foretold the glory of Anne of Austria.

The set was transformed into a countryside, a perspective described by Ménestrier as "a wood whose width & depth seemed to surpass the [size of the] Theater more than a hundred times and there appeared in this wood an Augur seated on his throne."

Act I, Scene 1: "The Augur, Endymion, Eurydice, Nurse, and Chorus of Augurs enter to foretell the happy wedding of Eurydice, and they perform many ceremonies used by the Ancients. They see two turtledoves in the air, which are pursued by vultures. This is taken for an evil omen, but Eurydice says that she pays no attention to it, because she is sure of the love of her Orpheus, and so the Augur leaves with his chorus, and she remains with her father, and they sing a three-part Canzona with the nurse."

Scene 2: "Orpheus arrives all happy, and sings with his bride words of tenderness and love. The two lovers sing and dance together (Ménestrier: 'Singing in so gay a manner that they show, both by their song and by the dance with which they accompany it . . .'). Her father, touched by such fervent love, also sings a Canzona for happiness, and they leave."

Scene 3: "Aristaeus and the Satyr. Aristaeus laments the marriage of his beloved Eurydice with Orpheus, and then sings a canzona about jealousy, while the Satyr (Ménestrier: 'dancing with his goat feet') answers him with a song to the contrary. Finally [Aristaeus] invokes the aid of Venus, the friend of his father Bacchus, and he sees her descend from heaven in a most beautiful machine (Ménestrier: 'in a cloud with her son Cupid, the Graces, and a troupe of little cupids who sing the praises of this goddess and her son')."

Scene 4: "When Venus, Cupid, and the Graces with six other cupids around, has descended she sees Aristaeus so sorrowful. She consoles him and says that she wishes to help him, and to do so better she will go to the temple of Proteus to transform herself into an old woman to be able to induce Eurydice to respond to his love. She commands the Graces to beautify Aristaeus, so that he may be more pleasing to his beloved, and leaves."

The Chigi score adds an aria for the Satyr and omits the following two scenes of the *relazione*:

[Scene 5: "While singing the Graces beautify Aristaeus with many ornaments and scented powders, and set him in order (Ménestrier: 'starting to curl his hair, they sang about the difference between cleanliness and negligence'). He leaves to find Venus."]

[Scene 6: "The Satyr, also desirous of being beautified by the Graces, sits down, and laughing they play a thousand tricks on him (Ménestrier: 'they did him a thousand harms while roughly braiding his hair all tousled and bristly'). Finally he tells them not to laugh because he has had great luck in love. Being rich he has discovered, that with women self-interest is more powerful than love. They call him a liar, they pull his hair, and they powder his whole face with scented powder. He complains that they wanted to blind him, he chases them, they flee, and the scene ends."]

Scene 7 of the *relazione* picks up as Scene 5 of the score. "The scene changes to a portico with a great temple (Ménestrier: 'When the perspective was opened, we saw a table superbly set'), where the wedding of Orpheus is being celebrated. There enter in sight of the audience to sit at a beautiful and rich table Hymen, Juno, Apollo, Endymion, Eurydice, Orpheus, a chorus of nymphs and shepherds who sing, a chorus of Hymenids bearing torches who did a beautiful dance. And while the one and the other [choruses] awaited the toasts there arrived Momus the god of slander, who laments that the feast should be celebrated without him, saying that one can't enjoy oneself without speaking ill of someone. [Omitted in the score: Juno tells him to sit down and say something. He makes a great invective against great Mother Nature, who wasted so much gold and so many jewels and concealed the leftovers deep in the earth, all to see poor mortals in poverty. Apollo tells him that he would have replied to this but now there was no time.] He charged Momus to sing a song, and he intemperately sang one about taking a wife, saying, that if she's ugly it's a great misfortune, and if she's beautiful it's a great danger, and so whether you marry or not in any case you repent it. There follows the dance, in this all the torches of the Hymenids go out, which is taken for a bad omen. They all invoke the aid of the gods, and leave with a sinfonia. (Ménestrier: 'Some nymphs and shepherds danced a ballet around the table, but the torches that they bore to celebrate this wedding having gone out [. . .] and the astonished shepherdesses leaving their dance sought the help of the gods in an hymn full of tenderness')."

Act II opens in a city full of beautiful palaces, the basic seventeenth-century urban stage set, "where one could note all the beauties of architecture," Ménestrier adds.

Scene 1: "Venus and Aristaeus: the scene changes to a city full of beautiful palaces. Venus transformed into an old woman with Aristaeus; they discuss his loves. Then they see Eurydice enter with the Nurse, and in order not to show that he is wait-ing for her, Aristaeus pretends to be learning a song about hope from the old woman."

Scene 2: "Eurydice, coming on [with her Nurse], regrets meeting Aristaeus, who wishes to love her against her will. The old woman approaches her and keeps asking her where she is going so sadly. She answers her, that having had evil portents about her wedding, she was going to the temple to beg pity from the gods. The old woman answers, that she could provide the remedy, and that was, that if she wished to change the portents she should change her husband. She marvels at this, and to confirm the firmness of her love she sings a very beautiful song in praise of Orpheus. Aristaeus is saddened by hearing his rival so praised, but the old woman answers, that there are other countenances not less handsome than Orpheus, and she shows her Aristaeus, whom [Eurydice] does not wish to see or hear. But being so implored both by the old woman, and by her nurse, finally she is induced to hear his laments. She commiserates his state, but she cannot remedy it, for her honor will not permit it. The old woman replies that honor is an expedient found for the advantage of women, but Eurydice refusing such a lying expedient, she sings the praises of honor and the firmness of her faith and leaves. The Nurse stays for a bit, touched, and comforts Aristaeus, and urges him to faithfulness because persistence wins. To instruct him she sings a song about hope and leaves."

Scene 3: "The Satyr, who has heard the whole discussion in hiding, and having understood that to cheer herself up Eurydice wished to dance in the Garden of the Sun, says, why so much conversation, let's go and steal her by force. Aristaeus is persuaded, and they leave."

Scene 4: "Momus, Cupid, Juno, Apollo. Momus sings the complaints that everyone everywhere makes of the tyranny of love, and therefore he exhorts [Cupid] to change his customs, otherwise in a short time his kingdom would be at sword's point. Juno enters, and makes a similar complaint in the name of women. Apollo descends, and makes other complaints. Cupid answers them all, and assures them to show that it is the opposite of that which they say he relates the desire of his mother Venus to betray Orpheus and deceive Eurydice, but that he would not do such a wrong to so faithful a pair of lovers, and that instead he will deceive his mother. Being informed of that promise they sing together the praises of Cupid, and leave.

Scene 5: "Cupid remains, complaining that the Graces are so late in bringing Orpheus as he had commanded. He sees Orpheus and the Graces coming. The Graces who are bringing Orpheus beg him to sing. He offers the excuse that because he is melancholy, and for the bad omens that hover over him, he would rather weep than sing. Cupid comes forward and sings, exhorting him to be happy, for when it thunders not always does it lighten. He consoles him, revealing to him the evil invention of Venus and that to do him harm she transformed herself into an old woman, but that he would be his champion and protector, and that [Orpheus] should not doubt, and for that reason he should go to reveal everything to Eurydice. He thanks him and leaves."

Scene 7: "At this point Venus arrives, and the Graces as spies reveal to Venus all of Cupid's conspiracy with Orpheus. Venus in anger wants to beat Cupid, who mocks her. They make a few turns. Finally Cupid takes flight and flees to heaven. Venus, still disguised as an old woman, ends the scene with an aria in praise of inconstancy in love and goes to resume her divine form."

Scene 8: "(Ménestrier: 'A temple having changed in a moment the aspect of the theater') Endymion, the Augur, and his chorus, who are going to make a sacrifice to Venus to calm her anger against Orpheus, and Eurydice [missing in the score] encounter Juno, who dissuades them from sacrificing to Venus, since Cupid had promised to Momus, to Apollo, and to her to be favorable to Orpheus and to Eurydice, but that in exchange they should sacrifice to her, as the goddess of weddings, and she sings her own praises, and they leave."

Scene 9: "Eurydice, the Nurse, and chorus of nymphs. The scene changes to a garden (Ménestrier: 'The scene changed immediately'). They come to do the pre-arranged dance, but because it was too early they put themselves under the greenery to rest; the nymphs sing a lullaby." Their song is a *sommeil* or sleep-scene, a genre found already in Monteverdi's *Incoronazione* (= *Il Nerone*).

Scene 10: "In this you see the Dryads arrive, she wakes, they begin the dance, which was a beautiful saraband, singing the praises of Love, and his power (Ménestrier: 'When the Dryads had arrived they awakened her, and danced with castanets a ballet that Eurydice found so pleasant that she joined in with her Nymphs')."

Scene 11: "The same, Aristaeus, and the Satyr, who in the dance come to steal Eurydice, who flees, and then a poisonous serpent hurls itself at her leg. It bites her, from which she is dying. Aristaeus [comes] as if to help her, she refuses, indeed she orders him to leave. He sings a lament of despair and leaves, while she meanwhile feeling great pain calls to her aid Apollo the god of medicine and father of her bride-groom. All this time she is failing, she wishes to see Orpheus before she dies. They send for him but he does not arrive in time. Since the poison reaches her heart, it takes her life, the nymphs make a sorrowful lament."

Scene 12: "The heavens open and the palace of the Sun appears (Ménestrier: 'The palace of the Sun which then comprised the decoration of the theater'), and [Apollo] above the Zodiac, who turning through the heavens wishes to descend to succor Eurydice, but he does not arrive in time, since he sees that she is already dead, and the earth is opened to receive her. He bewails her death and promises that Orpheus will go to the Inferno to get her back. The nymphs remove all their garlands from their heads, putting them on the body of Eurydice, which the earth swallows up. The act ends with weeping."

Act III begins with another transformation.

Scene 1: "The scene changes to a terrible landscape (Ménestrier: 'a terrible desert, caverns, and rocks with a cave in the form of a path, at the end of which through the darkness one discovered a bit of daylight'). Orpheus sings a sorrowful lament for the death of his bride and regrets that he does not have an even greater supply of tears. Then he hears a bizarre song, he approaches, and sees the Fates, whom he begs to reattach the thread of Eurydice's life. They excuse themselves, saying that they cannot do that. He says that they do not know the power of his singing joined with the sound of his lyre, and beginning to sing and play, the Fates are touched and exhort him to descend to the Inferno, for surely he will obtain his beloved bride. They show him the way.

Scene 2: "The Augur, his chorus, Endymion, and the nurse. Together they lament the death of Eurydice and the loss of Orpheus, for they do not know what has become of him. They go to invoke the aid of heaven."

Scene 3: "Aristaeus sings a great lament for the death of Eurydice. He feels the earth shake, the day darkens, the earth opens, and the ghost of Eurydice rises in a rage and rebukes him for his boldness, since he tried to stain her purity. Terrified, he trembles, calls for help, she hurls herself at him to kill him. She repents, and so that he should remain alive as an example of such a crime, she strikes him in the head with a snake and makes him lose his wits, and her ghost disappears."

Scene 4: "Momus and the Satyr enter singing a burlesque song against melancholy. They see Aristaeus, who is running madly here and there. They observe him, and finally realize that he has gone mad. He does numberless crazy things and extravagances. He imagines himself to be Decaulion, he throws rocks, he sees the Satyr and Momus enter and thinks that he has produced new beings. Then he imagines that the Satyr is Eurydice and sings her a most amorous song. And then in an access of pride he makes the sound of the trumpet with his mouth to one of them, to the other [the sound] of the drum, and sings a song of war. When that is finished he goes to hurl himself [from a cliff] and dies (Ménestrier: '[Eurydice] pursues him holding a snake and drives him mad, his music expressing his madness, fills the fourth scene with terror')." Aristaeus's war-song, to the accompaniment of Momus imitating trumpets and the Satyr imitating drums, seems a grotesque parody of the Prologue.

Scene 5: "Juno sends Jealousy and Suspicion to suggest to Proserpina that she attempt to return Eurydice to Orpheus, otherwise she may expect a thousand wrongs to her marriage bed from Pluto, giving her the example of Jove. They [Jealousy and Suspicion] leave."

[Scene 6]: "Then Venus enters all happy. Singing of the victory she had over Juno by killing Eurydice, at the same time she was avenged on the sun, who had revealed her amours with Mars. Juno rebukes her, they struggle together, and one leaves from one side and the other from the other.

Scene 7: "The scene changes to the Inferno. Jealousy and Suspicion enter the Inferno, and they wonder to see that kingdom empty of inhabitants. [Omitted in the score: A little devil tells them that they have all rushed to see a living man who had entered there.] Then Proserpina enters singing of the happiness she experiences in that infernal place owing to the love by which she loved and was loved in return by Pluto, but Jealousy begins to insinuate her passions. Since Suspicion has found Eurydice there, they exhort [Proserpina] to make Pluto send her out of the Inferno. She promises."

Scene 8: "In this Pluto enters berating Charon because he has brought Orpheus into the Inferno. [Charon] makes the excuse that he could not resist the force of his sweet song. Proserpina begs him to hear such sweet harmony. The whole chorus begs Pluto for the same. Finally he commands Charon to bring [Orpheus] into his presence.

Scene 9: "Orpheus enters singing and begging Pluto to give him back his beloved Eurydice. Pluto, touched by the sweetness of his song and of his lyre, played offstage by 12 viole,[49] which made an excellent harmony, concedes him his beloved but with the decree that as long as he is within the Inferno he must never turn back to look at her. Orpheus sings in thanksgiving, and Eurydice appears, and sings of her happiness and the faith of her husband, and they leave. Pluto, who sees the whole Inferno rejoicing, commands that they do a dance, which was most beautiful and extravagant, because there appeared first four dragons, with four harpies. At the end of their dance they left eight eggs, from which eight little devils emerged and danced. And the harpies and the dragons flew and then there entered four great snails with four phantoms, and from the phantoms issued four great lanterns, and then issued forth four great owls, and the devils hunted with beautiful and most extravagant and fine variations. The dance was played by pipes, and cornetts, and bagpipes (Ménestrier: 'A ballet of all the monsters of Hell, under a hundred extravagant figures of owls, of bucentaurs, of harpies, and other beasts enlivened this scene')." The *Gazette de Renaudot* described the ballet as a dance of monsters, "under the form of bucentaurs, of owls, of turtles, of snails, and several other strange animals and hideous monsters . . . to the sound of cornetts, with strange steps and a similar music."[50] The music for the ballet is not included in the score.

Scene 10 [added to Scene 9 in the score]: "Charon comes to bring the news to Pluto that Orpheus has broken the law, and therefore they have taken back Eurydice, who enters weeping."

Scene 11 [9 continued in the score]: "Eurydice sings a great lament [omitted in the score] before Pluto, who commands that she be brought to the Elysian Fields to be consoled."

Scene 12 [transferred to Scene 10 and last in the score]: "The scene changes to a pleasant countryside and beautiful forest with a very beautiful sea. Orpheus enters alone, singing a great lament, and one saw the trees walking to his sweet song, the

---

[49] The use of offstage string chords to represent the sound of the singer's lyre goes back at least to Marco da Gagliano's *La Dafne* of 1608.

[50] ". . . sous la forme de bucentaures, de hiboux, de tortües, d'escargos, et de plusieurs austres animaux estranges et monstres les plus hideux . . . au son des cornets à bouquin, avec des pas exttravagans et une musique de mesme": Prunières, 127.

rocks that moved, and all the animals came to hear him: lions, tigers, panthers, bears, wolves, stags, ostriches, peacocks, and other birds. At the end he says that he wishes to go away to die (Ménestrier: 'he communicates his sorrow to the trees and to the animals who dance to the sound of his lyre')."

Scene 13 [transferred to Scene 9 in the score]: "Bacchus comes with his chorus happily singing and dancing. Venus appears from the sea crying for revenge, because she has heard from Suspicion that Eurydice had returned to the world. She persuades Bacchus that he too wishes to avenge himself for the death of his son Aristaeus caused by Eurydice and Orpheus. Bacchus commands the bacchantes to kill Orpheus, and that they be the more maddened he commands them to get drunk and leaves weeping with Venus. The bacchantes do a beautiful dance while drinking and leave."

Last scene [in the score this opens with Scene 12 of the *relazione*: "Orpheus continues with several sorrowful airs on his lyre, that he plays so melodically that at its harmony joined with the sweetness of his voice, he makes the rocks move, the trees and the wildest beasts dance, so that one sees lions, panthers, other wild beasts come to caper on stage around him[51]]: A great machine descends with Jove within, with all the gods and a great chorus. Jove commands that the lyre of Orpheus be immortalized and that he have a place in the heavens." [Mercury reveals that the lyre of Orpheus is none other than the fleur-de-lis of unvanquished France, a speech included only in the score]. "The whole chorus sings, and it ends (Ménestrier: '[Jove] wills that his lyre be made a constellation in the firmament, at which the entire theater resounds with a melodious hymn to explain that perfect virtue must be entirely detached from the earth and expect its reward only from heaven. Thus at the end of this piece they made a moral instruction from this entertainment')."

*   *   *   *

The astonishing achievement of Torelli was perhaps somewhat more economical than it seemed. The machines were a few basic types, varied more by superficial decoration than by function. The most important one was a substantial descending machine capable of accommodating the chariot of Victory, the descent of Venus with her suite, and the final appearance of all the gods. A trap was also required for the

---

[51] *Gazette de Renaudot:* "Orphée s'entretient de plusieurs airs lugubres sur sa lyre, qu'il touche si mélodiquement qu'à son armonie jointe à la douceur de sa voix, il fait mouvoir les rochers, danser les arbres et les animaux les plus farouches, de sorte que l'on vit des lions, des panthères, d'autres bêtes furieuses venir sauter sur le théâtre à l'entour de lui" (Prunières, 128). This anticipation of *Zauberflöte* recalls the grotesque ballets that Balbi had created for *La finta pazza* to amuse the child king.

tomb which opened for Eurydice. Cupid's departure in flight was probably accomplished by the standard wire mechanism. For the sets, the painted perspective of Act I/1 opened for the following scene. Several scenes, such as II/8–9, were transformations effected in full view of the audience, coordinated perhaps by Torelli's device of the "gran ruota."[52] The heavens opened—another standard effect—on the palace of Apollo, whose Zodiac-chariot was perhaps the machine employed for a similar effect in the *Finta pazza* of 1645.[53]

Torelli had already created scenes that parallel those of *L'Orfeo*. The *Grotta dei venti* of *Bellerofonte* (1642) bears a strong resemblance to the cave of the Fates; the temple of Juno, with its salomonic columns, is particularly impressive; garden-scenes include a formal garden and a bosky dell. *La Venere gelosa* (1643) contained a number of forest- or garden-sets, a machine with a palace of Venus, and an infernal grotto. Perhaps G. F. Grimaldi's set for the Prologue of the Barberini *Il trionfo della Pietà* (1656: see Chapter 8), with its opposing fortresses of Understanding and Pleasure, owed something to Torelli's sets for the Prologue of *L'Orfeo*.[54]

Along with the sets and machines, the dances were the principal attraction of the opera for its audience, although Anne of Austria had a copy made of the music so that four of her singers could perform the *ariette* for her.[55] Venanzio Leopardi wrote to the duke of Modena: "what most delights, there are eight dances of every sort composed by an Italian Ballet Master" — "Jean Baptiste Balbi called Tasquin" — "danced by twelve of the principal masters of Paris."[56] Prunières suggests that the ballet-music missing from the score may have been furnished by French composers, and that the Infernal ballet — "Qui và la danza" in the score — is likely to have been a French concoction. No matter who composed them, some *airs de ballet* have been omitted from the score or, more accurately, from the lost original of Ms. Chigi Q. V. 58. In 1641 the shadowy but well-informed M. de St. Hubert wrote, "I would wish that the Airs not be composed until the subject was complete, and the dance-entries

---

[52] Bisaccioni's *Cannochiale* attributes to Torelli the invention of a "great wheel" that coordinated the movements of flats in scene-changes, but this invention has been traced to Giovanni Battista Aleotti as early as 1618 (Adami, *Scenografia*, 40).

[53] Prunières, 75.

[54] For Torelli's sets and machines for *Bellerofonte* see Molinari, *Le nozze degli dèi*, pls. 69–77; for *Il trionfo* (mistitled), pls. 98–101; for *La Venere gelosa* see *Illusione et pratica teatrale* (Venice: Neri Possa, 1975), item 20.

[55] See n. 46 above.

[56] "[Quel] che più diletta, vi sono da un Maestro Ballarino Italiano composti otto balletti d'ogni genere ballati da dodici maestri principali di Parigi": letter of 22 February 1647, in Prunières, 381.

arranged, so that they [the airs] were made to fit, & following the actions that the dancers must make and depict."[57]

Of *L'Orfeo*, Prunières observed with Gallic understatement that "the role of the Barberini in this matter has thus been exaggerated a bit."[58] And indeed, although the opera reflected Mazarin's experience of the Barberini productions and drew on members of Cardinal Antonio's household, it also reflected the influence of Venetian opera and created a network of performers extending far beyond the Barberini sphere.

One element, however, seems to have gone unremarked so far. There are two ancient sources for the story of Orpheus and Eurydice: Virgil, *Georgics*, IV; and Ovid, *Metamorphoses*, X–XI. The core elements of the story are the same in both versions: Eurydice dies bitten by a snake, Orpheus follows her to the underworld and enchants even its most terrifying denizens with his song. Pluto and Proserpina release Eurydice with the caveat that Orpheus not look back at her until they have reached the upper world. He disobeys and loses her forever.

Virgil's account of the Orpheus legend occurs in the fourth and final book of his great agricultural poem the *Georgics*. It is surrounded by a framing device lacking in Ovid's version and presents a significant variant in the description of Eurydice's death.

The subject of Book IV is the art of beekeeping. In the course of the treatise Virgil introduces the story of the shepherd Aristaeus, son of Apollo and the river-nymph Cyrene, who has lost all his bees through famine and disease. His mother advises Aristaeus to capture and bind the ever-changing deity Proteus to discover why his bees have died. Proteus reveals to Aristaeus that "The anger that pursues you is divine,/Grievous the sin you pay for. Piteous Orpheus/It is that seeks to invoke this penalty/Against you—did the Fates not interpose—/Far less than you deserve, for bitter anguish/At the sundering of his wife. You were the cause:/To escape from your embrace across a stream/Headlong she fled, nor did the poor doomed girl/Notice before her feet, deep in the grass/The watcher on the bank, a monstrous serpent." (Ovid simply states: "as the bride went walking/Across the lawn, attended by her naiads,/A serpent bit her ankle, and she was gone.")[59]

Cyrene interprets Proteus' words to Aristaeus: "the whole source of the plague/Lies in this story; this it is that caused/The nymphs with whom she used to dance

---

[57] "Ie voudrois que lon ne fit point les Airs que le subiet ne fust parfaict, & les entrées reiglées, afin que l'on les fist à propos, & suivant les actions que les danseurs doivent faire & representer": M. de St. Hubert, *La maniere de composer et faire reussir les ballets* (Paris: François Targa, 1641/Geneva: Minkoff, 1993), 11.

[58] "On a d'ailleurs un peu exagéré le rôle des Barberini en cette affaire": Prunières, 106, n. 3.

[59] Ovid, *Metamorphoses*, trans. Rolfe Humphries (Bloomington: Indiana University Press, 1955), 10, 2:1–111; 11, 2:1–84.

her rounds/In the high woods to send this wretched blight/Upon your bees. You as suppliant/Must sue with gifts for peace and venerate/Those not unyielding spirits of the forest,/For they will grant you pardon as you pray/And will forget their anger." Aristaeus sacrifices four bulls and four heifers. On the ninth day after the sacrifice he returns to the grove, to witness a miracle: ". . . throughout the putrid flesh/Of the oxen's innards bees are buzzing, swarming,/Bursting from holes in the flanks, and trailing off/In a huge cloud to mass at the top of a tree/And hang in clusters from the sagging branches."[60]

The story of Aristaeus as recounted by Virgil thus becomes a kind of pre-Prologue and a post-Epilogue to Buti's reworking of the Orpheus myth. The whole story of Orpheus and Eurydice is encapsulated in the context of the loss of a flock of bees and its eventual regeneration. With Francesco and Taddeo Barberini (Antonio was not present) and Anna Colonna prominently on display in the audience of *L'Orfeo*, the opera augured not only explicitly the victory of the French forces but implicitly the eventual return of the Barberini.

---

[60] Virgil, *The Georgics*, trans. L. P. Wilkinson (New York: Viking Penguin, 1982), 4, 2:452–527.

Appendix

BIBLIOTECA APOSTOLICA VATICANA MS. BARB. LAT. 4059[61]

[fol. 131] / L'Orfeo / Personaggi dell'opera / La Vittoria [S]—s.r Atto Melani / Giove [T]—S. Giacomo Mellani fr[at]ello / Giunone [MS]—s.a Margherita Costa Venere [S]—s.a Caterina Martinij fiorentina / Amore [S]—Domenichino Milanese / Le Gratie trè [SSS] / Il. s.r Marc'Antonio d'Este / Il s.r Dom[eni]co del med[esi]mo / Un Paggio di Cappella / Apollo [A]—Il s.r Mazzante fiorentino / Imeneo [S]—Il S.r Marc'Antonio d'Este

Le Parche trè le med[esi]me Gratie / Plutone [B]—S.r D. Alessandro fiorentino / Proserpina [S]—s.r Dom[eni]co d'Este / Caronte [B]—s.r Venantio [Leopardi] d'Este Bacco [S]—s.r Stefano di Bentivoglio / La Gelosia [A]—s.r Panfilo / Il sospetto—s.r Marc'Antonio d'Este / Orfeo [S]—s.r Atto Melani / Aristeo fig[li]o di Bacco Amante no[n] gradito d'Euridice [S] / Marc'Antonio Pasqualini [fol. 131v] Satiro confidente d'Aristeo [B]—s.r Gio: Batt[ist]a Milanese / Euridice [S]—s.ra Checca Costa / Endimione P[ad]re d'Euridice [B]—s.r Stefano di Bentivoglio / L'Augurre [B]—s.r D. Alessandro / Momo [T]—s.r Napolione / Venere tramuta in vecchia [T] s.r Fran[ces]co Venetiano / Armate francese—60. in scena / Choro di soldati assalitori—16. / Choro di soldati difensori—8. / Choro di Ninfe, e Pastori cantanti, e ballanti—24. / Choro d'Imenei trà Cantori, e ballarini 24. / Choro di Driadi 6. cantanti, e 24 ballanti—30. / Choro Infernale—10. Choro di Baccante trà cantanti, e ballanti 24. / Choro Celeste Tutti [.]

*   *   *   *

Avanti all'aprir' della Scena fù fatta una sinfonia con 20. Viole, 4 Cimbali, 4. Tiorbe e 4. Violini; 2. Liuti, e 2. Chitarre, che sonavano tutti.

Alzate le tende à suono di 4. Trombette, che sonavano à guerra, e tamburri, fù vista l'Armata francese, che combattevano una Città forte, e si vidde bellissimi abbattim[en]ti. Il Choro, che formava un'squadrone fermo cantava da guerra e l'altro Choro cantava alla difesa finalm[en]te con un'Ariete buttato à terra un'muro entrò gridando Vittoria Vittoria parte dell'Armata, e piantorno sopra i merli della [fol. 132] fortezza presa li standardi Reali di francia al grido della Vittoria comparve essa Vittoria nel Cielo sopra un' bellissimo Carro, tutto pieno di trofei, che fece il Prologo, accenando

---

[61] Barb. lat. 4059 appears by kind permission of the Biblioteca Apostolica Vaticana: S = soprano; MS = mezzo soprano; A = alto ; T = tenor; B = bass.

l'opera, e disse alcune lodi del Rè, e della Regina in 4. Strofe, p[er] ogn'una c'era il ritornello delle 20. Viole col resto degl'altri strom[en]ti, finite le d[ett]e 4. Strofe cantorno tutti gl'applausi al Rè, et à suon di canzonetta, che facevano le trombette si ritirò l'essercito, trasmutandosi la scena da luogo di Guerra in una bella Campagna boschereccia. [Ménestrier, 196: ". . . des Vers à l'honneur des Armes du Roi, & de la sage conduite de la Reine sa Mere. Ce Prologue n'étoit pas de l'action d'Orphée, il faisoit une piece detachée, ce que les Italiens se sont permis assez souvent en ces representations . . ."].

*   *   *   *

Atto P[rim]o Scena p[ri]ma / Aug[ur]re, Endimi[o]ni, Euridice, Nutrice, e Choro dall'Aug[ur]i escono p[er] fare augurare alle felici nozze d'Euridice, e fanno molte cerimonie usate dagl'Antichi, veggono p[er] aria due Tortorelle, che gli Avoltoij le p[er]seguitava. Si piglia p[er] cattivo Aug[uri]o, mà Euridice dice, che no[n] lo stima, perche sia certa dell'Amore del suo Orfeo, e così l'Aug[ur]re parte col suo Choro, et essa resta col P[ad]re, e colla Nutrice cantando una Canzona à trè in questo. [Ménestrier, 196: "on fit voir dés la premiere Scene un Bocage, dont l'étenduë & la profondeur sembloit surpasser plus de cent fois le Theatre, & il parut dans ce Bocage un Augure assis dans sa chaire . . ."].

2.a Scena / Viene Orfeo tutto lieto, e fà colla sposa parole di tenerezza, e d'amore, Cantano insieme li dui Amanti [Ménestrier, 197: "chantant d'une maniere si gaye qu'ils témoignoient, & par leur chant & par la Danse dont ils l'accompagnerent . . ."] il P[ad]re intennerito da si fervente amore anch'egli canta p[er] allegrezza una Canzona, e partono.

3.a Scena / Aristeo, e'l Satiro. / Aristeo si duole del maritaggio della sua amata Euridice con'Orfeo, e poi canta una Canzona sopra la Gelosia, il Satiro [Ménestrier, 197: "dansant avec ses pieds de Bouc"] ne risponde [fol. 132v] una in contrario, finalm[en]te invoca l'aiuto di Venere, amica di Bacco suo p[ad]re, e la vede venire dal Cielo in una machina assai bella [Ménestrier, 198: "dans un nuage avec Cupidon son Fils, les Graces, & une troupe de petits Amours qui chantoient les loüanges de cette Désse, & de son Fils"].

4.[a] Scena / Venere, Amore, e le Gratie con 6. altri Amoretti intorno, calata giù vede Aristeo cosi addolorato, lo consola, e dice volerlo aiutare, e p[er] far' meglio sarebbe andata al tempio di Proteo à trasmutarsi in Vecchia p[er] poter cosi indurre Eur[idi]ce alla corrispondenza del suo Amore, comanda alle Gratie, che abbelliscano Aristeo, acciò possa più piacere all'Amata, e parte.

5.a Scena / Le Gratie cantando abbelliscono Aristeo con molte galanterie à polvere d'odori, et accomodano [Ménestrier, 198–99: "se mettant à le friser, chanterent la difference qu'il y avoit entre la propreté & la negligence"], parte p[er] trovar' Venere.

6.a Scena / Il Satiro desideroso anch'esso d'essere abbellito dalle gratie si mette à sedere, e quelle ridendo li fanno mille burle [Ménestrier, 199: "elles lui firent mille maux en peignant rudement sa chevelure mêlé & toute herissée"] finalm[en]te gli d[ice] che no[n] si ridano, p[er]che lui hà havuto di gra[n] fortuna in amore p[er]che lui essendo ricco hà provato, che colle Donne può più assai l'interesse, che l'amore; esse gli danno delle mentite, li tirano li Capelli, e l'infarinano tutto il Viso colla polvere d'odore[;] esso si lamenta, che l'hanno avuto à cercare, gli corre appresso, fuggono, e finisce la scena.

7.a Scena / Si muta la scena in un' Portico con un' gra[n] Tempio [Ménestrier, 199: "Cependant la Perspective s'étant ouverte, fit voir une table superbement servie"], ove si celebrano le nozze d'Orfeo[;] escano in vista del Popolo à sedere in una bella, e ricca mensa [fol. 133] Himeneo, Giunone, Apollo, Endimione, Euridice, Orfeo, Choro di Ninfe, e Pastori, che cantano, Choro d'Imenei colle faci in mano, che fecero una belliss[im]a danza, e mentre si attendeva à far brindisi, l'un, e l'altro, soprevenne Momo Dio della Maldicenza, et lamenta, che senza lui si facciono le feste, dicendoli, che no[n] si può stare allegram[en]te se n[on] si dice male di qualch'uno. Giunone li dice, che si metta à sedere, e dica qualche cosa, fà una invettiva contra la gra[n] m[ad]re Natura, che à formar il Sole, [et] le stelle habbia sprecato tant'oro, e tante gemme, e gl'avanzi habbia nascosto nel profondo della terra, tutto cio p[er] vedere in povertà i miseri mortali; Apollo gli dice, che haverebbe risposto à questo, mà che all'hora no[n] era tempo, incaricò Momo, che cantasse una canzona, et egli incontinente ne disse una sopra il pigliar moglie, dicendo, che s'è brutta e gra[n] miseria, e s'è bella e gra[n] pericolo, e cosi uno ò la pigli, ò no[n] la pigli d'ogni modo se ne pente. Seguita il ballo, in q[ue]sto si smorzano tutte le faci à gl'Imenei, si prende p[er] cattivo Augurio, invocano gl'aiuti dei Dei, e partono con sinfonia [Ménestrier, 199: "Des Nymphes & des Bergeres danserent un Ballet autour de la table, mais les torches qu'ils portoient pour celebrer cet Hymené s'étant éteintes, . . . & les Bergeres étonées quittant leur danse, reclamerent par un Hymne plein de tendresse, les secours des Divinites"].

Atto 2.o Scena P[rim]a / Venere, et Aristeo / Si muta la scena in una Città piena di belli Palazzi [Ménestrier, 199–200: "une superbe decoration de Palais, où l'on pouvoit remarquer toutes les beautez de l'Architecture"] Venere cangiata in vecchia con Aristeo discorrono de suoi amori, in questo vede d'uscire Euridice colla Nutrice, e p[er] no[n] mostrar' d'attenderle, finge Aristeo d'apprendere dalla Vecchia una Canzona sopra la speranza[.]

[fol. 133] 2.a Scena / Euridice in uscir' si duole d'incontrarsi con Aristeo, che p[er] forza la vuole amare, la Vecchia se'l avvicina, la và ripigliando con' domandarle dove vadi così mesta, lei li risponde, et havendo havuto sinistri auguri nelle sue nozze, andava al Tempio p[er] impetrar mercede dagli Dei, risponde la vecchia, che lei poteva dare il remedio, et era, che volendo cangiare augurio cangiasse marito, lei si ammira di questo, e p[er] autenticare la fermezza dell'amor'suo canta una assai bella canzona d'encomij delle lodi di Orfeo; Aristeo si attrista in sentire lodar tanto il suo rivale, mà la vecchia ripiglia, che sono altri visi no[n] men belli di Orfeo, e li mostra Aristeo, ch'essa no[n] vuol vedere, nè sentire; ma' tanto pregato, e dalla vecchia, e dalla Nutrice, finalm[en]te s'induce à sentire i suoi lamenti, et essa compassionando il suo stato, però no[n] può darsi rimedio, che l'honor suo no'l p[er]mette, ripiglia la vecchia, che l'honore è una lisca ritrovata p[er] avantaggio delle Donne, ma rifiutato da Euridice si bugiarda ritrovata, canta le lodi dell'honore, e la fermezza della sua fede, e se ne và, resta p[er] un'poco la nutrice che intennerita conforta Aristeo, e l'essorta alla costanza p[er]che chi dura la vince, li canta p[er] ammaestram[en]to una canzona sopra la speranza, e se ne và.

[fol. 134] 3.a Scena / Il Satiro, che in disparte haveva inteso tutto il discorso, et haveva inteso, che Euridice p[er] rallegrarsi voleva fare una danza nel Giardino del sole disse che tante ciarle, andiamo, e rubbamela à forza, Aristeo s'induce, e partono.

4.a Scena / Momo, Amor, Gionone, Apollo / Momo canta le lamentat[io]ni, che tutti universalm[en]te facevano della tirannia d'amor, e però l'essortava à cangiar' maniere, altrim[en]te in poco tempo suo Regno si giocarebbe di Spadone, esce Gionone, e fà una simile lamentat[io]ne in nome delle donne; Apollo scende, e fa altre lament[atio]ni, Amore risponde à tutti, e sincera se stesso, anzi p[er] far vedere, che è il contrario di quello, che dicono racconta il desiderio, che hà Venere sua m[ad]re di tradire orfeo, et ingannare Euridice, mà che lui no[n] farebbe un'simil torto à coppia d'amanti si fedele, e che più tosto ingannerà sua m[ad]re, che questi, essi avertati [?] da quella promessa cantano insieme le lodi d'Amore, e partono[.]

5.a Scena / Resta Amore, dolendosi, che le gratie tardino tanto di condurre Orfeo si come l'haveva imposto[,] in questo li vede venire / Amore, Orfeo, le Gratie / Le Gratie conducendo Orfeo lo pregano, che voglia cantare, egli si scusa, che p[er] star malinconico, e p[er] li cattivi aug[u]ri che li sovrastavano, haveva più voglia di piangere, che di cantare, in questo si fà avanti Amore, è canta, essortandolo à stare allegram[en]te, che no[n] sempre quando tuona, saetta, lo consola, disco-prendoli la mala invent[io]ne di Venere [fol. 134v] e che per farli del male si era tramutata in Vecchia, mà che esso sarebbe stato suo fautore, e protectore, e che no[n] dubitasse, e che p[er] ciò andasse a palesare ad Euridice il tutto, egli lo ring[razi]a, e parte.

7.a Scena [*sic*] / In questo sopragiunse Venere, e le Gratie fanno la spia disco-
prendo à Venere tutto il trattato d'Amore, quel che era passato con'Orfeo, Venere in
collera vuol' battere Amore, che di lei si burla, fanno un'pezzo di girata; finalm[en]te
Amore prende un'Volo, e fugge in Cielo[.]

8.a Scena / Endimione, Augure, e suo Choro [Ménestrier, 201: "Un Temple ayant
changé tout d'un coup la face du Theatre"], che vanno p[er] fare un'sacrificio à Venere
p[er] placarla dall'ira contro Orfeo, et Euridice s'incontrano in questo Giovane [recte:
Giunone], che li dissuade di far' sacrificio à Venere, atteso che Amore haveva pro-
messo à Momo, ad Apollo, et à lei di esser favorevole ad Orfeo, et ad Euridice, mà
che in cambio facessero sacrifitio à lei, come Dea delle nozze, e canta le sue proprie
lodi, e partono.

9.a Scena / Euridice, La Nutrice, e Choro di Ninfe. Si muta la scena in un'
Giardino [Ménestrier, 202: "La Scene changea aussitôt de face"]. Vengono p[er] fare
la destinata danza, mà p[er]ch'era troppo per tempo mettersi sotto una verdura p[er]
riposarsi, le ninfe cantano una Canzona da dormire.

x.a Scena / In questo vedete venire le Driadi, si sveglia, si dà principio alla
danza, che fù una sarabanda belliss[i]ma, cantandosi le lodi d'Amore, e sua potenza
[Ménestrier, 202: "Les Dryades arrivées l'éveillerent, & danserent avec des Castag-
netes un ballet qu'Euridice trouva si agreable qu'elle s'y mêla avec ses Nymphes"].

[fol. 135] xi.a Scena / Li med[esi]mi, Aristeo, e satiro, che nella danza vengono
p[er] rapire Euridice, la quale fugge, et in questo un'serpente velenoso se gli avven-
tacchia nella gamba; la morde, che p[er] ciò ne more; Aristeo, come p[er] aiutarla,
ella ciò nega, anzi li commanda, che se ne reparta, fà un'lamento in disperat[io]ne,
e parte, ella intanto sentendosi estremo dolore chiama in soccorso Apollo Dio della
medicina, e P[ad]re del suo sposo, và tuttavia mancando, desidera di vedere Orfeo
prima di morire, inviano p[er] esso, mà no[n] giunge à tempo, poiche il veleno giunto
al Cuore, la priva di vita, le ninfe fanno un'doloroso pianto[.]

12.[a] Scena / S'apre il Cielo, vedesi il Palazzo del Sole [Ménestrier, 202–03: "Le
Palais du Soleil qui faisoit alors la decoration du Theatre"], et esso sopra il Zodiaco,
che girando p[er] lo Cielo vuol' discendere p[er] venire à soccorrere Euridice, mà
non giunge in tempo, poiche la vede già morta, e la terra si apriva p[er] riceverla,
piange la sua morte, e promette, che Orfeo andarà a recuperare nell'Inferno, le Ninfe
si levano di testa tutte le loro Ghirlande, che mettono sopra il corpo d'Euridice, che
la terra inghiottisce, finisce l'atto piangendo.

Atto 3.o Scena p[ri]ma / Si muta la scena in Paese horrido [Ménestrier, 203:
"un desert affreux, des cavernes, & des rochers avec un antre en forme d'allée, au
bout desquels à travers l'obscurité, se découvroit un peu de jour"] / Orfeo fà doloroso

lamento della morte della sua Sposa, e si duole, che le lagrime no[n] siano in assai mag[gio]re copia, sente in q[u]esto un'canto stravagante[,] s'avvicina, e vede le Parche, alle quali [fol. 135v] prega, che voglino riattacare il filo della vita d'Euridice[;] esse si scusano, che ciò no[n] possono fare, lui dice, che esse no[n] sanno la forza del suo canto congionto col suono della sua lira, e mettendosi à cantare, et a suonare inteneriscono le Parche, che l'essortano, che scenda all'Inferno, che sicuram[en]te otterà l'amata sposa[;] esse l'insegnano la strada[.]

2.a Scena / Aug[ur]i suo Choro End[imion]e et Nutrice. / Piangono insieme la morte d'Euridice, e la perdita d'Orfeo, che no[n] sanno, che ne sia, vanno p[er] invocare l'aiuto del Cielo.

3.a Scena / Aristeo fà un'gra[n] lamento p[er] la morte d'Euridice, in questo sente tremar' la terra, oscurarsi il giorno, s'apre il terreno, e sorge l'ombra d'Euridice infuriata, a sgridarlo della sua temerità, che habbia tentato di voler' macchiare la sua purità, lui atterito, trema, invoca aiuto, ella se l'avventa p[er] volerlo ammazzare, si pente, et acciò resti al Mondo p[er] essempio di tanto delitto lo delitto [sic] lo p[er]cuote in testa con un'serpente, e li fà p[er]dere il senno, e sparisce l'ombra[.]

4.a Scena / Momo, e il satiro escono cantando una Canzona burlesca in biasimo della malinconia, veggono Aristeo, che corre in quà, et in là furioso, l'osservano, e finalm[en]te si accorgono essere divenuto matto, fà infinite pazzie, e stravaganze, s'imagina d'essere Decaulioni, getta delle pietre, vede uscire il satiro, e Momo, e crede haver prodotto [fol. 136] nuova gente, s'imagina poi, che il satiro Euridice sia, e li canta una assai amorosa Canzona, e poi dato in fierezza ad uno gli fà fare il suon' colla bocca della tromba, all'altro del tamburro, e canta una Canzona da Guerra, e finita, và à precipitarsi, e more [Ménestrier, 203: "[Euridice] le poursuivit un serpent à la main, & le fit devenir furieux, son chant exprimant sa fureur, remplit de terreur la quatriéme Scene"].

5.a Scena / Giunone invia Gelosia, e'l sospetto à suggerire à Proserpina, che prova di far rendere Euridice ad Orfeo, altrim[en]te aspetti da Plutone mille torti al letto maritale, dandogli l'essempio di Giove, esse partono, in questo vede venire Venere tutta allegra, che cantando della Vittoria havuta contro Giunone p[er] haver' fatto morire Euridice, s'era in' un'med[esi]mo tempo vendicato del sole, che scop[er]se già l'amori suoi con Marte. Giunone la sgrida, contrastano insieme, e partono una di quà, et l'altra di là.

7.a Scena [sic] / Si è muta la Scena in Inferno. / La Gelosia, e il Sospetto, entrano nell'Inferno, e si meravigliano di vedere quella Reggia vota d'habitatori, un'piccolo demonietto gli dice, che tutti sono accorsi à veder un'huomo vivente, ch'era entrato là, in questo viene Proserpina cantando la felicità, che ella prova in quel luogo infernale mercè dell'amore, con che amava et era riamata da Plutone, mà la Gelosia incomincia à suggerire le passioni sue, il Sospetto ancora p[er] ritrovarsi ivi Euridice, l'esortano à farsi, che Plutone la mandi fuori dell'Inferno, ella promette.

8.a Scena / In questo viene Plutone sgridando Caronte p[er]che hà introdotto Orfeo nell'Inferno, egli si scusa, che alla forza del suo dolciss[im]o canto no[n] hà potuto [fol. 136v] resistere; Proserpina lo prega à voler' sentire si dolce armonia[;] Tutto il Choro prega p[er] il med[esi]mo[;] Plutone, al fine, comanda à Caronte, che l'introduca avanti al suo cospetto.

9.a Scena / Viene Orfeo cantando, e pregando Plutone à renderli la sua amata Euridice, Plutone intenerito dalla suavita del suo canto, e della sua lira, la quale era dadentro sonata con 12 viole, che faceva una boniss[i]ma armonia li concede l'amata, però con leggi, che p[er] entro l'inferno no[n] se habbi ma à voltare indietro à mirarla, Orfeo canta in ringratiam[en]to, et Euridice comparve, e canta le sue felicità e la fede del suo marito; e partono; Plutone, che vede tutto l'inferno in allegria comanda, che si facci una danza, la quale fù bell[issi]ma, e stravagan[tissi]ma, p[er]che comparve p[ri]ma quattro dragoni, con quattro Arpie, alla fine della loro danza lasciorno ott'ova, dalle quale uscirno otto diavoletti; et ballorno, e l'Arpie, e li draghi volorno e poi uscirno 4. Lumaconi con 4. fastasme, e dalli fantasme uscirno 4. lanternoni, e poi uscirno 4. Civettoni, e li diavoli fecero la caccia con belliss[i]me, è stravagant[issi]me mutanze, e fini, fù sonato il Ballo da Piferi, e cornetti, e cornamuse [Ménestrier, 204: "Un ballet de tous les Monstres d'Enfer, sous cent figures extravagantes de Hiboux, de Bucentaures, de Harpyes, & d'autres bêtes égayerent cette Scene"].

x.a Scena / Caronte viene à dar' nuova à Plutone, che Orfeo haveva rotta la legge, e p[er]ciò gl'havevano ritolta Euridice, la quale viene piangendo[.]

xi.a Scena / Euridice fà un'gra[n] Lamento avanti à Plutone, il quale comanda che sia menata a'i Campi Elitij ad esser consolata[.]

[fol. 137] xii.a Scena. / Si muta la scena in un'amena Campagna, e bella boscareccia col' mare assai bello / Viene Orfeo solo, facendo un'gra[n] lamento, e si vidde venire al suo dolciss[i]mo canto gl'Alberi, che camminano, i scogli, che si movevano, e vennero tutti gl'animali ad ascoltarlo; Leoni, Tigri, Pantere, Orsi, Lupi, Cervi, Struzzi, Pavoni, et altri Ucelli, alla fine dice di voler' andare à morire à parte [Ménestrier, 204: "[fait] part de sa douleur aux arbres & aux animaux qui dansent au son de sa Lyre"].

xiii.a Scena / Viene Bacco col suo Choro cantando, e ballando, e stando alle-gram[en]te, in questo comparve Venere dal mare gridando Vendetta, p[er]che haveva inteso dal Sospetto, che Euridice era tornata al Mondo, Persuade Bacco, che anch'egli voglia vendicarsi della morte di Aristeo suo fig[l]io precipitato per cagione di Euridice, e d'Orfeo; Bacco comanda alle Baccante, che ammazzino Orfeo, et acciò siano più infuriate, comanda, che s'imbriachono, e parte piangendo con Venere; Le baccante fanno una belliss[i]ma danza bevendo, e partono.

Scena ultima / Cala una gran machina dentro Giove, con'tutti li Dei, et un'gra[n] Choro. Giove comanda, che sia immortalata la lira d'Orfeo, et egli habbia luogo nel Cielo, tutto il Choro canta, e fenisce [Ménestrier, 205: "[Jupiter] voulut que sa Lyre fit une constellation dans le firmament, sur quoi tout le Theatre retentit d'un Hymne melodieux pour exprimer que la vertu parfaite se doit entierement détacher de la terre & n'attendre sa recompense que du Ciel. C'est ainsi que l'on fit sur la fin de cette piece une instruction morale de ce divertissement"].

[fol. 137v] Il giorno seguente nell'istesso Teatro / La scena fù convertita in una gra[n] sala tutta ben'dipinta, e messa in oro con'dodici lampadari di Christallo di Monte, faceva la più bella vista, che giàmai si sia veduta, e calò una machina, dove ci erano à sonare 24. Violini, andorno da 30, ò 40 Dame; ò più tosto Dee, che tale parevano, si p[er] la bellezza, si anche p[er] gl'ornam[en]ti di Gioie inestimabili; Madamisella d'Orleans sola portava indosso p[er] trè milioni di Gioie, trà diamanti, e p[er]le; erano però della Regina, e l'altre erano parim[en]te tutte coperte di Diamanti, io credo, che in tutto il resto d'Europa no[n] vi sia altretanto, andorno con'un Ponte dentro della bella Sala, e vi andorno parim[en]ti altretanti cavalieri, che no[n] erano men adornati delle Donne poiche un'Cav[alie]re haveva nel Cappello una gran'treccia di grosse p[er]le, e il vestito tutto ricamato di p[er]le disse valer 200. mila scudi, insomma le richezze sono inesplicabili, si danzò tutta la notte, danzo il rè, e P[ri]n[ci]pe di Gales, e'l P[ri]n[ci]pe Roberto Palatino

Questa relat[io]ne scritta in fretta la compatiscano.

Barberini Redux: The Return to Rome and the Pamphilj Wedding

... a most cutting reply, that Bernini gave to a Personage who was highly-placed, and unfriendly to the House of Barberini. He had figured on the urn of [the pope's] Sepulcher here and there some Bees, which gracefully alluded to Urban's arms: the Personage referred to looked at it, and turning to the Cavaliere in the presence of others, said with a smile, *Sir Cavaliere, Your Lordship wished with the placement of these Bees here, and there, to show the dispersion of the House of Barberini* (at that time the members of the House were displeased with the Pope, and had retired to France) to which without a moment's hesitation Bernini answered, *Your Lordship well knows, that bees when they have been scattered return to swarm at the sound of a Bell*, meaning the great Bell of the Campidoglio, which sounds after the death of each pope.

Domenico Bernini, Vita del Cavalier Gio. Lorenzo Bernino

During the exile of the Barberini at the French court the family household machinery in Rome continued to function. In March of 1646 Cardinal Antonio ordered from Aix the payment of significant sums to his household musicians Luigi Rossi and Marc'Antonio Pasqualini in connection with the preparations for *L'Orfeo* (see Chapter 6). Despite Cardinal Francesco's absence, the 1646 Quarantore was celebrated in his titular church of San Lorenzo in Damaso and was visited by the pope. Money was remitted to Cardinal Antonio for travel expenses and such extraordinary items as the funeral of Don Taddeo in 1647 (see Chapter 9).

Innocent X's price for the restitution of Barberini family's possessions, their reintegration into their privileges and offices, and the cancelling of lawsuits against them was their departure from the French court for the papal territory of Avignon and a letter of submission. In September of 1646 the pope issued a motuproprio declaring the Barberini innocent of all the accusations against them and reinstating them in their offices and dignities. In mid-November he received letters from the Barberini cardinals announcing their presence in Avignon.

At the beginning of 1647 Camillo Pamphilj renounced the red hat that his uncle had bestowed on him two months after his election, in order to marry a double heiress: Olimpia Aldobrandini, in her own right princess of Rossano, and widow of Paolo Borghese.[1] Innocent and his sister-in-law Donna Olimpia (who had hoped for a marriage with the more pliable Lucrezia Barberini) expressed their disapproval by boycotting the ceremony, and the newly-married couple was forbidden to return to Rome. It was not unheard-of for an unordained cardinal-deacon to renounce the *galero* to marry for dynastic reasons, as Ferdinando Gonzaga had done in 1615 and Maurizio of Savoy in 1642, but the last cardinal-nephew to resign his dignity had been Cesare Borgia. In October Innocent bowed to the will of Donna Olimpia by making her fifteen-year-old nephew, Francesco Maidalchini, a cardinal, in place of the disgraced Camillo.

On 27 February 1648 Cardinal Francesco Barberini returned to Rome, ostensibly sent by the king of France (i.e. Mazarin) to treat of "negotii gravissimi" with Innocent X, who seemed pleased at Francesco's return. When he had left, the cardinal had blond hair; after his two years of exile he came back "hoary and white," with "mustaches, long hair and a big collar in the French style," where previously he had been "shaved like a cleric of the Oratorio."[2] By the end of the year Francesco was reintegrated into the life of papal Rome, appearing prominently with the French ambassador at the celebrations for the election of the new king of Poland.

The Treaty of Westphalia, signed on 24 October 1648, finally ended the Thirty Years' War, but the exclusion of the papal representative, Fabio Chigi, from any significant participation in the deliberations also marked the final failure of Urban VIII's attempts to make the papacy the fulcrum of European power. The treaty was denounced impotently by Innocent X in the bull *Zelo Domus Dei* as "null, void, invalid, iniquitous, unjust, damnable, reprobate, empty, void of meaning and effect for all time."[3]

---

[1] On her musical patronage see Alexander Silbiger, "Michelangelo Rossi and His *Toccate e Correnti*," *Journal of the American Musicological Society* 36 (1983): 18–38, esp. 25–26.

[2] Gigli, 522: "Tornò il Card. Barberino tutto bianco, et canuto, dove che quando partì di Roma era di pelo biondo"; Costantini, Faz3i: "Lunedì mattina il Papa tenne concistoro ove concorse tutta Roma per vedere il cardinal Francesco con la zazzera francese, che prima andava raso come un chierico dell'Oratorio"; Ameyden: "il ritratto del Cardinale Barberino in stampa che si vende per le botteghe con li mostacci, zazzera e collarone alla francese."

[3] Quoted in C. V. Wedgwood, *The Thirty Years' War* (London: Jonathan Cape, 1938), 526.

The following February saw Mazarin embroiled in the first Fronde. France and Spain continued to battle on Italian soil, with the papacy accused of clandestine support for Spain.

The long story of the Wars of Castro against the Farnese dukes of Parma ended in 1649, when the pope conquered the city and ordered it razed to the ground. A column was erected on the spot with the legend, "Hic fuit Castrum" ("Here stood Castro"). (One wonders why the Barberini have been immortalized as worse than barbarians — "Quod non fecerunt barbari fecerunt Barberini" — for removing some bronze from the porch of the Pantheon while Innocent X Pamphilj's destruction of an entire city has passed unreproached.)

At the end of 1649 the Holy Year was ushered in by the festive ringing of the Roman church bells three times a day, culminating on Christmas Eve in the opening of the Holy Doors in the four major basilicas. (Since Cardinal Antonio Barberini was still in France, the Holy Door of Santa Maria Maggiore, of which he was archpriest, was opened by the young Cardinal Francesco Maidalchini, who made a mess of the ceremony.) Because of the Holy Year, the usual Carnival festivities were cancelled, although a few "Comedie" were presented in private palaces or outside the city. Instead, major relics, such as the Cathedra Petri, the Veronicle, the Holy Lance, and relics of the True Cross, were exposed in St. Peter's and other churches.

The traditional Quarantore celebrations for the Holy Year were particularly splendid, including ones in Carlo Rainaldi's Santa Maria in Campitelli and the Oratorio of the Collegio Romano. On 24 February (Giovedì Grasso, as was customary) in his basilica of San Lorenzo in Damaso Cardinal Francesco presented a Quarantore designed by Pietro da Cortona (fig. 7.1). The diarist Gigli reported that "the high altar was adorned with painted and gilded wooden architecture, and a great quantity of lighted flares of white wax."[4] Giovanni Simone Ruggieri's published diary of the Holy Year provides a more detailed description:

> . . . the Most Eminent Signor Cardinal Francesco Barberini Vice-Chancellor surpassed expectations, and almost performed the impossible, having had erected by the famous Painter named Pietro da Cortona, a superb, and magnificent structure, in the form of a Monstrance [Custodia], that all silvered rose above the High Altar in proportioned length, and width to fill all the empty space of the Tribune, and the Chapter Choir of that

---

[4] Gigli, 579; BAV, AB, Comp. 71.

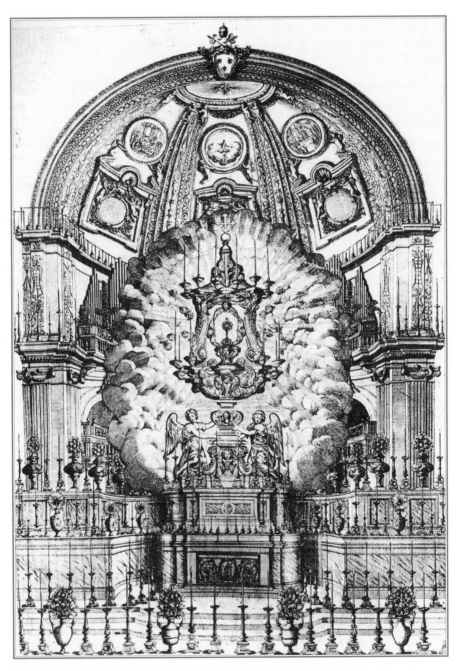

FIG. 7.1   Pietro da Cortona, *Quarantore in S. Lorenzo in Damaso, 1650*
(Rome, I.N.G.)

Church, surrounded by thick, and well placed clouds with an
infinity of candles, and of lights. . . .[5]

On 27 February Quarantore were celebrated in St. John Lateran, Santa Maria
Maggiore, and the Gesù. The Jesuits presented a magnificent apparato, also designed
by Rainaldi, depicting the temple of Solomon, with *prospettive* by Giovan Maria Mariani
and animated figures by Domenico Rainaldi.[6]

On 14 April, Maundy Thursday, Cardinal Francesco Barberini sang mass in
the Cappella Sistina in the presence of the pope. After mass he carried the sacrament
in procession through the Sala Regia to the Easter sepulcher in the Cappella Paolina.
The sepulcher was designed by Giovanni Maria di Bitonto, perhaps with the collaboration of Borromini, with whom Bitonto worked on the prospettiva of Palazzo Spada
in 1653–56. The walls were decorated with paintings and inscriptions:

> Above that colonnade, which in the said Hall corresponds in
> a direct line facing the aforesaid door of the Paolina, was a
> fine false Portico of silver with many lights around, which had
> in its recess a papal Tiara surrounded by little clouds with this
> motto. *Regimen ab alto.* Around the Hall at due distances were
> placed many statues in relief on their pedestals all touched up
> with silver, that held large lighted candles in their hands . . .
> The Most Holy Sepulcher . . . simulated a long perspective of
> rich, and well-ordered columns of the Doric order all touched
> up with gold, and shining silver . . .[7]

---

[5] . . . "l'Eminentissimo Signor Cardinal Francesco Barberini Vicecancelliere superò l'espettatione, e quasi
l'impossibile nell'apparato d'esso, havendo fatto erigere dal famoso Pittore chiamato il Signor Pietro da
Cortona un superbo, e magnifico edificio, in forma di Custodia, che sopra l'Altar Maggiore tutta inargentata
sorgeva in proportionata lunghezza, e latitudine ad empire tutto il vacuo della Tribuna, e del Choro del
Capitolo d'essa Chiesa, circondato da spesse, e ben collocate nuvole con infinità di cerij, e di lumi . . .":
Giovanni Simone Ruggieri, *Diario Dell'Anno del Santiß. Giubileo M.D.C.L. Celebrato in Roma Dalla Santita
di N. S. Papa Innocentio .X.* (Rome, 1651), 53–54.

[6] Probably the closest thing to the Quarantore apparati in current use are the Christmas crêches in
Roman churches, often with animated figures and perspective effects.

[7] Ruggieri, 78–79: "Sopra qual colonnato, che in detta Sala viene à corrispondere per dritta linea in
faccia alla sudetta porta della Paolina, era un bel Portico finto d'argento con molti lumi intorno, che
teneva nel suo vacuo un Regno del Papa circo[n]dato da alcune nuvolette con questo motto. *Regimen
ab alto.* Intorno alla Sala nelle loro debite distanze scompartite erano poste molte statue di rilievo sopra
i loro piedistalli tocche tutte d'argento, che tenevano grossi cerij accesi in mano . . . Il Santiss. Sepolcro
. . . [f]ingeva un longo sfondato di ricche, e ben ordinate colonne tocche tutte d'oro, e d'argento strillente
d'ordine dorico . . . ."

During Lent several confraternities presented splendid processions accompanied by music, sometimes polychoral. The renewed favor of Spain under Innocent X was demonstrated by the revival of the traditional procession on Easter Eve—suspended since 1625—to the Spanish national church, San Giacomo degli Spagnoli in Piazza Navona. The entire Piazza, including the Pamphilj palace and Bernini's unfinished Fountain of the Rivers, was worked into a magnificent composition of arches, columns, towers, and cupolas, lights and fireworks, with numerous choirs of musicians. A special altar for the sacrament was erected in front of old Sant'Agnese in Agone, the Pamphilj family church (not yet replaced by Borromini's sabotaged design) (fig. 7.2). The Spanish nation spent more than 12,000 scudi on the event.[8]

Fig. 7.2   Carlo Rainaldi, Giovanni Paolo Schor et al., *Piazza Navona Decorated for Easter, 1650* engraved by Dominique Barrière (Museo di Roma)

[8] See Francesco Luisi, "S. Giacomo degli Spagnoli e la festa della Resurrezione in piazza Navona," *La cappella musicale nell'età della Controriforma*, ed. Oscar Mischiati and Paolo Russo (Florence: Olschki, 1993), 75–103.

Processions of pilgrims and confraternities from towns such as Velletri and the Barberini fief of Monterotondo, sometimes contending bodily for the right of way, continued throughout the Holy Year; as it moved toward its end more pilgrims arrived from beyond the Alps. In June Cardinal Francesco participated in a procession at the Dominican church of Santa Maria sopra Minerva with eleven other cardinals. On 31 July the Jesuits celebrated the feast of St. Ignatius with "music of importance," and Cardinal Ludovisi blessed Orazio Grassi's gigantic new church (not yet finished) dedicated to the saint. On 4 August the Dominicans celebrated the feast of their patron at Santa Maria sopra Minerva with music for ten choirs and twenty-five cardinals in attendance. On Saturday, 6 August, the Feast of the Transfiguration, the Jesuits celebrated "il primo superbissimo Vespero" sung by members of the Cappella Pontificia and others in Sant'Ignazio. Vespers was intoned by Grassi, who had begun the Galileo affair by his denunciation of the scientist before Urban VIII in 1631 (see Chapter 3).[9]

In September of the Holy Year Innocent raised another nephew, Camillo Astalli, to the cardinalate, conferring on him the Pamphilj name and arms and the rank of cardinal padrone, the same office that Francesco Barberini had held under Urban VIII. Donna Anna Colonna Barberini marked the Anno Santo by opening a monastery dedicated to Maria Regina Coeli on the Lungotevere. Consecrated five years later in 1655, the building was destroyed in the nineteenth century to make way for the prison of the same name (see Chapter 9).

A less edifying aspect of the Holy Year was the rivalry between the Chapter of San Giovanni in Laterano and the Chapter of Santa Maria Maggiore, who wished to recite their own office on a visit to the Lateran. When they arrived in procession the Lateran Chapter did not come out to meet them, but instead strippped the altars of the basilica and put out the lights. When the Chapter of the Lateran came to Santa Maria Maggiore, sweepers were set to work to fill the church with dust; garbage (and possibly worse) was dropped through the holes in the ceiling of the Cappella Paolina where the confetti symbolizing roses was scattered on 6 August, the feast of the Madonna of the Snow and the basilica's Feast of Title (real rose petals now fall). On Christmas Eve the Holy Doors of the four great basilicas were again walled up, to the sound of hymns and psalms and final triumphant salvoes from Castel Sant'Angelo.

With the Holy Year completed, the Romans were able to celebrate Carnival of 1651 with the usual masking and races on the Corso. In June the water was turned on in Bernini's Fountain of the Rivers in Piazza Navona, and at Donna Olimpia's urging the pope issued an edict banning from the piazza the army of *matriciani*, fruit- and

---

[9] Ruggieri, *Diario*, 177–78.

vegetable-sellers, peddlers, booksellers, old-clothes men, "Jews and others," that did business there, except on market days.[10] In September the French ambassador presented a series of banquets in honor of the fourteenth birthday of Louis XIII. In October the Spanish ambassador riposted by celebrating the birth of a daughter to Philip IV of Spain, for which Bernini designed two brilliant fireworks displays: the first represented an elephant and castle (the Infanta of Castile?), the second the Devil in a canebrake (fig. 7.3).[11]

The Polish nation, which had received significant favors under Urban VIII, celebrated a number of notable events. In September of 1651 king Casimir won an important victory over the Turks. In February of 1652 his candidate Marcello Santacroce was named cardinal, along with two future popes, Fabio Chigi and Pietro Ottoboni. In March the birth of a son to the king was celebrated with a mass "con Musica solenissima" attended by Cardinal Francesco Barberini.

After a temporary rift, Innocent X was reconciled with Donna Olimpia through the good offices of his sister, the saintly nun Suora Agata Pamphilj. The pope also effected a greater reconciliation through a Pamphilj-Barberini marriage. (This was also intended to insure Barberini protection for Donna Olimpia after the eventual death of Innocent X.) Gigli reported that the Barberini cardinals had spent all the "great riches" that they had brought to France. (At one point Cardinal Francesco had to borrow 8,000 scudi from the painter Giovanni Francesco Romanelli.)[12] In addition, they had promised Mazarin to marry off Don Taddeo's eldest son Carlo, now Prince of Palestrina and Prince Prefect of Rome, to a niece of Mazarin. With the return of the Barberini to papal favor, Innocent X wished to create the second son, abbate Maffeo, a cardinal in return for the renunciation of the office of Prince Prefect to Innocent's nephew Prince Camillo Pamphilj. The question was settled by a kind of musical chairs: Carlo was made a cardinal and retained the title of Prince Prefect for life; he unwillingly ceded the title of Prince of Palestrina to the twenty-two-year-old Maffeo, who was to marry Olimpia Giustiniani, granddaughter of Donna Olimpia Maidalchini and ten years Maffeo's junior. Maffeo's abbacy was passed to a third brother, Nicolò.

Maffeo Barberini and Olimpia Giustiniani were married on 15 June 1653 by the pope in the Sistine chapel in the presence of the College of Cardinals. The wedding united the Barberini and the Colonna (through the bridegroom's mother, Anna

---

[10] Edict in Gigli II, fig. 42.

[11] See Elena Povoledo, "Gian Lorenzo Bernini, l'elefante e i fuochi artificiali," *Rivista Italiana di Musicologia* 10 (1975): 499–518.

[12] Silvia Bruno, "I Barberini e il loro *entourage* in Francia," *I Barberini e la cultura europea*, 317–30, esp. 321.

FIG. 7.3 Gian Lorenzo Bernini, *Trinità de' Monti, Fireworks for the Birth of a Daughter to Philip IV of Spain*, engraved by François Collignon (Rome, Biblioteca Casanatense)

Colonna) with the Pamphilj, Ludovisi, and Giustiniani families, and with two other papal families in the person of Olimpia Aldobrandini Borghese, wife of Innocent's nephew Camillo Pamphilj, all of whom were represented at the banquet following the ceremony. Little Olimpiuccia was promised a dowry of 100,000 scudi, and the Barberini also received other benefits, such as the remission of the fine of 1,000 scudi a day levied on Cardinal Antonio, who was still in France.[13]

Antonio had hoped that the whole Barberini family would definitively ally itself with the French crown. Francesco repudiated this alliance in insulting terms, refusing the three French candidates for Lucrezia Barberini's hand. On 4 April 1653 Antonio, who felt "despised and ill-treated" wrote bitterly to Francesco from Paris:

> I finally see with wonder and extreme affliction that Your Eminence strains the obligations that you yet confess to these [French] Majesties and you take no thought for the reasons that concern yourself and our House, instead you despise toward me even those [reasons] of humanity, you have thrown yourself into the resolution of leaving this royal service and what is still worse, under the very pretext of ill intentions on the part of this Kingdom; and although similar monstrous actions are capable of justly extinguishing every warm feeling in my heart toward one who behaves and treats me in such a way, nonetheless as one firm in the precepts of our Religion I wish to desire in a Christian way that there may not occur to Your Eminence and to our House the harm that appears too obviously connected with so formidable a change.[14]

Carlo Barberini returned from France to Rome on 22 June 1653, after his brother's wedding had been solemnized. He was immediately made a cardinal, an occasion whose protocol was marred by the refusal of Cardinal de' Medici, dean of the Sacred College, to receive any members of the Barberini family. (The Medici

---

[13] See Chapter 8 on the opera celebrating the rapprochement between the Barberini and Pamphilj families.

[14] Costantini, "Fazione Urbana," h1: "Vedo finalmente con meraviglia et afflitione estrema che V. Em.za sforzati gl'oblighi che pur confessa a queste Maestà e non curate le ragioni che risguardano lei medesima e la nostra Casa, anzi dispreggiate verso di me fin quelle dell'humanità, si è precipitata nella resolutione di ritirarsi da questo real servitio e quel che ancora è peggio, sotto l'istesso preteso de mal intentionati di questo Regno; e benché simili monstruosità habbiano di che estinguere per giustitia ogni buon sentimento nelle mie viscere verso chi si governa e mi tratta di tal sorte, voglio nondimeno come ben fermo ne' dettami della nostra Religione desiderar christianamente che non succedano all'Em.za V. et alla nostra Casa i pregiuditii che paiono troppo evidentemente connessi a si formidabile mutatione."

had been offended by the election of a subject, the Tuscan Maffeo Barberini, to the papacy.) On 12 July 1653, the last member of the family, Cardinal Antonio, returned unexpectedly from France, to the great joy of the populace.[15] He moved back into the Quattro Fontane palace, and when he went to call on the pope, who greeted him warmly, in all the streets where he passed the artisans called out, "Viva Cardinal Antonio!" His ante-chamber, the room where distinguished guests waited for an audience with the padrone of a palace, was filled with the cream of Roman society. The Barberini were so far back in favor that it was rumored that on the death of Innocent, Francesco would be elected pope with the support of the emperor, the king of France, and the Venetians.[16]

The situation was summed up by Galeazzo Gualdo Priorato in a book published in 1678.

> Through the French expeditions against Piombino and Orbetello, the House of Barberini, in short was re-established by the same pope and then by a strange metamorphosis was re-embraced, and the comedy of their wanderings was ended in a close union and family relationship with a great-niece of the same Pope married to Don Maffeo Barberino to whom Don Carlo Prince of Palestrina renounced his primogeniture being promoted to the purple, with which he could honorably remove himself from the obligation in which he found himself to take no other wife than the Contessa Martinozzi niece of Mazarin.[17]

Maffeo Barberini and his new bride (and her grandmother Olimpia Maidalchini) first lived in the Pamphilj palace on Piazza Navona. The departure of the French ambassador allowed them and Cardinal Carlo to join their uncle Antonio in the Quattro

---

[15] Costantini, "Fazione Urbana," h2, Francesco Barberini to Lucrezia Barberini, 12 July 1653: "Stamani è arrivato il Sig. Card. Antonio et doppiamente all'improviso."

[16] Margaret Murata, "A Topography of the Barberini Manuscripts of Music," *I Barberini e la cultura del Seicento*, 375–80, esp. 379, cites an oratorio in the Barberini fondo, the "Predica del Sole," as being written between 1648 and 1655 and documenting the Barberini-Pamphilj rapprochement; a setting of the same text by Marco Marazzoli is found in the Chigi manuscripts.

[17] Costantini, "Fazione Urbana," Faze1: ". . . restò in breve dallo stesso Pontefice ristabilita e poscia con strana metamorfosi riabracciata e terminata la commedia delle loro peripetie in una stretta unione e parentella con una pronepote dello stesso Pontefice maritata a Don Maffeo Barberino a cui Don Carlo Principe di Pellestrina rinunciò la primogenitura essendo promosso alla porpora, col che poté honorata-mente sottrarsi dall'impegno in cui si trovava di non prender altra moglie che la Contessa Martinozzi nepote di Mazazrino."

Fontane palace. The sailing was far from smooth for the ill-matched couple. The child-bride first barricaded herself in her room, then insisted on separate beds for the first month of marriage. Cardinal Antonio, forbidden to mount the arms of France, a foreign sovereign, on his palace because Carlo and Maffeo now ranked as papal nephews, left the Quattro Fontane and rented Palazzo Bonelli in Piazza Santi Apostoli (now the headquarters of the Christian Democratic party), where he displayed three immense shields with the arms of the pope, the king of France, and the Popolo Romano. The pope, who had been ill, went to Viterbo to recuperate, leaving the care of the Congregations and other serious matters to Cardinal Francesco, "whom he wished very well."[18]

The renewed fortunes of the Barberini seemed to mirror the misfortunes of the Pamphilj. In February of 1654 Innocent summarily removed his nephew Cardinal Camillo Pamphilj from his palace and from Rome, despite the intercession of Cardinal Francesco and Cardinal Chigi. Pamphilj's brother and adherents were also banished, his furniture and horses were sold publicly, and sc. 40,000 of his in the Monte di Pietà were sequestered.

Cardinal Francesco's Quarantore celebration in San Lorenzo in Damaso for 1654 was presented with "spesa et apparato straordinario" ("expense and extraordinary apparato") and was again visited by the pope, as in the days of Urban VIII. Innocent also visited the Quarantore in the Gesù designed by Giovan Maria Mariani and presented by the Congregation of the Nobles at the expense of its Prefect, Maffeo Barberini: "one saw a Perspective of reflections, with a great countryside and garden beautifully painted."[19] The apparato depicted a miracle in which a hive of bees constructed a temple of beeswax with an altar to enshrine a particle of a consecrated Host that a peasant had placed there to increase the yield of honey. The combination of the Barberini bees with the Pamphilj dove and fleur-de-lis symbolized the reconciliation and union of the two families.[20]

Prince Maffeo did not neglect the secular side of Carnival. He processed through the streets of Rome enthroned on a high chariot, costumed as the Sun, holding a scepter and the reins of four horses in his hand. At the foot of the throne sat an eagle, the emblem of his wife's family, the Giustiniani, gazing up unharmed at the Sun (fig. 7.4).

---

[18] Gigli, 689: "al quale voleva grandissimo bene."

[19] Ibid., 697: ". . . dove si vedeva una Prospettiva di riflessi, con una gran campagna, et Giardino vagamente dipinto. . . ."

[20] Cf. the *Relazione dell'Apparato . . .* 1654, quoted in Francesca Barberini and Micaela Dickmann, *I Pontefici e gli Anni Santi nella Roma del XVII secolo* (Rome: Bozzi, 2000), 50; Fagiolo dell'Arco, *La festa barocca*, 365–66; Gigli, 697.

Fig. 7.4 *Chariot of the Sun* (Prince Maffeo Barberini in his
Carnival Chariot in 1654) detail of Filippo Lauri–
Filippo Gagliardi, *Giostra delle Caroselle* (1656)
(Museo di Roma). See fig. 8.8

The Four Seasons preceded the chariot, which was accompanied by more than a
hundred servants in cloth of gold liveries who lighted torches as night fell.[21]

As the Barberini continued to rise in Innocent's favor, his own family's fortunes
proportionately declined. Cardinal Camillo Pamphilj was ordered to retake his own
name of Astalli and lost his status as cardinal padrone. The pope also deprived him
of his incomes from abbacies and pensions and the Legateship of Avignon, and many

---

[21] Fagiolo, *La festa barocca*, 366; Gigli, 697–98.

of Astalli's household were questioned and imprisoned. In March of 1654 Innocent raised Giovanni Battista Spada to the cardinalate at the request of Francesco Barberini. (He had promised to name a cardinal chosen by the Barberini, but as usual Francesco and Antonio could not agree—Antonio proposed his nephew Nicolò and Francesco suggested Monsignor Rasponi—and Spada was a compromise.) The pope's health declined, and there was famine and unrest in the city.

In April of 1654 Lucrezia Barberini left Rome for a forced marriage to Francesco I d'Este, duke of Modena, accompanied by her brothers Cardinal Carlo and Prince Maffeo.[22] The pope, recovering from a serious illness, was greatly in favor of the match, which reconciled the Barberini with one of their principal enemies in the War of Castro. Innocent received Lucrezia in a private audience, presented her with splendid gifts and the Golden Rose, and promised to make one of the duke's two sons by a previous marriage a cardinal. Although Innocent had forbidden Anna Colonna to enter the monastery of Discalced Carmelites that she had founded, at Lucrezia's intercession he allowed her mother to establish clausura in the monastery for three nuns and a prioress, further enriching it with new dispensations.[23] The pope's irritation with his own relatives continued: his nephew Camillo and the Princes Ludovisi and Giustiniani, the husbands of Camillo's sisters, were all in disgrace for leaking to the Spanish authorities the pope's designs on the kingdom of Naples.

In May of 1654 a fire broke out in Campo dei Fiori. Driven by the wind, it burned the block of buildings (insula) facing Cardinal Francesco's palace of the Cancelleria. "At this noise there appeared outside his Palace Cardinal Francesco Barberini, with his nephew Cardinal Carlo, and with great diligence and charity he made all those poor people who had fled from the fire enter his Palace, and had them clothed . . . and then having dressed them anew he gave each of them 200 scudi." The Cardinal

---

[22] Lucrezia was the beloved daughter of the pious Anna Colonna, who was estranged from her brothers-in-law by her demands for the restitution of her dowry. Lucrezia seems to have had a genuine vocation for the religious life, which was violated by Cardinal Francesco's insistence on an Italian dynastic marriage. He had her kidnapped from France to Italy and then forced her into marriage with Francesco d'Este. The cardinal summed up his attitude in a letter to Lucrezia of 30 December 1652: ". . . conforme vorrebbe la vostra et mia convenienza, ch'è di dimandarmi consiglio et di pigliarlo, non di dirmi risolutioni" ("your and my convenience should be in conformity, which is for you to ask me for advice and to take it, not to tell me what you have resolved"). The sad story is told at length in Costantini, "Fazione Urbana," h1. The celebrations in Modena for Lucrezia's arrival were described by Girolamo Graziani, *Descrizione delle allegrezze fatte dalla città di Modena per le nozze del Serenissimo Padrone e della serenissima Principessa Lucrezia Barberini* (Modena: Bartolomeo Soliani, 1654).

[23] Anna continued to live in her Palazzo dell'Olmo, near the Colonna family palace on Piazza Santi Apostoli, and died there (Giuseppe Sacchi Lodispoto, "Anna Colonna Barberini ed il suo monumento nel monastero di Regina Coeli," *Strenna dei Romanisti* 43 [1982]: 460–78, esp. 467–68).

also opened his guardaroba to the destitute, gave his helpers drink, and spent the night going about the quarter encouraging the people to evacuate their houses and save their goods.[24]

In September Cardinal Antonio made one of his rare public appearances, thanking the College of Cardinals as Camerlengo on behalf of the pope for their commemoration of the eleventh year of his reign. The celebrations were premature, for in December Innocent fell mortally ill. He remained lucid enough to discuss possible successors with the senior cardinals, including the Barberini. At the end of the month Donna Olimpia Maidalchini left the Apostolic Palace, sighing, "So soon, so soon!" and moved to the Quattro Fontane to join her granddaughter and Maffeo Barberini. When she attempted to re-enter the Vatican (which Gigli says was despoiled of even a bowl and a spoon with which to feed the dying pope some broth), Bernini's friend the Jesuit Giovanni Paolo Oliva told her to go about her business and marched her out. The pope hung on until 7 January 1655, dying with his eyes open and his tongue protruding. It was Cardinal Antonio Barberini, the principal target of Innocent's persecution a decade earlier, who as Camerlengo had the duty of verifying the pope's death by tapping him on the forehead three times with a ceremonial hammer while calling him by his baptismal name. A papal ceremonarius then smashed the Fisherman's Ring in the presence of the cardinals.

In his summary of Innocent's reign the chronicler Gigli did not spare the pope's hostility to "virtuous" persons, his avarice, and his submission to his dread sister-in-law. Gigli states that Innocent's anger at his own family was repaid when neither Donna Olimpia nor her children would assume the expenses of burial, although they financed a solemn lying-in-state according to an entry in the Cartari-Febei diary for 10 January 1655: "In St. Peter's they were working on the Pope's catafalque, for the last three days of the exequies, which is being done at the expense of his heirs." The splendid castrum doloris was designed by Andrea Sacchi.[25] Innocent's body was stored in a closet until his maggiordomo and a previous maggiordomo whom he had dismissed paid the modest sum of five scudi necessary for the pope's burial.

The conclave for the election of a new pope began on 18 January with a mass of the Holy Spirit sung by Cardinal Francesco Barberini as vice-dean of the Sacred

---

[24] : Gigli, 707: "A questo rumore comparve fuori del suo Palazzo il Card. Francesco Barberino, con il Card. Carlo suo Nepote, et con grandissima diligenza et carità fece entrare nel suo Palazzo tutti quei poverelli, che erano fuggiti dal fuoco, et li fece tutti vestire, et procurare, et poi havendoli tutti vestiti di nuovo gli donò anco 200. Scudi per uno."

[25] "In S. Pietro si lavorava per il catafalco del Papa, per li tre giorni ultimi dell' esequie, che si fa a spese de gl'heredi" (Fagiolo, *La festa barocca*, 366–67).

College, and the sixty-nine cardinal electors were locked in the next evening. Owing to the claims of twenty-two possible candidates, a long conclave was predicted. Cardinal Barberini himself was a strong candidate, and numerous other names were also floated. Cardinal Sacchetti, Cardinal Francesco's ostensible choice and a fervent Barberini client, was eventually excluded by the Spanish crown (proving the old Roman axiom, "Chi entra nel conclave papa esce cardinale," "The man who goes into the conclave as pope comes out as a cardinal"). The conclave was enlivened by such events as a fist-fight between Cardinal Astalli and Cardinal Decio Azzolino, and by the delirium of Cardinal Bernardino Spada, who left the conclave claiming that he had been elected pope. Finally, on 7 April—nearly three months after the opening of the conclave—following a series of votes favoring Cardinal Fabio Chigi, Cardinal Antonio Barberini cut the Gordian knot by vesting Chigi as pope, kissing his feet, and leading him to the altar of the Sistina for the ritual homage of the cardinals. Chigi, a Sienese, took the name of a previous pope from Siena and became Alexander VII. His election opened the last phase of Barberini 1glory in Roman spectacle.

BARBERINI *TRIUMPHANS*: ROMAN ENTERTAINMENTS FOR QUEEN CHRISTINA OF SWEDEN

In memory of Babs Johnson (Georgina Masson)

CHRISTINA ON THE WAY TO ROME

Christina of Sweden entered the orbit of the Barberini family long before she arrived in Rome in December of 1655. Urban VIII Barberini was the reigning pope when her father was killed in 1632 at the battle of Lützen, and he presided over the sometimes indecorous rejoicing at the unexpected disappearance of the Protestant champion. Gustavus Adolphus' death was commemorated by Cardinal Antonio Barberini's musician Luigi Rossi in a dramatic cantata, "Un ferito cavaliere," which was circulating at the highest levels in France by 1641.[1] Christina knew the work of Rossi and other composers in the Barberini households, such as Marc'Antonio Pasqualini and Giacomo Carissimi, and three Italian musicians traveled to Rome in her suite. Cardinal Francesco Barberini's librarian Lucas Holstenius, himself a convert, was dispatched by Alexander VII as special internuncio to escort the queen from Innsbruck to Rome. Her journey was monitored from Rome by Alexander VII through Giulio Rospigliosi.

Christina had abdicated the throne of Sweden in June of 1654 and went first to the Spanish Netherlands, where she remained for more than a year. She was privately converted to Catholicism in Brussels on Christmas Eve of 1654. She left for Rome with a large suite at the end of September 1655, traveling by way of Innsbruck, where

---

[1] Prunières, *L'Opéra italien*, 25.

she publicly proclaimed her conversion in November. There she was entertained with a lavish performance of the opera *L'Argia*, a libretto of Giovanni Filippo Apollini set by Antonio Cesti, the queen's first direct experience of Italian opera.

Christina's arrival in Ferrara on 22 November 1655 marked her entry into the papal states, and the pope sent four nuncios to welcome her and to accompany her to the outskirts of Rome. One of these was Archbishop Annibale Bentivoglio, a son of the great Ferrarese family that had been long associated (sometimes disreputably) with the Barberini. His father, Marchese Enzo, and his uncle, Cardinal Guido, had been artistic mentors of the younger Barberini in the 1630s. To Guido is attributed the published account of Cardinal Antonio Barberini's memorable joust of 1634, in which Annibale's brother Cornelio had ridden as *mantenitore* or champion. Cornelio had continued his father's theatrical activities by such spectacles as *Le pretensioni del Tebro e del Po*, presented in 1642 for Don Taddeo Barberini (see Chapter 4). During Christina's stay in Ferrara, Cornelio and his wife, Costanza Sforza, revived the Ferrarese theatrical tradition by entertaining her with *L'Oritia*, a "dramma morale" with music and machines presented in the theater of the Accademia degli Intrepidi located in the "teatro della sala grande" of the ducal palace. On Christina's departure, Cornelio, his wife, and their son joined Archbishop Annibale in her entourage.[2]

Outside Rome, Christina exchanged her four nuncios for two cardinal legates of royal birth, and on 23 December she entered the City in state through the Porta del Popolo, refurbished by Bernini, expertly managing the beautiful palfrey that formed part of the pope's lavish gifts (fig. 8.1).[3] She was welcomed by Cardinal Francesco Barberini at the head of the College of Cardinals and by a cross-section of Roman power: Cardinal Carlo and Prince Maffeo Barberini, the great-nephews of Urban VIII; Prince Camillo Pamphilj, nephew of Innocent X; his wife Olimpia Aldobrandini, princess of Rossano, great-niece of Clement VIII and Gregory XV and widow of Paolo Borghese, a nephew of Paul V.[4] (Alexander VII was still holding his own family, the Chigi, at bay in Siena.)

---

[2] Luciano Capra, "La regina Cristina a Ferrara," in *Queen Christina of Sweden: Documents and Studies*, ed. Magnus von Platen (Stockholm: Norstedt, 1966), 74–82; esp. 78–79 (Analecta Reginensia, 1). On Ferrarese theaters see Elena Povoledo, "Ferrara" s.v., *Enciclopedia dello spettacolo* 5 (Rome: Le Maschere, 1958).

[3] Per Bjurström, *Feast and Theatre in Queen Christina's Rome* (Stockholm: Bengtsons, 1966) (Analecta Reginensia, 3), 12–17, who incorrectly identifies Prince Maffeo Barberini as Nicolò and as Prior (rather than Prefect) of Rome, a title in fact held by his brother Carlo. See also Georgina Masson, "Papal Gifts and Roman Entertainments in Honour of Queen Christina's Arrival," in *Queen Christina of Sweden: Documents and Studies*, ed. von Platen, 244–61.

[4] Georgina Masson, *Queen Christina* (New York: Farrar, Straus & Giroux, 1968), 251.

MARIA ALEXANDRA CHRI STINA SVECIÆ REGINA.

Magnus Alexandro quem soluit in Vrbe Philippus,
Froenas imperÿs, Regia Virgo, tuis. D. H. Q.
Ioseph. Teſtan Inu Fecit.

At uictrix at Regna domes maiora relictis,
Dat Tibi Alexander Nomen, et omen Equus.
Gio. Iacomo Roſſi, le Stampa e le Vende in Roma alla Pace.

Fɪɢ. 8.1   Giuseppe Testana,
Queen Christina's Entry into Rome

For Christina's first visit to St. Peter's on the same day, the church was hung with tapestries furnished by Cardinal Barberini as archpriest of the basilica. According to the chronicler Giacinto Gigli, "before all the pilasters between the chapels were as many choirs of musicians as there were in Rome."[5] The diarii of the Cappella Pontificia (whose protector was Cardinal Antonio Barberini) record the singing of the antiphon "Ista est speciosa [inter filias Jerusalem]" at the queen's entrance and a *Te Deum* for six choirs, "with their organs," of Orazio Benevolo, conducted by the composer.[6] (This may have been sung to satisfy Christina's curiosity, since Paolo

---

[5] Giacinto Gigli, *Diario*, 751: "avanti tutte le pilastrate tra le cappelle erano tanti cori di musici quanto n'erano in Roma."

[6] BAV, CS, Diario 73, fol. 33v: Mons. Scanaroli intoned "il Te Deum quale fu seguitato dalli musici di S. Pietro e di tutte le Basiliche di Roma Catredali [!]; et Regie; et altri spartiti in 6 chori ben adornati con suoi organi, la compositione del Te Deum fu del Sig.re Horatio Benevoti. . . ."

Giordano Orsini had written to assure her that Benevolo was the equal of Carissimi as a composer.)[7]

On Christmas Eve of 1655, a year after her private abjuration of heresy in Brussels, the queen attended the traditional banquet in the Vatican for the cardinals, and on Christmas Day she was confirmed by Alexander VII, taking as her confirmation names Alexandra Maria. On St. Stephen's day she dined with the pope in public, to the accompaniment of a sermon by Bernini's friend the Jesuit Padre Giovan Paolo Oliva and the customary vocal and instrumental music provided by the Cappella Pontificia.[8] Later in the day Christina took up residence in Palazzo Farnese, which was furnished by the pope with a lavish gift of household supplies. For most of January the queen visited religious institutions, but with the approach of the Carnival season at the end of the month the Barberini inaugurated their festivities in honor of the royal convert.

THE PRINCE'S CARNIVAL OF 1634

The Barberini were the obvious choice to lead the celebrations for visiting royalty. The senior Barberini cardinals, Francesco and Antonio, had played key roles in the election of Alexander VII the previous April, and their association with Giulio Rospigliosi, whom the new pope named Secretary of State on 1 January 1656, went back more than three decades. The Barberini had a long tradition of symbolic spectacle and were the only family in Rome who possessed appropriate performing space for royal entertainments: both the theater building at the Quattro Fontane (a feature unparalleled in any other Roman palace) and the temporary outdoor theater created in front of the palace's north wing accommodated more than three thousand spectators.

The Barberini also had an obvious family model for their entertainments for Christina of Sweden, which were remembered as "the Queen's Carnival," in the "Prince's Carnival" of 1634. These festivities had been created by the Barberini to honor the visit to Rome of Alexander Charles Vasa, brother of King Vladislao of Poland and a Catholic cousin of Christina. For the occasion Cardinal Francesco Barberini presented an expanded version of the sacred opera *Il Sant'Alessio*, first produced in 1631

---

[7] Masson, *Queen Christina*, 125.

[8] BAV, CS, Diario 73, fol. 36: "diversi Mottetti a 2, e a 3, a 4 et a 8" sung by five sopranos, three altos, three tenors, and two basses, with Marco Marazzoli at the organ (Jean Lionnet, "Christine de Suède et la chapelle pontificale, un espoir deçu?," *Cristina di Svezia e la Musica* [Rome: Accademia Nazionale dei Lincei, 1998], 311–20, esp. 315).

or 1632 (see Chapter 3).[9] The opera, performed in Cardinal Francesco's antechamber in the Quattro Fontane palace, had a text by Giulio Rospigliosi set by Stefano Landi. The production was enriched by the machines that Francesco Guitti, an intimate of the Bentivoglio family, had created for Don Taddeo Barberini's *Erminia sul Giordano* of the previous year. (The creation of spectacular effects by the re-use of existing materials was part of the game of Roman opera.) Cardinal Antonio Barberini planned a magnificent joust in Piazza Navona, which he presented despite Alexander Charles' unexpected departure. Both events were commemorated in elaborately illustrated vanity publications, the opera by a full score and the joust by a detailed *relazione, La Festa Fatta in Roma* included in the published works of Guido Bentivoglio.

That the 1656 celebrations harked back to those of 1634 is suggested by a Barberini manuscript description of the Carosello presented for Christina. Ignoring completely the fact that the Prince of Rossano had produced a joust as recently as 1651, the description of the 1656 production recalls the sæcular games of the Roman Empire, supposedly celebrated only when the last spectator of the previous games had died: "a regulated shooting of pistols, accompanied by Machines, and by Music, and concluded with the beauties of Caroselli. Actions the one no longer seen in Rome, the other not practiced for so long, that few or none preserve the memory of it."[10]

Beneath their splendid trappings, the 1634 celebrations embodied a coherent political and social program (see Chapter 3). Several strands intertwined in the re-worked version of *Il Sant'Alessio*, most notably in the new prologue composed for the occasion (see figs. 3.5–3.6). The themes of the prologue are familiar ones in the Barberini program: the identification and transformation of Old and New Rome; Rome as the symbol of the papacy; Counter-Reformation admonitions to rulers; the choice of rule by love rather than by force. The new prologue's emphasis on gratu-itous clemency in absolute power may have been intended to soften the perception on the part of civilized Europe of the role played by the Barberini in the trial and condemnation of Galileo Galilei the previous year.

Cardinal Antonio's joust (a quintain run or *giostra del saracino*) was preceded by two *veglie* or evening entertainments. The celebration combined music, dance, splendid costumes, a great deal of poetry, and the climactic appearance of a machine in the form of a great ship, accompanied by a boatful of musicians (see figs. 3.3–3.4). The event was intended to present the Barberini as Renaissance princes of aristocratic

---

[9] See Chapter 3, n. 11.

[10] BAV, Ms. Barb. lat. 4913, fol. 103v: ". . . abbattimento regolato di pistole, accompagnato [104] dalle Machine, e della Musica, e terminato con le vaghezze de Caroselli. Attioni l'una non più in Roma veduta, l'altra già per tanto tempo non praticata, che poco ò nessuno ne conserva la ricordanza."

lineage rather than—as they were—successful wool-merchants from the Valdarno. By combining their emblems (the sun and the laurel) with those of the Roman baronial Colonna family (columns, sirens), the Barberini imaged their incorporation into the Roman patriciate through the marriage of Taddeo Barberini with Anna Colonna.

In 1656 the Barberini were not the autonomous agents of two decades earlier but were bound increasingly closely to the Pamphilj. The thaw that accompanied the return of the Barberini culminated in the arranged marriage between the twenty-two-year-old Maffeo Barberini and the twelve-year-old Olimpia Giustiniani, granddaughter of Innocent's all-powerful sister-in-law, Donna Olimpia Maidalchini.[11] Owing to both the scarcity and the generally unsatisfactory performance of the Pamphilj males, Maffeo became *de facto* papal nephew.

The Queen's Carnival of 1656: The Program

Symbolic spectacles were a corporate effort in seventeenth-century Rome. The patron initiated the process, perhaps suggesting in addition a subject or programmatic message. If the content were particularly complex, as in the case of Pietro da Cortona's ceiling fresco in Palazzo Barberini, an intellectual from the patron's household circle would elaborate a program. In the case of an opera, a writer would produce a libretto embodying the patron's wishes. This was handed over to the composer(s), who sometimes modified it for musical purposes. A small army of copyists, vocal and instrumental musicians, choreographers and dancers, engineers, set- and machine-designers, painters, tailors, shoemakers, instrument tuners, moving-men, and miscellaneous artisans (including nuns who made artificial flowers of silk) swung into action to realize the production. The entire effort was directed and co-ordinated by an overseer, called the *corago*, something like a modern theatrical producer/director. Sometimes an outsider was called in to perform this task, as Enzo Bentivoglio did for the 1628 Medici-Farnese wedding celebrations in Parma, but often the librettist became the stage director (and continued to do so into the time of Verdi).[12]

A contemporary *avviso* notes that the subject of the first opera presented by the Barberini in 1656 had been suggested by the pope, and the diario of the Cappella Pontificia refers offhand to "The Comedy that is being done by order of Our Lord"

---

[11] On the Quarantore apparato of 1654 in the Gesù celebrating the reconciliation of the two families see Chapter 6 above. Giovan Maria Mariani's set featured the bees of the Barberini together with the Pamphilj emblems of three lilies, rising from a hedge of flowers, and a dove of peace.

[12] On the role of the *corago* see the important treatise *Il Corago o vero alcune osservazioni per metter bene in scena le composizioni drammatiche*, ed. Paolo Fabbri and Angelo Pompilio (Florence: Olschki, 1983).

("La Commedia che si fa p[er] ordine di N[ostro] S[ignore.")[13] In 1656, therefore the Barberini were apparently acting as agents of Alexander VII in carrying out a program suggested by the pope and fleshed out by Rospigliosi, but constructed on the model of their entertainments in 1634.

In seeking to understand the papal program behind the 1656 celebrations, we must remember that Alexander VII was confronted by a dilemma. On the one hand, the former Queen of Sweden, the prize Catholic convert of the century, had to be entertained and displayed with all the dignity due her rank—"that she be made all the possible demonstrations to the advantage and glory of the Catholics," as the pope himself put it.[14] On the other hand, the headstrong young woman of unknown theological tenets, doubtful companions, masculine habits and dress, and openly "Amazonian" tendencies, had to be instructed how to live suitably in the city where, by default, she would become the ranking female resident. A note of caution had already been sounded by Archbishop Bentivoglio. In writing to Rospigliosi, who was carefully monitoring Christina's progress toward Rome, Annibale had noted: "If I had anything to wish for in her it would be . . . some greater devotion in substance and in appearance. To my way of thinking the fact that she knows too much does not render her completely credulous about the miracles of the saints, and the veneration of their relics." He also informed Rospigliosi that the autocratic Christina was displeased with the credit given the Jesuits for her conversion because "it diminishes her Glory of having herself alone known how to recognize the true path to convert herself into the bosom of our holy Church."[15]

Rospigliosi and the pope were aided in their delicate task by one thing: Christina herself was a virtuoso at employing symbolic spectacle. Both her assertion that the Peace of Westphalia was a personal achievement of her father and herself, and her determined refusal ever to marry were conveyed to the world at large in the form of ballets where Christina displayed her self-image in her choice of roles such as Pallas and Diana. She therefore would presumably be quick to perceive the messages transmitted by the celebrations. (Whether she would pay any attention to them was, of course, another question.)

---

[13] BAV, CS, Diario 74, fol. 4v (9 January 1656).

[14] ". . . che se gli facessereo tutte le possibili dimostrationi ad avantaggio e gloria de Cattolici" (quoted by Capra, "La regina Cristina," 74).

[15] "S'avessi da desiderare alcuna in lei sarebbe . . . nella sostanza e nell'apparenza qualche maggior devotione. A mio creder il troppo sapere non la rende del tutto credula verso i miracoli de' santi, e nella venerazione delle loro reliquie"; ". . . le venga scemata la Gloria d'aver ella sola saputo conoscere la vera strada per ridursi nel grembo della nostra santa Chiesa" (Capra, "La regina," 78).

By means of the sugared pill of musical spectacle, the pope wished to insinuate important doctrinal points: theological orthodoxy expressed in submission to the power of Rome; the contemplation of death (a personal obsession of Alexander VII); the doctrine of free will as opposed to Protestant predestination; the validity of the Sacraments—especially those hotly attacked by the Protestants, such as Penance; womanly modesty and deference to male authority; and austerity of life.

Politically, the papal program showed a strong Habsburg (and therefore anti-French) bias. France had attempted to block Alexander's election, and Rospigliosi had served for nine years as nuncio to the Habsburg court in Madrid. As cardinal, Alexander had been an observer at the Peace of Westphalia, whose disregard of the Church he bitterly opposed. Although France and Sweden were traditional allies, Christina had made the principal acts of her conversion in Brussels and Innsbruck and was thus a Habsburg client. The uneasy relations between France and the papacy perhaps explain the conspicuous absence from the 1656 celebrations of Cardinal Antonio Barberini, who had been cardinal protector of France until 1644 and later accepted from Mazarin the *cordon bleu*, the archbishopric of Reims, and the post of Grand Aumônier of France. Antonio gave the palace at the Quattro Fontane, of which he had been the sole tenant, to his nephew Maffeo, and rented Palazzo Bonelli near the palace of his Colonna in-laws at Santi Apostoli, on whose façade he conspicuously displayed the French royal arms.

Enlarging on the model of the 1634 celebrations, in 1656 the Barberini fulfilled the papal program by offering Christina not one but three operas, as well as a tourney or Carosello. Of the operas, *La vita humana overo Il trionfo della Pietà*, a moralizing allegory, was composed especially for the occasion. The sentimental comedy *Dal male il bene* had been produced two years earlier, and a second sentimental comedy, *Le armi e gli amori*, had apparently been composed but not yet performed.[16] The festivities are documented by printed *argomenti*, manuscript libretti and scores, and in addition a printed score for *La vita humana* (a distinction shared with only two other Barberini opera productions, *Il Sant'Alessio* and *Erminia sul Giordano*).[17] The celebrations are

---

[16] See Wolfgang Witzenmann, "Die römische Barockoper *La vita humana overo Il trionfo della pietà*," *Analecta Musicologica* 15 (1975): 158–201, esp. 159. Murata, *Operas for the Papal Court*, 348, 369, 386 lists no performances of these works after 1656, but the *Enciclopedia dello spettacolo* (8 [1961], cols. 1118–19) mentions an otherwise undocumented performance of *Le armi* in 1654, and states that the Barberini theater closed with subsequent performances of *La vita* in 1657 and perhaps 1658. A letter of Giacomo Rospigliosi, 16 February 1660, mentions a performance of *La vita* in Rome but does not say where (Murata, *Operas*, 388).

[17] Dedication to Christina by Marco Marazzoli (Rome: Mascardi, 1658). Between September 1656 and April 1657 Cardinal Francesco spent sc. 46 for the printing of 46 folios by Maurizio and Amadio Balmonti;

described in *avvisi* and in printed and manuscript accounts, and their expenses are detailed in Barberini financial records. The sets of *La vita humana* were engraved for the printed score, and the Carosello is commemorated in a splendid painting by Filippo Gagliardi and Filippo Lauri that remained in Palazzo Barberini until 1959. These sources have been employed by scholars such as the late Georgina Masson, Per Bjürstrom, Margaret Murata, and Wolfgang Witzenmann, but reading them in the light of the 1634 Barberini celebrations can still provide some new insights into the origins and message of the Barberini festivities for Christina.

The Queen's Carnival: Creation

By mid-October of 1655 Christina's arrival in Rome was certain enough for Alexander VII to commission from Bernini the coach destined as his principal gift to the queen.[18] Christina left Innsbruck, where she had publicly proclaimed her conversion, on 8 November, headed for Rome by way of Ferrara and Loreto. The *relazione* submitted to Cardinal Francesco Barberini by Giovanni Francesco Grimaldi, the designer of the festivities, allows us to dovetail the creation of the entertainments with the queen's progress. Toward the end of November, Grimaldi began to design the opera-sets according to the directions of Rospigliosi, the librettist of all three works, and Marco Marazzoli, the composer of *La vita humana*. This is confirmed by Cardinal Francesco's accounts, which record on 18 November a payment of sc. 150 for the first of a series of "expenses made and to be made on behalf of the Commedia" ("spese fatte e da fare in ordine alla Commedia"). (The final total was sc. 7285.86.[19]) At the beginning of December, Grimaldi began drawing and painting the canvas sets for *La vita*, working every day except Christmas and St. Stephen's until Candlemass, 2 February. He also made a plan, side-views, and elevations for the theater for the Carosello and designed the habits, helmets, and horse-trappings for the riders

---

the *tipografo* was Vitale Mascardi. Francesco paid G. F. Grimaldi for designing the scenes and G. B. Galestruzzi for engraving them; BAV, Barb. lat. 9907 contains three drawings by Grimaldi which served for the engravings. Two studies by Grimaldi for the third scene are found in British Library 106 1t-10-1A-130 and 107 At-10-1a-130 (reproduced in Masson, "Papal Gifts"). Five "piastre da intagliare" went to Carlo Orlandi; Giacomo de' Rossi was paid sc. 9,55 for printing "n.o 1350 folii of scenes." If each figure is considered a single folio, and there were five folios per volume, the print run was about 274 copies (Petrucci Nardelli, "Il Card. Francesco Barberini senior e la stampa a Roma," 167–68).

[18] Masson, "Papal Gifts," 244.

[19] BAV, AB, CFB, Comp. 85, fol. 42: Masson, "Papal Gifts," 260, n. 63.

and attendants. In addition, Grimaldi designed and made models of the two new chariots for the Carosello, those of Sdegno (Scorn) and Amore (Love), and reworked a mechanical Dragon and Maffeo Barberini's chariot of the Sun, both built for previous festivities. Finally, he designed the triumphal arch facing the queen's box for the musicians of the Carosello and all the ornaments of the outdoor theater. (After such an effort Grimaldi must have been disappointed when the sc. 380 that he had requested—and had certainly earned—was discounted to sc. 300.)[20]

By 9 January 1656 the singers Bonaventura Argenti and Domenico Palombi (both in the cast of *La vita humana*), Domenico del Pane (in *La vita humana* and *Dal male il bene*), and Marazzoli (composer of part of *Dal male* as well as all of *La vita humana*) were being excused from service in the Cappella Pontificia for "La Commedia che si fa p[er] ordine di N. S."; the following week several members of the Cappella were absent for rehearsing "certi Chori."[21] With three operas and the music for the Carosello to prepare in less than two months, both space and time must have been at a premium, and the movers' bills show a lively traffic of instruments and costume-trunks between St. Peter's, Rospigliosi's house and the shop of the harpsichord-builder and technician Giuseppe Boni (both in Borgo), the queen's residence of Palazzo Farnese, and Cardinal Francesco's palace, the Cancelleria. The bill for tuning harpsichords submitted by Boni vividly evokes the stress of the rehearsals, some eighty in number:

> For having kept in order various Harpsichords for all the rehearsals that all together are about eighty times more or less[;] some rehearsals are of the Vita humana, and L'armi e gl'Amori and Dal male il bene[;] in these rehearsals I had to go to [the house of] Mons. Rospigliosi, and S.r Marco of the Harp [Marazzoli], and S.r Lodovico Lenzi, and I took care of the Harpsichords and was always present and also at the rehearsals in the Cancelleria.[22]

---

[20] BAV, AB, CFB, gius. 7616–7665, fol. 270.

[21] BAV, CS, Diario 74, fol. 4v, 15 January 1656.

[22] BAV, AB, CFB, gius. 7616–7665, fol. 163: "Per haver accomodato diversi Cimbali p[er] tutte le prove che in tutto sono da ottanta volte in circa più presto più che meno qualche prove sono della Vita humana, e l'armi e gl'amori e dal male il bene in queste prove mi bisognava andare da Mons.re Rospigliosi, e dal S.r Marco dell'Arpa, e dal S.re Lodovico Lenzi, e si accomodava li Cimbali e si stava sempre assistenti e anco le prove della Cancelleria."

LA VITA HUMANA OVERO IL TRIONFO DELLA PIETÀ

La vita humana was premiered on Monday, 31 January 1656, in the great theater off the north wing of Palazzo Barberini.[23] (The queen attended another performance on Thursday, 3 February; the last performance, again in her presence, was given on Monday, 7 February.) In addition to Rospigliosi's libretto, Marazzoli's music, and Grimaldi's sets and costumes, the opera also featured choreography by Luca Cherubino. Rospigliosi directed all three opera productions, and Marazzoli supervised his music for *La vita humana*. Christina was present in a specially constructed box under a baldacchino, and the audience included eighteen cardinals and prelates. G. B. Muzzarelli, an observer from Modena, described the scene:

> When the Queen had been ushered into a cabinet of damask together with the Cardinal [Francesco] at the head of the large box, while they awaited the lowering of the curtain, the Cardinal was seen circling around the theater, now from one side, now from the other, with that admission showing in it a like nature of great joy, taking more pleasure in losing his temper than in helping the prince [his nephew Maffeo].
> The theater, they say, seats four to five thousand persons. The ladies were on the floor in front of the stage, against which there arose a large staircase, which from the same, two boxes stretched like two arms up to the stage, in one of which sat the Queen a bit farther forward, [the box] covered with damask as I said.[24]

As the inaugural production and the only opera composed specifically for the celebrations, *La vita humana* was clearly intended to set their keynote. The personages of the allegory are symmetrical. Innocence and Guilt (sopranos), backed by antiphonal choruses of the Virtues and Vices, contend for Human Life, also a soprano.

---

[23] On 28 February the Barberini entertained the queen at a magnificent banquet.

[24] G. B. Muzzarelli, 4 II 1656: "[. . .] Introdotto [!] la Regina in un gabinetto di damasco insieme con il Signor Cardinale a capo dello palco grande, mentre per attendere il callare della tela, vedevosi il Signor Cavaliere [recte: Cardinale] Barberino girar il teatro hora da una parte, hora dall'altra con quale amissione mostrando in esso simil'natura di gran giubilio, essendo più gusto nell'inanimarsi che secondare il principe.

"'Il teatro e capace dicevano di quattro in cinque milla persone. Le dame stavano nel piano avanti la scena, contro della quale si alzava una gran scalinata, che dalla medesima, come due braccie porgevano due palchi sin alla scena, in uno dello quale [delli quali?] stava la Regina puoco più fuori, coperta [!] di damaschi come detto" (as transcribed in Jarrard, *Architecture*, 224, from Modena, Archivio di Stato, Cancelleria Ducale, Amb, Roma 263).

The companion of Human Life, Understanding (contralto), is the ally of Innocence; Pleasure (tenor), is the henchman of Guilt. Since this was the most important of the productions, the cast featured virtuoso singers from the Cappella Pontificia. Innocence was sung by the soprano Domenico Palombi or Domenico Rodomonte,[25] Human Life by the soprano Bonaventura Argenti, Guilt by the soprano Domenico del Pane, Pleasure by the tenor or alto Francesco de' Rossi, and Understanding by the soprano Lodovico Lenzi. Aurora in the Prologue was sung by the soprano Giuseppe Sorilli. Innocence was dressed in white taffeta with lace and flowers, and Guilt appeared in black and gold.[26]

One observer noted that the opera "turned out to be very beautiful, so much the more since there were only five musicians [in fact six] who sang it," while another described them as "all exquisite Singers both for music, and in the elegance of acting."[27]

In 1660 Rospigliosi's nephew Giacomo described the work as "totally moral, and it has no plot, because it was not the intention to make a story but rather one might say a collection of little arias heard together, and joined by a pair of recitatives."[28] As if to compensate for the fact that the opera is indeed "totalmente morale, e non ha nodo," the libretto contains such incidents as lively battle-scenes, sleeping-draughts resulting in feigned death, disguises, transformations, and reversals of fortune or peripateia.

Musically, as Giacomo Rospigliosi's comment suggests, the opera is the most tuneful of the three presented. The score contains a number of "ariette," often strophic. Many of these airs are lively pieces in triple meter, some with passacaglia interludes; hyperglycemic duets and trios in thirds and sixths are frequent. There are even charming strokes of frivolity (e.g. I/3) and humor, when Pleasure issues an edict

---

[25] Rodomonte was at San Luigi dei francesi in 1646 (Lionnet, "La musique," 70).

[26] Masson, "Papal Gifts," 256.

[27] Murata, Operas, 387; the Florentine ambassador, the spectacle-designer Tommaso Guidoni, is quoted in Jarrard, Architecture, 244, n. 62: ". . . riuscita assai bella, tanto più che non erano che cinque soli musici che l'hanno cantata" (Jarrard gives the date as 3 January 1656, evidently an error for 31 January); Gualdo Priorato, 288: ". . . tutti Musici isquisiti nella musica, e nella leggiadria del recitare."

[28] ". . . totalmente morale, e non ha nodo, perche non fu l'intenzione di fare intreccio ma piutosto si puo dire una raccolta d'ariette udite insieme, e concatenate con un paio di recitativo" (quoted by Murata, Operas, 388). The "totally moral" nature of the festivities was criticized by Atto Melani in a letter of 20 November 1655: "Penso che la Regina non abbi da vedere in Roma, feste di quella [di Innsbruck] più bella, perché se bene si preparano gran cose, sono però gesuitate e bachettonerie e fuori del primo ingresso non penso ch'abbi da essere altro di buono" ("I think that the Queen will not see celebrations more beautiful than that [of Innsbruck] in Rome, because although they are preparing great things, however they are Jesuiteries and pious humbugs and aside from her initial entry I don't think there will be anything else good") (quoted in Tamburini, Due teatri, 239).

(I/6). In Act II Rospigliosi addressed a long speech to the queen, comparing her to Saint Bridget of Sweden and prophesying new crowns for her—a clear reminiscence of the address to Alexander Charles in the 1634 prologue of *Il Sant'Alessio*. The apparent death of Understanding in Act III provides the opportunity for another genre piece, a moving lament sung by Human Life.

Reporting on the opera, one *avviso* praised the variety of the sets, which changed "ogni mezzo quarto d'ora" ("every half quarter-hour"). The stage effects included "cavalli vivi e veri, con uomini a cavallo in atto di giostra, camelli vivi, e elefanti, bovi, caccie di tori sopra palchi, e cose di gran maraviglia" ("real live horses, with men on horseback performing a joust, live camels, and elephants, oxen, bull hunts on platforms, and things of great wonder").[29] The opera concluded with an unusually realistic "lontananza where there appeared the Vatican Palace, the façade and dome of S. Pietro, Borgonuovo, and Castel Sant'Angelo full of lights, and which emitted fiery lightnings, and the Catherine-Wheel [girandola] accompanied by the firing of a great quantity of fireworks."[30] (The depiction of the girandola was particularly appropriate, as it was customarily performed on the Feast of Peter and Paul, 29 June, the celebration of the power of the papacy.) The scene would certainly have appealed to the "soldier's daughter" who at the age of two had clapped her hands and laughed at the sound of cannon fire.[31]

Was Christina aware of a bit of backstage drama reported in a contemporary life of Grimaldi?

> Giovan Francesco [Grimaldi] was much envied by Bernini, in token of which in the Barberini opera one night he had the tubes [for the stage fountain] plugged up and the ropes for the sets under the stage cut secretly. When this became known Bernini suffered great displeasures and had a great public scolding from the prince for it.[32]

---

[29] *Fidelissima discrizzione* [1656], 1751, p. 135.

[30] ". . . lontananza dove apparivano il Palazzo Vaticano, la facciata e cuppola di S. Pietro, Borgonovo, e Castello Sant'Angelo ripieno de lumi, e che mandava fuori li fulgori di fuoco, e la girandola accompagnata con lo sparo di gran quantità di mortaletti." A similar scene had concluded the opera *La Genoinda/ L'Innocenza difesa* given by Cardinal Francesco in the Cancelleria in 1641 (Murata, *Operas*, 299). Masson, "Papal Gifts," 256, cites payments for "a pierced tin reflector, 23 palmi long, for the transparency of the Castle," "for making three large holders to take three torches each, for the reflector of the Castle . . . four large tin flasks for resin."

[31] Masson, *Queen Christina*, 38.

[32] Bologna, Biblioteca Universitaria, Ms. 245, c. 161v: ". . . Gio[van] Fran[ces]co era invidiato assai dal Bernini, a segnio che nell'opera de Barbarini fece una notte segretamente turare li condotti e tagliare di

The author of another *avviso* reacted like Atto Melani and found the opera
"long, and as many say, tiresome for being completely serious, and worthy more of
a Church than a Theater."[33] According to this account, the queen attempted to con-
ceal her boredom by chatting with her neighbors. In compensation, the Barberini
cardinals and Prince Maffeo "exerted themselves greatly that day, in setting things
in order, so that they themselves suffered great weariness." Cardinal Francesco,
"through rushing around wishing to behave like a youth suffered a fainting-fit, so
that it was necessary to hurry with restoratives." The queen had been told that the
opera was entirely the work of Rospigliosi, but hearing that "it had been the idea of
the pope" ("era stato pensiero del Papa"), she made a point of attending the other
performances, at which Cardinal Francesco continued to bustle about as he had done
at performances in the 1630s and "was seen several times to hurl himself on someone
who had entered without his knowing how."[34]

G. B. Muzzarelli's verdict was somewhat grudging:

> The costumes were noble, well proportioned, the scenes were
> beautiful, but with few changes and even fewer machines, as
> the characters were few, but the three sopranos exquisite in
> their parts. At the end, after the dance there were the likenesses
> of the Catherine-wheel of Castello, but not very respectable
> for invention, at the same time they fired off fireworks with-
> out, and within they made lightnings of fire appear, and they
> succeeded better in the semblance of the girandola.[35]

---

sotto il palco le corde delle scene. Saputosi il Bernini ci passò de gran disgusti e ne ebbe una gran bravata
dal prencipe in publico." C. 167v: Grimaldi "fece poi le comedie della regina di Svezia che erano così
belle che non furno più vedute in Roma. Era d'una fontana e per invidia li fu messo un merangholo
dentro il condotto . . ." (Grimaldi "then made the comedies of the queen of Sweden that were so beautiful
as had never been seen in Rome. There was a fountain and for jealousy there was put a merangolo in
the pipe . . .") (quoted in Anna Maria Matteucci, Rosella Ariuli, *Giovanni Francesco Grimaldi* [Bologna:
CLUEB, 2002], 287, 292).

[33] ". . . lunga, e come molti dicono tediosa per essere tutta grave, e degno piu tosto di Chiesa che di
Teatro . . ." (Murata, *Operas*, 387).

[34] "Li Signori Cardinali Barberini, et il Principe di Pellestrina stentorno grandemente quel giorno,
nell'ordinare le cose, tanto che patirono in se stessi grandissime fatiche, con poco gusto degl'altri, et il
Cardinale Francesco per il gran moto volendo sempre fare da giovene patì un diliquio, si che fu necessario
correre con ristorativi . . . fu visto più volte scagliarsi adosso a qualch'uno ch'era entrato senza sapere il
come . . ." (Murata, *Operas*, 387–88).

[35] "Li abiti erano nobili, ben proportionati, le scene furono belle, ma di puocho mutatione e meno machine,
come puochi li personaggi, ma per l'esquitezza loro nelle parti delli tre soprani. In fine, dopo il balletto
fossero la similitudine della girandola di Castello, ma non molto riguardevole d'inventione, nell'istesso

F_{IG}. 8.2   G. B. Grimaldi, engr. G. B. Galestruzzi, *La vita humana*, Proscenium
(Biblioteca Apostolica Vaticana)

Grimaldi's sets for *La vita humana* are well known from G. B. Galestruzzi's
engraved plates for the printed score, although these contain occasional conflations
or slight inaccuracies (which also occur in other Barberini opera engravings).[36] The
first plate (fig. 8.2) depicts the proscenium, surmounted by the new private arms of
blue and silver that Christina had assumed on her abdication, the Vasa wheat-sheaf
on two bendlets under a crown royal; the drop-curtain shows a villa and a garden,
the villa resembling Bernini's early reworking of Santa Bibiana. The fore-edge of the
stage supports vases embellished with the Barberini bees alternating with jets of water,
with a larger jet in the center. Below this is a fountain decorated with tritons, whose
water gushes from a double scallop-shell. We learn from the plumber's accounts
that this was real water—the engraving shows it overflowing onto the floor—pumped
from the nearby garden of the palace through an elaborate system of tubing (the
water-supply sabotaged by Bernini).[37]

---

tempo facevano sparare mortaletti di fuori, e di dentro facevano apparir i lampi del fuoco, et meglio
riuscirono nell'apparenza della detta girandola . . ." (Jarrard, *Architecture*, 224–25).

[36] See Hammond, *Music and Spectacle*, 337–38, n. 33.

[37] BAV, AB, CFB, gius. 7616–7665, fol. 144.

Muzzarelli reported:

> Above the same boxes, where one could easily make two others of the same, there was an apparato of striped taffeta with a colonnade of painted cloth where the lights stood, with a cornice above of painted cloth, which went to join them with that of the proscenium of the painted set with architecture of a colonnade, and above a great coat-of-ams of the Queen with two eagles [angels with trumpets in the engraving] with above it the motto formed of lights "Il Trionfo della Pietà."[38]

The engraving of the first scene, for which a drawing also exists, combines the Prologue and Act I/1 (figs. 8.3–8.4). In the Prologue, the sun rises on a darkened stage and Aurora descends on a machine, scattering pieces of silvered paper to represent dew. In his detailed *relazione* of Christina's reception in Rome Galeazzo Gualdo Priorato described it thus:

> When a curtain had fallen there appeared night depicted in a shadowy stage-set. The dawn began to rise, afterwards bit by bit the sun, which then lighted up the entire theater with wondrous artifice. Dawn scattered from her silvered chariot a quantity of perfumed flowers, and waking the shepherds to there work it served as a most graceful prologue. After which their remained in a most pleasing perspective [prospettiva] a City with two opposed fortresses, one of Understanding, the other of Pleasure.[39]

---

[38] G. B. Muzzarelli: "Sopra detti medesemi palchi, dove commodamente se ne potrebbero fare due altri medesemi, era apparato di taffetoni rigati con colonato di tela dipinto [!] dove stavano le lumiere, con un cornicione sopra di tela dipinta, che le andava ad unire con quello del frontispizio della scena dipinta con architettura di colonato, e sopra un grande armone della Regina da due aquile, con il motto sopra formato di lumi Il Trionfo della Pietà" (as transcribed by Jarrard, *Architecture*, 224).

[39] Galeazzo Gualdo Priorato, *Historia della Sua Reale Maestà Cristina Alessandra, Regina di Svezia* (Rome: Reverenda Camera Apostolica, 1656), 288: "[abbassata] una tenda apparve in ombrosa scena figurata la notte. Cominciò a sorgere l'aurora, doppo a poco a poco il sole, che illustrò poi con mirabil artificio tutto il teatro. L'aurora spargendo dall'argentato suo carro quantità di fiori odoriferi, e risvegliati i pastori all'opere servì di prologo graziosissimo. Dopo di che rimase in vaghissima prospettiva una Città con due rocche opposte all' incontro, una dell'Intendimento, l'altra del Piacere."

Fig. 8.3   Grimaldi, *La vita humana*, sketch for Prologue
(Stockholm, Nationalmuseum)

FIG. 8.4 Grimaldi, engr. Galestruzzi, *Prologue/Act I* from *La vita humana*

As we might expect, Muzzarelli's account is more critical:

> . . . in describing the introduction of the scene I forgot the fortress, nor did I mention what was more important, that later on there appeared a fine seashore on a chariot, but from the confines of which in a cloud there appeared Dawn who sang the prologue, and it is sufficient to say that it was by Bonaventura [Argenti].[40] There was no other machine except this one, in whose rising the sun began to shine, at whose beginning it aroused great expectation, but did not fulfill it, since the reflections that it made on the sea were greater, and they truly made a fine marvel, but the proportion of the sun could not produce such, and in the increasing of the sun in proportion the scene was being more illuminated, than had appeared corresponding to the Dawn . . .[41]

---

[40] Gualdo Priorato identifies Aurora as Giuseppe Sorilli (ibid., 288).

[41] "[. . .] nel descrivere l'introduttione della scena io mi sono scordato per la rocca, ne ho detto quello che più importava, che più oltre appariva una bella marina su carreto, pero dai confini della quale entro

The sunrise machine seems to be a version of Bernini's famous device, which was apparently widely imitated. Christina herself saw a similar one in Modena in 1657, somewhat Jesuitically exclaiming that she "had never seen anything more beautiful, and more majestic."[42]

Act I/1 shows the opening exchange between the defenders of the opposed fortresses of Virtue and Vice. The banners and scrolls displayed by the two castles set up both the color-scheme and the ideological opposition of the entire celebration. From the keep of Vice fly a sea-blue and silver flag with a siren and a scroll with the words, "It is permitted if it pleases" ("Lice se piace"). Virtue flies a red-and-gold crown of thorns and a scroll, "It pleases if it is permitted" ("Piace se lice"). The audience would have recognized the first motto as a quotation from Guarini's idyllic drama, *Il pastor fido*, of which the second motto was the Christian repudiation. The third plate (fig. 8.5) represents a forest with three figures. The set seems to have been built on that of the previous act by adding flats of trees in front of the castles and changing the backdrop from a seashore to mountains. The fourth engraving (fig. 8.6) shows the garden of Pleasure, reworked from Grimaldi's original design, with three figures. The final plate (fig. 8.7) depicts the Vatican quarter and the Catherine-wheel of Castel Sant'Angelo.

There are some loose ends among the score, the engravings, and the descriptions of the opera. Muzzarelli places the final scene after a "balletto," and Gualdo Priorato noted that *La vita humana* ended with "various interludes of ballets, and concerts of music, and instruments . . . then concluding with a ciacona wonderfully danced by two excellent ballerini, and with the appearance of the play of a girandola."[43] The printed score breaks off with a trio in the garden of Pleasure. Mazzocchi's autograph score indicates dance-music after the first and second acts but not at the end. This last may have been furnished by "Carlo del Violino" (who may be identified either with the well-known cantata composer Carlo Caproli or with Carlo Manelli), paid

---

una nuvola apparisce l'Aurora che fece il prologo, e basta il dire che fosse D[!]onaventura. Non vi fu altra macchina che questa, nell'alzarsi della quale principio[ò] a spuntare il sole, nel cui principio diede grande aspettatione, ma non corrispose a pieno, maggiore essendo i riflessi che faceva nel mare, et facevano veramente meraviglia fine, ma la proportione del sole non poteva produce [!] tali, e nel crescer del sole approportione si andava più illuminando la scena, che n'era apparsa corrispondente all'Aurora . . ." (quoted in Jarrard, *Architecture*, 224).

[42] Quoted in ibid., 225, where it is given as "Queen Christina of *Spain*'s visit to Modena."

[43] ". . . diversi intermedii di balletti, e concerti di musica, e d'instrumenti . . . concludendo poscia con una ciacona danzata mirabilmente da due eccellenti ballerini, e coll'apparenza del gioco di una girandola" (Gualdo Priorato, *Historia*, 288). The ciaccona in Francesco Cavalli's *Le nozze di Teti e Peleo* of 1639 is written over a "Zefiro" bass (Alm, "First Steps on the Venetian Stage").

FIG. 8.5   Grimaldi, engr. Galestruzzi, *Forest Set* from *La vita humana*

FIG. 8.6   Grimaldi, engr. Galestruzzi, *Garden of Pleasure* from *La vita humana*

Fig. 8.7 Grimaldi, engr. Galestruzzi, *Castel Sant'Angelo and Girandola* from *La vita humana*

on the same bill as Luca Cherubino, the ballet-master.[44] Presumably Cherubino was one of the dancers of the ciaccona, perhaps with Francesco Marti, another *maestro di ballo* named in the Barberini accounts.[45] Dances must have figured largely in *Dal male il bene* as well, since the shoemaker's bill includes dancing shoes for ten named dancers and twelve unspecified pages for dancing "in the Spanish style" in "the Spanish comedy."[46]

---

[44] BAV, AB, CFB, Comp. 85, fol. 52: "sc. 18 a Luca Cherubino m[aest]ro di ballo p[er] il balletto fatto nella Comedia intitolata La Vita humana, e gli altri sc. 6:20 in doble due di Spagna a Carlo che suonava il violino." Caproli's possible presence is interesting, since he had ties both to Cardinal Antonio Barberini and to the Pamphilj: see Prunières, *L'Opéra italien*, 152–54, and the entry by Eleanor Caluori in *The New Grove Dictionary* (London and New York: Macmillan, 1980). M. de St. Hubert states that the music is composed to fit the choreography already created, as in the case of Emilio de' Cavalieri's "O che nuovo miracolo" in the 1589 Florentine intermedi.

[45] BAV, AB, Comp. 356, DMB, LMG AA, 1653–57, carta 307 left: sc. 6 to Fran.co Marti "m[aest]ro di ballo ad un Sonatore, che sonava alle Comedie."

[46] Masson, "Papal Gifts," 256.

In their discussions of *La vita humana*, Per Bjurström and Wolfgang Witzenmann have somewhat obscured the message of the work by misidentifying characters in the engravings. Bjurström described the figures in the third plate (reading from left to right) as Innocence, Pleasure, and Understanding, and the ones in the fourth as Pleasure, Innocence, and Human Life—scarely the "vaga donzella" of the text.[47] Witzenmann identified them as Life, Pleasure, and Understanding in the third, and Pleasure, Life, and Innocence in the fourth.[48] With a bit of poetic license, plate three in fact depicts Life and Understanding, who have been onstage in II/5, overhearing Pleasure's monologue in II/7. Engraving four represents the concluding trio of the printed score, sung by Understanding, Life, and Innocence (III/5). Innocence appropriately wears a plumed helmet, recalling the figure of Rome in the 1634 prologue of *Il Sant'Alessio* (see fig. 3.5).

With the characters assigned correctly, the messages that Alexander VII and Rospigliosi addressed to the queen by means of the opera are clarified. The principal theme of the work, as the typography of the printed title-page shows, is *Il trionfo della Pietà*—that credulity whose deficiency in Christina worried Archbishop Bentivoglio, and on which the Pope himself admonished her. The opera depicts Human Life as female and therefore frail: she cannot attain Innocence (which, as a state to be achieved by action, corresponds to the removal of Original Sin by the action of baptism) except by relying on masculine Understanding and fleeing from Pleasure. (Christina's reputation for libertine living was already causing the papacy concern.) As the final appearance of Innocence in Roman armor reminds us, the true seat of Innocence is Rome itself, and she sets up the final scene-change (misplaced by Bjurström) with the words "Con voci festeggianti/Andiam di Pietro di venerar la mole" ("With festive voices let us go to reverence the great stronghold of Peter") (III/5). Like Christina and Alexander Charles Vasa, Life, Innocence, and Understanding are all pilgrims to Rome.

The opera contains other theological messages directed at any lingering Protestantism in Christina's beliefs. In I/4, while Vita is pondering a moral choice, she asks Innocence, "Non sono libera?" and Innocence confirms the doctrine of Free Will with a curt "Si." Act III emphasizes the doctrine of penitence with the presentation of a ring carved with a death's head. (On his election, Alexander VII had commissioned from Bernini a statue of a skull, and he slept in a coffin.) In III/4 the enchantment by which Guilt and Pleasure counterfeit Innocence and Understanding is broken when Innocence sings, "Regna Dio, vive Dio, trionfa in Cielo" ("God rules,

---

[47] Bjurström, *Feast and Theater*, 28.

[48] Witzenmann, "Die römische Barockoper," 172–73.

God lives, He triumphs in Heaven"), an echo of the inscription on the base of the obelisk in front of St. Peter's, "Christus vincit, Christus regnat, Christus imperat" — itself a medieval ruler-acclamation.[49] (From the *giustificazioni* for the opera we learn that the disguises of Guilt and Pleasure had little strips of lead sewn on them, to make sure that they fell dramatically at the moment of transformation.)[50]

Behind the moralizing allegory of *La vita humana* we may perhaps discern the outline of a similar work, *La Rappresentazione di anima e di corpo* of Emilio de' Cavalieri (d. 1602), "composer of the first surviving play set entirely to music," to a text by Agostino Manni. *La Rappresentazione* was published by Alessandro Guidotti in Rome with a dedication to Cardinal Pietro Aldobrandini and an extended and informative preface about performance practice dated 3 September 1600. The work was performed in Rome some time before November of 1600. The protagonists of the psychomachia are Anima and Corpo. Time is passing, and the Soul longs for eternal peace, while the Body tempts her with the good things of the world. On the side of the good are arrayed Counsel and Intellect, supported by a Guardian Angel and Blessed Spirits. They are opposed by Pleasure, the World, Worldly Life, and the Damned Souls. At the conclusion Anima and Corpo are united in their desire to climb the path to Heaven, and the work ends with a sung and danced ballo, a kind of sacred parallel of "O che nuovo miracolo," the concluding balletto of the 1589 Florentine intermedii.

Dal male il bene; Le armi e gli amori

Dal male il bene, first performed at the Palazzo Barberini in Carnival of 1654, was the first theatrical production of the Barberini since their return from France: the immense theater built by Francesco and Antonio had lain unused (like many another seventeenth-century court theater) since Cardinal Antonio's spectacular *Il palazzo incantato* of 1642.[51] The libretto of *Dal male* was adapted by Rospigliosi and his nephew Giacomo from a Spanish play, *No ay bien sin ageno daño* of Antonio Sigler de Huerta, and was set by Marazzoli and Antonio Maria Abbatini. The *giustificazioni* for the 1656 performance reveal an emphasis on the Spanish setting of the opera. Several bills for the slippers for twenty-two dancers specify that they were "for the

---

[49] See Ernst Kantorowicz, *Laudes Regiae: A Study in Liturgical Acclamations and Medieval Ruler Worship* (Berkeley: University of California Press, 1946).

[50] BAV, AB, CFB, gius. 7616–7665, fol. 267: "Piombo in laminette . . . acciò calassero subito."

[51] The reference to Masson, "Papal Gifts" that Jarrard gives for her statement that Grimaldi restored the theater is non-existent.

Spanish comedy" or "for dancing in the Spanish style." Spanish swords and costumes were also supplied.[52]

It has been stated that *Dal male il bene* was originally presented at the Quattro Fontane palace in February of 1654 in honor of Maffeo Barberini and Olimpia Giustiniani, who had been married on 15 June 1653. A library catalogue by the voluminous note-taker Carlo Cartari (1614–97), prefect of the University of the Sapienza, does indeed list the *argomento* of an unnamed "opera performed in Rome for the marriage of prince Barberini and the Pamphilj."[53] However, a letter of Giulio Rospigliosi dated 14 February 1654 states that *Dal male il bene* was composed later and thus had no connection with the wedding:

> . . . a few days before Christmas [1653] Cardinal Barberino
> informed me, that the Signora Donna Olimpia wished Cardinal
> Carlo Barberini to have a bit of comedy in music done for this
> Carnival, but the Cardinal added to me that he would be pleased,
> if the Abate my nephew would do something taken from some
> Spanish comedy, as it followed with a bit of direction, that he
> had from me. The comedy is titled *Dal male il bene.*[54]

The commission embodies an exquisite balance of power. Donna Olimpia Maidalchini, grandmother of the new wife of Maffeo Barberini, conveys to Rospigliosi through Cardinal Francesco Barberini, the *de facto* head of the family, her wish that Cardinal Carlo, head of the younger generation, present a work based on a Spanish source for the entertainment of Maffeo and Olimpia Giustiniani in their new palace.

---

[52] Masson, "Papal Gifts," 256.

[53] Arnaldo Morelli, "La musica a Roma nella seconda metà del Seicento attraverso l'archivio Cartari-Febei," *La musica a Roma attraverso le fonti d'archivio*, ed. Bianca Maria Antolini, Arnaldo Morelli, Vera Vita Spagnolo (Lucca: Libreria Musicale Italiana, 1994), 107–36, esp. 108, n. 2. Cartari's index of the library of Cardinal Rocci (d. 1651) lists an unnamed "Argomento dell'opera recitata in Roma per le nozze del prencipe Barberino e la Panfilia, Roma, 1654."

[54] ". . . pochi giorni prima di Natale il Signor Cardinal Barberino mi accennò, che la Signora Donna Olimpia desiderava che il Signor Cardinal Carlo Barberino facesse fare un poco di commedia in musica per questo carnevale, e però il Signor Cardinal mi soggiunse haverebbe havuto gusto, che l'Abate mio nipote facesse qualche cosetta cavata da alcuna commedia spagnola, come è seguito con un poco di direzione, che ha havuto da me. La commedia è intitolata *Dal male il bene*." Murata, *Operas*, 52, identifies the Donna Olimpia of Rospigliosi's letter as the young Olimpia Giustiniani Barberini, but in the Rome of Innocent X "Donna Olimpia" *tout court* must surely refer to Donna Olimpia Maidalchini. The synopsis of *Dal male il bene* was printed in 1654 by the Reverenda Camera Apostlica without dedication or title; the title-page bears the Pamphilj dove and the Barberini bees in sign of the reconciliation of the two families by the marriage (Rome, Biblioteca Corsiniana 172.G.13: Franchi, *Drammaturgia romana*, 308).

Dal male il bene is significantly different from the earlier Barberini productions. As Rospigliosi noted, it was received with great approval because "although there were no machines, what touched the exquisiteness of the music, of the performers, of the costumes, and of the sets could not be greater."[55] The absence of machines was an anomaly in the tradition that had fostered the marvels of Francesco Guitti, Andrea Sacchi, and Bernini himself. The choice of a sentimental comedy in a bourgeois setting contrasts with the sacred, heroic, pastoral, or moralizing subject-matter of earlier Barberini operas. Rospigliosi's experience as nuncio in Madrid and his familiarity with the Spanish court allowed his Barberini patrons to slide gracefully into a new accommodation with the hispanophile Pamphilj by means of a Spanish comedy. From the opening appearance of Fortuna in the prologue, the opera proclaimed the rehabilitation of the Barberini and their reconciliation with Innocent X, in token of which each act ends with some variant of the proverb, "Dal male il bene," "All's well that ends well."

There is some possibility that, as was customary, the 1654 version of the opera was retouched, in this case to make it more appropriate to Christina's attendance by tacking on a moralizing conclusion. The music director of the 1656 production was one of the composers, Antonio Maria Abbatini (Marazzoli was the other composer).[56] The Pistoiese Gioseppe Fede, in the service of Prince Ludovisi, sang the role of Elvira, as he had in the original production, and a "castrato dell'Abbatini" (Domenico del Pane) appeared as Fortuna.[57] Gualdo Priorato wrote that the opera "rather contained a plot of various amorous incidents, in which by chance Virtue, and Love interweaving themselves, gave us to know, that quite often good comes out of evil, from misfortunes are born better fortunes, proving the saying, that we would be in danger, if we were not in danger."[58] Perhaps Christina was moved to apply this maxim to her own experience, since a repeat performance, costing Cardinal Francesco sc. 185.86 for new sets by Abbatini's brother Guidobaldo (the rather modest sum suggests that the original sets were reworked), was arranged for the queen in Palazzo Farnese.[59]

---

[55] ". . . se bene non si erano macchine, quello che tocca all'esquitezza della musica, de' recitanti, de gl'habiti, e delle scene non puo esser maggiore": letter of 14 February 1654, quoted in Murata, *Operas*, 349.

[56] Witzenmann, "Römische Barockoper," 160. The 1654 production had been stage-managed by Giacomo Rospigliosi and "Signor Mancini," and the text manuscript BAV, Vat. lat. 13355, which contains minutely detailed stage-directions, may have served as a prompt copy (Murata, *Operas*, 53–57).

[57] Murata, *Operas*, 348–50.

[58] Gualdo Priorato, *Historia*, 286–89: ". . . conteneva pur un nodo di varij accidenti amorosi, ne quali intrecciandosi a caso la Virtu, e l'Amore, si dava a conoscere, che ben spesso dal male ne risulta il bene, dalle disgratie sovente nascono le maggiori fortune, comprobandosi il detto, che pericolati faressimo, se pericolati non fossimo."

[59] BAV, AB, CFB, Comp. 85, fol. 74v.

The third Barberini opera, *Le armi e gli amori*, was premiered on Sunday, 20 February, and repeated the next day in the presence of the queen. Another Spanish-derived work, it was adapted by Rospigliosi from Calderón's *Los empeños de un acaso* and set to music by Marazzoli, with sets by Giovanni Maria Mariani.[60] The music of the opera was directed by the singer Lodovico Lenzi, who had been sent to Madrid at Rospigliosi's request in 1645 and was to be entrusted with the direction of the Rospigliosi-Abbatini opera *La comica del cielo* (with sets by Bernini) in 1668.[61] *Le armi e gli amori* was sung by rather obscure singers (five of them named Francesco), including Francesco Federici "di S. Pietro" and Francesco "del Principe di Gallicano" (Pompeo Colonna). Mariani was paid "for having worked 73 days and 26 evenings for the commedia *'dell'Armi e gli Amori.'*" The sets included a garden with "eight nude figures of women or dryads, under a pergola painted in gouache," and a gallery with "seven figures of gods, in yellow chiaroscuro touched with gold," six heads of gods, and ornaments of putti with the Vasa wheat-sheaves.[62]

The source of the text is elegantly acknowledged in the play within a play that forms the prologue to the opera. We are told that the theater is full and the audience is impatiently awaiting the beginning, but the leading lady is still in her dressing-room. A song with a passacaglia bass introduction repudiates the laments, complaints, and sighs of earlier operas and proposes instead a drama of love and arms, "Now hear the boast with Italian notes of a wandering swan, who pours out on the banks of the Manzanares his song, not mortal, but divine." Nor was the object of the celebration forgotten: "Also you are honored by the high presence of royal Christina, to which the festive waves of the Tebro bow, shall arouse her glories."[63] Gualdo Priorato observed that "the content . . . turned on the simultaneous combination of various events both amorous, & warlike, which reciprocally accompany the fortunes of the followers of Mars, and Venus."[64] In both these operas, where the plot was neither "totalmente morale" nor "senza nodi," the musical emphasis was more upon recitative for declaiming the text than upon independently melodious *ariette* or ensembles.

---

[60] On Mariani as a designer of Quarantore apparati see n. 11 above and Chapter 6.

[61] Murata, *Operas*, 7, 389.

[62] BAV, AB, CFB, Comp. 85, fol. 63v; Murata, *Operas*, 368–70; Masson, "Papal Gifts," 257.

[63] "D'un cigno peregrino, che scioglie in riva al Manzanaro il canto mortal nò, mà divino, con Italiche note hor s'oda il vanto . . . Anche l'alta presenza, à cui l'onde festose del Tebro inchina v'honorà della real Christina sveglieran le sue glorie."

[64] ". . . il contenuto . . . versava nel simultaneo concorso de' varij avvenimenti insieme amorosi, & armigeri, che vicendevolmente sogliono accompagnare le fortune de' seguaci di Marte, e di Venere" (Gualdo Priorato, 300–01).

THE *GIOSTRA DELLE CAROSELLE*

For a variety of reasons, the Carosello or joust that concluded the Barberini celebrations for Christina's arrival has received less close attention than the three operatic productions. First, the authors of the work are unknown. Its sources do not specify whose was the initial impulse (the pope? Rospigliosi? the Barberini?), who created from this the finished allegorical program, who served as *corago*, who wrote the libretto.[65] The composer(s) of the ninety-eight and one-half sheets of music "which was sung on the chariots of the joust" ("che si cantava sop[r]a li carri della giostra") that were copied is unknown; as in the case of almost every other chivalric celebration, not one note of it appears to have survived (but see Chapters 1 and 4).[66] We only know that Giovanni Francesco Grimaldi created the decoration of the temporary outdoor theater, the costumes, the triumphal arch for the musicians, and the machinery, all depicted in the Lauri–Gagliardi painting (fig. 8.8).

Although the chivalric spectacle—appropriate to a secular prince—was presented under the auspices of young Maffeo Barberini, his uncle Cardinal Francesco, still the dominant figure of the family, sustained the bulk of the expenses. (Maffeo's previously unavailable accounts record expenses of sc. 1429.50 between 1 February and 30 June.)[67] It is not always remembered that the patrons of such chivalric spectacles did not shoulder all the expenses: participants also paid. For the 1656 Carosello the

---

[65] Elena Tamburini, "La lira, la poesia, la voce e il teatro musicale del Seicento: Note su alcune vicende biografiche e artistiche della baronessa Anna Rosalia Carusi," *La musica a Roma attraverso le fonti d'archivio*, 419–31, esp. 419, n. 1, claims that Barone Carlo Ventura del Nero organized the 1655 [!] Carosello. She cites BAV, AB, Gius. 7538–7615, c. 150, where the reference does not appear; fol. 17 contains items "consignati Al s.r Baron del Neri." Jarrard (*Architecture*, 236) says the major influence on the Carosello was Cardinal Rinaldo d'Este's description of the *Gara delle stagioni* (which she misspells throughout), sent to Cardinal Antonio Barberini on 21 December 1655 (BAV, Barb. lat. 7394). This seems unlikely since the Barberini already possessed a model in the 1634 Giostra, and since Cardinal Francesco seems to have been the principal mover of the 1656 celebrations. In fact, Cardinal d'Este's letter to Cardinal Francesco (not to Antonio) (BAV, Barb. lat. 7394, fol. 129v, 21 December 1655) merely describes the lighting of piazze in Modena. Muzzarelli described the Carosello as "most noble for the appearance and for the illumination, and for being carried out very competently but it was not of much consideration. There were four considerable machines among the others the dragon of Tissimo. Every knight of the 24 Personages had contributed 500 scudi" ("nobilissima per la comparsa e per l'illuminazione, e per l'operatione assai compitentimente ma non fù da molta consideratione. Vi furono quattro macchine riguardevole fra l'altro il drago di Tissimo. Ogni cavallieri [!] delle 24 Personaggi habbia concorso di scudi 500" (as transcribed in Jarrard, *Architecture*, 236, n. 78). However, Cardinal Francesco also deposited money at the Monte di Pietà for the credit of the Cavalieri della Giostra (Masson, "Papal Gifts," 251).

[66] BAV, AB, Comp. 356, MB, LMG AA, carta 307 [left]: To Belard[i]no Terrentij sc. 17.23 "p[er] haver copiati foglij 98 1/2 di musica, che si cantava sop[r]a li carri della giostra."

[67] BAV, AB, Comp. 356, carta 307: see Appendix.

Fɪɢ. 8.8   Filippo Lauri–Filippo Gagliardi, *Giostra delle Caroselle* (1656) (Museo di Roma)

Modenese Muzzarelli noted, "Each knight of the 24 Personages contributed 500 scudi" —a total of 12,000 scudi.[68] Although the allegory of the Carosello itself displays some anomalies—notably the uncomfortably large role played by Sdegno, Scorn, in a celebration of Christina—it is possible to interpret the event as a reasonably coherent summation of the Barberini celebrations for Christina's arrival.

By knocking down several houses, Grimaldi had created on the long side of the prince's or north wing of the Quattro Fontane palace an outdoor theater in the form of a rectangular courtyard accommodating some three thousand spectators. Christina's box was set up in the center of the palace façade, and two rows of boxes ran around the cortile, with additional seats under them on the long side facing the queen. The painting shows the west side of the courtyard with the entrance of Cortona's theater and rows of seats masking its façade. Directly in front of the queen was the triumphal arch, 50 palmi romani (11 meters) long and 35 palmi (8 meters) high. "At the height of the said *portone* in four great windows, with false gelosie, there extended a Choir for the musicians, who with a variety of instruments, made exquisite melodies."[69] Although the *mantenitore* or champion customarily entered from one side and the *venturieri* or challengers from the other, all the participants and the gigantic *carri* must have entered through the triumphal arch. The theater was decorated with herms, mentioned in Grimaldi's *giustificazione*. The illumination, which alone cost more than sc. 1000, was provided by flaming vases and iron stars, also eliminated from the painting, and the carved and painted wooden herms which held candles.[70] The spectacle began in darkness, after which the entire theater was illuminated at once.

---

[68] Muzzarelli, quoted in Jarrard, *Architecture*, 236. BAV, AB, Comp. 356, carta 307: "devono dare @ p[ri]mo febraro s[cu]di duecento m[one]ta buoni al s[acro] m[onte] della Pietà pagati con m[andat]o no. 1300 alli ss.ri March[es]i Gio:B.a Costaguti, e Stefano Pignatelli due delli Deputati di d[ett]a Giostra dalla parte dell'Amazzoni" ("they must give on February 1 two hundred scudi in cash to the Sacro Monte di Pietà [the papal pawnshop] paid with the pay-order no. 1300 to the marchesi Giovanni Battista Costaguti and Stefano Pignatelli two of the Deputies of the said Giostra from the side of the Amazons").

[69] Gualdo Priorato, *Historia*, 302: "Nella sommità di detto portone in quattro gran fenestre, con finte gelosie, si stendeva un Coro per i musici, che con varietà d'instrumenti, fecero melodie isquiste." Don Maffeo's accounts for the joust record payments to carpenters for the scalinata and teatro, fees for accommodating borrowed benches, wood for the herms. Payments for refreshments mention sugar, ice, cedri, and lemons.

[70] Expenses for the lighting in Don Maffeo's accounts: "16 girelle date p[er] tenere le stelle di filo di ferro nel teatro della giostra"; to Servio Servi for 26 stelle, illumination, and "altre girelle che reggevano d[ett]e stelle"; "tavole d'abeto per dipingere li termini che reggevano le padelle nel teatro della giostra"; sc. 41.55 to Gio. F.co Grimaldi Pittore "p[er] haver dipinto li suoi Huomini li termini, et arco che stavano nel teatro della giostra"; [left] padelle to burn around theater; payments to Servio, to Cap. Giuseppe Rasponi a cavalier; ciambelle, "fattura et altre fatte per le padelle."

A traditional formal scheme underlay the sometimes confusing superficial richness of the Carosello. As the Barberini manuscript account notes, it combined two standard types of entertainment: a battle between two opposing squadrons (as opposed to the joust, in which a single champion took on a series of challengers), and a display of decorated *carri* or chariots: "a regulated shooting of pistols, accompanied by Machines, and by Music, and concluded with the beauties of Caroselli."[71]

Despite threatening weather, the joust began at the third hour after sunset on 28 February with a prologue by the musicians. After a ceremonial entry and presentation of each squadron, enriched by the entries of their respective chariots, the two groups fought. The entrance of another machine halted the action, after which a second combat took place. The opposing sides were reconciled by a final chariot-entrance.

The combatants were arranged in two squadrons of twelve each, preceded by eight trumpeters on horseback and accompanied by 120 grooms. The first squadron, the Knights, wore Roman costumes in Christina's new heraldic colors of turquoise and silver, with "with crests of feathers so ample, and ostentatious, that one did not know how in the waving of the air so spacious and heavy an affair could be held on the head."[72] The feathers alone had cost each knight more than sc. 200, and their crests were further embellished with rosettes of mirror and spun glass depicting the Vasa wheat-sheaf. A chariot of blue and silver, as high as the queen's box, was drawn in by three singers representing the Graces; on the chariot sat a fourth singer costumed as Rome (=Amor). The Graces "supported with sweetest song the harmonious sentiments of Amor" ("secondarono con soavissimo canto gli armoniosi sentimenti d'Amore"), who proclaimed that Love is the soul of the universe and its throne is the heart of the queen. The second squadron comprised a troop of Amazons in fiery red and gold with touches of black, headed by Prince Maffeo Barberini wearing a headdress containing more than six hundred feathers. The Amazons' chariot, also in red and gold, was drawn by three singers representing the Furies and was surmounted by a singer costumed as Sdegno. The two groups processed so as to confront each other for "a delightful, and more than curious dialogue also in music, each of

---

[71] BAV, Ms. Barb. lat. 4913, fol. 103v: ". . . abbattimento regolato di pistole, accompagnato [104] dalle Machine, e della Musica, e terminato con le vaghezze de Caroselli." A printed "argomento," bound in gold lace, was distributed: BAV, AB, Comp. 356, carta 307 [left] sc. 18 to Ignatio Lazzari stampatore "p[er] haver stampato gli argomenti della d[ett]a giostra"; [right] payment for "merletto d'oro" to put around the joust programs.

[72] ". . . cimieri di penne così ampli, e pomposi, che non si sà come tra l'ondeggiamento dell'aria potessero sostenere in capo una macchina si spatiosa, e grave" (Gualdo Priorato, *Historia*, 304).

the sides at the end calling its own Warriors to arms for the decision."[73] The Amazons drew up at the head of the theater toward the garden, the Knights opposite them in front of the theater, each squadron followed by its chariot. The combatants removed their mantles and replaced their headdresses with lighter ones, the chariots retired, and the grooms surrounded the field with lighted torches. "The choir of Musicians placed . . . above the arch . . . as from time to time it made harmonious sinfonie, so it gave way to the sound of the trumpets." ("Il coro de' Musici situato . . . sopra l'arco . . . come di quando in quando faceva armoniose sinfonie, cosi cedette al suono delle trombe") (fig. 8.9).

FIG. 8.9   Lauri–Gagliardi, *Giostra delle Caroselle*
            detail of Musicians' Gallery
            (Museo di Roma)

The weapons of battle were pistols (perhaps in compliment to Christina, who was a crack shot), and the combatants advanced on each other in groups increasing from three to twelve, "whence between the smoke, the fire, and the noise of the weapons, we enjoyed the appearance of a fray, and a most delightful mêlée" ("onde trà il fumo, il fuoco, e lo strepitar delle armi, si godè la sembianza d'una mischia, e di una zuffa

---

[73] ". . . un dilettevole, e più che curioso dialogo pure in musica, chiamando in fine da ciascuna delle parti, per la decisione, i proprij Guerrieri all'armi" (Gualdo Priorato, *Historia*, 307).

vaghissima"). Then appeared Hercules (Alcide), whose labors were depicted on the triumphal arch. He was mounted on a Dragon that Grimaldi had recycled from a previous occasion, its effectiveness newly enhanced by sixteen tin fangs, two great lanterns to light its eyes, and a lining of leaded tin to enable it to breathe fire by means of fireworks.[74] After Alcide had sung from the arch, he entered the *teatro* on the Dragon. "Con voce sonora, e grave," he stopped the combat, offering to the contestants the apples of the Hesperides. After this, "which unrolled in an orderly fashion with sweet music," the Dragon processed around the field to the sound of "the Trumpets of the whole Theater to which the Choirs of Musicians responded in alternation."[75] The contestants fought the Dragon—this time with the nobler weapons of sword and shield—for possession of the apples. The entertainment culminated in the entrance of the chariot of the Sun, accompanied by twenty-four damsels representing the hours. On the chariot sat a singer, Apollo, who expressed Rome's sentiments for Christina, which were echoed by the musicians. "The Choirs of Musicians with the Instruments therefore repeated his last notes, and then the trumpets, more joyful than ever, began the concluding march." The performers left the field "with an artful mixture of voices and instruments and trumpets."[76]

The chariot of the Sun had been the hit of the 1654 Carnival. In its original version, Prince Maffeo Barberini, surrounded by servants in cloth of gold, was enthroned as the Sun with a scepter in his hand, holding the reins of four horses. At the foot of the throne the eagle of the Giustiniani gazed at the Barberini sun, and before the chariot rode the Seasons (see fig. 7.4).[77]

The source of the allegorical confection of the 1656 Carosello is to be sought in Cesare Ripa's *Iconologia*, of which the Barberini owned at least three copies.[78] Ripa depicts "Amor di virtù" as a naked youth with wings, crowned with one laurel wreath

---

[74] BAV, AB, CFB, gius. 7616–7665, fol. 147v: "foderato di latta stagniata tuta la bocha del drago . . . et fattogli sedici denti Grandi di latta . . . doi Canoni di latta per tirare li razzi alla Bocha del drago . . . doi lucerne Grande . . . per dar lume al ochi del Drago" ("for having lined the whole mouth of the dragon with tin . . . and made sixteen Large tin teeth . . . two tin Cannons to fire off the fireworks in the Mouth of the dragon . . . two Great lanterns . . . to light the eyes of the dragon"). Don Maffeo's accounts for the joust record expenditures for for masks, pistols, pozzolana for the cortile, gunpowder for the "carro del Drago"; pistol holsters (calze da pistola); wigs and powder; boots (stivaletti).

[75] ". . . che sortì ordinatamente con musica soave" ("le Trombe di tutto il Theatro alle quali alternativam[en]te rispondevano i Chori de Musici" (BAV, Ms. Barb. lat. 4913, fols. 118v–119).

[76] "Repplicarono perciò l'ultime sue note i Chori de Musici con gli Istromenti, e successivam[en]te le trombe intimarono più che mai liete l'ultima marcia" "con una artificiosa meschianza di voci e stromenti e di trombe" (BAV, Ms. Barb. lat. 4913, fol. 119).

[77] Gigli, *Diario Romano*, 697–98.

[78] Hammond, *Music and Spectacle*, 125.

and holding three more in his hands.[79] "Sdegno" is portrayed as an armed man in red with flames, his legs covered with lion skins, and a hat in the shape of a bear's head. His face is red and "sdegnoso," and he carries broken chains in his hand. Sdegno is not exclusively a negative personification. Although his red color and flames show that Sdegno is "a lively boiling of the blood" ("un vivace ribollimento del sangue"), and his arms and legs indicate that "he can be so powerful in man by the operation of the less noble passions, that man becomes like the brute beasts, and the wild savages" ("può esser si potente nell'huomo per opra delle passioni meno nobili, che si renda simile à gli animali brutti, & alle fiere selvaggie"), the broken chains suggest that "Scorn arouses the forces, & the strength to overcome all obstacles" ("lo sdegno suscita la forza, & il vigore per superare tutte le difficoltà")—not an undesirable attribute in a ruler.[80] The accompanying Furies are described by Ripa as they appear in Dante: ugly, dressed in black with bloodstains, belted and hatted with serpents. They carry a branch of cypress in one hand, a trumpet belching flames and black smoke in the other.

The corrective for the negative qualities of Sdegno lies in the figure of Hercules, represented with a lion skin, a club, and a dragon circling an apple tree. Hercules is the type of "Virtù heroica." His domination of the dragon signifies moderation in concupiscence, the sublimation of the passions that overpower Sdegno. Hercules' club stands for Reason, and his lion skin is emblematic of generosity and strength of soul. (A statue of Hercules on the Campidoglio represented him with three apples, symbolizing "moderation in Anger, temperance in Avarice, generous disdain for delights and pleasures."[81] In the *speculum principis* tradition Hercules was the type of the ruler's choice between Virtue and Vice—an admonition that figured prominently in the decorative program of Palazzo Barberini.[82]

The chariot of the Sun, in Ripa's description, contains a naked "giovanetto ardito" with gilded hair and rays. His right arm is stretched out and holds three figurines, the Graces. A bow and arrow are in his left hand, and a dragon under his

---

[79] Cesare Ripa, *Iconologia* (Rome: Faeji, 1603), facsimile ed. Erna Mandowsky (Hildesheim: Olms, 1984), 18–19.

[80] Ripa, *Iconologia*, 446. Sdegno and Amore had already appeared in another Barberini production, *L'Armida/L'Amore trionfante dello sdegno*, a libretto of Ascanio Pio of Savoy set by Cardinal Antonio's musician Marco Marazzoli. This was premiered in the Teatro Grande di Corte of Ferrara, February 1641, then repeated for Don Taddeo, who stayed in Ferrara from 5–14 January 1642, on 11 January in the Teatro Obizzi (see Chapter 4).

[81] ". . . moderazione dell'Ira, temperantia dell'Avaritia, generoso sprezzamento delle delitie e piaceri" (Ripa, *Iconologia*, 506–07).

[82] Scott, *Images*, figs. 6, 81, 96–97.

feet. His chariot is adorned with jewels and gold and throws off a great light; it is accompanied by the twenty-four hours of the day, each of which takes the tiller of the chariot for her appointed time.[83]

Christina's Roman pilgrimage was the result of her conversion, and so the dominant images of the two productions created especially for the queen's arrival—*La vita humana* and the Carosello—are those of combat and choice, which can be diagrammed as a series of oppositions:

La vita humana		*Carosello*	
Virtues	Vices	Knights	Amazons
Understanding	Pleasure	Amor=Roma,Graces	Sdegno, Furies
Innocence	Guilt	Hercules	Dragon
Piety	Heresy		
red/gold	blue/silver	blue/silver	red/gold

These oppositions are represented musically by the antiphonal choruses of Virtues and Vices in *La vita humana* and by the alternating choirs and the opposition of military and courtly instruments in the joust. Even in the secondary operas, Virtù and Love are opposed in *Dal male il bene*, while *Le armi e gli amori* contrasts Mars and Venus.

The symbolic opposition of colors is reciprocal. In *La vita humana*, blue and silver are associated with the Vices, Pleasure, Heresy, and Guilt; red and gold with the Virtues, Understanding, Innocence, and Piety. In the Carosello, blue and silver characterize the Knights, Rome, Love, and the Graces, while red and gold are associated with the Amazons and the largely negative figures of Sdegno and the Furies. The symbolism of the Amazon squadron may be inappropriate to the celebration of a royal convert but not to the celebration of a famous equestrian. Maffeo Barberini chose to ride as chief of the Amazons, and a glance at the Lauri–Gagliardi picture shows that the red and gold of Sdegno and the Amazons dominated the entire production. Christina employed both combinations. Although the tinctures of her new arms as a private person were blue and silver (the latter an unusual choice for royalty), at her state entry into Rome her body-guards wore scarlet capes decorated with crosses in the Vasa black and gold. (The papal colors were also red and gold.)[84] At one level, therefore, the opposition of colors might stand for the two sides of Christina's nature: the private person, a woman with all the frailties assigned to women, and the sovereign—neuter or even an honorary male, as in the case of Elizabeth I.

---

[83] Ripa, *Iconologia*, 51–52, 203–14.

[84] Bjurström, *Feast and Theatre*, 16.

The messages of the two original 1656 productions dovetail. The plot of the sacred opera *La vita humana* demands a moral choice between mutually exclusive alternatives. The chivalric Carosello presents the two sides of Christina's nature—woman and sovereign—as complementary and harmonizes them under the dominion of the Sun, identified in the Carnival of 1654 as "the emblem of Pope Urban, and of his family the Barberini" ("l'impresa di Papa Urbano, e della sua famiglia Barberina"). However, the Sun was not only a personal emblem of the Barberini, but a more general symbol of the papacy as well. The final statement of the celebrations that the Barberini orchestrated for Alexander VII in 1656 depicted the warring elements in Christina's nature and her personal history reconciled under the beneficent rule of the Roman papacy.

EPILOGUE

The threads briefly gathered in the 1656 celebrations soon unravelled. *La vita humana* was Marazzoli's last opera, and the 1656 celebrations were the last echo of the Barberini symbolic spectacles of the reign of Urban VIII. Like some diminished figure in the golden haze of *Le temps retrouvé*, Cardinal Francesco had given for Christina his last performance of the epic rages that had so delighted the chroniclers two decades earlier. The Barberini theater fell into disuse; over the years it was adapted to a variety of purposes including serving as a studio for the sculptor Bertel Thorwaldsen before being torn down in the 1930s to make way for an apartment building (fig. 8.10). (A bit of the façade survives.) Christina took over the Barberini's role as patron of opera, promoting artists such as Alessandro Scarlatti and Filippo Juvarra, presenting performances in her own private theater, and resisting Innocent XI's attempts to destroy operatic life in Rome. Giulio Rospigliosi became her friend, and the queen and Cardinal Azzolino regarded his election as Clement IX in 1667 as a personal triumph. Despite Christina's attempts on the thrones of Poland and Naples, the crowns that Rospigliosi had prophesied for her in *La vita humana* (wisely not specifying whether they were to be earthly or heavenly) continued to elude her. The womanly modesty, piety, and submission to the papacy that Alexander VII and Rospigliosi counseled to the queen in 1656 were fulfilled only in part in her later career in Rome. In at least one case, the murder of the wretched Gian Rinaldo Monaldeschi, Sdegno completely overthrew the Herculean control of Reason in the queen's character, and the immediate cause of her death was a stroke caused by her rage at an attempt to abduct a female opera-singer under her protection.

FIG. 8.10   Pietro da Cortona, *The Teatro Barberini Before its Demolition*

The magnificent Lauri–Gagliardi painting of the 1656 joust passed into Barberini family legend. When Georgina Masson, taking tea with Prince Barberini at the end of World War II, asked what the picture represented, he replied, "That's the party my family gave for Christina of Sweden," adding, "we still have the bills in our archive, including the one for the feathers." Years later, Miss Masson was writing her book on Queen Christina and attempted to recover this material from the Barberini Archive, which had been transferred to the Vatican and was in a state of chaos. She recounted the story to the Belgian Sub-Prefect of the Biblioteca Vaticana as evidence that the documents must exist. "Madame," he replied coldly, "les princes italiens ne s'occupent pas de Libri mastri generali." Recalling the scene, she would crow triumphantly, "But I found it, and at the end was the bill for the feathers, just as old Enrico had said!"

Appendix

Excerpts from the accounts of Don Maffeo Barberini for the 1656 festivities:

BAV, AB, MB, Comp. 356, LMG AA. opening 307 left:
"Spese p[er] la giostra, e Comedie del p[rese]nte anno devono dare @ p[ri]mo febraro s[cu]di duecento m[one]ta buoni al s[acro] m[onte] della Pietà pagati con m[andat]o no. 1300 alli ss.ri March[es]i Gio: B.a Costaguti, e Stefano Pignatelli due delli Deputati di d[ett]a Giostra dalla parte dell'Amazzoni"

26 Feb.: sc. 26 to a droghiere for sugar, sc. 39 to an indoratore per "oro trito p[er] truffare il Carro d'oro, e rosso" / sc. 126.04 to a segatore for the tavolini of the scalinata, and Teatro for the joust / sc. 6 to Fran.co Marti "m[aest]ro di ballo ad un Sonatore, che suonava alle Comedie" / sc. 5.30 for a segatore who sawed wood for the scalinata / sc. 3.92 to a bottigliere for "cedri e limoni et altre in tre comedie," wood for "palchetti fatti sotto il n[ost]ro Palazzo, tavole d'abeto prese per dipingere li termini, che reggevano le padelle nel teatro della giostra," "2 store[?] servite, dove si lavoravano li carri" / payments for 16 "girelle date p[er] tenere le stelle di filo di ferro nel teatro della giostra" / payments to falegname for fitting benches borrowed elsewhere, to facchini for carrying and returning them / sc. 200 for droghiere for sugar to make water for comedies and joust / sc. 4.15 to the credenziere for men who helped at the credenza on the occasion of the banquet given for the cavaliers on the last day of Carnival / expenses for masks, four pistols for the joust, gold for the carro of red and gold / to the arcibugiero for gunpowder for the carro del Drago, pozzolana for the cortile of the joust / to Belard[i]no Terrentij sc. 17.23 "p[er] haver copiati foglij 98 1/2 di musica, che si cantava sop[r]a li carri della giostra" / to Servio [Servi] for 26 stelle and "altre girelle che reggevano d[ett]e stelle" / sc. 41.55 to Gio. F.co Grimaldi Pittore "p[er] haver dipinto li suoi Huomini li termini, et arco che stavano nel teatro della giostra" / to a worker in the bottiglieria, to facchini for pulling the carri two evenings / payment for merletto d'oro to put around joust programs / calze da pistola for the joust / 20 tapestries borrowed for the palchetti

opening 307 right, sc. 797.83 carried over: entries for wigs and powder for the joust, pozzolana, colors, for painting terms and arch / payments to festarolo for palchetti and stairs / sc. 18 to Ignatio Lazzari stampatore "p[er] haver stampato gli argomenti della d[ett]a giostra" / repayment to spenditore Lodovico Tentone; payments to a nevarolo, sc. 42.70 for stivaletti for joust, to a legname, "tocche d'argento" for caroselli, for padelle to burn around the theater / payments to Servio, to Cap. Gioseppe Rasponi a cavalier; ciambelle, "fattura et altre fatte per le padelle."

The last entry is dated 30 June, with a total of sc. 1429.50.

"THY HAND, GREAT ANARCH . . .": MUSIC AND SPECTACLE IN BARBERINI FUNERALS 1644–80

For Maria Giulia Barberini and Idalberto Fei

Thy hand, great Anarch, lets the curtain fall,
And universal darkness buries all.

Alexander Pope, *Dunciad*

Certain manifestations of Barberini patronage of music and spectacle reached their climax during the reign of Urban VIII, to be followed by a glorious afterglow in the festivities that the family presented in 1656 to welcome Christina of Sweden. The ensuing decline of interest in such events on the part of the older members of the family is apparent in the fact that Cardinal Francesco, the promoter of most of the great operatic spectacles presented in the 1630s and 40s and 1656, by 1674 was one of the two cardinals (the other was Benedetto Odescalchi, the future Innocent XI, "papa minga" — "the pope who says no" in the dialect of his native Milan) who led the campaign for closing the Teatro Tordinona, Rome's only public opera theater.[1]

---

[1] August 1675: comedies of *istrioni* will not be presented in the Teatro Tor di Nona, "havendo li sig.ri cardinali Francesco Barberini et Odescalchi rappresentato a N. S.re li scandali e li danni che ne nascono" ("the lords cardinals Francesco Barberini and Odescalchi having apprised Our Lord of the scandals and damages that arise from them"). As cardinal, Odescalchi "non mancava mai una sera durante i cinqu'anni [*recte* quattro] che la Regina mantenne il suo palco al Teatro" ("never missed an evening during the five years that the Queen [Christina] maintained her box in the Theater"), but on his election in 1676 "mutando tutto ad un tratto d'umore e di condotta, intraprese di distruggere il Teatro ove egli aveva costume di prendere tanto piacere" ("changing all at once in humor and behavior, he undertook the destruction of

Not unexpectedly, while the Barberini interest in worldly spectacle waned, funeral ceremonies began to loom larger as, one by one, the senior members of the family died off: Urban VIII, his brother Antonio, his nephew Don Taddeo, Taddeo's widow Anna Colonna, and finally the cardinal-nephews Antonio and Francesco.

In 1683 Claude-François Ménestrier described the typology of the seventeenth-century funeral, differentiating "invitation, cortège, service, funeral elegy, and burial." The decorations of the church were to correspond architectually to these aspects of the funeral: the outside façade to the invitation, the nave to the cortège, the altars to the service, the inscription to the funeral elegy, and the catafalque to the burial.[2] This allegorical representation culminated in "the luminous vision of the 'castrum doloris' which celebrated the triumph of death and the triumph of the religious and temporal power personified by the deceased."[3] (To see how little the typology of aristocratic funerals changed over the next two centuries, it suffices to read the first chapter of Federico De Robertis' *I Viceré* of 1894.)

We tend to take an analytical rather than a synthetic view of these ceremonies, but for a moment we may allow our imaginations to recreate the effect of the church, darkened by funereal draperies but illuminated by hundreds of candles; the great catafalque and the splendidly macabre decorations; and the solemn music of chant or polyphony.

A complete funeral celebration comprised the Office for the Dead (Matins with its three Nocturns, Lauds, the Little Hours, Vespers, and Compline), and the Requiem mass. In the case of important religious or secular personages, solemn absolutions were sometimes performed at the end of the mass, by five cardinals for a pope and five bishops for a cardinal.

Marcello Fagiolo has individuated seven typologies of apparati:

1. catafalques in the shape of an antique circular temple; beginning in Rome, these were employed throughout Europe for sovereigns.

---

the Theater where he had been accustomed to take so much pleasure") (*Istoria segreta*, cit. Alberto Cametti, *Il teatro di Tordinona poi Apollo* [Tivoli, 1938], 63ff.).

[2] Claude-François Ménestrier, *Des decorations funebres* (Paris: De La Caille, 1683); Silvia Carandini and Maurizio Fagiolo dell'Arco, *L'effimero barocco* (Rome: Bulzoni, 1978), 2:322; quoted by Matteucci and Ariuli, *Giovanni Francesco Grimaldi*, 90. The library of Urban VIII contained printed *relazioni* of funerals, especially those whose decorations influenced the design of Bernini's baldacchino such as the funerals of Paul V and Cosimo II de' Medici (Sebastian Schütze, "La biblioteca del cardinale Maffeo Barberini: Prolegomena per una biografia culturale ed intellettuale del Papa Poeta," *I Barberini e la cultura europea del Seicento*, 37–46, esp. 42.

[3] Carandini, cit. Matteucci and Ariuli, *Giovanni Francesco Grimaldi*, 90.

2. tempietti or ciboria on a central plan (octagons etc.) surmounted by cupolas or baldachins.

3. ædicolæ on raised steps resembling a pyre (*pyra*): these were especially connected with kings of Spain.

4. pyramidal constructions as the basis for a trionfo of the deceased, who is represented in the form of a colossal statue or a winged image supported by angels, Fame, or other allegorical figures.

5. pyramids, recalling the marvels of Egypt: these were variously interpreted as a symbol of immortality, of the soul, or of heaven. According to Cesare Ripa's *Iconologia*, the pyramid symbolized apotheosis, the "bright, & high glory of Princes, who with magnificence make sumptuous and great buildings, with which this glory is shown."[4] The most notable example is Bernini's catafalque for the Duke of Beaufort (1669).

6. catafalques surrounded by four obelisks or guglie, employed for sovereigns or condottieri.

7. catafalques with mixed installations or inventions.[5]

As the celebrations of the Prince's Carnival of 1634 provided a model for the 1656 festivities, so the Requiem ceremonies for benefactors of the Jesuit Order that Cardinal Antonio presented on 17–19 November 1639 as part of their centenary celebrations may serve as a pattern in describing later Barberini funerals.

The castrum doloris for the Gesù (fig. 9.1) was designed by Antonio's favorite artist Andrea Sacchi, and its glory was such as to fan the already existing envy of Bernini.[6] According to the Roman chronicler Giacinto Gigli, "they made a very high Catafalque [about eighteen meters] with four Pyramids in the corners with many Inscriptions, and Statues, and figures representing dead bodies with papier-mâché bones: and all the Church was hung with black from the vault to the ground, but the black cloths were not complete, but the pilasters remained white, and the black was between one pilaster and another so that the *apparato* appeared at the same time

---

[4] "[C]hiara, & alta gloria de i Principi, che con magnificenza fanno fabriche sontuose, e grandi, con le quali si mostra essa gloria" (Ripa, *Iconologia*, 198); Maurizio Fagiolo dell'Arco, *La festa a Roma*, 2:29–37.

[5] Marcello Fagiolo, "Introduzione alla festa barocca: il Laboratorio delle Arti e la Città Effimera," *Le capitali della festa*, ed. Marcello Fagiolo, 22.

[6] Maurizio Fagiolo dell'Arco, *La festa barocca*, 311.

FIG. 9.1 Andrea Sacchi, *Catafalque for the Benefactors of the Gesù* (1639),
engraving by Johannes Valdor
(Rome, Biblioteca Apostolica Vaticana)

sad, and happy"[7]—a sort of *demi-deuil*. Among the personifications represented by the statues were Charity, Religion (her head veiled, like that of the Nile in Bernini's Fountain of the Rivers, to indicate "the obscurity of the Faith"), Benignity, and Liberality. Eternity and Immortality accompanied Adam and Eve, who were held prisoner by a great figure of Death. The catafalque was surrounded by four smoking extinguished candle-obelisks [Gigli's *piramidi*] complete with snuffers, while two skeletons with torches flanked the urn that surmounted the catafalque. The ensemble thus constituted a Triumph of Death, which was brought into the world by Sin through the fall of Adam and Eve, and which overcomes earthly powers. Death in turn is vanquished by Faith, here symbolized by the figures of Eternity and Immortality and by a grisaille panel depicting Pope Gregory the Great interceding for the souls in Purgatory.

URBAN VIII (1644)

Solemn exequies could be performed after the burial of the actual corpse. In the case of a pope, "the Body of the Dead pope was displayed for three days in S. Pietro, and the Exequies were celebrated for nine days."[8] The corpse was dressed in red pontifical mass vestments with two cardinal's hats at its feet. The papal funeral ceremonies were celebrated at length not only for solemnity but also to give nonresident cardinals time to reach the City for the ensuing conclave. For each of the first six days the singers of the papal chapel sang in the presence of the College of Cardinals in the Cappella della Pietà a Requiem mass "all in Plainchant," intoned by the sopranos without improvised counterpoint (*contrapunto*), "according to the style of our Cappella," and sung andante or "with care" ("con sollecitudine"). The Tract and the Sequence of the mass were sung by three pairs of sopranos.[9] On the last three days of mourning the daily pontifical Requiem mass was followed by solemn absolutions with incense and holy water at the specially erected catafalque.

---

[7] "... fecero un Catafalco altissimo con quattro Piramidi nelle cantonate con molte Scrittioni, et Statue, et figure rappresentanti corpi morti di ossa fatti di cartone: et tutta la Chiesa apparata di negro dalla volta sino a terra, ma però non erano i panni neri intieri, ma rimanevano i pilastri bianchi, et il nero era tra un pilastro e l'altro acciò comparisse l'apparato mesto insieme, et allegro" (*Diario*, 322–23).

[8] Gigli, *Diario*, cit.; Fagiolo, *La festa*, 248. The public display of the pope's corpse, like the ceremony in which the cardinal Camerlengo (in this case Antonio Barberini) tapped three times on the forehead of the corpse, calling the pope by his baptismal name, demonstrated that the pontiff was indeed dead. The Fisherman's Ring was later broken by a ceremonarius in the presence of the cardinals.

[9] Andrea Adami, *Osservazioni per ben regolare il coro dei cantori della Cappella Pontificia*, 93–95.

The absolutions, beginning with the chant "Non intres" ("Enter not into judgment with thy servant, O Lord, for in thy sight shall no man living be justified"), were performed by the celebrating cardinal and four other cardinal bishops to the accompaniment of responsories sung by the Cappella Pontificia. On the tenth day a Mass of the Holy Ghost opened the conclave to elect a new pope.[10]

Urban VIII died on 29 July 1644. Gigli reports that during the ensuing exposition of the pope's body in St. Peter's, "there was great tumult . . . and one smelled a stench from the cadaver, very great the first day."[11] The diary of the puntatore of the Cappella Pontificia, an official elected annually and charged with recording and fining absences, under the date of 29 July notes that while Urban was lying in state the choir sang the responsory "Subvenite sancti Dei all in plain chant [and] with great gravity it was finished." Under the date of 6 August the puntatore mentions in passing that "the Pyramid"—the castrum doloris—"which they are making in the midst of San Pietro for the aforesaid funeral [is] not finished." It was completed the next day, and the five responsories for the absolutions were sung by the Cappella.[12] The conclave began on 9 August with the singing of Gregorio Allegri's eight-part setting of *Veni Creator Spiritus*.[13]

The Cappella Pontificia, now usually called the Cappella Sistina, was the pope's private musical establishment, which sang when he officiated in church and also provided music for such secular occasions as banquets and anniversaries. (The regular choir of San Pietro was the Cappella Giulia, linked to the place rather than to the person of the pope.) P. P. Sevin depicted the musicians of the Cappella Pontificia performing at the banquet offered by Clement IX Rospigliosi to Christina of Sweden on 9 December 1668 (fig. 9.2).

The Cappella maintained a number of special performance practices. All the parts were sung by male voices, the upper ones by falsettists or castrati, who also played the leading role in chant-intonations. Instruments, even organ continuo, were not permitted when the Cappella performed in church, and its repertory was conservative. The basis of the repertory was plainchant, either performed "con molta gravità secondo lo stile della nostra Cappella" in measured rhythms rather the current rhythmically free style, or employed as the basis for contrapunto, improvised

---

[10] Adami, *Osservazioni*, 90–95, 147–15; BAV, CS, Diario 63, fol. 43v.

[11] Gigli, *Diario*, 427.

[12] BAV, CS 63, fols. 48–48v: "Subvenite sancti Dei tutto in canto fermo co[n] molta gravità è finito"; "non esser' finita la Piramide, che si fa in mezzo à San Pietro per il sud[dett]o funerale." According to Fagiolo, *La festa*, 248, the erection of a catafalque in St. Peter's became customary from this time on.

[13] BAV, CS 63, fols. 50–50v.

FIG. 9.2   P. P. Sevin, *Musicians of the Papal Chapel Performing*
at the Banquet of Clement IX Rospigliosi
for Christina of Sweden
(Stockholm, Nationalmuseum)

polyphony.[14] The polyphonic repertory of the Cappella was dominated by the liturgical music of Palestrina, but the composer-members of the Cappella also provided music in a more up-to-date style for other occasions, such as the banquet for Christina. A final echo of the Cappella's performance practice has been preserved in one of the Lamentations for Holy Week sung by the last castrato in the choir, Alessandro Moreschi, and recorded well over a century ago, in April of 1904.

Like that of the 1639 Jesuit ceremony, Pope Urban's catafalque was designed by his nephew Antonio's protégé Andrea Sacchi, who received sc. 200 from the Reverenda Camera Apostolica.[15] The "piramide" of the puntatore book may refer to obelisks, conceivably ones recycled from the 1639 Gesù commemoration. The diary of Bernini's associate Carlo Cartari, rettore of the Sapienza, describes in detail a much more complex construction, painted to imitate porphry and bronze: sixteen columns in four divisions surrounding a tholus and interspersed with medallions and other decorations. At the center of the tholus was an urn with cushions of gold brocade.[16] Cardinal Francesco Barberini's account-books for 1645 record sc. 76.28 for a lead coffin (great personages were traditionally entombed in an outer coffin of wood and an inner one of lead with an inscription) and sc. 390.10 for "esequie," including the catafalque (sc. 25), black hangings (sc. 10.55), candles (sc. 261.15), gilding (sc. 66.60), and music and masses (the healthy sum of sc. 120), plus sc. 31 to the sacristan.[17]

CARDINAL ANTONIO BARBERINI THE ELDER (SANT'ONOFRIO) (1646)

The diary of the puntatore of the Cappella Pontificia for 1646 records: "Wednesday 12 [September 1646] at the twenty-first hour [three hours before sunset] the exequies of the Most Eminent Sig. Cardinal Sant'Onofrio Barberini at Santo Andrea della Valle. The Sacred College was present[;] all [the singers were] present with all the

---

[14] For an example of contrapunto see Hammond, *Music and Spectacle*, 136.

[15] Fagiolo, *La festa*, 326.

[16] RAdS, Cartari-Febei, b. 73, fol. 151, quoted in Fagiolo, *La festa*, 326. Whether the two writers are describing the same monument is unclear, but as Jennifer Montagu has pointed out (*Roman Baroque Sculpture: The Industry of Art* [New Haven and London: Yale University Press, 1989], 183), such discrepancies between sources are not uncommon. Cartari regarded the catafalque for Innocent X as "much inferior to the one made for the exequies of Urban" (quoted by Fagiolo, *La festa*, 366).

[17] BAV, AB, CFB, Computisteria 82, fols. 164, 209v. Bernini's tomb of Urban VIII was unveiled in March of 1647 (Gigli, *Diario*, 497).

signori giubilati [pensioned members of the Cappella]."[18] Giacinto Gigli noted in his diary that the Capuchin Antonio (called Cardinal Sant'Onofrio to distinguish him from his nephew Antonio) died in his nephew's palace at the Quattro Fontane and that his body was taken to the family chapel in Sant'Andrea della Valle, where "the office was performed with great solemnity on the 12, and when the office was finished [the body] was carried to be buried in the Church of the Conception of the Capuccini [Santa Maria della Concezione, on what is now Via Veneto], which Church with its Convent was built by Pope Urban at his urging for the said Friars. His body was accompanied by the Orfanelli, and by 23. Companies of sacchi [confraternities], and 13. Friaries with 250. torches of white wax."[19]

Unlike the other Barberini, Gigli adds, Antonio was praised for his generosity to pious works. He left the residue of his estate to the Propaganda Fede, and nothing to his relatives. His gravestone at the entrance to the choir of the Capuccini bears the famous inscription, "Here lie ashes, dust, and nothing."

The funeral ceremonies for a cardinal were clearly laid out.[20] They resembled those for a dead pope, except that the pontifical absolutions for cardinals were given by bishops instead of cardinals. The body was to be transported to the nearest church and placed on "a high platform on a pall of 'broccato lugubre,'" vested in purple mass vestments according to its rank in the College, with two cardinal's hats at its feet. At the foot of the catafalque was a table with a white cloth, holding two lighted candelabra, a cotta, a black stole and cope, holy water and a sprinkler, and a thurible and incense boat. The church was draped in black with the customary arms and trophies. The corpse was attended by four masters of ceremonies, cursors with silver maces, and two grooms [palafrenieri] from the cardinal's household holding banderoles of black taffeta. In the early afternoon ["dopo desinare"] of the next day all the Friaries were to go to the church to sing the Office of the Dead, dividing the Nocturns of the Office among them. During the Office visiting cardinals, vested in mourning purple, after praying before the Sacrament, went to the feet of the corpse, said an Our Father, and sprinkled it with holy water.[21] An engraving of 1689 shows

---

[18] BAV, CS, Diario 65, f. 66r: "12 Mercredi (7bre 1646) a hore 21 l'esequi[e] del E.mo Sig.e Cardinal Sant Onofrio Barberini a Santo Andrea della Valle. Presente il Sacro Collegio tutti presenti con tutti li S.ri Giubilati."

[19] Gigli, *Diario*, 479–80: ". . . fu fatto l'offitio con gran solennità alli 12., et finito l'offitio, fu portato a sepellire alla Chiesa della Concettione de' Capuccini, la qual Chiesa con il Convento fu ad instanza sua edificata da Papa Urbano per li detti suoi Frati. Fu il suo corpo accompagnato dalli Orfanelli, et da 23. Compagnie di sacchi, et 13. Fratarie con 250. torcie di cera bianca."

[20] Girolamo Lunadoro, *Relatione della Corte di Roma* (Venice: Brigonei, 1661), 175–78.

[21] Funeral of Cardinal Sannesi, 21 February 1621, in *Päpstliches Zeremoniell*, ed. Wassilowsky and Wolf, 115.

a cardinal performing the same office for Christina of Sweden (fig. 9.3), with the table clearly visible.

For funerals "con pompa" the burial of a cardinal in his titular church could be accompanied by a procession of friaries with lights, prelates and Apostolic Protonotaries mounted on their mules, members of the papal household, and servants. "For some Cardinals who are of great families, and have rich relatives, they then perform their exequies in the Church where they are buried, with beautiful catafalques, where the entire Sacred College attends the sung Mass."[22] Such ceremonies were always performed around sunset. For interments "senza pompa" the corpse was carried to its resting place secretly in a carriage two hours after sunset.

*   *   *   *

The Roman Way of Death

Prima, a Ppalazzo, tanti frati neri
La notte e'r giorno a bbarbottà orazzione!
Pe Rroma, quer mortorio bbuggiarone!
Cqua, tante torce e ttanti cannejjeri!

Messe sú, mmesse ggiú, bbenedizzione,
Bòtti, diasille, prediche, incenzieri,
Sonnetti ar catafarco, arme, bbraghieri,
E sempre Cardinali in priscissione!

G. G. Belli, "Le Ssequie de Leone
Duodescimosiconno a Ssan Pietro" (1831).[23]

Most accounts of Roman Baroque funerals concentrate on the artistic and spectacular aspects of the events: music, spoken and written commemorations, decorations and their depictions. At least one seventeenth-century Roman source shows the reverse of the medal, the details of the behind-the-scenes preparations, down to the prices

---

[22] Lunadoro, *Relatione*, 177: "Ad alcuni card. che son di gran famiglia, e hanno parenti ricchi, gli si fanno poi l'esequie nella Chiesa dove son sotterrati, con belli catafalchi, dove assiste tutto il Sacro Collegio alla Messa cantata . . ."

[23] "First, in the [Apostolic] Palace, so many black friars / Mumbling prayers night and day! / Throughout Rome, that buggering funeral! / Here [San Pietro], how many torches and candelabra! // Masses up, masses down, benedictions, / Artillery, *Dies Irae*, sermons, incensing, / Sonnets to the catafalque, coats of arms, piles of things, / And always Cardinals in procession!" / G. G. Belli, "The Exequies of Leo the Twelfthy-Second at St. Peter's."

Fɪɢ. 9.3 Nicolas Dorigny, *Cardinal Asperging the Corpse of Christina of Sweden Lying in State in S. Maria in Vallicella* (Stockholm, Nationalmuseum)

of the goods and services involved. *Il Perfetto Mastro di Casa, Libro Terzo* of Francesco Liberati (Rome: Per Angelo Bernabò dal Verme, 1668; reprint, Sala Bolognese: Forni, 1974) was written as an instruction book for the maestro di casa, the head of the household of a cardinal or a great prince. As the former maestro di casa of Cardinal Bichi, Liberati writes from experience. He offers detailed advice for situations new to the novice maestro: the forms of celebration for the creation of a cardinal padrone; the furnishings, equipment, and services for the cardinal participating in a papal conclave; and the ceremonies at the death of the cardinal padrone. Of these events, the first "is performed with enthusiasm, and splendor," the last "with sorrow and parsimony; but nonetheless the one, and the other are of great expense."[24]

Liberati's instructions presuppose the following sequence of events. First, a lying in state of the corpse, vested pontifically, in its own palace. Next, a procession at night to the parish church of the cardinal's residence, which was decorated for the exequies that were to take place the next day; bells were rung as part of the ceremonies. Participants included five mendicant orders who sang the office of the dead, the singers and clergy of the Cappella Pontificia, various masters of ceremonies, the papal bailiffs (cursori), the clergy of the churches involved, and perhaps sundry professional mourners (beccamorti). After the funeral, the body was taken in procession to the church where it was to be entombed and the funeral decorations were removed. Cardinal-deans and great princes were entitled to a cavalcade, "where all the Household [Camera] of the pope, & other persons participate."[25]

Liberati establishes a tone of hard-headed realism at the outset of his discussion: ". . . when your Padrone has died, you will immediately see appear before you Festaroli, Printers of the arms of the dead, Merchants of black cloth, & others, who hiding behind honeyed words, will try to get the job. . . ."[26] Liberati advises the maestro di camera to pay the funeral debts immediately, "and particularly the workmen, and the Artisans, who are needier than the others, and quicker to complain about it . . . As soon as the Funeral is finished pay off your debts, and also come to terms with the Masters of Ceremonies, Musicians, Cursori, and then with the other tradespeople who took part in the exequies, for you can be sure that early next morning you will

---

[24] 3:231: "La prima delle quali si fà con gusto, e splendidezza, e la seconda con dispiacere, & avaritia; ma sono tuttavia l'una, e l'altra di grandissima spesa . . ."

[25] 3:269: "Alli Signori Cardinali Decani, overo Priincipi grandi si suol far la Cavalcata, che c'intervengono tutta la Camera di Nostro Signore, & altre persone."

[26] 3:251: ". . . succeduta la morte del suo Padrone, verrà subbito compargli avanti Festaroli, Stampatori d'armi da morte, Cimatori de' panni neri, & altri, che difendendosi in parole melate, si studieranno per haver l'impiego . . ."

find all of them at your door."[27] (To avoid this, it was customary for the maestro di casa to set up an account with a bank, which would pay the creditors from a list furnished by the maestro.)

On the death of the cardinal padrone, the maestro di casa's first responsibility was to order from the Banderaro, the vestment-maker, episcopal mass vestments of purple taffeta, the color of mourning for cardinals: tunic, dalmatic, chasuble, stole, maniple, silk gloves, liturgical stockings ["Sandali"], and shoes, as well as two cushions of the same material. (The obligatory simple miter of white damask had already formed part of the new cardinal's trousseau.)[28] The maestro should also purchase "a pectoral Cross, and a ring, both of gilded brass with false stones to be buried with the corpse, and they are worth about three scudi."[29] Other furnishings included a carpet with a fringe of black velvet, which could be borrowed if the cardinal's heirs did not want to buy a new one; the original owner's arms on the borrowed carpet were to be covered by the cardinal's arms in silver paper. Four banderoles of black taffeta with black staves were to be provided for four of the cardinal's grooms (palafrenieri), beginning with the dean of the grooms (decano dei palfrenieri), to hold at the corners of the coffin.

The coffin itself was to be ordered from the carpenter. Its dimensions were 9 x 12 palmi (roughly 7' x 9'), and it was supported on two trestles, the one under the head two palmi (18") higher than the one at the foot. The case of cypress, which cost 3.50 scudi, was put inside a leaden case costing 4 1/2 baiocchi per pound [libra] of metal, "with the arms, and letters carved with the name, and family name, title, and age of the deceased cardinal."[30]

Liberati describes the festaroli, the artisans who rented the draperies for the church and hung and dismantled them, as the most aggressive and rapacious of the tradesmen, and he insists repeatedly that the maestro di casa must not make a commitment to them without previously agreeing on a price.

---

[27] 3:265: "Deve il Maestro di casa sopra il tutto usar puntualità in pagare li creditori, e particolarmente gli operarij, e l'Artisti, che sono più degli altri bisognosi, e più facili à lamentarsi; subbito dunque finita la fontione del Mortorio sodisfaccia i suoi debiti, e compisca parimente con li Signori Mastri di Cerimonie, Musici, Cursori, e poscia con gli altri mercenarij, che v'interven[n]ero nell'essequie, assicurandosi che il giorno seguente la matina à buon hora, gli trovarà tutti intorno alla sua porta."

[28] 3:235: "Una Mitra bianca di damasco . . ."

[29] 3:252–53: ". . . l'infrascritte robbe di taffettà pavonazzo, che servono per l'esequie, cioè Tonicella, Dalmatica, Pianeta, Stola, Manipolo, guanti di seta, Sandali, scarpe episcopali, e due coscini . . . d'una Crocetta pettorale, e d'un anello ambedue d'ottone indorato con pietra falsa da sepellirsi insieme con il cadavero, e vagliano trè scudi in circa."

[30] 3:268: "Per la Cassa di piombo, con arme, e lettere scolpite col nome, e cognome, titolo, & età del defonto Cardinale, si suol pagare baiocchi quattro, e mezzo la libra."

The festarolo was to hang cloths in the nave and tribune of the church, on the inner and outer façades, and to attach the cardinal's arms and the morti or figures of death, which were furnished by the coloraro. (As well as the morti, the coloraro also provided arms of the cardinal, two thousand small ones and two hundred large ones.)[31] The festarolo was to cover the benches for the assisting cardinals, drape the baldacchino over the high altar of the church, provide covering and cushions for a double kneeling-desk before the Sacrament, and cover the catafalque with black taffeta bearing the cardinal's arms.

Liberati warns that the festarolo will claim sc. 120–130 as the going rate, but sc. 25 is what the Dominican church of Santa Maria sopra Minerva, Liberati's paradigm church, paid the festarolo for decorating its two greatest festivals. To the festarolo's objection that more time is available for such occasions, Liberati answers that "the labor of the exequies [is] done, and dismantled within twenty-four hours at most without special decoration [disegno], & architecture . . ."[32] (This implies that not all funerals employed the elaborate and purpose-built decorations characteristic of the great Barberini ceremonies.) Liberati also criticizes the cimatori and the Jews who rent cloth: they inflate their bills, pleading "the carrying, and the carrying back, the sewing, and the unsewing of the cloths."[33]

As always in seventeenth-century Rome, candles were an important expense. The maestro di casa was to provide twelve candles of a pound each for the high altar and Sacrament altar of the church where the funeral was celebrated, as well as two candles of four pounds each for "the little table in front of the bed where the Corpse will be placed."[34]

Gratuities in the form both of candles and money were given to the various participants in the ceremonies. Each of the five orders of mendicant friars who sang the office of the dead received a bundle of thirty candles of thirty ounces each and a scudo apiece.[35] As a group, the singers of the Cappella Pontificia received forty-five pounds of wax and fifteen scudi in cash.[36]

---

[31] 3:259–60.

[32] 3:257: ". . . il lavoro dell'essequie facendosi, e sfacendosi in termine di ventiquattro hore alla peggio senza disegno, & architettura. . . ."

[33] 3:258–59: ". . . la portatura, e la riportatura, coscitura, e discuscitura de' panni. . . ."

[34] 3:262: "Di più due candele di quattro libre l'una per il tavolino avanti al letto dove sarà collocato il Cadavero."

[35] 3:263, 267.

[36] 3:263, 266.

DON TADDEO BARBERINI (1647)

Don Taddeo, Prince Prefect and Prince of Palestrina, died in exile in Paris on 14 November 1647, "at 44 years of age, dead without doubt owing to the sufferings, and torments sustained in the persecution of his House," as Gigli noted.[37] Under the heading "Conti di Francia" in Cardinal Antonio's financial records there appear entries of sc. 314 "for expenses made for the funeral of the Most Excellent Sr. Prince Don Taddeo, that is a lead case; and for the carpenter" and a further payment of sc. 10.54 "to various People, that is tradesman [mercante], barber, embroiderer, and painter."[38] The painter may have been Paolo Gismondi (1612–c.1685), who frescoed a sacristy in Sant'Agnese in Agone c. 1664.[39] Although no details of Taddeo's exequies are given, the sum recorded suggests at least a dignified commemoration despite the decline in Barberini fortunes.

ANNA COLONNA BARBERINI (1658)

Taddeo's widow, Anna Colonna, died on 31 October 1658. Her principal benefaction was her foundation of Santa Maria Regina Coeli, a convent of Discalced Carmelites located on the Lungara in the place now occupied by the prison of the same name. Although the first stone of the building, which was designed by Taddeo's architect Francesco Contini,[40] was laid in 1642, permission to admit nuns was not obtained from Innocent X until 1654 on the occasion of the forced marriage of Anna's daughter Lucrezia to the duke of Modena. Most of the decoration of the convent was carried out after Anna's death by her heir, her third and favorite son Nicolò, also a Carmelite, who spent more than 3,000 scudi on her monument and furnishings for the convent chapel.[41]

---

[37] Gigli, *Diario*, 510.

[38] BAV, AB, CAB, Comp. 280, fol. 70: "per spese fatte per il funerale dell'Ecc.mo S.re P[ri]n[ci]pe D. Taddeo, cioè cassa di piombo; et al falegname"; "a Diversi, cioè mercante, barbiere, raccamatore, e pittore." On Gismondi see Silvia Bruno, "I Barberini e il loro *entourage* in Francia," *I Barberini e la cultura europea del Seicento*, 317–30, 321.

[39] Anthony Blunt, *Guide to Baroque Rome* (New York: Harper & Row, 1982), 5.

[40] On Contini, see Waddy, *Seventeenth-Century Roman Palaces*, 289–90; and Lorella Masella and Zaira Fornari, "L'attività architettonica promossa dalla famiglia Barberini a Palestrina attraverso l'opera di Francesco Contini," *I Barberini a Palestrina*, ed. Peppino Tomassi (Palestrina, 1992).

[41] Marilyn Dunn, "Piety and Patronage in Seicento Rome: Two Noblewomen and Their Convents," *The Art Bulletin* 76 (1994): 644–63, esp. 651, n. 68. In *Les tapisseries des Barberini et la décoration d'intérieur dans la Rome baroque* (Turnhout, Belgium: Brepols, 2005), 66, Pascal-François Bertrand turns Lucrezia Barberini into her mother's sister, thus creating a non-existent "Lucrezia Colonna" (see Waddy, 169).

In her will, Anna expressed her confidence that Contini would execute her intentions for "my resting place facing the little window for the Communion of the nuns with my statue according to my thought as know Sig.re Francesco Contini my architect and mastro Gabriele Renzi my stone-cutter [scarpellino]."[42] As originally constructed, Anna's sepulchral monument consisted of two columns with gilded Corinthian capitals sustaining an entablature holding up a broken pediment consisting of curved scrolls and a triangular central element, surmounted by two angels brandishing the trumpets of Fame (fig. 9.4).[43] This framed a statue after a model by the otherwise unknown Jacomo Antonio Galli showing the Prefetessa in gilded bronze kneeling in prayer before a fictive prie-dieu of black marble, for which he was paid sc. 40 by Nicolò Barberini.[44] The monument was originally placed facing the small window through which the nuns received communion. At present the statue (now dated to 1659) and the black marble kneeling-desk with its inscription are preserved in the Albright–Knox Gallery in Buffalo, New York (fig. 9.5).

The convent of Regina Coeli was demolished around 1877 and the sepulchre was returned to the Barberini family. The statue was put on display in the Quattro Fontane palace and the rest of the monument stored in the palace cellar. Around 1884 Monsignor Giuseppe de Bisogno purchased the complex for an altar in the chapel of the palace he was building in Prati. When his palace was in turn demolished in 1962 the altar was returned to storage, where it is said still to exist.[45] Soon after World War II the Barberini sold the statue to the art-dealer Joseph Brummer, from whom the Museum acquired it in 1946.

The decorations for Anna's exequies, celebrated eleven days after her burial in Regina Coeli, included a catafalque comprising a cupola on eight columns with painted images of Charity, Prudence, Piety, and Constancy below, two crowns surmounted

---

[42] "[il] mio deposito incontro al finestrino della Communione delle monache con la mia statua conforme sa il mio pensiero il Sig.re Francesco Contini mio architetto e mastro Gabriele Renzi mio scarpellino" (Giuseppe Sacchi Lodispoto, "Anna Colonna Barberini ed il suo monumento nel monastero di Regina Coeli," *Strenna dei Romanisti* 43 [1982]: 460–78, esp. 471).

[43] The ensemble is reminiscent of Pietro da Cortona's door for the Barberini theater: see Merz, *Pietro da Cortona and Roman Baroque Architecture*, 25.

[44] For a terra cotta "ritratto della bo[na] me[moria] dell'Ecc. D. Anna Colonna Barberini Prefetessa comprensivi dei modelletti e promettendo di assistere al modello in cera e getto di metallo per la perfezione dell'opera" ("portrait of the Most Excellent D. Anna Colonna Barberini Prefectess of blessed memory comprising small models and promising to assist at the modeling in wax and the casting in metal for the perfecting of the work") (Lodispoto, "Anna Colonna," 475).

[45] Personal communication from an officer of the Banco di Roma; see Lodispoto, "Anna Colonna Barberini," 474.

FIG. 9.4 *Altar of Anna Colonna Barberini Monument*
(reconstruction after Lodispoto)

Fig. 9.5   Gabrielle Renzi, *Sepulchral Monument of*
Anna Colonna Barberini
(Buffalo, New York, Albright–Knox Gallery)

by the Barberini bees at the top, and possibly a portrait.[46] Anna's body was buried in a small room below the pavement in front of the high altar of the chapel; I do not know where her remains are to be found today.

   In addition to Nicolò's splendid ceremonies in Regina Coeli and exequies in two other Carmelite churches, Santa Maria della Scala and its daughter foundation Santa Maria della Vittoria, Anna's other two sons underwrote a rather mingy commemoration in Sant'Andrea della Valle, site of the Barberini family chapel. (She had been compelled to bring legal action against the Barberini for the restitution of her dowry.) The 1658 accounts of Anna's second son, Maffeo, prince of Palestrina,

---

[46] Dunn, "Piety and Patronage," 651, n. 68.

list sc. 64.33 paid to his elder brother, Cardinal Carlo, for "Spice-seller, Armorer, decorator [the festarolo, who rented draperies for churches and palaces and hung them and took them down], rental of black Cloths, carpenter, sung Mass, silver panels on loan brought and carried back all used for the funeral done in the Church of Sant'Andrea della Valle on the occasion of the death of the Most Excellent Donna Anna Colonna our Mother."[47]

SUOR INNOCENZA BARBERINI (1666)

In 1666 the Barberini funerals reached a low point indicated by a note in Cardinal Francesco's Giornale for 30 April, recording the miserable sum of sc. 5.60 to one who celebrated "several low and sung masses in various Churches, for the Soul of M[ad]re Suor Innocenza Barberini sister of His Eminence."[48] Sister Innocenza, in the world Camilla Barberini, was born in 1598 and was a nun of the convent of the Most Holy Incarnation together with her sister Clarice.

CARDINAL ANTONIO BARBERINI THE YOUNGER (1671)

Quite different were the exequies of their brother Cardinal Antonio, who died on 4 August 1671 at Nemi as the result of a stroke following a "Pantagruelian meal."[49] Funerals were celebrated for Antonio "in almost all the Churches of this great City."[50] Eight commemorations, each reflecting a different aspect of his career, seem to have been particularly important. The diary of the puntatore of the Cappella Pontificia for 1671 records: "Monday 31 [August] there was no service because the sacristy went

---

[47] BAV, AB, DMB, Comp. 379, 100: "Spetiale, Armarolo, festarolo, nolo di Panni neri, falegname, Messe, Messa cantata, sporti d'argento prestati portati e riportati il tutto servito p[er] il funerale fatto alla Chiesa di S. Andrea della Valle in occ[asion]e della morte dell'Ecc.ma Sig.ra D. Anna Colonna n[ost]ra M[ad]re."

[48] BAV, AB, CFB, Comp. 74, p. 39: "più messe basse e cantate in diverse Chiese, p[er] l'Anima della m[ad]re Suor Innocenza Barberini, sor[e]lla di S.E." Several devotional works, such as the engraving of the catafalque for the benefactors of the Jesuits, were dedicated to the sisters. The date of Antonio's death is given as 3 August in a list of protectors of the Ospedale della SS. Trinità de Pellegrini, as 4 August by the *Dizionario biografico degli italiani*.

[49] The gargantuan menu is quoted in Karin Elizabeth Wolfe, "Cardinal Antonio Barberini the Younger (1608–1671): Aspects of His Art Patronage" (Ph.D. thesis, Courtauld Institute, University of London, 1999), 182–83.

[50] BAV, Barb. lat. 4913, the apparato of the church of the Archconfraternita degli Orfani, 4 September 1671, fol. 29.

to the Propaganda Fede where were done the exequies of the Sig. Cardinal Antonio formerly our protector."[51] (Antonio had become cardinal protector of the Cappella in 1639.) Presumably the ceremony took place in Borromini's chapel of the Re Magi.

Other exequies for Cardinal Antonio were performed in the Church of the Arciconfraternita degli Orfani on 4 September. A funeral in Santa Maria Maggiore on 18 September was sponsored by Cardinal Giacomo Rospigliosi, who had succeeded Antonio as archpriest of the basilica in 1668. Giacomo was a nephew and occasional collaborator of the Barberini's former opera librettist Giulio Rospigliosi, later Pope Clement IX (d. 1669), who was buried in the basilica. The ceremony in Sant' Andrea della Valle on 26 September emphasized the presence there of the family chapel, begun by Urban VIII when still a cardinal. The funeral in the Gesù (September, date apparently unspecified) reflected Antonio's long-standing patronage of the Order. Cardinal Francesco also underwrote a funeral in his titular church of San Lorenzo in Damaso,[52] and his nephew Cardinal Carlo presented a funeral in the cathedral of Pesaro. Yet another funeral was celebrated at the Ospedale della SS. Trinità de' Pellegrini, of which Antonio was protector.[53] Although he was also the protector of the Dominican Order, there seems to be no record of a funeral in a Dominican church such as S. Maria sopra Minerva, for which Antonio had funded the building of the novitiate. In addition, the Congregation of the Virtuosi of the Pantheon resolved to "fare un poco d'esequie per riconoscere l'obligatione che la Congregazione ha a detta Eminenza . . . con la maggiore lautezza possibile" ("to make a bit of exequies to recognize the obligation of the Congregation to the said Eminence . . . with the greatest splendor possible").[54]

The expenses of the ceremonies in the Gesù and Sant'Andrea della Valle were paid by Francesco out of Antonio's estate. Disbursements are recorded for catafalques in both churches (sc. 300) and sc. 1600 for the ceremony in the Gesù.[55] Other expenses included the renting of black cloths, "arms of death," gesso and paintings for the catafalques. The engraver Domenico [Dominique] Barrière received sc. 45 for the catafalque in the Gesù (fig. 9.6) and other "printed writings" ("scritti a stampa"). Both the payment to Barrière and the inscription on the engraving of the catafalque

---

[51] BAV, CS 89, fol. 25r: "31 Lunedì (Agosto 1671) non fu servitio per che la sacrestia andò a Propaganda Fede dove furono fatto l'essequie per il S. Card.e Antonio gia n[ost]ro Protettore."

[52] BAV, AB, CFB, Comp. 89, 194.

[53] RAdS, Ospedale della SS. Trinità de Pellegrini, b. 546, letter "G"; I owe this important reference to the kindness of Dr. Karin Wolfe.

[54] Quoted in Wolfe, "Cardinal Antonio Barberini," 188.

[55] BAV, AB, CAB, Comp. 237, pp. 5, 8, 13–14.

FIG. 9.6 G. B. Contini, *Funeral Apparato for Cardinal Antonio Barberini in the Gesù,*
engraved by Dominique Barrière (Rome, Biblioteca Apostolica Vaticana)

indicate Giovanni Battista Contini (1641–1723), the son of Don Taddeo's architect and an assistant to Bernini, as the designer of the decorations.[56]

In contrast to the triumph of death of the 1639 commemorations in the Gesù, the decorations for Antonio's funeral there celebrated his earthly life. Barrière's engraving shows that the base of the catafalque was in the shape of an X, adorned with trophies and the cardinal's arms and surmounted by a tower of candles at each corner. According to the Latin relazione by the Jesuit Carlo Bovio, who also wrote the funeral oration, the four statues of female figures supported by a central element represented Beneficence, Magnanimity, Prudence, and Piety. These held up a drapery with the portrait of Antonio in a winged frame. The accounts contain payments for the four statues "representing four virtues and other works of sculpture, and models" and "Death, and small coats of arms in paper" (presumably papier-mâché).[57]

The ceremony of the Arciconfraternita degli Orfani, celebrated in Santa Maria in Aquiro on 4 September 1671, featured an apparato designed by Mattia de' Rossi, another of Bernini's assistants. Skeletons carried the insignia of Antonio's numerous dignities in Italy and France, where he had been archbishop of Reims, premier peer, Grand Almoner, and knight of the St.-Esprit and St.-Michel. A chariot of death carried away all the cardinal's earthly honors. The catafalque had four pedestals, three orders of stairs, and in the middle a high pyramid with a cardinal's hat. The mass was sung by Bishop Giuseppe Maria Suarez, "Vicario del Reverendissmo Capitolo di S. Pietro," and music played a prominent role: "in addition to the regular Musicians of the Church, from 12. other Outside Musicians, part from the Cappella Pontificia, and part from other principal Churches of Rome."[58] The employment of musicians from other organizations to supplement those of the Archconfraternity suggests the performance of polyphonic music as well as plainchant.

---

[56] Comp. 237, 25, 31–32, 38, 39. A pupil of his father and of Bernini, Contini worked with Fontana on the funerals of Alexander VII and Clement IX (but see Fagiolo, La festa, 479). Payments for the two catafalques are found in BAV, AB, CAB, Libro mastro, busta 220, fols. 130 left/right.

[57] BAV, AB, CAB, Comp. 237, 5–38. Fagiolo, La festa barocca, 494, ascribes the expenses of the ceremony to the Jesuits, but the inscription on the engraving attributes the "Cenotaphium funeri celebrando" to the Cardinals Francesco and Carlo and Don Maffeo.

[58] BAV, Barb. lat. 4913, fols. 30–37: "et oltre i Musici ordinarij della Chiesa, da 12. altri Musici Forastieri, parte della Cappella Pontificia, e parte d'altre Chiese Principali di Roma." The preacher, Joseph-Marie Suarès [Suarez], had encountered Cardinal Francesco Barberini in Avignon in October of 1625. In 1627 the cardinal summoned him to Rome, where he became librarian of the Barberini library, bishop of Vaison (1633), and vicar of St. Peter's and domestic prelate (1666). At his death in 1677 Suarès was buried in St. Peter's in a marble tomb paid for by Cardinal Francesco (Jérôme Delatour, "Abeilles thuaniennes et barberines: les relations des savants français avec les Barberini sous le pontificat d'Urbain VIII," I Barberini e la cultura europea del Seicento, 155–72, 161).

The funeral in Santa Maria Maggiore on 18 September featured "un bel catafalco" by Giovan Antonio de' Rossi (1616–95), widely active in Rome as an architect.[59] The church was hung with dark cloths and brilliantly illuminated by more than four hundred flares [fiaccole].

The catafalque for the 26 September ceremony in Sant'Andrea della Valle was again the work of Giovanni Battista Contini. As was customary, payments trickled on long after the expenses—at least until August of 1674—that they recompense: stucco work, carpenter, sculptures, gilding on the catafalques, rental of cloth, paintings, and a lead coffin for Antonio, who seems to have been stored away in the cathedral of Sant'Agabito in his nephew Maffeo's fief of Palestrina.[60]

In 1632 Cardinal Antonio had been elected protector of the Ospedale della SS. Trinità de Pellegrini in succession to Cardinal Ludovisi, and his possesso was celebrated on 17 January 1633. Owing to Antonio's absences in France, the popes designated a series of co-protectors, ending with Cardinal Carlo Barberini. On Antonio's death the guardians of the Ospedale voted unanimously for "esequie con pompa."

The "Memoria" describing the occasion does not seem to include a date among its copious details. The façade of the church was elaborately decorated with black cloth, arms, skeletons, and an inscription. Inside, the church was hung from the windows down with black cloth, leaving the cornice and other stucco ornaments free (like the demi-deuil effect of the 1639 Gesù decorations). Twenty-four silvered papier-mâché candelabra, each holding three fiaccole, were placed on the main cornice. Over each chapel there hung a skeleton of cloth held by a cherub of silvered papier-mâché, with the cardinal's arms in the middle chapel on either side of the church and lights on the pilasters. On the cornice under the central altarpiece (Guido Reni's "Holy Trinity") were placed twelve apostles in silver from the Cappella Pontificia.

The catafalque itself, "larger than usual," was furnished with many silver candlesticks and twelve silver torchières at the corners and others on the ground. At the top of the catafalque there was an urn covered with an embroidered cloth, and on that a cardinal's hat on a brocade cushion.

---

[59] Wolfe, "Cardinal Antonio Barberini," 189; Blunt, *Guide*, 311.

[60] "Trasferito il suo corpo a Palestrina, fu sepolto nella sua Cattedrale nella Cappella di S. Lorenzo con questa bellissima iscrizione: Il Peccatore a norma della sua testimentaria disposizione" ("when his body had been transferred to Palestrina, he was buried in its Cathedral in the Chapel of S.Lorenzo with this beautiful inscription, "The Sinner," according to his testamentary disposition"); *Repertorio di tutti li Cardinali che sono stati Protettori della Venerabile Arciconfraternita della Santissima Trinità de' Pellegrini* (RAdS, Ospedale della SS. Trinità de Pellegrini, b. 546, letter "G"), quoted in Wolfe, "Cardinal Antonio Barberini," Appendix 4, 262–68.

The Requiem mass was celebrated pontifically by Mons. Suarez. Music for two choirs was provided by "musici di cappella" (whether the cappella of the church or more likely the Cappella Pontificia is not specified) at the modest fee of 12 scudi (20 scudi was the usual compensation). In the context of seventeenth-century Roman church music, bi-choral settings were a rather commonplace solution.[61]

Cardinal Carlo's catafalque in the cathedral of Pesaro (fig. 9.7) was designed by the local nobleman Paolo Emilio Cassio. The text of the engraving by Santi Bartoli indicates that Carlo presented the ceremony in his capacity as legate *a latere* to the Province of Urbino, which had reverted to the papacy under Urban VIII in 1631 and was the source of the Della Rovere title of Prince Prefect of Rome that Carlo had inherited from his father (see Chapter 2). However, the phrase "cum ritu solemni parentaret Patruo Francisco Cardinali Barberino" ("with a solemn rite his Uncle Cardinal Francesco Barberini made this offering to the dead") on the engraving reveals that here as elsewhere, although the hands were the hands of Esau—in this case Carlo—the voice was the voice of Jacob, uncle Francesco.[62]

---

[61] "Si fece pertanto parare tutta la Chiesa dalle fenestre a basso di panni di lutto, lasciandosi scoperte tutte le cornici ed altri ornamenti di stucco; si distribuirono sopra il cornicione 24 gran candelabri di carta pesta di colore giallo allumati di oro trito con pendoncini di roverso nero, ciascuno de' quali reggeva tre fiacole cioè quella di mezzo di tre libre e l'altre di due libre l'una; sopra ciascuna cappella pendeva una morte in tela retta da un cherubino di carta pesta inargentato, e nella cappella di mezzo nell'uno e l'altro lato della Chiesa vi era l'arme di Sua Emza. in tela d'Imperatore retta parimente da un cherubino, ed a tutti li pilastri un lustrino grande inargentato con candela di una libra. In tutte le attacature di detti cherubini, quadri dell'armi e delle morti e de' lustrini vi era un fioco grande fatto di tocca d'argento . . . Il detto catafalco fu posto nel mezzo sotto la cupola in maggior grandezza del solito armato di gran numero di candelieri di argento con 12 torcieri di argento sopra detto catafalco alle cantonate di esso, con altri torcieri di argento in terra intorno al detto catafalco, nell'ultima cima del quale vi era una urna coperta con la nostra coltre ricamato, e sopra di essa il cappello Cardinalizio posato sopra un cuscino grande di broccato . . . Cantò la messa di requie Mons. Vescovo Suarez Vicario del Rmo. Capitolo di S. Pietro, pontificalmente con musici di cappella a due cori; il Padre Bompiani della Compagnia di Gesù fece l'orazione latina." Quoted in Wolfe, "Cardinal Antonio Barberini," 262–68.

[62] The engraving is reproduced in Fagiolo, *La festa*, 494, where Carlo is mis-identified as Antonio's brother and the sponsor of the funeral in Sant'Andrea della Valle. Carlo also commissioned the completion of a statue of Urban VIII by Lorenzo Ottoni for Pesaro Elena (Bianca di Gioia, *Le collezioni di scultura del Museo di Roma: Il Seicento* [Rome: Campisano, 2002], 201).

FIG. 9.7   Paolo Emilio Cassio, *Funeral Apparato for Cardinal Antonio Barberini, Pesaro, Duomo,*
engraved by Pietro Santi Bartoli
(Rome, Biblioteca Apostolica Vaticana)

CARDINAL FRANCESCO BARBERINI (10 DECEMBER 1679)

Francesco survived his youngest brother by eight years, in which he absorbed Antonio's vast artistic inheritance and made significant alterations to the palace at the Quattro Fontane.[63]

As in the case of Antonio, funerals were celebrated for Francesco in several Roman churches, among them St. Peter's, Santa Maria in Cosmedin, and his titular church of San Lorenzo in Damaso. The expenses of these funerals were sustained by his nephew Cardinal Carlo, whose Libro mastro records payments for "wax, decorations [apparatura], coats of arms . . . masses celebrated, for the music, charitable gifts to the poor of the Ospedale of Monte Filicaia," for copper and for an engraver, and for paper for printing.[64]

The diary of the puntatore for the Cappella Pontificia for 1679 records: "13 [December] Wednesday Santa Lucia there was not the customary service[;] after supper were performed the exequies of the Most Eminent S.re Cardinal Barberino at S. Lorenzo in Damaso, from whence his body was carried with the customary cavalcade to the sacristy of S. Pietro with great solemnity, both of friars, and confraternities[,] it reached there about the second hour of night."[65]

The presence of the Cappella Pontificia implied polyphonic music, but the puntatore's statement also confirms Lunadoro's account, that the orders of friars played a significant part in cardinalatial funerals. Since Francesco was the cardinal protector of the Franciscan Order, they had a prominent role in his exequies. The friars assembled at their church of the Araceli and went in procession to Francesco's titular church of San Lorenzo in Damaso; upon entering they divided into two antiphonal choirs.

---

[63] Waddy, *Roman Baroque Palaces*, 351–71.

[64] CCB, Libro mastro, busta 297, ff. 241 sinistra e destra, f. 241: "Spese fatte in occ[asion]e della morte della gl[orios]a mem[oria] Dell Em. Card. Franc.o Barberini n[ost]ro Zio (1680).

    9 Genn[aio] 898 sc. 898.70 per pag[are] alli Gio. Dom[enic]o e Bernardino Valentini droghieri per prezzo di 3268 cera bianca di Venetia sc. 898.70

    Febraro sc. 207.40 per tanti spesi e pag[a]ti per il funerale fatto in S. Pietro

    Detto sc. 75.25 per tanti spesi in cera, apparatura, arme attacate alla facciata, messe fatte celebrare, per la musica, dati per carita a' poveri d[ell']ospedale di Monte Filicaia [?] et altro per il funerale et essequie fatte in S. Maria in Cosmedin

    1682: 31 dicembre sc. 18.50 . . . per tanti pagati . . . cioè sc. 15 a Pietro de Santis intagliatore, e sc. 3.50 per il rame dell'intaglio fatto per l'iscrittione del funerale dell'Em Fran.co

    Destra: 31 dicembre sc. 6.97 buoni ad Ignatia, e Fratelli Passarini . . . per carta da stampare, et altro dato dalla sua bottega in serv[izio] del funerale" Totale: sc. 1199.85.

[65] BAV, CS 98, fol. 40v: "13 (Dicembre 1679) Mercodi Santa Lucia non si servì al solito il dopo pranzo furono fatte l'Essequie dell'Em.mo S.re Cardinal Barberino a S. Lorenzo in Damaso, di dove fu trasportato il suo corpo con la solita cavalcata alla sacrestia di S. Pietro con grandissima solennita, si di fraterie, come anche di confraternita la giunsi circa li due hore di notte."

Their singing—the special chant dialect of the Franciscan Order—was sufficiently impressive to warrant an unusual comment from the author of the relatione: "the Office was begun with the customary Plainchant used by the Order, for which by reason of the tenderness they conceived many wept . . . the *Requiem* was intoned by the Father Cantors, to whom in unison the fullness of both Choirs responded with the customary Song."[66]

The friars of the Araceli were known for their performance of chant. In 1640 the avant-garde composer, traveler, and musical connoisseur Pietro Della Valle frankly admitted, "I go much more willingly where I hear them sing well." The choirs of the Dominicans at the Minerva and of Sant'Agostino "at least render a bit of good sound to my ears . . . nor do the Zoccolanti of the Aracoeli displease me, . . . indeed they give me some pleasure with those sonorous low basses [bassoni sonori] of theirs."[67] A century later, the chanting of the Araceli friars prompted the conception of the greatest historical work of the eighteenth century, Edward Gibbon's *Decline and Fall of the Roman Empire.* "It was at Rome, on the 15th of October 1764, as I sat musing amid the ruins of the Capitol, while the barefooted friars were singing vespers in the temple of Jupiter, that the idea of writing the decline and fall of the city first started to my mind."[68]

Cardinal Francesco, for forty-seven years archpriest of St. Peter's and member of the Congregatione of the Fabbrica, was buried in the sacristy of the basilica (fig. 9.8). Francesco's monument in the sacristy by Lorenzo Ottoni combines the exaltation of its subject with symbols of Death.[69] The inscription is flanked by herms and surmounted by a winged skull, while a bust of the deceased, wreathed in laurel branches, is accompanied by two angels, one bearing the cardinal's arms and the other trumpeting his fame.

---

[66] *Il Calice d'oro ingemmato,* BAV, Barb. SSS.I.4, int. 18, 6–7: "fù incominciato l'Ufficio con il solito Canto fermo usato dalla Religione, per il che molti per tenerezza concepita piangevano . . . da Padri Cantori fù intonato il Requiem, à quali unitamente corrispose nel solito Canto la pienezza d'ambi i Cori." There was a long tradition of varying chant performance according to the circumstances—slow and low in pitch for mournful occasions, higher and faster for joyful ones; e.g. in the Holy year of 1625: "they sang the litanies musically but with sad notes" ("cantavano li [!] letanie musicalmente ma con note meste, e devote") (Giovanni Briccio, *Le solenni e devote processioni,* quoted in Rose Marie San Juan, *Rome: a city out of print* [Minneapolis and London: University of Minnesota Press, 2001], 275, n. 11).

[67] Pietro Della Valle, *Della musica dell'età nostra* in Angelo Solerti, *Le origini del melodramma* (Turin: Fratelli Bocca, 1903), 148–79, esp. 175–76.

[68] Edward Gibbon, *Autobiography,* ed. Dero Saunders (New York: Meridian, 1961), 154.

[69] Bianca di Gioia, *Le collezioni di sculture,* 199–201: the *Vita* of Ottoni written by Pascoli says that "the depository of the vicecancelliere [Francesco] in the Sacristy of S. Pietro" (therefore a tomb and not merely

FIG. 9.8   Lorenzo Ottoni, *Sepulchral Monument of Cardinal Francesco Barberini*
(S. Pietro in Vaticano, sacristy)

*   *   *   *

The church of Santa Rosalia next to the Barberini palace in Palestrina was begun by Don Taddeo Barberini as an ex-voto to the Santuzza for her intercession against the Plague. It was designed by Francesco Contini and was inaugurated on 7 November 1660. Cardinal Francesco Barberini the younger, Taddeo's grandson, made it into a sepulchre for members of the family not buried in Sant'Andrea della Valle. In 1704 he installed in the adjacent Cappella dei Depositi the bodies of Don Taddeo and Cardinal Antonio in mausolea designed by Bernardino Cametti.[70] Taddeo's tomb features Cametti's bust showing him wearing the Prince Prefect's tiara designed by Pietro da Cortona (see fig. 2.4), while Antonio's bust is inserted into a pyramid on which a white marble angel is writing "Aeternitati vixit" (fig. 9.9).

The sometimes unquiet spirits of the great Barberini were now at rest. *Requiem aeternam dona eis, Domine, et lux perpetua luceat eis.*

---

a sepulchral monument) was commissioned by Cardinal Carlo Barberini (+1704). This is confirmed by Moroni: "He was buried in the old sacristy of the Vatican basilica, not in that of San Lorenzo in Damaso, as Sperandio has it" (*Dizionario di erudizione storico-ecclesiastica* 4:108). Its inscription dates the monument, which was moved to the corridor leading into the sacristy in the eighteenth century, to 1682. Sebastian Schütze, *Gian Lorenzo Bernini: Regista del Barocco* (Milan: Skira, 1999), 296, proposes 1680 as the date; other scholars have dated it as late as 1704, the death of Cardinal Carlo, whose Libro Mastro Generale B for 1682 records a payment of sc. 663.66 but does not indicate the payee. On 28 May 1679, 60 baiocchi were paid to Giuseppe Giorgetti for "Haver fatto la forma nel viso Al Em.mo Sig.re Card.le Fran.co Barberino e fatta con ogni diligenza con gesso et altra materia" ("Having made the mould of the face of the Most Eminent Cardinal Francesco Barberino and made [it] with all diligence with plaster and other materials"). In discussing Ottoni's busts of Francesco and Antonio, Bianca Di Gioia states that Francesco "visse a lungo con i fratelli Antonio e Taddeo" ("lived for a long time with his brothers Antonio and Taddeo") in the Quattro Fontane palace (197). In fact, Francesco never lived there, Taddeo inhabited the palace only between 1632 and 1634, and Antonio moved in only after Taddeo's departure. She also confuses Cardinal S. Onofrio (Antonio senior) with Antonio junior (201).

[70] *Itinerario mostra: I prìncipi della Chiesa* (Milan: Edizioni Charta, 1998), 176.

FIG. 9.9   Bernardino Cametti, Lorenzo Ottoni,
          Sepulchral Monument of Cardinal Antonio Barberini
          (Palestrina, Santa Rosalia)

Appendix

BARBERINI FUNERALS

Outline (after Montserrat Moli Frigola, "Donne, candele, lacrime e morte: Funerali di regine spagnole nel seicento," *Barocco romano e barocco italiano* [Rome: Gangemi, 1985], 135–58, 147):

1. date
2. typology of the celebrations
3. place/-es of the celebrations
4. typology of the apparato
5. commissioner/-s
6. celebrant or celebrants
7. chronicler/relazione of the celebration
8. funeral oration
9. poetical compositions
10. musical compositions
11. artists and artisans
12. participants in the celebration
13. written sources
14. visual sources
15. monuments
16. bibliography

Abbreviations:

AB	Archivio Barberini
BAV	Biblioteca Apostolica Vaticana
CAB	Cardinal Antonio Barberini
CCB	Cardinal Carlo Barberini
CFB	Cardinal Francesco Barberini
Comp.	Computisteria
CS	Cappella Sistina
DMB	Don Maffeo Barberini
LMG	Libro mastro generale
RAdS	Rome, Archivio di Stato

Bianca di Gioia	Elena Bianca di Gioia, *Le collezioni di scultura del Museo di Roma: Il Seicento* (Rome: Campisano, 2002)
Cartari	Carteggio Cartari-Febei, RAdS
Fagiolo	Maurizio Fagiolo dell'Arco, *La festa barocca* (Rome: Edizioni De Luca, 1997)
Fagiolo/Roma	Maurizio Fagiolo dell'Arco, *La festa a Roma*, 2 vols. (Turin: Umberto llemandi & c., 1997)
Gigli	Giacinto Gigli, *Diario di Roma*, ed. Manlio Barberito, 2 vols. (Rome: Colombo, 1994)
Hammond	Frederick Hammond, *Music and Spectacle in Baroque Rome* (New Haven and London: Yale University Press, 1994)
Lunadoro	Girolamo Lunadoro, *Relatione della Corte di Roma* (Venice: Brigonci, 1661)
Prìncipi della Chiesa	*Itinerario mostra: I prìncipi della Chiesa* (Milan: Edizioni Charta, 1998)
Waddy	Patricia Waddy, *Seventeenth-Century Palaces: Use and the Art of the Plan* (New York; Cambridge, MA: Architectural History Foundation/MIT Press, 1990)

I would like to thank Dr. Michael Erwee for his assistance.

I. Urban VIII (+29 July 1644)

1. 29 July-8 August 1644
2. catafalque, office of the dead, requiem, absolutions
3. San Pietro
4. possibly 2 apparati: "piramide" (CS, Diario 63) and tholus (Cartari)
5. Reverenda Camera Apostolica (Cardinal Antonio Barberini, Chamberlain, Cardinal Francesco Barberini, Vice-Chancellor)
6. cardinals, Cappella Pontificia
7. BAV, CS diario 63; Cartari, RAdS, busta 73, fol. 151; Gigli, 322–23; Venice, Archivio di Stato, Senato III, dispacci, filza 121
8. Felice Contelori, *Oratio in funere Urbani VIII* (Augsburg, 1644)
9. G. Naudé, *Panegyricus* (Paris, 1644)
10. responsories etc. sung in Gregorian chant by the Cappella Pontificia, psalms sung in procession with the body (BAV, AB, Comp. 70)
11. Andrea Sacchi

12. cardinals, Cappella Pontificia: BAV, CS 63, fols. 48–48v: "Subvenite sancti Dei tutto in canto fermo co[n] molta gravità è finito"; "non esser' finita la Piramide, che si fa in mezzo à San Pietro per il sud[dett]o funerale."

13. BAV, AB, CFB, Comp. 82; BAV, CS Diario 63, puntatore della Cappella Pontificia; Cartari, RAdS, busta 73, fol. 151; Gigli, 322–23

14. — — —

15. Bernini, tribune of S. Pietro

16. Fagiolo, 326; Hammond, 282; Laurie Nussdorfer, *Civic Politics in the Rome of Urban VIII* (Princeton, NJ: Princeton University Press, 1992), 228–53

II. Cardinal Antonio Barberini the elder (Sant'Onofrio) (+11 September 1646)

1. 12 September 1646
2. "esequie" (CS); "offitio" (Gigli)
3. Barberini Chapel, Sant'Andrea della Valle; Chiesa della Concettione de' Cappucini
4.–6. — — —
7. BAV, CS, Diari 65, fol. 66r: "12 Mercredi (7bre 1646) a hore 21 l'esequi[e] del E.mo Sig.e Cardinal Sant Onofrio Barberini a Santo Andrea della Valle. Presente il Sacro Collegio tutti presenti con tutti li S.ri Giubilati."
8. funeral oration
9.–11. — — —
12. Cappella Pontificia, Orfanelli, 23 Compagnie di sacchi, 13 Fraterie
13. CS Diario 65
14. — — —
15. Stone engraved with the words "Hic jacet cinis, pulvis, et nihil."
16. Gigli, 479–80

III. Don Taddeo Barberini (+14 November 1647)

1. late 1647
2. — — —
3. [Paris]
4. — — —
5. Cardinal Antonio Barberini
6.–10. — — —

11. carpenter, tradesman, barber, embroiderer, painter: perhaps the painter Paolo Gismondi

12. — — —

13. BAV, AB, CAB, Comp. 280: "Conti di Francia" of Cardinal Antonio Barberini; Gigli, 510; BAV, AB, CAB, Comp. 280, fol. 70: "per spese fatte per il funerale dell'Ecc.mo S.re P[ri]n[ci]pe D. Taddeo, cioè cassa di piombo; et al falegname"; "a Diversi, cioè mercante, barbiere, raccamatore, e pittore."

14. — — —

15. Palestrina, S. Rosalia: bust: Bernardino Cametti (see fig. 9.9), tomb: Lorenzo Ottoni

16. Bianca di Gioia, 12, 17, 195–206; *Prìncipi della Chiesa*, 176

IV. Anna Colonna Barberini (+31 October 1658)

1. ?November: exequies 11 days after her burial

2. tomb, catafalque, requiem masses, sepulchral monument

3. Rome, convent of Regina Coeli; S.M. della Scala; S.M. della Vittoria; Sant'Andrea della Valle

4. catafalque, sepulchral monument, ecclesiastical furnishings

5. Nicolò Barberini (Regina Caeli, S.M. della Vittoria, S.M. della Scala); Carlo and Maffeo Barberini (Sant'Andrea della Valle)

6.–9. — — —

10. sung mass

11. spetiale, armarolo, festarolo, rental of black cloths, carpenter, silver panels; Gabrielle Renzi (scarpellino); Jacomo Antonio Falli (model of the portrait of the Prefetessa); monument designed by Francesco Contini; payments for the monument by Nicolò Barberini 1659–61

12. "le monache [of Regina Coeli] mi doveranno fare il funerale in d[ett]a chiesa e convento" (testament of Anna Colonna, 28 June 1656)

13. BAV, AB, DMB, Comp. 379: Libro di mandati di Maffeo Barberini, 100: "Spetiale, Armarolo, festarolo, nolo di Panni neri, falegname, Messe, Messa cantata, sporti d'argento prestati portati e riportati il tutto servito p[er] il funerale fatto alla Chiesa di S. Andrea della Valle in occ[asion]e della morte dell'Ecc.ma Sig.ra D. Anna Colonna n[ost]ra M[ad]re."

14. — — —

15. Gabrielle Renzi, statue and fictive kneeling-desk (Albright–Knox Gallery, Buffalo, New York, USA; see figs. 9.4 and 9.5); altar, present whereabouts unknown

16. Marilyn Dunn, "Piety and Patronage in Seicento Rome: Two Noblewomen and Their Convents," *The Art Bulletin* 76 (1994): 644–63; Giuseppe Sacchi Lodispoto, "Anna Colonna Barberini ed il suo monumento nel monastero di Regina Coeli," *Strenna dei Romanisti* 43 (1982): 460–78.

V. *Suor Innocenza dell'Incarnazione (Camilla) Barberini (+26 March 1666)*

1. April 1666
2. low masses and sung masses
3. Rome, "various churches"
4. ———
5. Cardinal Francesco Barberini
6. an unnamed priest
7.–12. ———
13. BAV, AB, CFB, Comp. 74, Giornale H del cardinale Francesco:. 39: "più messe basse e cantate in diverse Chiese, p[er] l'Anima della m[ad]re Suor Innocenza Barberini, sor[e]lla di S.E."
14.–15. ———
16. Pio Pecchiai, *I Barberini* (Rome: Biblioteca d'Arte Editrice, 1959), 153–54; cf. Waddy, 27, 129–30, 331

VI. *Cardinal Antonio Barberini (+4 August 1671)*

Exequies celebrated in Rome, "in almost all the Churches of this great City"; Lunadoro, 175–78

A. Rome, Propaganda Fede
   1. 31 August 1671
   2. "essequie" (CS Diario 89)
   3. Propaganda Fede
   4.–6. ———
   7.–11. ———
   12. Cappella Pontificia
   13. BAV, CS, Diario 89, fol. 25r: "31 Lunedi (Agosto 1671) non fu servitio per che la sacrestia andò a Propaganda Fede dove furono fatto l'essequie per il S. Card.e Antonio gia n[ost]ro Protettore."
   14.–16. ———

B. Rome, Chiesa dell'Arciconfraternita degli Orfani (=S. Maria in Aquiro, "Domus Arciconfraternitatis Orphanorum" [Cesare d'Onofrio, *Roma nel Seicento* (Florence: Vallecchi, 1969), 88])

    1. 4 September 1671

    2. funeral, catafalque, apparato

    3. S. M. in Aquiro

    4. cartelloni with insignia of the dignities of the deceased; chariot of death; catafalque with 4 pedestals, 3 orders of stairs, pyramid

    5. Arciconfraternita degli Orfani

    6. mass sung by Bishop Giuseppe Maria Suarez, Vicar of the Chapter of S. Pietro

    7. BAV, Barb. lat. 4913

    8. Giovanni Lotti; homily by P. Issi Somarco

    9. — — —

    10. "oltre i Musici ordinarij della Chiesa, da 12. altri Musici Forastieri, parte della Cappella Pontificia, e parte d'altre Chiese principali di Roma" (BAV, Barb. lat. 4913)

    11. Mattia de' Rossi

    12. See 10

    13. See 7

    14. — — —

    15. Palestrina, S. Rosalia: bust by Bernardino Cametti and tomb by Lorenzo Ottoni (see fig. 9.8)

    16. See n. 7: Bianca di Gioia, 195–206; not listed by Fagiolo; *Prìncipi della Chiesa*, 158

C. Rome, Santa Maria Maggiore

    1. 18 September

    2. "solemn exequies": funeral, catafalque

    3. Santa Maria Maggiore

    4. — — —

    5. Cardinal Giacomo Rospigliosi, Archpriest of the Basilica (1668) in succession to Antonio

    6. — — —

    7. Cartari, RAdS, busta 83, fols. 159–60; see n. 37

    8.–10. — — —

    11. Cartari: "vi fu installato un bel catafalco del Rossi" (Giovan Antonio de' Rossi: Wolfe, "Cardinal Antonio," 189); ASV, Archivio Rospigliosi #60 (Libro Mastro

Generale and Rubricelli): c. 144 (30 September 1671): portrait of Antonio by Michelangelo Maruli "esposto in detto funerale," sc. 19.50 to "musici che hanno cantato nella messa di requiem," total sc. 147.70; P. Mentinoia sculpta, G. Baldesi for pitture, catafalco, Lolli, gilder, festarolo: total ca. sc. 1900

12.–15. — — —

16. Cartari, RAdS, busta 83, fols. 159–60; Fagiolo, 494

D. Rome, Sant'Andrea della Valle

1. 26 September

2. catafalque

3. Sant'Andrea della Valle (family tomb)

4. catafalque, "panni lugubri," illumination

5. Cardinals Carlo and Francesco Barberini (the first incorrectly identified by Fagiolo, 474, as "fratello del defunto")

6. — — —

7. Cartari, RAdS, busta 83, fols. 163–64

8.–10. — — —

11. G. B. Contini

12. — — —

13. BAV, AB, CAB, Comp. 237; Karin Elizabeth Wolfe, "Cardinal Antonio Barberini the Younger (1608–71): Aspects of his Art Patronage" (Ph.D. thesis, Courtauld Institute, University of London, 1999), 189

14. — — —

15. family chapel

16. BAV, AB, CAB, Comp. 237, 5, 8, 13–14; Cartari, RAdS, busta 83, fols. 163–64; Fagiolo, 494

E. Rome, Chiesa del Gesù

1. September (BAV, AB, CAB, Comp. 237, 14: sc. 600 per il "funerale che si farà fare da Noi nella Chiesa del Giesu")

2. [Office, Requiem]

3. Chiesa del Gesù

4. catafalque, black draperies, arms of death

5. Cardinal Francesco Barberini

6. — — —

7. Carlo Bovio, S.J., *In funere eminentissimi principis Antonii Barberini S.R.E. Cardinalis Camerarii & . Honorarii Tumuli ac Funebris Pompæ Descriptio, & Oratio* . . . (Rome: Nicolai Angelo Tinassi, 1671, BAV)

8. Carlo Bovio, S.J.

9.–10. — — —

11. G. B. Contini; "Fr. Laurenti Pittore" for 2 catafalques; Lolli, gilder for 2 catafalques

12. — — —

13. BAV, AB, CAB, Comp. 237

14. engraving n. 7 by "Domenicus Barriera" (Dominique Barrière) (see fig. 9.5)

15. — — —

16. BAV, AB, CAB, Comp. 237; Fagiolo, 494

F. Rome, S. Lorenzo in Damaso

1. September-October

2. funeral

3. S. Lorenzo in Damaso

4. catafalque

5. Cardinal Francesco Barberini

6.–12. — — —

13. BAV, AB, CFB, Comp. 89, 194; Comp. 90, 3v.

14.–16. — — —

G. Pesaro, duomo

1. ?

2. funeral

3. Pesaro cathedral

4. catafalque

5. Cardinals Francesco and Carlo Barberini

6.–10. — — —

11. Paolo Emilio Cassio

12. — — —

13. *Relatione dell'apparato* . . . (Pesaro, 1680) (BAV, Barb. SSS. I. 4, int. 6)

14. engraving by Pietro Santi Bartoli (see fig. 9.6)

15. — — —

16. Fagiolo, 494

H. Rome, Ospedale di SS. Trinità de' Pellegrini

1. ?

2. pontifical Requiem, catafalque, decorations of façade and church

3. SS. Trinità de' Pellegrini

4. "Si fece pertanto parare tutta la Chiesa dalle fenestre a basso di panni di lutto, lasciandosi scoperte tutte le cornici ed altri ornamenti di stucco; si distribuirono sopra il cornicione 24 gran candelabri di carta pesta di colore giallo allumati di oro trito con pendoncini di roverso nero, ciascuno de' quali reggeva tre fiacole cioè quella di mezzo di tre libre e l'altre di due libre l'una; sopra ciascuna cappella pendeva una morte in tela retta da un cherubino di carta pesta inargentato, e nella cappella di mezzo nell'uno e l'altro lato della Chiesa vi era l'arme di Sua Emza. in tela d'Imperatore retta parimente da un cherubino, ed a tutti li pilastri un lustrino grande inargentato con candela di una libra. In tutte le attacature di detti cherubini, quadri dell'armi e delle morti e de' lustrini vi era un fioco grande fatto di tocca d'argento . . . Il detto catafalco fu posto nel mezzo sotto la cupola in maggior grandezza del solito armato di gran numero di candelieri di argento con 12 torcieri di argento sopra detto catafalco alle cantonate di esso, con altri torcieri di argento in terra intorno al detto catafalco, nell'ultima cima del quale vi era una urna coperta con la nostra coltre ricamato, e sopra di essa il cappello Cardinalizio posato sopra un cuscino grande di broccato . . . Cantò la messa di requie Mons. Vescovo Suarez Vicario del Rmo. Capitolo di S. Pietro, pontificalmente con musici di cappella a due cori; il Padre Bompiani della Compagnia di Gesù fece l'orazione latina."

"Consequently they had the whole Church decorated from the windows down with mourning draperies, leaving all the cornices and other stucco ornaments uncovered; on the main cornice they distributed 24 large candelabra of papier-mâché of a yellow color illumined by gold leaf with little pendants of black reversed, each of which supported three torches [fiaccole] that is the one in the middle of three pounds and the others of two pounds apiece; over each chapel there hung a skeleton of cloth supported by a cherub of silvered papier-mâché, and in the middle chapel on each side of the Church there were the arms of His Eminence in Imperial cloth also supported by a cherub, and on all the pilasters a large silvered ornament [lustrino] with a candle of one pound. In all the attachments of the said cherubim, pictures of arms and skeletons and of the lustrini there was a large tassel made of silver braid [tocca d'argento] . . . The said catafalque of a larger size than the usual was placed in the middle under the cupola furnished with a large number of silver candlesticks with 12 silver torchieres above the said catafalque at its corners, with other silver torchieres on the ground around the said catafalque, at the top of which there was an urn covered with our pall [coltra], and on that the Cardinal's hat placed on a large brocade cushion . . . Mons. Bishop Suarez Vicar of the Most Reverend Chapter of St. Peter's, sang the requiem mass pontifically, with musicians from the chapel in two choirs; Father Bompiani of the Company of Jesus made the Latin oration."

5. Primicerio and guardians of SS. Trinità

6. Mons. Vescovo Suarez, Vicario del R[erendissi]mo Capitolo di S. Pietro

7. "Repertorio di tutti li Cardinali che sono stati Protettori della Venerabile Arciconfraternita della Santissima Trinità de' Pellegrini" (RAdS, Ospedale della SS. Trinità de Pellegrini, b. 546, letter "G"), quoted in Karin Elizabeth Wolfe, "Cardinal Antonio Barberini," Appendix 4, 262–68; "Trasferito il suo corpo a Palestrina, fu sepolto nella sua Cattedrale nella Cappella di S. Lorenzo con questa bellissima iscrizione: Il Peccatore a norma della sua testimentaria disposizione"

8. Latin oration by Padre Bompiani, S. J.

9. — — —

10. "musici di cappella a due cori"; sc. 12 "Al Maestro di Cappella per la Musica"

11. carpenter, sc. 14.50; gilder, sc. 9.50; painter for retouching the arms and painting a large skeleton over the door of the church, sc. 2; festarolo, sc. 60; wax, sc. 63.75; 27 *canne* of *tocca d'argento*, sc. 9.40

12. Mons. Suarez, primicerio and guardians of the Ospedale, members of the households of Cardinals Antonio and Carlo Barberini

13. See 7

14. — — —

15. inscribed tablet in the small refectory of the Ospedale

16. See 7

I. Rome, Virtuosi del Pantheon

A resolution adopted on 13 September 1671: "Fu proposto che stante la morte del Signor Cardinale Antonio Nostro Protettore sarebbe stato ben fare un poco d'esequie per riconoscere l'obligatione che la Congregazione ha a detta Eminenza, e fu risoluto a viva voce che si debbano fare le dette esequie con la maggiore lautezza possibile": from the archive of the Virtuosi, Libro delle Congregazioni, vol. 1654–1701, quoted in Wolfe, "Cardinal Antonio Barberini," 188.

VII. Cardinal Francesco Barberini (+10 December 1679)

1. 15 December 1679 (incorrectly 1680 in Fagiolo, 509)

2. funeral

3. S. Lorenzo in Damaso (also S. M. in Cosmedin, S. Pietro, Pesaro)

4. ?catafalque

5. Cardinal Carlo Barberini

6. Franciscan friars from S. M. in Araceli, Cappella Pontificia

7. *Il Calice d'oro ingemmato;* BAV, AB, CCB, LMG, busta 297

8. BAV, Barb. lat. 4913, fols. 25–38. According to an *avviso*, on 13 January 1680 Innocent XI Odescalchi pronounced a "bella oratione" in praise of Cardinal Francesco at a concistory, exhorting the cardinals to emulate Francesco's "esatezza delle funzioni ecclesiastiche" and his liberality to the poor (BAV, Barb. lat. 6422, fols. 25, 45v)

9. — — —

10. Franciscan liturgical chant; music by the Cappella Pontificia: see nn. 44–45

11.–12. — — —

13. *Il Calice d'oro ingemmato,* BAV; BAV, AB, CCB, LMG, busta 297; *L'Ercole trionfante nella caduta . . .* (Pesaro: Stamperia Camerale, 1680); *Relatione dell'Apparato* (Pesaro, 1680, both in BAV, Barb. SSS. I. 4); BAV, Barb. lat. 4729, fols. 341–44 [Andrea Nicoletti], *Memorie circa la persona del signor cardinale Francesco Barberini per fare l'oratione funebre in Pesaro*

14. 31 December 1682: "sc. 18.50 . . . cioè sc. 15 a Pietro de Santis intagliatore, e sc. 3.50 per il rame dell'intaglio fatto per l'iscrittione del funerale dell'Em Fran.co" (engraving not traced)

15. S. Pietro, Sacristy: tomb and bust by Lorenzo Ottoni from a death mask made by Giuseppe Giorgetti (see fig. 9.7), dated between 1682 (inscription) and 1700–1704

16. Bianca di Gioia, 199–201; Fagiolo, *La festa,* 509; Lunadoro, 175–78; G. Moroni, *Dizionario di erudizione storico-ecclesiastica da S. Pietro sino ai nostri giorni,* vol. 4 (Venice, 1840), 108; *Prìncipi della Chiesa,* 172–73

*   *   *   *

The following musical examples were played during the original talk:

1. Gregorian chant: Subvenite Sancti Dei, occurrite angeli Domini: Suscipientes animam eius: Offerentes eam in conspectu Altissimi. V. Suscipiat te Christus, qui vocavit te: et in sinum Abrahae angeli deducant te. Suscipientes . . . (Gloria Dei Cantores, *Gregorian Requiem,* 1995).

2. Gregorian chant: Incipit Lamentatio Jeremiae Prophetae. Aleph. Quomodo sedet sola civitas plena populo: facta est quasi vidua domina Gentium: princeps provinciarum facta est sub tributo. Beth. Plorans ploravit in nocte, et lacrimae eius in maxillis eius: non est qui consoletur eam ex omnibus caris eius: omnes amici eius spreverunt eam, et facti sunt ei inimici. Ghimel. Migravit Judas propter afflictionem, et multitudinem servitutis: habitavit inter gentes, nec invenit requiem: omnes persecutores eius apprehenderunt eam inter angustias. Daleth. Viae Sion lugent eo quod non sint qui veniant ad solemnitatem: omnes portae eius distructae: sacerdotes eius gementes: virgines eius squallidae, et ipsa oppressa amaritudine. He. Facti sunt hostes eius in capite, inimici eius locupletati sunt: quia Dominus locutus est super eam propter multitudinem iniquitatum eius: parvuli eius ducti sunt in captivitatem, ante faciem tribulantis. Jerusalem, Jerusalem, convertere ad Dominum Deum tuum (Alessandro Moreschi, *Moreschi—The Last Castrato*, recorded in Rome, 11 April 1904).

3. Palestrina, Missa Papae Marcelli, version for two choirs by Francesco Soriano: Kyrie eleison (*Messa per San Silvestro*, 1613, William Byrd Choir, recorded in the Cappella Sistina, 1984).

4. Franciscan chant, ca. 1300: Tota pulchra es, Maria, et macula originalis non est in te. Tu, gloria Jerusalem. Tu, laetitia Israel. Tu, advocata peccatorum. O Maria, virgo prudentissima, mater clementissima. Ora pro nobis, intercede pro nobis ad Dominum Jesum Christum (*Franciscan Road*, Monastery of St. Saviour's, Jerusalem, 1999).

5. Gregorian chant: In paradisum deducant te angeli: in tuo adventu suscipiant te martyres, et perducant te in civitatem sanctam Jerusalem. Chorus angelorum te suscipiat, et cum Lazaro quondam paupere aeternam habeas requiem (*Gregorian Requiem*).

Bibliography

CÆRIMONIALE / EPISCOPORVM / . . . / VENETIS APVD CIERAS M.D.C. XIII.

LA CONTESA / TORNEO / FATTO IN FERRARA PER LE NOZZE / Dell'Illustrissimo Signor / GIO. FRANCESCO SACCHETTI / Coll'Illustrissima Signora / D. BEATRICE ESTENSE TASSONA. / IN FERRARA. / Appresso Francesco Suzzi Stampatore Camerale. 1632 [I-FEc. E. 12. 5. 20].

[Girolamo Graziani]. DESCRIZIONE DELLE ALLEGREZZE FATTE DALLA CITTÀ DI MODENA PER LE NOZZE DEL SERENISSIMO PADRONE E DELLA SERENISSIMA PRINCIPESSA LUCREZIA BARBERINI. Modena: Bartolomeo Soliani, 1654.

[Costanzo Ricci]. LA / MASCHERA TRIONFANTE / NEL GIVDICIO DI PARIDE / RAPPRE-SENTATO / DALLA MAGNANIMITA' DELL'ECCELL.O / PRINCIPE PREFETTO / BARBARINO. / ALL'EMINENENTISS. PRINCIPE IL CARD. / ANTONIO BARBERINO / LEGATO &c. Bologna, N. Tebaldini, 1643.

MISSALE / ROMANVM / EX DECRETO SANCROSANCTI / Concilij Tridentini restitutum / . . . VENETIS. APVD. IVNTAS, n. d. [1623].

OPLOMACHIA / DI / Bonauentura Pistofilo nobile Ferrarese / . . . / In Siena 1621. / Per Hercole Gori.

DE / PRÆFECTO VRBIS / LIBER / auct. / FELICE CONTELORIO. Rome: Reverenda Camera Apostolica, 1625.

RITVALE / ROMANVM / PAVLI QVINTI / Pontificis Maximi . . . Venice: Cieras, 1615.

DEL TORNEO ULTIMAMENTE FATTO IN BOLOGNA ALL'EMIN. SACCHETTI DESCRITTIONE PANEGIRICA DEL COMM. GIO. BATTISTA MANZINI ALL'EM. PADRONE IL SIG. CARD. CAPPONI. Bologna, 1639.

IL TORNEO / DI BONAVENTURA PISTOFILO / NOBILE FERRARESE . . . In Bologna per il Ferrone . . . [1626].

Adami, Andrea. *Osservazioni per ben regolare il coro dei cantori della Cappella pontificia*. Rome: Rossi, 1711; fascimile ed. Giancarlo Rostirolla, Lucca: Libreria Musicale Italiana, 1988.

Adami, Giuseppe. "L'ingegnere-scenografo e l'ingegnere-venturiero." In *Barocke Inszenierung*, 158–89.

_____. *Pietro Paolo Floriani tra spalti e scene*. Loreto: Tecnostampa, 2006.

_____. *Scenografia e scenotecnica barocca tra Ferrara e Parma (1625–1631)*. Rome: "L'Erma" di Bretschneider, 2003.

Ademollo, Alessandro. *I teatri di Roma nel secolo decimosettimo*. Rome: Pasqualucci, 1888; reprint, Rome: Borzi, 1969.

Alm, Irene. "First Steps on the Venetian Stage." Unpublished paper.

_____. "Theatrical Dance in Seventeenth-Century Venetian Opera." Ph.D. diss., University of California, Los Angeles, 1993.

I Barberini e la cultura europea del Seicento. Edited by Lorenza Mochi Onori, Sebastian Schütze, and Francesco Solinas. Rome: De Luca Editori d'Arte, 2007.

Barberini, Francesca, and Micaela Dickmann. *I Pontefici e gli Anni Santi nella Roma del XVII secolo*. Rome: Bozzi, 2000.

Barbieri, Patrizio. "I 'doi bellissimi organi' di S. Lorenzo in Damaso." *Amici dell'organo* (September 1984): 46–53.

Barocke Inszenierung. Edited by Joseph Imorde, Fritz Neumeyer, and Tristan Weddigen. Emsdetten and Zurich: Edition Imorde, 1999.

Bernini, Domenico. *Vita del Cavalier Gio. Lorenzo Bernino descritta da Domenico Bernino suo Figlio*. Rome: a spese di Rocco Bernabò, 1713; reprint, Perugia: Ediart, 1999.

Bernini in Vaticano. Rome: De Luca, 1981.

Bertrand, Pascal-François. *Les tapisseries des Barberini et la décoration d'intérieur dans la Rome baroque*. Turnhout: Brepols, 2005.

Bianca di Gioia, Elena. *Le collezioni di scultura del Museo di Roma. Il Seicento*. Rome: Campisano, 2002.

Bjurström, Per. *Feast and Theatre in Queen Christina's Rome*. Analecta Reginensia, 3. Stockholm: Bengtsons, 1966.

Blunt, Anthony. *Guide to Baroque Rome*. New York: Harper and Row, 1982.

Bruno, Silvia. "I Barberini e il loro *entourage* in Francia." In *I Barberini e la cultura europea del Seicento*, 317–30.

Burke, Peter. "Rome as Center of Information and Communication." In *From Rome to Eternity: Catholicism and the Arts in Italy, ca. 1550–1650*, ed. Pamela M. Jones and Thomas Worcester, 253–69. Leiden, Boston, and Cologne: Brill, 2002.

Caluori, Eleanor. "Marco Marazzoli." *The New Grove Dictionary of Music and Musicians*. London: Macmillan, 1980.

Cametti, Alberto. "I musici di Campidoglio." *Archivio della Reale Società Romana di Storia Patria* 48 (1925): 95–135.

_____. *Il Teatro di Tordinona poi Apollo*. Tivoli, 1938.

Capra, Luciano. "La regina Cristina a Ferrara." In *Queen Christina of Sweden: Documents and Studies*, ed. Magnus von Platen, 74–82. Analecta Reginensia, 1. Stockholm: Norstedt, 1966.

Carandini, Silvia, and Maurizio Fagiolo dell'Arco. *L'effimero barocco*. 2 vols. Rome: Bulzoni, 1978.

Caroso, Fabritio. *Il ballarino* (1581).

_____. *Nobiltà di dame* (1600), trans. and ed. Julia Sutton. Oxford: Oxford University Press, 1986.

Carter, Tim. *Monteverdi's Musical Theatre*. New Haven and London: Yale University Press, 2002.

Cavazzini, Patrizia, ed. *Agostino Tassi (1578–1644): Un paesaggista tra immaginario e realtà*. Rome: Iride, 2008.

_____. *Palazzo Lancellotti ai Coronari: Cantiere di Agostino Tassi*. Rome: Istituto Poligrafico e Zecca dello Stato, 1998.

Cavicchi, Adriano. "Appunti sulle relazioni tra Frescobaldi e l'ambiente musicale marchigiano: L'intavolatura di Ancona." In *Girolamo Frescobaldi nel IV centenario della nascita*, 87–106.

Cipolla, Carlo. *Cristofano e la peste*. Bologna: Il Mulino, 1976.

Cochrane, Eric. *Florence in the Forgotten Centuries*. Chicago: University of Chicago Press, 1974.

Coelho, Victor. *The Manuscript Sources of Seventeenth-Century Italian Lute Music*. New York: Garland Publishing, 1995.

Il Corago o vero alcune osservazioni per metter bene in scena le composizioni drammatiche. Edited by Paolo Fabbri and Angelo Pompilio. Florence: Olschki, 1983.

Costantini, Claudio. "Fazione Urbana: Sbandamento e ricomposizione di una grande clientela a metà Seicento." *Quaderni* (January 2006); version online at www.quaderni.net.

Delatour, Jérôme. "Abeilles thuaniennes et barberines: Les relations des savants français avec les Barberini sous le pontificat d'Urbain VIII." In *I Barberini e la cultura europea del Seicento*, 155–72.

Dethan, Georges. *Mazarin et ses amis*. Paris: Berger-Levrault, 1968.

Dizionario biografico degli Italiani. Rome: Istituto della Enciclopedia Italiana.

Donisi, Enrica. "Pietro Paolo Sabatini nella Roma barocca tra mecenatismo e didattica." In *Tullio Cima, Domenico Massenzio e la musica del loro tempo*, ed. Fabio Carboni, Valeria De Lucca, and Agostino Ziino, 49–73. Rome: IBIMUS, 2003.

Drake, Stillman. "Galileo Gleanings XII: An Unpublished Letter of Galileo to Peiresc." *Isis* 53 (1962): 201–11.

Dunn, Marilyn. "Piety and Patronage in Seicento Rome: Two Noblewomen and Their Convents." *The Art Bulletin* 76 (1994): 644–63.

Ecorcheville, Jules. *Vingt Suites d'orchestre du XVIIe siècle français*. 2 vols. Berlin: Liepmannsohn and Paris: Fortin, 1906.

Elliott, J. H. *The Count-Duke of Olivares*. New Haven and London: Yale University Press, 1986.

Enciclopedia dello Spettacolo. 11 vols. Rome: Le Maschere, 1954–68.

Fabris, Dinko. *Mecenati e musici: Documenti sul patronato artistico dei Bentivoglio di Ferrara nell'epoca di Monteverdi (1585–1645)*. Lucca: Libreria Musicale Italiana, 1999.

Fagiolo dall'Arco, Marcello, ed. *Le capitali della festa*. 2 vols. Rome: De Luca Editori d'Arte, 2007.

Fagiolo dall'Arco, Maurizio, ed. *La festa a Roma dal Rinascimento al 1870*. 2 vols. Turin: Allemandi, 1997.

_____. *La festa barocca: Corpus delle feste a Rome /1*. Rome: Edizioni De Luca, 1997.

Faustini, Agostino. *Libro delle Historie Ferraresi*. Ferrara: Gironi, 1646; reprint, Bologna: Forni, 1967.

Fosi, Irene. *All'ombra dei Barberini: Fedeltà e servizio nella Roma barocca*. Rome: Bulzoni, 1997.

Franchi, Saverio. *Annali della stampa musicale romana dei secoli XVI-XVII*; I/1: *Edizioni di musica pratica dal 1601 al 1650*. Rome: IBIMUS, 2006.

_____. *Drammaturgia romana: Repertorio bibliografico cronologico*. Rome: Edizioni di Storia e di Letteratura, 1988.

Freitas, Roger. *"Un Atto d'ingegno:* A Castrato in the Seventeenth Century." Ph.D. diss., Yale University, 1998. Ann Arbor: UMI, 2000.

Frey, Herman-Walther. "Die Gesänge der sixtinischen Kapelle an den Sonntagen und hohen Kirchenfesten des Jahres 1616." In *Melanges Eugène Tisserant*, 6:395–437. Studi e Testi, 236. Città del Vaticano: Biblioteca Apostolica Vaticana, 1964.

Gàl, Fiorenza Rangoni. *Fra' Desiderio Scaglia Cardinale di Cremona: Un collezionista inquisitore nella Roma del Seicento*. Gravidona: Nuova Editrice Delta, 2008.

Galilei, Galileo. *Le opere di Galileo Galilei*, ed. Antonio Favaro. 20 vols. Florence: Barbera, 1890–1909.

Gheyn, Jacob de. *Wapenhandelinghe van Roers Musquetten ende Spiessen* (1607), ed. David J. Blackmore as *The Renaissance Drill Book*. London: Greenhill Books; Mechanicsburg, Pennsylvania: Stackpole Books, 2003.

Gibbon, Edward. *Autobiography*, ed. Dero Saunders. New York: Meridian, 1961.

Gigli, Giacinto. *Diario di Roma*, ed. Manlio Barberito. 2 vols. paged continuously. Rome: Colombo, 1995.

Girolamo Frescobaldi nel IV centenario della nascita. Edited by Sergio Durante and Dinko Fabris. Florence: Olschki, 1986.

Grisar, Johannes, S. J. "Päpstliche Finanzen, Nepotismus und Kirchenrecht unter Urban VIII." In *Miscellanea Historiae Pontificiae*, 207–366. Rome, 1943.

Gualdo Priorato, Galeazzo. *Historia della Sua Reale Maestà Cristina Alessandra, Regina di Svezia*. Rome: Reverenda Camera Apostolica, 1656.

Gundersheimer, Werner L. "Patronage in the Renaissance: An Exploratory Approach." In *Patronage in the Renaissance*, ed. G. F. Lytle and Stephen Orgel, 3–23. Princeton, 1981.

Hammond, Frederick. "Bernini and the 'Fiera di Farfa.'" In *Gianlorenzo Bernini: New Aspects of His Art and Thought: A Commemorative Volume*, ed. Irving Lavin, 115–78. University Park, PA; London: Pennsylvania State University Press, 1985.

_____. *Girolamo Frescobaldi*. Cambridge, MA: Harvard University Press, 1983; revised Italian version Palermo: EPOS, 2002.

_____. "Girolamo Frescobaldi and a Decade of Music in Casa Barberini." *Analecta Musicologica* 19 (1979): 94–124.

_____. "More on Music in Casa Barberini." *Studi Musicali* 14 (1985): 235–61.

_____. *Music and Spectacle in Baroque Rome.* New Haven: Yale University Press, 1994.

Harper, James Gordon. "The Barberini Tapestries of the Life of Pope Urban VIII: Program, Politics, and 'Perfect History' for the Post-Exile Era." Ph.D. diss., University of Pennsylvania, 1998. 2 vols. Ann Arbor: UMI, 1999.

Herklotz, Ingo. "The Accademia Basiliana. Greek Philology, Ecclesiastical History and the Union of the Churches in Barberini Rome." In *I Barberini e la cutura europea del Seicento*, 147–54.

Hope, Charles. "Artists, Patrons, and Advisers in the Italian Renaissance." In *Patronage in the Renaissance*, ed. G. F. Lytle and Stephen Orgel, 293–343. Princeton, 1981.

Illusione et pratica teatrale. Venice: Neri Pozza, 1975.

Jarrard, Alice. *Architecture as Performance in Seventeenth-Century Europe: Court Ritual in Modena, Rome, and Paris* (Cambridge: Cambridge U. P., 2003).

Johnson, Catherine, et al., eds. *Vatican Splendour: Masterpieces of Baroque Art.* Ottawa: National Gallery of Canada, 1986.

Kantorowicz, Ernst. *Laudes Regiae: A Study in Liturgical Acclamations and Medieval Ruler Worship.* Berkeley: University of California Press, 1946.

Kerwin, W. Chandler. *Powers Matchless: The Pontificate of Urban VIII, the Baldachin, and Gian Lorenzo Bernini.* New York: Peter Lang, 1997.

Kleinman, Ruth. *Anne of Austria.* Columbus, OH: Ohio State Press, 1985.

Lavin, Irving. "Lettres de Parmes (1618, 1627–28) et débuts du théâtre baroque." In *Le lieu théatral à la renaissance*, 105–58. Paris: Centre national de la recherche scientifique, 1968; reprint, 1986.

_____. "Urbanitas Urbana. The Pope, the Artist, and the Genius of the Place." In *I Barberini e la cultura europea del Seicento*, 15–30.

Lavin, Marilyn Aronberg. *Seventeenth-Century Barberini Documents and Inventories of Art.* New York: New York University Press, 1975.

Leman, Auguste. *Recueil des instructions générales aux nonces ordinaires de France de 1624 à 1634.* Paris: Champion, 1920.

Leone, Rossella, et al., eds. *Il Museo di Roma racconta la città.* Rome: Gangemi, 2002.

Leone, Stephanie C. *The Palazzo Pamphilj in Piazza Navona: Constructing Identity in Early Modern Rome.* London and Turnhout: Harvey Miller Publishers, 2008.

Lionnet, Jean. "Christine de Suède et la chapelle pontificale, un espoir deçu?" In *Cristina di Svezia e la Musica*, 311–20. Rome: Accademia Nazionale dei Lincei, 1998.

_____. "Les événements musicaux de la légation du Cardinal Flavio Chigi en France (1664)." *Studi Musicali* 25 (1996): 127–53.

_____. Liner notes for Luigi Rossi, *Orfeo.* Harmonia Mundi France 90135860.

_____. "Una svolta nella storia del Collegio dei Cantori Pontifici: Il decreto del 22 giugno 1665 contro Orazio Benevolo; Origine e Conseguenze." *Nuova Rivista Musicale Italiana* 17 (1983): 72–103.

Lodispoto, Giuseppe Sacchi. "Anna Colonna Barberini ed il suo monumento nel monastero di Regina Coeli." *Strenna dei Romanisti* 43 (1982): 460–78.

Luisi, Francesco. "S. Giacomo degli Spagnoli e la festa della Resurrezione in piazza Navona." In *La cappella musicale nell'età della Controriforma*, ed. Oscar Mischiati and Paolo Russo. Florence: Olschki, 1993.

Lunadoro, Girolamo. *Relatione della Corte di Roma*. Venice: Brigonci, 1661.

Marder, T. A. *Bernini's Scala Regia at the Vatican Palace*. Cambridge: Cambridge University Press, 1997.

Masella, Lorella, and Zaira Fornari. "L'attività architettonica promossa dalla famiglia Barberini a Palestrina attraverso l'opera di Francesco Contini." In *I Barberini a Palestrina*, ed. Peppino Tomassi. Palestrina, 1992.

Masson, Georgina. "Papal Gifts and Roman Entertainments in Honour of Queen Christina's Arrival." In *Queen Christina of Sweden: Documents and Studies*, ed. Magnus von Platen, 74–82. Analecta Reginensia, 1:244–61. Stockholm: Norstedt, 1966.

———. *Queen Christina*. New York: Farrar, Straus and Giroux, 1968.

Matteucci, A. M., and Rossella Ariuli. *Giovanni Francesco Grimaldi*. Bologna: CLUEB, 2002.

Ménestrier, Claude-François. *Des decorations funebres*. Paris: De La Caille, 1683.

Mersenne, Marin. *Correspondance du P. Marin Mersenne, religieux Minime*, ed. Cornélis de Waard. Paris: Beauchesne, 1933–77.

Merz, Jörg Martin. *Pietro da Cortona and Roman Baroque Architecture*. New Haven and London: Yale University Press, 2008.

Miller, Stephen R. "Music for the Mass in Seventeenth-Century Rome: Messe Piene, the Palestrina Tradition, and the Stile Antico." Ph.D. diss., University of Chicago, 1998. 2 vols. Ann Arbor: UMI, 1999.

Mochi Onori, Lorenza. *Palazzo Barberini: La Galleria Nazionale di arte antica: Origine e sistemazione del museo*. Rome: Abete Industria Poligrafica, 1998.

———. "Un ritratto di Taddeo Barberini di Carlo Maratta (1625–1713)." In *Studi di Storia dell'Arte in onore di Denis Mahon*, 322–25. Milan, 2000.

Molinari, Cesare. *Le nozze degli dèi: un saggio sul grande spettacolo italiano del Seicento*. Rome: Bulzoni, 1968.

Monaldini, Sergio. "'La montagna fulminata' Giostre e tornei a Bologna nel Seicento." In *Musica in torneo nell'Italia del Seicento*, 103–33.

———. *L'Orto dell'Esperidi: Musici, attori e artisti nel patrocinio della famiglia Bentivoglio (1646–1685)*. Lucca: Libreria Musicale Italiana, 2000.

Montagu, Jennifer. *Roman Baroque Sculpture: The Industry of Art*. New Haven and London: Yale University Press, 1989.

Montevecchi, Benedetta, and Sandra Vasco Rocca. *Suppellettile ecclesiastica*. Florence: Centro Di, 1988.

Moore, James H. *Vespers at St. Mark's: Music of Alessandro Grandi, Giovanni Rovetta and Francesco Cavalli*. 2 vols. Ann Arbor: UMI, 1981.

Morelli, Arnaldo. "La musica a Roma nella seconda metà del Seicento attraverso l'archivio Cartari-Febei." In *La musica a Roma attraverso le fonti d'archivio*, 107–36.

Moroni, Gaetano. *Dizionario di erudizione storico-ecclesiastica*. 130 vols. Venice: Emiliana, 1840–61.

Murata, Margaret. *Operas for the Papal Court 1631–1668*. Ann Arbor: UMI, 1981.

_____. "A Topography of the Barberini Manuscripts of Music." In *I Barberini e la cultura del Seicento*, 375–80.

_____. "Why the First Opera Given in Paris Wasn't Roman." *Cambridge Opera Journal* 7 (1995): 87–106.

La musica a Roma attraverso le fonti d'archivio. Edited by Bianca Maria Antolini, Arnaldo Morelli, and Vera Vita Spagnolo. Lucca: Libreria Musicale Italiana, 1994.

Musica in torneo nell'Italia del Seicento. Edited by Paolo Fabbri. Lucca: Libreria Musicale Italiana, 1999.

Nagler, A. M. *Theatre Festivals of the Medici 1539–1637*. New Haven and London: Yale University Press, 1964.

Nardelli, Franca Petrucci. "Il Card. Francesco Barberini senior e la stampa a Roma." *Archivio Romano di Storia Patria* 108 (1985): 133–98.

Negri, Cesare. *Le gratie d'Amore*. Milan, 1602.

The New Grove Dictionary of Music and Musicians. 2nd ed. London and New York: Macmillan, 2001.

Noehles, Karl. "Architekturprojekte Cortonas." *Münchner Jahrbuch der bildenden Kunst*, dritte Folge 20 (1969): 171–206.

Nussdorfer, Laurie. *Civic Politics in the Rome of Urban VIII*. Princeton: Princeton University Press, 1992.

Oberli, Matthias. *"Magnificentia Principis": Das Mäzenatentum des Prinzen und Kardinals Maurizio von Savoyen (1593–1657)*. Diss. Zurich 1998. Weimar: VDG, 1999.

Old Master Drawings. Christie's auction sale catalogue (1996).

Ovid (P. Ovidius Naso). *Metamorphoses*, trans. Rolfe Humphries. Bloomington: Indiana University Press, 1955.

Päpstliches Zeremoniell in der frühen Neuzeit: Das Diarium des Zeremonienmeisters Paolo Alaleone de Branca während des Pontifikats Gregors XV (1621–1623). Edited by Günther Wassilowsky and Hubert Wolf. Münster: RHEMA, 2007.

Parker, Geoffrey. *Europe in Crisis 1598–1648*. Ithaca: Cornell University Press, 1979.

Pirrotta, Nino. "Scelte poetiche di Monteverdi." In *Scelte poetiche di musicisti: Teatro, poesia e musica da Willaert a Malipiero*. Venice: Marsilio, 1987.

Pisano, G. "L'ultimo prefetto dell'Urbe, Don Taddeo Barberini." *Roma* 9 (1931): 103–20, 155–64.

Povoledo, Elena. "Ferrara." *Enciclopedia dello Spettacolo*, 5. Rome: Le Maschere, 1958.

_____. "Gian Lorenzo Bernini, l'elefante e i fuochi artificiali." *Rivista Italiana di Musicologia* 10 (1975): 499–518.

Il principe romano: Ritratti dell'aristocrazia pontifica nell'età barocca. Rome: Gangemi, 2007.

I principi della Chiesa: Itinerario mostra. Milan: Edizioni Charta, 1998.

Prunières, Henry. *L'Opéra italien en France avant Lulli*. Paris: Champion, 1913; reprint, 1975.

Redondi, Pietro. *Galileo eretico*. Turin: Einaudi, 1983.

Rice, Louise. "Urban VIII, the Archangel Michael, and a Forgotten Project for the Apse Altar of St. Peter's." *Burlington Magazine* 134 (1992): 428–34.

Ripa, Cesare. *Iconologia*. Rome: Faeji, 1603; facsimile ed., Erna Mandowsky, Hildesheim: Olms, 1984.

Ronan, Colin. *Galileo*. New York, 1974.

Rosand, Ellen. *Monteverdi's Last Operas: A Venetian Trilogy*. Berkeley, Los Angeles and London: University of California Press, 2007.

_____. *Opera in Seventeenth-Century Venice: The Creation of a Genre*. Berkeley: University of California Press, 1991.

Ruggieri, Giovanni Simone. *Diario Dell'Anno del Santiß. Giubileo M.D.C.L. Celebrato in Roma Dalla Santita di N. S. Papa Innocentio. X.* Rome, 1651.

Saint Hubert, M. de. *La maniere de composer et faire reussir les ballets*. Paris: Targa, 1641; reprint, Geneva: Minkoff, 1993.

San Juan, Rose Marie. *Rome: A City Out of Print*. Minneapolis and London: University of Minnesota Press, 2001.

Schettini Piazza, Enrica. "I Barberini e i Lincei: dalla mirabil congiuntura alla fine della prima Accademia (1623–1630)." In *I Barberini e la cutura europea del Seicento*, 117–26.

Schütze, Sebastian. *Gian Lorenzo Bernini: Regista del barocco*. Milan: Skira, 1999.

_____. "La Biblioteca del cardinale Maffeo Barberini: Prolegomena per una biografia culturale ed intellettuale del Papa Poeta." In *I Barberini e la cultura europea del Seicento*, 37–46.

Scott, John Beldon. *Images of Nepotism: The Painted Ceilings of Palazzo Barberini*. Princeton, Princeton University Press, 1991.

_____. "Patronage and the Visual Encominum during the Pontificate of Urban VIII: The Ideal Palazzo Barberini in a Dedicatory Print." *Memoirs of the American Academy in Rome* 40 (1995).

Silbiger, Alexander, ed. *17th Century Keyboard Music*, 12. New York: Garland Publishing, 1987.

Solerti, Angelo. *Le origini del melodrama*. Turin: Fratelli Bocca, 1903.

_____. *Musica, ballo e drammatica alla corte medicea dal 1600 al 1637*. Florence, 1905; reprint, New York: Blom, 1968.

Southorn, Janet. *Power and Display in the Seventeenth Century: The Arts and Their Patrons in Modena and Ferrara*. Cambridge: Cambridge University Press, 1988.

Sperandini, Giovanni Maria. *Feste, spettacoli e tornei cavallereschi nella Modena di Cesare d'Este (1598–1628)*. Modena: Edizioni Artestampa, Centro Studi Nonantolani, 2008.

Tamburini, Elena. *Due teatri per il principe: Studi sulla committenza teatrale di Lorenzo Onofrio Colonna (1659–1689)*. Rome: Bulzoni, 1997.

_____. "La lira, la poesia, la voce e il teatro musicale del Seicento: Note su alcune vicende biografiche e artistiche della baronessa Anna Rosalia Carusi." In *La musica a Roma attraverso le fonti d'archivio*, 419–31.

Toschi, Chiara Cavaliere. "Tracce per un calendario delle manifestazioni dell'effimero" and "Appendice documentaria." In *La chiesa di San Giovanni Battista e la cultura ferrarese del seicento*, 144–53. Milan: Electa, 1981.

Virgil (P. Virgilius Maro). *The Georgics*, trans. L. P. Wilkerson. New York: Viking Penguin, 1982.

Waddy, Patricia. *Seventeenth-Century Roman Palaces: Use and the Art of the Plan*. New York: The Architectural History Foundation; Cambridge, MA: MIT Press, 1990.

Walker, Thomas. "Echi estensi negli spettacoli musicali a Ferrara nel primo Seicento." In *La corte di Ferrara e il suo mecenatismo 1441–1598/The Court of Ferrara & its Patronage*, ed. Marianne Pade, Lene Waage Petersen, and Daniela Quarta, 337–51. Ferrara: Panini, 1990.

Walter, Eugene, as told to Katherine Clark. *Milking the Moon: A Southerner's Story of Life on This Planet*. New York: Crown Publishers, 2001.

Wedgwood, C. V. *The Thirty Years' War*. London: Jonathan Cape, 1938.

Weil, Mark S. "The Devotion of the Forty Hours and Roman Baroque Illusions." *Journal of the Warburg and Courtauld Institutes* 37 (1974): 218–48.

Wistreich, Richard. *Warrior, Courtier, Singer: Giulio Cesare Brancaccio and the Performance of Identity in the Late Renaissance*. Burlington, VT: Ashgate, 2007.

Witzenmann, Wolfgang. "Autographe Marco Marazzolis in der Biblioteca Vaticana (I)." *Analecta Musicologica* 7 (1969): 36–86.

_____. "Die römische Barockoper La vita humana overo Il trionfo della pieta." *Analecta Musicologica* 15 (1975): 158–201.

Wolfe, Karin Elizabeth. "Cardinal Antonio Barberini the Younger (1608–1671): Aspects of his Art Patronage." Ph.D. diss., Courtauld Institute, University of London, 1999.

Zaslaw, Neal. "The First Opera in Paris: A Study in the Politics of Art." In *Jean-Baptiste Lully and the Music of the French Baroque: Essays in Honor of James R. Anthony*, ed. John H. Heyer, 7–24. Cambridge: Cambridge University Press, 1989.

Ziino, Agostino. "Pietro Della Valle e la 'musica erudita.' Nuovi documenti." *Analecta Musicologica* 5 (1967): 97–111.

Ziosi, Roberta. "'L'Amore trionfante dello sdegno': un'opera ferrarese del 1642." Ph.D. diss., University of Ferrara, 1987.

_____. "I libretti di Ascanio Pio di Savoia: un esempio di teatro musicale a Ferrara nella prima metà del Seicento." In *Musica in torneo nell'Italia del Seicento*, 135–65.

Zirpolo, Lilian H. *Ave Papa Ave Papabile: The Sacchetti Family, Their Art Patronage, and Political Aspirations*. Toronto: Center for Reformation and Renaissance Studies, 2005.

Index

ABOUT THE AUTHOR

FREDERICK HAMMOND is Irma Brandeis Professor of Romance Culture and Music History at Bard College. A distinguished scholar of Italian music of the seventeenth century, he has held fellowships at the American Academy in Rome, the Harvard Center for Renaissance Studies (Villa I Tatti, Florence), and at the Gladys Krieble Delmas Foundation for Venetian Studies. In 1988 he was made a Cavaliere al merito della Repubblica (Italy). Among Frederick Hammond's publications are *Girolamo Frescobaldi* (Harvard University Press, 1983; Italian translation, EPOS, 2002); *Girolamo Frescobaldi: A Guide to Research* (Garland Publishing, 1988); *Music and Spectacle in Baroque Rome: Barberini Patronage under Urban VIII* (Yale University Press, 1994); and *Ambiente Barocco* (exhibition catalogue) (Yale University Press, 1999). Former harpsichordist for the Los Angeles Philharmonic, Professor Hammond is Music Director Emeritus of the Clarion Music Society and has recorded with Nonesuch, ABC Westminster, and Decca.